For those who suffered.
In hope of a better world.

The roots of evil

ERVIN STAUB is Professor of Psychology at the University of Massachusetts, Amherst. He has conducted extensive research and published many articles on helping, altruism, values, aggression, and motivation. He is author of the two-volume work, *Positive Social Behavior and Morality*. In 1990, Professor Staub was awarded the Intercultural and International Relations Prize of the Society for the Psychological Study of Social Issues (a division of the American Psychological Association).

The roots of evil

The origins of genocide
and other group violence

ERVIN STAUB
University of Massachusetts at Amherst

CAMBRIDGE
UNIVERSITY PRESS

PUBLISHED BY THE PRESS SYNDICATE OF THE UNIVERSITY OF CAMBRIDGE
The Pitt Building, Trumpington Street, Cambridge CB2 1RP, United Kingdom

CAMBRIDGE UNIVERSITY PRESS
The Edinburgh Building, Cambridge CB2 2RU, UK   http: //www.cup.cam.ac.uk
40 West 20th Street, New York, NY 10011-4211, USA   http: //www.cup.org
10 Stamford Road, Oakleigh, Melbourne 3166, Australia

First published 1989
First paperback edition 1992
Reprinted 1993 (twice), 1994, 1995, 1996, 1997, 1998

Printed in the United States of America

Typeset in Times

A catalogue record for this book is available from the British Library

Library of Congress Cataloguing-in-Publication Data is available

ISBN 0-521-42214-0 paperback

Contents

Preface

Before I first thought of writing this book, I had for many years been conducting research and writing articles and books on the psychological origins of people helping others in need. Psychologists call this altruism, or "prosocial behavior." In early 1979 I completed the second of my two-volume *Positive Social Behavior and Morality*, and that summer, during a sabbatical leave, I began to read seriously about the Holocaust.[1] I realized that a number of concepts that were useful for understanding why people did or did not help others in need were also useful for understanding the extreme destructiveness of the perpetrators of the Holocaust.

For example, a feeling of responsibility for other people's welfare greatly increases the likelihood of helping during an accident or sudden illness. This is partly a matter of personality, but it also depends on circumstances. A person helps more when circumstances focus responsibility on him or her. People help less when circumstances diffuse responsibility among a number of those who are present or focus it elsewhere (e.g., on a doctor who is present). I reasoned that harming and killing members of a group become possible when a feeling of responsibility for their welfare has been lost as a result of profound devaluation by a society or by an ideology adopted by the society.

It was clear to me that devaluation and loss of responsibility alone will not directly lead to genocide. Instead, an evolution must occur. Limited mistreatment of the victims changes the perpetrators and prepares them for extreme destructiveness. This was first suggested to me when in my laboratory children whom we involved in prosocial acts became more willing to help others. Research indicates that adults are also changed by their own prior actions. People learn by doing. Extreme destructiveness, it seemed to me, is usually the last of many steps along a continuum of destruction.

I was also struck by the influence of bystanders who knew of or witnessed the persecution of Jews. In Denmark, in the French Huguenot village of Le Chambon, and in a few other places where bystanders resisted Nazi persecution of Jews, the persecutors changed their behavior. Research strengthened my belief in the power of bystanders. What one bystander said during an emergency defined the meaning of the situation and influenced others' helping. What a bystander did affected others; passivity reduced and action increased helping.

I felt I had the beginnings of an understanding. I knew, however, that the Holocaust had been described as an incomprehensible evil. This view, it seemed to me, romanticized evil and gave it mythic proportions. It discouraged the realistic understanding that is necessary if we are to work effectively for a world without genocides and mass killings and torture.

During the next few years I read and taught courses, first about the Holocaust, then about other genocides and "lesser" cruelties such as mass killings and torture (for a discussion of definitions see Chapter 1). I began to write and lecture on how genocides and mass killings in general come about and to work on this book. This process also led to further exploration of the development of human caring and connection and to an attempt to specify an agenda for creating caring and connection within and between groups.

The reasons for undertaking this task were not disinterested. Their origins are in my personal experience. It took me many years to begin to pay attention to this; my resistance may have been a defense against feelings of loss and sorrow that I was not ready to deal with. I was fortified in this by the professional stance of the disinterested social scientist.

As a Jewish child in Budapest, I was six years old in the horrendous summer of 1944, when the Nazis took over four hundred thousand Hungarian Jews to Auschwitz, where most were murdered on arrival. My immediate family – my parents, my sister, and I – miraculously survived until the end of the war in one of the "protected" houses created by Raoul Wallenberg. Wallenberg, whose heroic deeds are by now well known, was a Swede who accepted a mission to come to Hungary and attempt to save Jewish lives.[2] His strategy was to create, in his capacity as a Swedish diplomat, "letters of protection" that guaranteed Hungarian Jews Swedish citizenship after the war. The Hungarian authorities allowed a few thousand such documents; many false ones were also created. Some other embassies – the Swiss, the Spanish – followed Wallenberg's example.

Wallenberg managed to buy houses into which people with letters of protection could move. Although there were constant raids on these houses by Hungarian Nazis (the Arrow Cross), many women and children survived. (My father was in a forced labor camp. He escaped when his group was on its way to Germany and was its sole survivor. He hid with us in the protected house and was undetected during several raids on the house.)

I was also powerfully influenced by a Christian woman who worked many years for my family. I love her and consider her my second mother. Maria Gógàn took my sister and me into hiding at one point, when it seemed that all Jews would be collected for "deportation" (that is, taken to Auschwitz for extermination). She procured food for us and the others in the protected house. In the midst of cruelty and violence she risked her life for others, not only for our family, but even for strangers.

These early experiences are one source of my intense and lifelong concern with kindness and cruelty. But even after I had begun to integrate my past experiences with my scholarly interests, I remained reluctant to mention them in lectures or articles. I thought that the origins of my concerns should not matter, and I feared that audiences and readers might discount the validity of what I had to say. I hope that readers will see such experiences as motivating my study of the issues discussed in this book, but not as determining my conclusions.

I have several reasons for mentioning my childhood experiences here. In 1985 I published an article about the psychology of perpetrators and bystanders.[3] Reviewers, who recommended publication, objected that I analyzed the Holocaust along with seemingly much lesser cruelties, for example, the disappearances in Argentina, where between nine and thirty thousand people were tortured and then killed. The Holocaust literature confirms my sense that some readers, given their own personal suffering and identification with victims, may feel that the tremendous tragedy of the Holocaust is diminished when it and other genocides and mass killings are studied together.

I deeply appreciate the horrors of the Holocaust: the Nazis' obsession with eliminating the Jews as a people, the murder of six million in factories of death, and the great brutality with which victims, who in no way provoked the perpetrators, were treated. Still, extreme evil defies comparisons of magnitude. What is the degree of evil in the act of torturers who insert a tube into a man's anus or a woman's vagina and seal into it a rat, which then tries to get out by gnawing its way through the victim's body? This method of torture was used in Argentina. I intend to make no comparisons of the magnitude of horrors; I do wish, however, to enhance our understanding of the commonalities (and differences) in the *psychological and cultural origins* of mass killings and genocides.

I also fear that some readers may see me as exculpating killers; I have no such intention. Understanding the motives of those who perpetrate genocide may seem to blunt outrage because the individual and group changes that lead to increasingly vicious acts may become not only more comprehensible, but even seemingly natural. Although outrage is easier to feel in the face of uncomprehended evil, to understand is not necessarily to forgive. In fact, understanding can *increase* our awareness of the culpability of perpetrators of great evil because we can see them as human beings, not as beasts without moral capacity.

Perpetrators make many small and great decisions as they progress along the continuum of destruction. They choose leaders, adopt ideologies, create policies and plans, and engage in harmful and violent acts. Their circumstances and characteristics (which themselves evolve) move them in certain directions. But human experience is always multidimensional and other directions are possible. Other aspects of the self and of experience can be guides to contrary choices. Choice clearly implies responsibility. We must maintain a double vision that both searches for understanding and acknowledges human responsibility. (These issues are discussed at several points, especially in Chapters 2 and 10.)

In the immediate aftermath of the Holocaust, people wondered whether the special characteristics of Germans as a people led them to perpetrate the Holocaust. However, the many atrocities committed by many states since World War II have led to a view that "Germanness" is no explanation. Many now doubt that cultural characteristics determine such conduct. In this book I reassert the importance of culture – not the old notion of "national character," but a certain pattern of characteristics that enhances the potential for group violence. The psychological processes leading to extreme destructiveness arise when this pattern combines with extreme difficulties of life.

Although this book includes a great deal of historical material, it is primarily a psychological work that attempts to draw on history in the service of psychological understanding of how genocides and mass killings come about.

I want to mention another bit of personal history. I was invited to give a lecture on the psychology of genocide at the University of Trier, in West Germany, in June 1987. At my request, my hosts very kindly arranged for me to talk with a group of students and with a group of people who lived under Hitler. A scheduled two hours with a group of twenty 60- to 75-year-old men and women turned into an intense four-hour discussion of their experiences in the Hitler era. We spoke in German, which I learned when I lived in Vienna between 1956 and 1959 and to my surprise remembered well. I am grateful for the willing participation of members of this group. I will refer in a few footnotes to this discussion and to a ninety-minute discussion with a larger group of students.

Acknowledgments

A book reflects many influences on the writer and the contributions and support of many people. At the University of Massachusetts, the continuing interest of Seymour Epstein, George Levinger, Susan Fiske and other colleagues in my attempts to understand the roots of human destructiveness has been more helpful than they might have imagined. The early intellectual influence of Walter Mischel, as well as Perry London, Eleanor Maccoby, and others at Stanford, during my graduate-school years (and subsequently) has also been important. The friendship and support of Lane Conn, a former colleague at Harvard, and Sarah Conn, a former student of mine there, have been of great value.

I am grateful to a number of scholars who read and commented on drafts of all or parts of the book. The sociologist Helen Fein, the historian David Wyman, and the German psychologist Wolfgang Stroebe, as well as two anonymous reviewers, commented on the whole book; the historian Robert Potash commented on the chapter on Argentina, and the anthropologist Joel Halpern commented on the chapter on Cambodia.

The book was typed and retyped on the computer as I revised and edited it. The staff of the psychology department at the University of Massachusetts at Amherst provided essential help. Melanie Bellenoit was involved from the beginning to the end; her contribution was outstanding and invaluable. Joanne Daughdrill, Amanda Morgan, Stacie Melcher and Jean Glenowicz also made significant contributions. Lisa Sheehy did an excellent job in collecting some materials on Turkey and Argentina and translating some Spanish sources. People routinely thank their families for help and support. Mine certainly deserves thanks. Once more they lived with me through years of the obsession of writing a book – an obsession perhaps more intense with this book – and with books about mass killing, genocide, and torture lying around the house. I am grateful to Sylvia, Adrian and Daniel for their forbearance and love. I hope that my continuing interest in and work on some of the positive aspects of human behavior provided relief for them, as I hope that my concern throughout this book with the roots and evolution of caring, helping, altruism, cooperation, and nonaggression will do the same for the readers of this book.

Finally, I appreciated the hospitality of the Department of Phychology at the London School of Economics and Political Science, where I worked on this book in the spring of 1987.

Part I

Psychological and cultural bases of genocide and other forms of group violence

1   An introduction

A central issue of our times is the murder, torture, and mistreatment of whole groups of people. The widespread hope and belief that human beings had become increasingly "civilized" was shattered by the events of the Second World War, particularly the systematic, deliberate extermination of six million Jews by Hitler's Third Reich. Millions of other noncombatants were also killed, systematically or randomly and carelessly.

The destruction of human groups has a long history. In many ancient wars inhabitants of cities were massacred, often with great brutality, and the cities razed to the ground. Many religious wars were extremely brutal, if not genocidal. Our own century has witnessed, in addition to two world wars, mass killings by colonial powers, the genocide of the Armenians, and the mass destruction of lives in the Soviet Union through repeated purges and deliberate starvation of peasants.

Genocides, mass killings, and other cruelties inflicted on groups of people have not ceased since the Second World War. Consider the millions killed by their own people in Cambodia and Indonesia, the killing of the Hutu in Burundi, the Ibo in Nigeria, the Ache Indians in Paraguay, and the Buddhists in Tibet, and the mass killings in Uganda. Dictatorial governments have recently tended to kill not only individuals but whole groups of people seen as actual or potential enemies. This trend is evident in the Argentine disappearances and the death squad killings in E1 Salvador and Guatemala.

How can human beings kill multitudes of men and women, children and old people?* How does the motivation arise for this in the face of the powerful prohibition against murder that most of us are taught? We must

* On October 12, 1987, NBC news presented a program on the killing of children in our modern age. According to this program, "Once children just died in the crossfire, now they are targets." While always among victims of genocide, in the last twenty years children have increasingly become direct targets, killed in order to terrorize communities into political passivity.

3

understand the psychological, cultural, and societal roots of genocide and mass killing if we are to stop such human destructiveness. As cultures, societies, and individual human beings we must learn how to live together in harmony and resist influences that turn us against each other. My analysis is intended as a contribution to these goals.

Genocide and war have much in common. In one, a society turns against a subgroup seen as an internal enemy; in the the other, a society turns against a group seen as an external enemy. Identifying the origins of genocide and mass killing will also help to enlighten us about sources of war, torture, and lesser cruelties such as group discrimination that can be steps to mass killing or genocide.

Aggression, violence, torture, and the mistreatment of human beings are all around us. But kindness, helpfulness, generosity, and love also abound. Some Christians in Nazi-occupied Europe risked their lives to save Jews and other persecuted people. Many nations helped in response to starvation in Cambodia at the end of the 1970s and Ethiopia in the mid-1980s, the destruction wrought by earthquake in Soviet Armenia in 1988, and other tragedies.

This book presents a conception of how a subgroup of a society, whether historically established or newly created (such as the "new people" in Cambodia, the name the Khmer Rouge gave the inhabitants of cities they forced into the countryside), comes to be mistreated and destroyed by a more powerful group or a government. The conception is then applied to the analysis of four instances: in greatest depth to the Holocaust, the extermination of six million Jews in Nazi Germany; to the genocide of the Armenians in Turkey in 1915–16; the genocide in Cambodia in the late 1970s; and the disappearance and mass killing of people in Argentina during those same years.

The approach and content of the book

A brief preview. Certain characteristics of a culture and the structure of a society, combined with great difficulties or hardships of life and social disorganization, are the starting point for genocide or mass killing. The resulting material and psychological needs lead the society to turn against a subgroup in it. Gradually increasing mistreatment of this subgroup ends in genocide or mass killing.

Under extremely difficult life conditions certain motives dominate: protecting the physical well-being of oneself and one's family and preserving one's psychological self, including self-concept and values; making sense of life's problems and social disorganization and gaining a new comprehension of the world, among others. It is difficult, usually, to fulfill these aims by improving the conditions of life. Instead, people often respond with thoughts, feelings, and actions that do not change real conditions but at least help them cope with their psychological consequences. These include devaluing other groups, scapegoating, joining new groups, and adopting ideologies – all of which may give rise to the motivation for, and diminish inhibition against, harming others.

What motives arise and how they are fulfilled depend on the characteristics of the culture and society. For example, a society that has long devalued a group and discriminated against its members, has strong respect for authority, and has an overly superior and/or vulnerable self-concept is more likely to turn against a subgroup.

Genocide does not result directly. There is usually a progression of actions. Earlier, less harmful acts cause changes in individual perpetrators, bystanders, and the whole group that make more harmful acts possible. The victims are further devalued. The self-concept of the perpetrators changes and allows them to inflict greater harm – for "justifiable" reasons. Ultimately, there is a commitment to genocide or mass killing or to ideological goals that require mass killing or genocide. The motivation and the psychological possibility evolve gradually.

Such a progression is made more likely by the passivity of bystanders – members of the society not directly affected and outside groups, including other nations. Active opposition by bystanders can reactivate the perpetrators' moral values and also cause them to be concerned about retaliation.

In the next chapter I will present a more detailed description of the core concepts. In subsequent chapters of Part I, I examine in greater detail each component of the conception, including the psychology of individual perpetrators, bystanders, and heroic helpers. In Part II, I apply the conception to a detailed analysis of the Holocaust; in Part III, to the analysis of the other genocides and mass killings.*

In Part IV, I discuss how, with some changes and extensions, this conception provides an understanding of the origins of war, the other major form of group violence. The difficult life conditions that lead to war may include internal problems, problems in the international order, and conflicts with other nations.

---

* Part of the overall conception I present and many of the specific concepts, ideas, and considerations also apply to individual violence within groups. One major difference is that the cultural and psychological influences that arise from the differentiation between "us" and "them," ingroup and outgroup, need not be involved in individual violence. Another is that personal (rather than societal) characteristics and circumstances (or the characteristics of and conditions in families) become of primary importance.

Genocide and mass killing are tragedies for the perpetrators also. Their characters are affected, and at times the cycle of violence makes them victims as well. To diminish the chance of such tragedies, we must identify elements of culture, institutions, and personality that reduce hostility and aggression and enhance caring, connection, helpfulness, and cooperation within and between groups. To promote these ends we must create crosscutting relations that allow members of different subgroups (and of different nations) to work and play together; we must help groups develop positive reciprocity in their relationships; and we must guide individuals and groups to act in others' behalf. In these and other ways we can create a progression, an evolution of caring, connectedness, and nonaggression in opposition to the continuum of destruction. How the young are socialized by parents and schools is also essential. In Chapters 17 and 18, I present an agenda for creating caring and nonaggressive persons and societies.

Differences and similarities and the selection of cases. This book searches for the origins of genocides and mass killings. The outcomes differ greatly (for example, in the number of people killed and methods of killing), and the influences that lead to genocide are not identical. Difficult conditions of life vary. Severe economic problems, political violence, war, and even rapid, substantial social change can result in social chaos and personal upheavals. Of the cultural-societal characteristics that have the potential to generate violence, only some may be influential in a given instance. The continuum of destruction takes various forms as well. In some cases a society has progressed along this continuum for decades or even centuries. In other cases, the progression develops over a much shorter time under the influence of difficult life conditions or of the ideologies adopted to deal with them.

Why did I choose the Holocaust, the genocides in Turkey and Cambodia, and the disappearances in Argentina for study and analysis? Each is significant in its own right, yet they differ in many ways. If we can identify commonalities in their origins, we can gain confidence in our understanding of the origins of genocides and mass killings in general.

The Holocaust is an instance of suffering and cruelty that informs our age. It gave rise to a deep questioning of the nature of individuals and groups, of human beings and human societies. For many, the evil embodied in the Holocaust is incomprehensible. For some, it is preferable not to comprehend, because comprehension might lead to forgiving.[1] But as I have noted, only by understanding the roots of such evil do we gain the possibility of shaping the future so that it will not happen again.

The genocide of the Armenians is the first modern genocide. Turkey and the Turks have never admitted that it happened. The say it was self-defense, the deportation of an internal enemy in time of war. For this reason alone, the Armenian genocide deserves attention. There are other important differences between the Holocaust and this genocide. The Holocaust made use of bureaucratic management and advanced technology in the framework of a totalitarian system. The genocide of the Armenians was less planned, with limited bureaucratic organization and very little advanced technology in its execution.

Paradoxically, in this highly technological age, we are horrified by the nontechnological brutality of the Cambodian genocide, its direct, primitive methods of murder on a large scale. In this case people were killed not because of their religious or ethnic origin, but for political reasons. Because of their past or because of their current deviation from rules, many people were deemed incapable of living in the type of society envisioned by the Cambodian communists. Because the victims were members of the same racial and ethnic group as the perpetrators, and even religion did not enter into their selection, the mass killing in Cambodia can be regarded as "autogenocide."

Five to six million Jews were killed in the Holocaust, probably about eight hundred thousand Armenians in Turkey, and between one and two million people died in Cambodia. The disappearances in Argentina cannot be compared in magnitude: between nine and thirty thousand people were killed. The Argentine victims were regarded as political enemies who endangered the state: communists, communist sympathizers, or left leaning.

There can be no exhaustive test of my conception of genocide, but I can provide significant confirmation by demonstrating substantial similarities in the psychological and cultural origins of these four disparate cases and the existence of extraordinary life problems.

The definitions of genocide and mass killing

The word *genocide* was introduced by the jurist Raphael Lemkin, who began a crusade in 1933 to create what was to become the Genocide Convention. In 1944, in a study of the Axis rule in occupied Europe, he proposed the term *genocide* to denote the destruction of a nation or an ethnic group, from the ancient Greek word *genos* (race, tribe) and the Latin *cide* (killing).[2] As a result of his efforts, on December 11, 1946, the General Assembly of the United Nations (UN) passed a resolution that said: "Genocide is a denial of the right of existence of entire human groups. . . . Many instances of such crimes have occurred, when racial, religious, political and other groups have been destroyed, entirely or in part."[3]

In subsequent work of UN committees on what became the Genocide Convention, passed on December 9, 1948, disagreements about content were substantial. The Soviet Union and other nations objected to the inclusion of political groups as victims of genocide, arguing that the etymology of the term should guide the definition: only racial and national groups could be *objectively* designated. Others argued that political groups are transient and unstable. Some objected that the inclusion of political groups in the convention "would expose nations to external intervention in their domestic concerns,"[4] and political conflict within a country could become an international issue. Those who wanted to include political groups pointed out that the meanings of words evolve. They wanted genocide to refer to the destruction of any group.[5] Even the inclusion of economic groups was suggested.

The Genocide Convention as finally adopted did not include political groups. It defined the crime of genocide as "acts committed with intent to destroy in whole or in part, a national, ethnical, racial or religious group" by killing members of the group, causing them serious bodily or mental harm, creating conditions calculated to bring about their physical destruction, preventing births, or forcibly transferring children to another group.[6]

Killing groups of people for political reasons has become the primary form of genocide (and mass killing) in our time. There is no reason to believe that the types of psychological and cultural influences differ in political and other group murders. In this book genocide means an attempt to exterminate a racial, ethnic, religious, cultural, or political group, either directly through murder or indirectly by creating conditions that lead to the group's destruction. Mass killing means killing members of a group without the intention to eliminate the whole group or killing large numbers of people without a precise definition of group membership. In a mass killing the number of people killed is usually smaller than in genocide.

For example, in Cambodia the scale of murder was genocidal, but the identification of who was to be killed somewhat imprecise, as it frequently is in political genocide. In Argentina the reasons were also political, but the number of victims was much smaller, and their identification even less precise – a mass killing rather than a genocide. The ideology that led to the killings in Cambodia demanded many more victims.[7]

Four mass killings/genocides

I will here briefly describe what happened in the Nazi Holocaust, in the genocide of the Armenians, in the autogenocide in Cambodia, and in the disappearances in Argentina.

The Holocaust

The word refers to the extermination of about six million Jews by Nazi Germany from June 1941 to 1945. Another five million people were also killed: political opponents; mentally ill, retarded, and other "genetically inferior" Germans; Poles; and Russians. Gypsies, like Jews, were to be eliminated; more than 200,000 were killed, probably many more.

The extermination of Jews had several phases.[8] After sporadic killings, a policy of extermination, the Final Solution, was created. The policy took shape in 1941; it was institutionalized in January 1942 at the Wannsee Conference. In 1941, *Einsatzgruppen* (literally, task forces; special mobile killing units) were established and sent to the eastern front. They lined up and shot groups of Jews at the edge of mass graves, which at times the victims were forced to dig. Later they filled trucks with Jews and drove them around until they died of the carbon monoxide that was routed back into the truck. About one and a half million people were killed in these ways.

More and more, the killing took place in specially constructed camps, most located in Poland. Some were strictly extermination camps. Jews were told they would be resettled and gathered from all over Europe; in territories not occupied by the Germans but allied with them, governments were asked to hand over their Jewish population. The Jews were herded into freight cars and transported to camps. After days on end without food, water, or medical care, some died on the way. On entering the camps they were told to undress for showers. Instead, they were gassed to death. Their bodies were removed by Jews assigned to special working units and were burnt first in open fires, later in great ovens.

Other camps were combined labor and extermination camps. The "selection" at Auschwitz is infamous. Those deemed capable of work or considered useful in cruel medical experiments were sent to the camp. Others were immediately taken to the gas chambers. Families were separated in this process.

Other modes of killing were part of camp life. Inmates were deliberately starved. Those who became weak or ill were sent to the gas chambers. Some were killed in camp hospitals with injections into the heart. Others died for real or imagined infractions of inhumane camp rules; they were hanged or suffocated in tiny airless prison cells.

In addition to the organized murders, there was both planned and capricious brutality in the treatment of inmates. Only the most limited bodily care was possible. Toilets were long rows of holes, with only seconds to use them. Inmates slept three or four to a bunk. They were ruled by other inmates who were former criminals and were exposed to degradations, mutilation in medical experiments, and torture.[9]

The genocide of the Armenians

In the midst of World War I, during the night of April 24, 1915, the religious and intellectual leaders of the Armenian community in Constantinople were taken from their beds, imprisoned, tortured, and killed. At about the same time, Armenians in the Turkish army, already segregated in "labor battalions," were all killed. Over a short time period Armenian men over fifteen years of age were gathered in cities, towns, and villages, roped together, marched to nearby uninhabited locations, and killed.[10]

After a few days, the women and children and any remaining men were told to prepare themselves for deportation. They were marched from Anatolia through a region of ravines and mountains to the Syrian Desert, where they were left to die. On the way, they were attacked by Turkish villagers and peasants, Kurds, and *chettis* – brigands who were freed from prison and placed in their path. The attackers robbed the marchers of provisions and clothes, killed men, women, and children, even infants, and raped and carried off women. Through it all, Turkish gendarmes urged the marchers on with clubs and whips, refused them water as they passed by streams and wells, and bayoneted those who lagged behind.

Telegrams to provincial capitals captured by the British army and reports by witnesses, including diplomats like Henry Morgenthau, the American ambassador to Turkey, provide evidence that the extermination of the Armenians was planned and organized by the central government.[11] Estimates of the number killed range from four hundred thousand to over a million; the actual number is probably more than eight hundred thousand.

The autogenocide (Khmer killing Khmer) in Cambodia

In 1975, after a five-year civil war, the communist Khmer Rouge, or Red Khmer, gained victory and power in Cambodia. They evacuated all the cities, including Phnom Penh, the capital, whose population had swelled with refugees to almost three million. All were brutally driven from the city and some were killed.

Whoever the small group of dominant communist leaders, Pol Pot and his followers, regarded as potential enemies of the ideal state that they wanted to build or as incapable of living in and contributing to such a state was killed. That included officers of the defeated army, government officials, intellectuals, educated people, and professionals such as doctors and teachers. Communists who became victims of infighting were often interrogated and tortured before being killed. The killings were not entirely systematic. There were more in some parts of the country than in others, more during certain periods than others. The killing actually intensified toward the end of the Khmer Rouge rule in 1979.

The populations of cities were driven into the countryside to build villages and irrigation systems and work the land. They were not allowed to settle in abandoned villages but had to build new ones from scratch. Peasants were allowed to keep some property, including small parcels of land. Those driven from the cities were allowed no property of any kind.

The people were forced to work very long days with little food. They were not allowed to forage in the forest, a customary source of food for Cambodian peasants. They were killed for the slightest infraction of the many and stringent rules, sometimes without warning. Parents were killed in front of their children, brothers in front of brothers. About two million people died from execution and starvation between 1975 and 1979.[12]

The disappearances in Argentina

In 1976 the armed forces took over the government in a coup. They intensified the war against guerrillas who had been committing murders and kidnapping people for ransom. The military began to kidnap and torture even people who were merely suspected of association with the guerrillas or regarded as left leaning or politically liberal. The selection of victims was indiscriminate; not even pregnant women were spared.

Most of those kidnapped and tortured were killed, alone or in mass executions. Some were drugged and dropped from helicopters into the ocean. The authorities gave away infants and young children of victims killed, often to military families, without informing relatives. When relatives asked about people who had disappeared, the authorities denied knowledge of their whereabouts. At least nine thousand were killed, with some estimates as high as thirty thousand.[13]

Is mass killing ever justified?

Are mass killing and genocide ever justifiable self-defense or understandable retaliation? How can they be? In both genocides and mass killings (but also frequently in war) the people killed include women, old people, children, as well as men who in no way harmed the killers. There may be antagonism or violence between some of the victims and the perpetrators. The perpetrators sometimes claim the victims provoked the mass killing.

There was some "provocation" in each of our four cases except the Holocaust. But how can hostility by some members of a group, often in response to repression or violence against them, justify the attempt to exterminate the whole group; or violence by a small group of people who oppose a system justify the "creation" of a large group whose members are then killed?

Nor are genocides and mass killings ever "rational" expressions of self-interest. The three genocides, at least, were highly destructive to the perpetrators. The fabric of society was impaired, many people essential to its functioning were killed, and desperately needed resources were used in the service of killing.*

---

* The frequently self-destructive nature of genocides makes it unlikely that its function is to reduce population surplus, as one author has suggested.[14] Certainly genocide does not seem to do this in an effective manner and does not appear to gain evolutionary advantage for the perpetrators.

2   The origins of genocide and mass killing: core concepts

I believe that tragically human beings have the capacity to come to experience killing other people as nothing extraordinary. Some perpetrators may feel sick and disgusted when killing large numbers of people, as they might feel in slaughtering animals, but even they will proceed to kill for a "good" reason, for a "higher" cause. How do they come to this? In essence, difficult life conditions and certain cultural characteristics may generate psychological processes and motives that lead a group to turn against another group. The perpetrators change, as individuals and as a group, as they progress along a continuum of destruction that ends in genocide. The behavior of bystanders can inhibit or facilitate this evolution.*

A conception of the origins of genocide and mass killing

Difficult life conditions

Human beings often face hard times as individuals or as members of a group. Sometimes a whole society or substantial and potentially influential segments of society face serious problems that have a powerful impact and result in powerful motivations.

Economic conditions at the extreme can result in starvation or threat to life. Less extreme economic problems can result in prolonged deprivation,

---

* *Psychological processes* include the thoughts and feelings of individuals, the meanings they perceive in events. *Culture* includes the thoughts, feelings, and ways of perceiving and evaluating events and people shared by members of a group – the shared meanings. Specific aspects of culture are shared rules, norms, values, customs, and life-styles. Culture is coded, maintained, and expressed in the "products" of a group: its literature, art, rituals, the contents of its mass media, and the behavior of its members. A result of shared culture is similarity in psychological reactions to culturally relevant events. *Society*, as I use the term, means the institutions and organizations of the group. These express the culture, embodying shared meanings that guide the life of the group. Thus, while devaluation of a group is a

deterioration of material well-being, or at least the frustration of expectations for improved well-being. Hostility and violence threaten and endanger life, whether political violence between internal groups or war with an external enemy. Political violence threatens the security even of people who are uninvolved. Widespread criminal violence also threatens life and security. War threatens the life of at least some individuals and affects many aspects of the life of a society. Rapid changes in culture and society – for example, rapid technological change and the attendant changes in work and social customs – also have the psychological impact of difficult life conditions. They overturn set patterns of life and lead to disorganization.

The meaning assigned to life problems, the intensity of their impact, and the way groups of people try to deal with them are greatly affected by the characteristics of cultures and social organizations. By themselves, difficult life conditions will not lead to genocide. They carry the potential, the motive force; culture and social organization determine whether the potential is realized by giving rise to devaluation and hostility toward a subgroup (or a nation; see Chapter 16).

Difficulties of life vary in nature, magnitude, persistence, and the accompanying disorganization and chaos in society. As a result, the impact also varies: the threat may be to life, to security, to well-being, to self-concept, or to world view. In all four cases I discuss, political violence, civil war, or external war was involved. Political violence may create a new political system that changes traditional ways of life and values; this has the impact of difficult life conditions. The new system can further cultural and social characteristics that contribute to genocide. In all four cases I will examine, changes in political systems preceded genocides and mass killings by less than a decade.

One important cultural characteristic is the rigidity or the adaptability of a society. Monolithic societies, with a limited set of acceptable values and ways of life, may be more disturbed by change. For example, the disruptive changes in technology, ways of life, and values under the shah probably contributed to the intensity of Islamic fundamentalism in Iran. Rigidity and flexibility partly depend on societal self-concept, the way

cultural characteristic, discrimination is embodied in social institutions such as schools or a military that segregates members of a group or uses them only for labor and does not give them weapons (as was the case with the Armenians in Turkey before the genocide). Society also includes political organizations and institutions. Occasionally culture and social organization can be discrepant, as when a repressive dictatorial system emerges in a democratic culture. But a truly great discrepancy of this kind is probably rare. In both Germany and the Soviet Union, the two great totalitarian states, the culture supported authoritarian rule or at least made it acceptable.

a group and its members define themselves. Greater rigidity makes the difficulties of life more stressful.

Psychological consequences: needs and goals

Difficult life conditions give rise to powerful needs and goals demanding satisfaction. People need to cope with the psychological effects of difficult life conditions, the more so when they cannot change the conditions or alleviate the physical effects. Hard times make people feel threatened and frustrated.* Threats to the physical self are important, but so are threats to the psychological self. All human beings strive for a coherent and positive self-concept, a self-definition that provides continuity and guides one's life. Difficult conditions threaten the self-concept as people cannot care for themselves and their families or control the circumstances of their lives.

Powerful self-protective motives then arise: the motive to defend the physical self (one's life and safety) and the motive to defend the psychological self (one's self-concept, values, and ways of life). There is a need both to protect self-esteem and to protect values and traditions. There is also a need to elevate a diminished self.

Disruption in customary ways of life, the resulting chaos, and changing mores can profoundly threaten people's assumptions about the world and their comprehension of reality. Because understanding the world is essential, people will be powerfully motivated to seek a new world view and gain a renewed comprehension of reality. Without such comprehension life is filled with uncertainty and anxiety.

When their group is functioning poorly and not providing protection

---

* I will use several motivational concepts, some in part interchangeably. *Motivation* designates an active psychological state that makes an outcome or end desirable, whether eating to diminish hunger or killing to feel powerful or avenge real or imagined harm. A *motive* is a characteristic of the individual or culture out of which active motivation arises. There are different kinds of motives. *Needs* are more intense and have a more imperative quality. They push an organism to action, either because they are required for survival or because they are essential to the wholeness and functioning of an individual or culture. *Goals* have desired outcomes that are self-enhancing and are sources of satisfaction. The more deeply a goal (acquisition of wealth, writing a great book, making a contribution to humanity) comes to be an important aspect of self-definition, the more imperative it becomes. Essential, unfilled goals thus become needlike in character. I will sometimes use the word *aim* to designate the outcomes that individuals desire as a result of the active motivation arising from their needs and characteristic (personal) goals.

Frustration is an emotion that results from interference with fulfilling a motive or from the failure to fulfill it. The emotional consequences are greater when the motive is more important. Difficult life conditions often frustrate basic goals, and needs.

and well-being, people's respect for and valuing of the group diminish; their societal self-concept is harmed. Because people define themselves to a significant degree by their membership in a group, for most people a positive view of their group is essential to individual self-esteem – especially in difficult times. The need to protect and improve societal self-concept or to find a new group to identify with will be powerful.

Persistent difficulties of life also disrupt the relationships among members of the group. They disrupt human connections. People focus on their own needs, compete with others for material goods, and feel endangered by others. The need for connection, enhanced by suffering, will be powerful.

These psychological reactions and motivations are natural and often adaptive. People are energized by a sense of personal value and significance, connection to other people, the feeling of mutual support, and a view of the world that generates hope. However, when these motivations are very intense and fulfilled in certain ways, they become likely origins of destruction.

Threats and frustrations give rise to hostility and the desire to harm others. The appropriate targets of this hostility are, of course, the people who caused the problems, but usually they cannot be identified. Often no one is to blame; the causes are complex and impersonal. At other times those responsible are too powerful, or they are leaders with whom people identify too much to focus their hostility on them. The hostility is therefore displaced and directed toward substitute targets. Hostility is especially likely to arise if people regard their suffering as unjust, as they often do, and especially if some others are not similarly affected.

Ways of coping and fulfilling needs and goals

Constructive actions have beneficial, practical effects and also help a person cope with the psychological consequences of life conditions. Unfortunately, it is often difficult to find and to follow a practically beneficial course of action. When this is the case, it is easy for psychological processes to occur that lead people to turn against others. The psychological needs must be controlled, or satisfied in other ways. People must unite without creating a shared enemy or an ideology that identifies enemies. Wisdom, vision, the capacity to gain trust, and effective institutions are needed to strike out on a constructive course of action.

Certain ways of seeing and evaluating events and people require no physical action (and any actions that follow from them usually do not change life conditions), but they help people satisfy at least the psychological needs and goals that arise from difficult life conditions. Some of these internal processes are basic psychological tendencies common to all human beings: differentiation of ingroup and outgroup, "us" and "them"; devaluation of those defined as members of an outgroup; just-world thinking, which is the tendency to believe that people who suffer, especially those already devalued, must deserve their suffering as a result of their deeds or their characters; and scapegoating, or blaming others for one's problems. Individuals differ in such psychological tendencies depending on their socialization and experience and resulting personality; societies differ depending on their history and the resulting culture.

Blaming others, scapegoating, diminishes our own responsibility. By pointing to a cause of the problems, it offers understanding, which, although false, has great psychological usefulness. It promises a solution to problems by action against the scapegoat. And it allows people to feel connected as they join to scapegoat others. Devaluation of a subgroup helps to raise low self-esteem. Adopting an ideology provides a new world view and a vision of a better society that gives hope. Joining a group enables people to give up a burdensome self, adopt a new social identity, and gain a connection to other people. This requires action, but it is frequently not constructive action.

Often all these tendencies work together. The groups that are attractive in hard times often provide an ideological blueprint for a better world and an enemy who must be destroyed to fulfill the ideology. Sometimes having a scapegoat is the glue in the formation of the group. But even if the ideology does not begin by identifying an enemy, one is likely to appear when fulfillment of the ideological program proves difficult. Thus these psychological tendencies have violent potentials. They can bring to power a violent group with a violent ideology, as in Germany, or shape an ideology, as they probably did in the case of the Pol Pot group that led the Khmer Rouge to genocide in Cambodia.

The continuum of destruction

Genocide and mass killing do not directly arise from difficult life conditions and their psychological effects. There is a progression along a continuum of destruction. People learn and change by doing, by participation, as a consequence of their own actions. Small, seemingly insignificant acts can involve a person with a destructive system: for example, accepting benefits provided by the system or even using a required greeting, such as "Heil Hitler." Initial acts that cause limited harm result in psychological changes that make further destructive actions possible. Victims are further devalued; for example, just-world thinking may lead people to believe that suffering is deserved. Perpetrators change and become more able and willing to act against victims. In the end people develop powerful commitment to genocide or to an ideology that supports it.

Deeply ingrained, socially developed feelings of responsibility for others' welfare and inhibitions against killing are gradually lost. Often the leaders assume responsibility, and accountability is further diminished by compartmentalization of functions and the denial of reality. The most terrible human capacity is that of profoundly devaluing others who are merely different. Often there is a reversal of morality, and killing them comes to be seen as good, right, and desirable. In the course of all this, new group norms evolve, and institutions are established in the service of genocide or mass killing. The progression may occur in a short time, although often intense devaluation has already developed by the time those who become the perpetrators of genocide appear on the scene.

Some people become perpetrators as a result of their personality; they are "self-selected" or selected by their society for the role. But even they evolve along the continuum of destruction. Others who were initially bystanders become involved with the destructive system and become perpetrators. Even bystanders who do not become perpetrators, if they passively observe as innocent people are victimized, will come to devalue the victims and justify their own passivity.

There are usually some people whose values or other personal characteristics make them oppose the treatment of the victims. Most such people, if they are to remain opposed, need support from others. With that support, some may come to resist the killing or the system that perpetrates it. Small initial acts can start a progression on a continuum that leads them to heroic resistance and to risking their lives to help the victims.

Cultural-societal characteristics

The characteristics of one's culture and society determine not only the consequences of difficult life conditions and the choice of avenues to satisfy needs, but also whether reactions to initial acts of mistreatment occur that might inhibit further steps along the continuum of destruction. Most cultures have some predisposing characteristics for group violence, and certain cultures possess a constant potential for it. Also, when life problems are more intense, a weaker pattern of cultural-societal preconditions will make group violence probable.

The cultural self-concept of a people greatly influences the need to protect the collective psychological self. A sense of superiority, of being better than others and having the right to rule over them, intensifies this need.

Collective self-doubt is another motivation for psychological self-defense. When a sense of superiority combines with an underlying (and often un-acknowledged) self-doubt, their contribution to the potential for genocide and mass killing can be especially high.

Nationalism arises partly from this combination of superiority and self-doubt. One form of nationalism is the desire to enlarge the nation's terri-tory or to extend the influence of its values and belief system. Another form is the desire for purity or "cleansing." Nationalism is often strength-ened under the influence of diffiult life conditions. Strong nationalism sometimes originates in the experiences of shared trauma, suffering, and humiliation, which are sources of self-doubt.[1]

Societal values can embody a positive or negative evaluation of human beings and human well-being. But even in societies that do value human welfare, an outgroup may be excluded from the moral domain.

"Us"–"them" differentiation is a basic human potential for which we even carry "genetic building blocks" (see Chapter 4). It is one source of cultural devaluation. Negative stereotypes and negative images of a group can become deeply ingrained in a culture. The needs I have described are often fulfilled by turning against such a "preselected" group. Its members are scapegoated and identified as the enemy of the dominant group's well-being, safety, and even survival, or as an obstacle to the realization of its ideological blueprint.

Strong respect for authority and strong inclination to obedience are other predisposing characteristics for mass killing and genocide. They make it more likely that responsibility will be relinquished and leaders will be followed unquestioningly. People who have always been led by strong authorities are often unable to stand on their own in difficult times. Their intense need for support will incline them to give themselves over to a group and its leaders.

A monolithic, in contrast to a pluralistic, culture or society is another important precondition. In a monolithic culture there is limited variation in values and perspectives on life. In a monolithic society strong authority or totalitarian rule enforces uniformity. The authorities have great power to define reality and shape the people's perception of the victims. Soci-eties with strong respect for authority also tend to be monolithic, and this combination makes adjustment to social change especially difficult.

In a pluralistic society with varied conceptions of reality and greater individual self-reliance, people will find it easier to change and gain new perspectives and accept new customs and mores. Reactions against initial harmful acts are more likely to occur and to inhibit the progression along the continuum of destruction.

As I have noted, an ideology with a destructive potential can become a guiding force, overriding contrary elements in culture or society. However, an ideology has to fit the culture if it is to be adopted by the people.

Partly but not entirely as a result of the above characteristics, societies vary in aggressiveness. Some have a long history of violence: aggression has become an accepted mode of dealing with conflict, even valued and idealized. Institutions that serve as the machinery for destruction may already exist.

Even more important than the current tendencies of a society is its deep structure. In the late nineteenth century, France might have seemed as likely as Germany to turn on the Jews. Anti-Semitism, as expressed in the Dreyfus affair, was widespread and racial ideologies attracted sympathetic interest. But the deep structure of anti-Semitism was stronger in Germany; for example, the medieval persecution of Jews was especially intense and cruel there.[2] There was also a long authoritarian tradition, as opposed to the celebration of individual freedom and rights by the French Revolution.[3] A deeply embedded anti-Semitism joined with other cultural characteristics and with difficult life conditions to create the conditions for genocide.

Why was there no Holocaust in Russia, where anti-Semitism was intense, the government was despotic, and life conditions near the end of World War I were difficult? Normally, there are a number of potential enemies. The Soviet leaders had an ideology that identified the wealthy as the enemy. This built on deep-seated class divisions in society. The ideology justified violence for the sake of the better world that the Communist Party and the new state were going to create. Eventually, it too led to the deaths of many millions under Stalin.

The role of bystanders

Another important factor is the role of bystanders, those members of society who are neither perpetrators nor victims, or outside individuals, organizations, and nations. In most societies there are some who are prepared to turn against other groups. It is the population as a whole that provides or denies support for this. The people's support, opposition, or indifference largely shapes the course of events.* Opposition from bystanders, whether based on moral or other grounds, can change the per-

---

* In 1985, during the trials of the Argentine military leaders for their role in the disappearances, many voices expressed dismay about the silence in Argentina at the time of the disappearances – a silence that expressed not just fear but acceptance.

spective of perpetrators and other bystanders, especially if the bystanders act at an early point on the continuum of destruction. They may cause the perpetrators to question the morality of their violent acts or become concerned about the consequences for themselves. Internal opposition from

Table 1. *The origins and motivational sources of mistreatment*

Environmental and cultural origins[a] $\longrightarrow$	Motivational consequences	Psychological and behavioral means of fulfilling motives
A. Difficult life conditions		
Economic problems (inflation, depression, etc.); political, criminal, or other widespread violence, including war; rapid changes in technology, social institutions, values, ways of life; social disorganization.	1. Retaliation and harm-doing (hostile aggression)	Mistreatment, aggression
	2. Defense of the physical self	Escape, nonaggressive self-defense, aggression; submission or giving up
	3. Motivation to overcome obstacles, to fulfill expectations and goals	Instrumental aggression, constructive (individual and/or communal) actions[b]
Experience of attack on or threat to life, physical safety, material well-being; to the fulfillment of goals and expectations; to the psychological self, ways of life, and values; to world view and comprehension of reality	4. Defense or elevation of psychological self (self-concept, values, ways of life); desire to relinquish burdensome identity	Devaluating, scapegoating; diminishing others by mistreatment or aggression; giving up self to new group or leader; adopting an ideology; acting constructively for change
	5. Desire for a feeling of efficacy, control, power	Same as no. 4
B. Cultural and personal preconditions		
Self-concept, goals and aims, value orientations; ingroup-outgroup differentiation, devaluation; orientation to authority; monolithic (vs. pluralistic) culture; emerging ideology; cultural aggressiveness; and others	6. Motivation to protect and elevate social identity (societal self-concept)	Protecting and elevating one's group, partly by diminishing other groups; adopting new group; see also means listed under no. 4
	7. Motivation to gain renewed comprehension of the world and of the self in the world	Adopting ideology; joining new group; acting to elevate and protect old group

Table 1. *The origins and motivational sources of mistreatment*

Environmental and cultural origins[a]	Motivational consequences	Psychological and behavioral means of fulfilling motives
C. *Societal-political organization*		
Authoritarian or totalitarian system; social institutions discriminating (vs. promoting harmony, cooperation, and altruism); institutions capable of carrying out mistreatment	8. Motivation to regain hope	Giving up self to new group or leader; adopting an ideology; acting constructively for change
	9. Need for feeling connected to other human beings	Joining group; promoting joint cause; creating strong ingroup by scapegoating; creating an experience of threat to the group
	10. Obedience to authority	Submission to authority, an agentic state

[a] The difficult life conditions, cultural and personal characteristics (preconditions), and organization of society shown in column one join to create the motives listed in column two. Especially the last two components also influence the methods employed (shown in column three) to fulfill these motives.
[b] Other results can be giving up or succumbing to feelings of hopelessness and depression.

bystanders may require great courage. Other nations are often passive, even though attempts to exert influence may require little courage or real sacrifice from them.

The role of motivation

My conception of the origins of genocides and mass killings (see Table 1) is based on a theory of motivation and action, *personal goal theory*, that I have developed in other publications.[4] According to this theory, both individual human beings and cultures possess a hierarchy of motives. Individuals and cultures do not always act on their most important motives. Circumstances can activate motives lower in the hierarchy. For example, the need for self-defense and the need for connection to other people can be important or relatively unimportant motives. The lower a motive is in an individual's or culture's hierarchy, the more extreme the life conditions needed to make it active and dominant.

Whether a motive is expressed in behavior depends on the skills and competencies of individuals, or on the social institutions. Even the intention to commit genocide cannot fully evolve without a machinery of destruction. Personal goal theory describes how individuals and cultures select goals to actively pursue and suggests ways to determine when it is likely that they will act to fulfill them.

This is a probabilistic conception. The combination of difficult life conditions and certain cultural preconditions makes it probable that motives will arise that turn a group against another. This combintion makes it probable that initial acts of harm-doing will be followed by further steps along the continuum of destruction. The behavior of bystanders can facilate or inhibit this progression. Genocide arises from a pattern, or gestalt, rather than from any single source.

The outcome of this evolution and the immediate cause of the genocide is that perpetrators come to believe either that the victims have something they want or (more likely) stand in the way of something they want. In Germany the victims threatened an imagined racial purity and superiority and stood in the way of the nation's (and humanity's) improvement. In Turkey the victims seemed to threaten a pure national identity and a return to past greatness. In Cambodia the victims were seen as class enemies or judged incapable of helping to create a particular type of communist society. In Argentina the victims were seen as threatening national security, a way of life, and religious ideals, as well as the perpetrators' own safety.

Leadership and followership

The genocide of the Jews could hardly have occurred without Hitler, but that does not mean the accident of his presence was responsible. There will always be individuals with extreme views, radical ideologies, and the willingness to use violence who offer themselves as leaders. Cultural preconditions, combined with difficult life conditions, make it probable that they will be heard and accepted as leaders. Hitler's ideology and mode of leadership fitted important characteristics of German culture, tradition, and society.

Leaders also vary in personal characteristics, charisma, organizational ability, and the like. But even here culture has a role. Non-Germans always had trouble comprehending Hitler's personal appeal.[5] Leadership is crucial to move people and give them direction, but it is a transactional process, a relationship between group and leader. Because of shared culture, what a leader offers often naturally fulfills cultural requirements. Leaders also intentionally adjust their style and vision to the group. Hitler's authoritarian leadership was effective in Germany (in the United States, for example, appeal to individualism seems required of a leader).

If difficult life conditions persist and the existing leadership and societal institutions do not help people cope at least with the psychological effects, the people are likely to turn to radical leadership. In general, our capacity to predict what kinds of leaders emerge and where they lead is limited. However, conditions conducive to genocide and mass killing are likely to give rise to the kind of leadership that plans and promotes these acts. If Hitler had not existed, Germans would probably still have directed violence against some subgroup or nation; the environmental and cultural preconditions were both present. But even in Germany, leaders might conceivably have emerged who provided more peaceful and cooperative solutions. Conversely, if Hitler had lived in a country with fewer of the cultural preconditions for genocide, he would have been much less likely to gain power. And if the society were not facing severe life problems, his capacity to influence would have been further reduced.

The individual and the system

Genocide is usually organized and executed by those in power, by a government or ruling elite. Governments will commit genocide if the way of thinking and motivations out of which genocide evolves are already consistent with the culture or if they become so under the influence of the government. What is the relationship between the characteristics of individuals and those of the system to which they belong? What is the relative contribution of each to cruelty (or kindness)?

Human beings have genetic propensities for both altruism and aggression. Which of these propensities evolves more depends on individual socialization and experience. A child in a family that is highly aggressive and antisocial will usually grow up aggressive and antisocial. In a family that prohibits the expression of anger (or joy) children will learn that it is wrong to express and even to feel anger (or joy).

Effective socialization of the young will create individuals whose personal values and conduct accord with those of the system. It is unlikely that Roman soldiers who killed enemies defeated in battle experienced remorse: their socialization and experience made killing defeated enemies and enslaving women and children normal operating procedures. In some societies violence against people seen as outsiders is a way of life. We do not assume that members of such a society should have resisted a way of life integral to their social-cultural system. We do not blame individual Mundurucú headhunters, because being a Mundurucú male meant being a headhunter.[6] When a long cultural continuity of this type exists, which creates synchrony between the characteristics of the individual and the group, the social organization, not the individual, is responsible. In the modern world, however, even violence-prone societies or subsystems of societies, such as the Argentine military, usually also hold and transmit moral and social values that prohibit violence. This creates individual responsibility. Usually person and system each carry a share of the responsibility.

Socialization and experience in most modern societies result in a wide range of personal characteristics, so there will be people whose values, sympathies, self-interest, and current needs suit a violent and inhumane system and others who are opposed to such a system. The degree of opposition and conformity to a new social order depends on the nature of the preceding society. But human malleability continues through life. People not initially involved in creating the new system often undergo *resocialization*. This can be slow or fast and may affect a smaller or larger segment of the population. The speed and amount of change depend on the degree to which the original culture and therefore personal characteristics are at variance with the new system, how effective the new system is at resocialization, and the magnitude of life problems and resulting needs.

When we ask how people could do this, we must not judge only by universal moral standards that represent our ideals but must also appreciate how people are influenced by systems. Ultimately, we must ask how to create cultures and social systems that minimize harm-doing and promote human welfare, in part by how they shape individuals.

The roots of evil

Evil is not a scientific concept with an agreed meaning, but the idea of evil is part of a broadly shared human cultural heritage. The essence of evil is the destruction of human beings. This includes not only killing but the creation of conditions that materially or psychologically destroy or diminish people's dignity, happiness, and capacity to fulfill basic material needs.

By evil I mean *actions* that have such consequences. We cannot judge evil by conscious intentions, because psychological distortions tend to hide even from the perpetrators themselves their true intentions. They are unaware, for example, of their own unconscious hostility or that they are scapegoating others. Frequently, their intention is to create a "better world," but in the course of doing so they disregard the welfare and destroy the lives of human beings. Perpetrators of evil often intend to make people suffer but see their actions as necessary or serving a higher good. In addition, people tend to hide their negative intentions from others and justify negative actions by higher ideals or the victims' evil nature.

Most of us would not regard it as evil to kill to defend one's own life or the life of one's family, or to protect others' lives. In contrast, most of us would regard terrorist violence against civilians (who are not responsible for the suffering of either the terrorists or those whose interests they claim to represent) as evil.

But any kind of group violence has evil potential. It is rarely directed only at people who cause suffering. Its aim is rarely just to protect people or alleviate their suffering. And its intensity and the circle of its victims tend to increase over time, as our discussion of genocide and mass killing will show. This is also evident in the history of torture. In the Middle Ages, when torture was part of the legal system, the circle of victims expanded over time. Starting with low-status members of society accused of a crime, progressively higher-status defendants and then witnesses were tortured in order to extract evidence from them.[7]

Ordinary psychological processes and normal, common human motivations and certain basic but not inevitable tendencies in human thought and feeling (such as the devaluation of others) are the primary sources of evil. Frequently, the perpetrators' own insecurity and suffering cause them to turn against others and begin a process of increasing destructiveness.

But the same needs and motivations that cause evil can be fulfilled, and probably more completely, by joining others. This may be a more advanced level of functioning, requiring more prior individual and cultural evolution toward caring and connection. The tendency to pull together as an ingroup and turn against an outgroup is probably more basic or primitive. Threats and stress tend to evoke more primitive functioning.

There are alternative views of the roots of evil, of course. Some believe that because power and self-interest are strong human motives, human beings are basically unconcerned about others' welfare and will therefore do anything to satisfy their own interests. Thomas Hobbes developed this view most fully, and Freud's thinking is congenial to it.

According to Hobbes, people must be controlled externally, by society and the state, to prevent them from harming others in fulfilling their own interests. According to Freud they must acquire a conscience through socialization, which then controls them from within. However, assumptions about human nature cover a wide range. Some regard humans as basically good but corrupted by society (Rousseau). Others regard them as good but capable of being shaped by experience with parents and other significant people in such a way that they become unloving and unconcerned about others (the psychologist Carl Rogers).

Human beings have varied genetic potentials, and the way they develop is profoundly shaped by experience. Human infants have a strong genetic propensity to develop powerful emotional attachment to their primary caretakers. However, the quality of attachment varies greatly. One widely used classification system differentiates between infants who are "securely attached" (who are secure and comfortable in their relationship to caretakers), those whose attachment is anxious/conflictful, and those whose attachment is avoidant.[8] Infants with secure attachment to their parents or caregivers develop more successful relationships with peers in preschool and early school years.[9]

Moreover, the behavior of the caretaker seems to powerfully affect the quality of attachment. Greater responsiveness to the infant's needs, more eye contact, and more touching and holding are associated with secure attachment.[10] While the infant's own temperament and actions are likely to influence – evoke or diminish – such caretaking behaviors, their principal determinant is the caretaker. Once a certain quality of attachment appears, it is still changeable. More or less stress in the life of the mother can change the quality of the infant's attachment, presumably because the mother's behavior changes.[11]

We have the potential to be either altruistic or aggressive. Security, the fulfillment of basic needs, the propagation of one's genes, and satisfaction in life can be ensured as much by connection to other people as by wealth and power. But feelings of connection to many or all human beings require a reasonably secure and trustworthy world or society.

Differences in socialization and experience result in different personal characteristics, psychological processes, and modes of behavior. Some people develop dispositions that make them more likely to act violently and do harm, especially in response to threat. At the extreme, the desire to diminish, harm, and destroy others can become a persistent characteristic of a person (or group). People may also learn to be highly differentiated, good in relation to some while evil in relation to other humans.

Groups as evil or good

Reinhold Niebuhr regarded human beings as capable of goodness and morality, but considered groups to be inherently selfish and uncaring.[12] It is a prevalent view that nation-states are only concerned with power and self-interest. Only fear prevents them from disregarding human consequences in pursuing power and self-interest.

I see evil in groups as similar, though not identical, to evil in individuals. It arises from ordinary motivations and psychological processes. Like individuals, groups can develop characteristics that create a great and persistent potential for evil. But they can also develop values, institutions, and practices that promote caring and connection (see Chapters 17 and 18).

Moral constraints are less powerful in groups than in individuals. Groups are traditionally seen as serving the interests of their members and the group as a whole, without moral constraints or moral obligations to others. There is a diffusion of responsibility in groups.[13] Members often relinquish authority and guidance to the group and its leaders. They abandon themselves to the group and develop a commitment that enables them to sacrifice even their lives for it.[14] This can lead to altruistic self-sacrifice or to joining those who turn against another group. Combined with the group's power to repress dissent, abandoning the self enhances the potential for evil.

But in both individuals and groups the organization of characteristics and psychological processes is not static but dynamic. As a result, very rarely are either evil or good immutable. Influences acting on persons and groups can change their thoughts, feelings, motivations, and actions.

The more predisposing characteristics a society possesses and the more it progresses along the continuum of destruction – the more the motivation for genocide and the associated institutions and practices develop – the less potential there is to influence the society peacefully. Here my view converges with that of Hobbes: there is a point at which only inducing fear by the use of power will stop perpetrators from destruction. At times not even that will work, because fanaticism overcomes the desire for self-preservation. Single individuals with a strong potential for evil might be checked by the social group. But who is to inhibit groups? Powerful nations or the community of nations have not customarily assumed this responsibility, perhaps because of the tradition that nations are not morally responsible.

Comparison of personal (and social) goal theory and other approaches

There is a substantial historical and descriptive literature on each genocide and mass killing that I examine in this book but surprisingly little analysis of the psychological, cultural, and social origins, except in the case of the Holocaust, but even here no in-depth psychological-cultural analysis exists. To provide a basis for comparison and contrast with my own conception, which uses personal goal theory as a starting point, focuses on motivation and social evolution (and might be called social goal theory), I will briefly discuss some prominent ideas about the origins of the Holocaust.

Compartmentalization of functions and euphemistic language. Raul Hilberg focused on bureaucratization of functions as an important facilitator of the Holocaust.[15] Germany had a tradition of bureaucracy with functions and responsibilities divided. Each person could focus on his or her job, without seeing the whole. A person could schedule trains transporting Jews to extermination camps and keep the relationship of this activity to the genocide out of awareness. As Scott Peck noted, the same division of functions and compartmentalization characterized officers in the Pentagon during the Vietnam War.[16]

Hannah Arendt and Raul Hilberg both emphasized the use of euphemistic language that veiled reality not only from outsiders but also from the perpetrators themselves.[17] Instead of extermination squads, there were Special Troops (Einsatzgruppen); the extermination of the Jewish people was described as the "final solution of the Jewish question." Euphemistic language was used even by the victims.

Bureaucratic compartmentalization and euphemistic language serve to deny reality and distance the self from violent actions and their victims. Denial of obvious reality, though it consumes much psychological energy, allows perpetrators to avoid feeling responsibility and guilt and allows victims to avoid feeling dread.

However, bureaucratization and euphemistic language are not the source of or the motivation for genocide or mass killing. Nor are they crucial. In Cambodia and Turkey there was little bureaucratic organization.

Obedience to authority and the authoritarianism of culture. Stanley Milgram's research on obedience to authority showed that many ordinary people can be induced, even by someone with limited authority, to administer what they believe to be extremely painful and life-threatening electric shocks.[18] Milgram suggested that people can enter an "agentic" mode in which they relinquish individual responsibility and act as agents of authority.

While obedience is an important force, it is not the true motive for mass killing or genocide. The motivation to obey often comes from a *desire* to follow a leader, to be a good member of a group, to show respect for authority. Those who willingly accept the authority of leaders are likely to have also accepted their views and ideology. Guided by shared cultural dispositions, the shared experience of difficult life conditions, shared motivations that result from them, and shared inclinations for ways to satisfy motives, people *join* rather than simply obey out of fear or respect. We must consider not only how those in authority gain obedience but how the motivations of the whole group evolve. Milgram's dramatic demonstration of the power of authority, although of great importance, may have slowed the development of a psychology of genocide, as others came to view obedience as the main source of human destructiveness.

The role of authority is also stressed by Erich Fromm and Alice Miller.

According to Fromm, individuals who grew up in the authoritarian culture of Germany would have trouble assuming responsibility for their own lives.[19] In trying times they could escape from freedom by following a leader, a group. Fromm identified an intrinsic desire for submission that arose from an inability to cope. In Alice Miller's view, children who grow up in punitive, authoritarian families do not develop separate, independent identities.[20] They cannot stand on their own but need guidance and leadership. With modification, these views can be incorporated into my "evolutionary" conception. A society's strong respect for authority is *one* source of genocidal violence. A tendency to like and obey authority is *one* characteristic of perpetrators.

Psychosocial consequences of World War I on German youth. German youth were influenced by war experiences, the deprivation of food and fathering, and chaotic conditions after the war. Children old enough to be influenced by authoritarian fathering before the war must have experienced a vacuum upon the return of their defeated, powerless fathers from the war. In this view, Hitler had extraordinary influence because he fulfilled important needs.[21] Erik Erikson suggested that he served as a rebellious older brother, with whom young Germans could join in rebellion.[22]

This thinking is congenial to my conception. The special needs of young Germans, which became part of their personality, may have made their problems especially difficult to bear. These needs may have joined the even more crucial long-standing characteristics of German culture to intensify the need for authority and the security it would provide.

The soldiers also suffered long-term effects from their experiences on the battlefield. The traumatic aftereffects of extended combat have long been recognized. Research on "posttraumatic stress disorder" in Vietnam veterans uncovered persistent personality changes. In many Vietnam veterans these changes are still evident in 1989, fifteen years after the end of the war. It was also fifteen years between the end of World War I and Hitler's rise to power. Posttraumatic stress probably made German veterans more susceptible to Hilter's appeal.

Anti-Semitism in Germany. Germany's long history of anti-Semitism has been offered as one reason for the genocide. Although of great importance, prejudice and even discrimination against a group can persist for a long time without resulting in large-scale violence. How devaluation and negative image produce extreme destructiveness must be explained.

The role of the family. One focus of Israel Charny is the role of the family, and the child's experiences in it that make him a "genocider."[23] I also stress the profound importance of the child's experience, in the family and with people in general, in shaping his or her personality and moral values. However, the nature of society and what happens in it are also highly important: the historical events and conditions that affect the whole group, the group's culture, and its motivations. How children are raised – for example, with severity or with benevolence – and family organization are among important aspects of the culture.

Hitler's personality and psychopathology. Hitler's illegitimate birth, his hatred of his father, his belief (probably false) that his paternal grand-mother was Jewish, his belief that a Jewish doctor caused the death of his beloved mother, his difficulties with women, his unusual sexual practices, and the suicides of women he had relationships with have been examined in great detail.[24]

The psychohistory of individuals is a worthwhile contribution to the understanding of human personality and the disposition to cruelty. How-ever, as an explanation of genocide it has limited value, for two reasons. First, as I noted earlier, there will always be people with extreme views who offer themselves as leaders. It is more important to understand followership – what leads a group to accept such a person as their leader. Second, fanatical devotion to an ideology has more *direct* influence on the actions of perpetrators than childhood experience or psychopathology. Hitler created a radical ideology out of building blocks in his experience and personality and developed a fanatical devotion to it (for a discussion of fanaticism, see Chapter 4). Knowledge of the childhoods and personalities of leaders and followers can inform us about their susceptibility to fanaticism but cannot explain mass killing and genocide.

The role of victims. That the victims played a part in their own destruction has been suggested, mainly by Arendt but also by Hilberg, Dawidowicz, Bettelheim, and others. The Germans set up Jewish councils, which main-tained order and helped organize the transportation of Jews for "resettle-ment," which really meant murder or slave labor ending in death. There was some resistance, but most Jews did as they were told. Victims were also mostly passive in the other three cases we shall consider. There are many reasons for this. Sometimes victims deny the reality to defend them-selves against the intense anxiety that would result from seeing the inten-tions of the harm-doers. More importantly, the victims face overwhelming, brutal force. Often, the population is also antagonistic, and they stand alone. As the continuum of destruction progresses, there is a parallel pro-gression of psychological changes in victims. They give up hope, moving along a continuum of victimization.

The behavior of victims affects the perpetrators' resolve. It can make the devaluation of victims, the evolution of a genocidal ideology, and its expression in action easier or more difficult. But it is not the origin of the motivations that lead to mass killing or the cause of victimization.

Complex analyses of the origins of the Holocaust. Especially in the last decade historians have offered increasingly complex analyses of economic and political forces that preceded the Holocaust and presumably contributed to it. They have examined the role of elites, the relationship between big business and Hitler, the nature and impact of mass politics, the circumstances of the collapse of the Weimar Republic, the unification of Germany under Bismarck within a highly authoritarian political framework, the rapid industrialization of Germany, and so on.[25] I believe, however, that the basic sources of genocide are cultural characteristics, difficult life conditions, and the needs and motives that arise from them. Many economic and political processes are affected by, or arise from, and in turn serve these needs. Leaders who consciously manipulate the people to serve their political purposes are likely to share these needs. Channeling frustration, offering scapegoats, and creating ideologies may help both members of the group and leaders to deal with their needs. Thus psychological needs and political purpose coincide. This integration of different motives is itself satisfying and may become a motive in its own right.[26]

Some further comparisons: (a) Continuity and discontinuity. In explaining genocide, some authors stress discontinuity between past and present. Dekmejian suggests that in situations of social turmoil new elites arise, who are usually highly marginal groups.[27] They respond to social conditions with a pervasive identity crisis, which leads them to adopt an extreme and rigid identity. Hartt stresses the importance of structural change "as exemplified in the concept of national upheaval – an abrupt change in the political community, caused, for example, by the formation of a state through violent conflict."[28]

In all four cases I discuss, a new government had come to power not more than eight years before the genocide or mass killing began, with new leadership groups except in Argentina. However, only in Cambodia did a violent civil war bring the new elite to power.

Changes in the form of government and the associated changes in society contribute to the likelihood of genocide by creating or intensifying difficult life conditions. Turkey and Germany changed from monarchy to some form of electoral system (followed in Germany by totalitarian rule), which required changes in the populations' societal self-concepts and world views. In Cambodia many changes took place in the preceding forty years, with the change just before the genocide the most wrenching. Lack of experience and of a tradition of rule would make new leaders insecure and threaten their identity as they face intense difficulties of life, which in part they have created. Their need to form their own identity and separate themselves from the traditions of the past may increase their readiness for violence. Nonetheless, the new leaders *and* their followers are rooted in the culture, frequently a homogeneous one with a limited set of dominant values. I see the shared needs and dispositions of the whole group and a cultural continuity as especially important in understanding the roots of genocide.

(b) The role of the state and social structure. Some authors touch on the role of state structure in genocide. The state is an organization with interests of its own. It needs to survive in a world of competing and often hostile (or perceived as hostile) nation-states. In this view, to maintain its power, to bring about obedience, and to unite the group, some states commit genocide.

But not all states do. Different organizations, including states, have different perspectives on reality, methods of operation, and motives. We must come to understand the origins of motives and the evolution of destructive tendencies as exemplified by elements of culture, ideologies, societal and institutional norms that allow destruction, and institutions that come to serve destruction and whose very nature may in extreme cases require violence.

Summary: a conception of motivation and evolution

Although genocide results from a number of influences working together, these influences (see Table 1) can be divided into a few important classes.

My focus is motivation, its origins and consequences. Individuals and groups have many needs, goals, and desires. Which ones will become active and exert influence at any given time? I will describe and employ personal goal theory to specify how an active motivation to harm a subgroup of society arises and how it intensifies in the course of a social evolution that ends in genocide. I will also discuss how the normal inhibitions against harming and killing people decline, partly by excluding victims from the moral universe.

The conception and its elaboration in the analyses of specific cases give us ways of identifying conditions under which genocide and mass killing are more or less probable. The conception may help us predict the occurrence of genocide and specify interventions by other nations that would inhibit mistreatment with genocidal potential. It provides a basis for a long-term agenda: the creation of caring, nonaggressive people and societies. In the next four chapters I discuss in detail different components of this conception of the origins of genocide.

3   The psychology of hard times: the effects of difficult life conditions

Psychologists have identified two primary conditions that instigate aggression: (1) frustration, which results from interference with goal-directed behavior or the failure to fulfill goals, and (2) attack on or threat to life, material well-being, or self-concept and self-esteem.[1] Other conditions have also been shown to increase aggression: heat, noise, crowding, the general level of arousal, and specifically sexual arousal.[2] These conditions and bodily states are most likely to intensify aggression if an inclination for it already exists because of prior frustration or attack or for other reasons. It is noteworthy that at least some of the physical conditions, such as crowding, and some of the bodily states, such as arousal due to stress, can be the result of difficult life conditions.[3]

Why do certain conditions make aggression probable? According to the sociobiologist E. O. Wilson, human beings have a genetic predisposition to respond aggressively when their survival and thereby the transmission of their genes are threatened.[4] Although no particular mode of aggression is genetically based, the probability increases that some aggressive response will result. Whereas a genetic potential for aggression obviously exists and probably a genetic predisposition as well, the great individual and group variation in aggressiveness suggests that environment and experience are more important.[5] In humans, feeling threatened is a psychological experience that results from the way events are construed. The meaning given to events by people can be partly based on their objective nature (e.g., lions attack, fires burn) but is mostly based on past experience, world views, personality, and views handed down by society. Research showing the relationship of aggression to parental socialization and family experience (see Chapter 4) supports this view.

In the psychological laboratory frustration and attack are normally limited in magnitude and duration and involve no real threat to survival.[6] Under these conditions instigation, particularly frustration, has less potency. Intense, persistent frustration of goals and expectations resulting from difficult conditions of life can be expected to have greater impact.

35

In psychological experiments, an aggressive response to instigation is most likely when (1) the subject is physically attacked, that is, pain is inflicted, usually by electric shocks; and (2) the subject's self-concept, self-esteem, or social image is threatened. Insult, verbal abuse, and criticism give rise to anger and aggression. Aggression is more likely when the actions of a frustrator seem to arise out of ill-will. Frustrating people by apparent carelessness or stupidity induces less aggression than frustrating them arbitrarily, presumably with a desire to harm.[7] It is in the latter case that victims can expect future attacks and self-defense is essential.

Motivations arising from threat, frustration, or difficult life conditions

Motives due to threat, frustration, or difficult life conditions depend both on the nature of instigation and the characteristics of individuals (and cultures). Are certain of these motives better served by aggression than by other means?

Motivational sources of human behavior

According to my theory of personal goals, there are four major sources of motivation.[8] First, in the course of their lives, people develop personal goals, desires that they want to fulfill, outcomes that they want to produce. Groups of outcomes that satisfy the desires – for example, for achievement, approval, or friendship – define personal goals. In most cases a "network of cognitions" – thoughts, beliefs, relevant knowledge – accompanies the desired outcomes and in part defines the goal.

Human beings are purposive creatures, who set aims for themselves and strive to fulfill them. The desire for certain outcomes is incorporated into our personalities. Each of us has a variety of personal goals, which can be arranged in a hierarchy according to their importance. Each may in certain circumstances become an active desire. Under normal conditions, in psychologically well-functioning people, personal goals are the most important sources of motivation.

Our *biological needs*, which include hunger, thirst, freedom from pain, survival, are another important type of motivation. When they are regularly satisfied, these needs are apparent only in the modulated form of personal goals. (A gourmet, for example, seeks food for pleasure, not survival). Deprivation makes biological needs a strong motive. Prior deprivation causes some people to be strongly motivated by the psychological presence of biological needs, even when they are currently fulfilled.

Goals involve a *desire* for outcomes; biological needs *push* for satisfaction. When important goals are persistently frustrated, they may come to resemble needs and exert a push for satisfaction. While personal goals can be internally activated, by thoughts and images, frequently conditions in the environment elicit or activate them: a task activates the goal to achieve; another's need activates the goal to benefit people. In contrast, needs tend to press for satisfaction even in the absence of relevant environmental conditions.

Social customs, rules, and standards also give rise to action or determine its direction and aim. Many customs and rules are second nature to us, we "automatically" follow them, without awareness. They may even define for us when to become angry and how to express our anger. They define our modes of interaction with others, including the respect (or lack of respect) we show to people who fill certain positions in society. When a custom or rule is strongly established, people will deviate from it only when another strong motivation requires deviation. Often we become aware of the influence of rules and customs only when there are compelling reasons to deviate from them. Whether we follow them automatically or consciously, adherence usually gives rise to good feelings and deviation to guilt, anxiety, or the fear of disapproval and punishment. This is especially true of norms that identify mutual social obligations.

Finally, *unconscious motivation* can guide the choice of our aims. In this case, we do not know why we choose the aim, and sometimes do not know the real aim. A motivation to fail may result from unconscious hostility to parents. Anger may be displaced from parents or people in authority to more acceptable objects.

All of us have certain motives: protection of our physical self from danger, attack, and deprivation; protection and enhancement of our self-image or self-concept and the associated values and ways of life. In people (or groups) whose self-concept is poor, negative, or under attack, the desire to protect the self-image will become a highly important motive; it may come to resemble a need pushing for satisfaction.

How do people select aims to act on?[9] Their personal goals and other motives form a hierarchy. The aims of individuals or groups *at a particular time* depend on the relative importance of their motives and the degree to which circumstances allow or call for the expression and fulfillment of each motive. Persistent life problems "activate" motives for self-protection, make them dominant, and over time needlike. Ordinary *self-related* goals, such as the desire for satisfying work or friendship, are replaced by *self-protective* goals, the desire to defend the physical or psychological self; *other-related* goals, the desire to benefit people or fulfill moral values, are less likely to become active.

Other-related goals arise from personal values; they resemble personal goals, except that their desired outcome is human welfare. At least two kinds of personal values are important. A *prosocial value orientation* involves concern about others and the desire to benefit them. Research shows that people with a stronger prosocial orientation give more help to others in need. A *moral rule orientation* embodies the desire to maintain or fulfill moral principles, norms, and rules.[10] When other-related goals are low in the hierarchy of motives, the environmental press must be greater if they are to become active; for example, the other person's distress must be more intense.

Under persistently difficult life conditions, lasting changes often occur in motive hierarchies. Self-protective and self-related goals become more important, and people become less open to others' need.

People judge others' need for help relative to their own well-being. They engage in *hedonic balancing*; they compare their "relative well-being," the discrepancy between their current welfare and their normal or usual well-being, with others' relative well-being, the discrepancy between others' current welfare and what they regard as others' normal, or usual, or customary well-being.[11] If their own relative well-being is worse, people are unlikely to help, even if they are in an absolute sense better off than a person in need. Even apart from comparisons, when people's own well-being is low, the need of others has to be great to gain their attention. The main exceptions are people with strong prosocial or moral values.

The defense of the physical and psychological self are basic goals, but they can be dormant for a person with a strong feeling of personal adequacy who lives under normal (nonthreatening) conditions. People with a weaker sense of their physical safety or weak self-esteem are easily threatened. Those with less faith in their own efficacy and less expectation of fulfilling their goals are easily frustrated. But even people with a strong individual or collective sense of physical and psychological safety will feel threatened when they face intense and persistent difficulties in life, and their primary motive can become defense of the individual or collective self.

Motivations for aggression: psychological states and processes that promote aggression

A variety of motives result from threat, attack, the perception of danger, and interference with the fulfillment of goals. Self-protective personal goals can become so intense that they develop the imperative, forceful quality of needs. Aggression is a likely response.

Proponents of the original "frustration-aggression" hypothesis, the first widely used theory of aggression in psychology, might regard all the motives that I specify below as the result of frustration. But I prefer a differentiated view, identifying a variety of motives that may generate aggression.

1. Instigation can give rise to anger, rage, and the desire for *retaliation* and *harm-doing*. Aggression as a means to serve this motive has been called hostile aggression. Anger, rage, and the desire to retaliate or harm can also be useful for mobilizing a person to remove the attack or threat, that is, for self-defense.

2. Instigating conditions can also directly give rise to the motivation for *self-defense*. Escape is one mode of self-defense, but it is often impossible or inconsistent with a person's self-conception and values or imposes further frustration by requiring extreme effort, such as moving away. Aggression is an effective self-defense, since it communicates that instigation does not pay and makes renewed instigation less likely.[12] It can also serve self-defense by reestablishing a balance of power with the instigators,[13] which reduces the likelihood of further harm-doing, reestablishes self-esteem and public esteem, and makes a cooperative relationship possible. In this way reciprocity or retaliation can serve the motivation for self-defense rather than the desire to harm. Other means of self-defense are subordination and attempts to initiate a positive, cooperative relationship with instigators.

3. Instigating conditions also give rise to the motive to *protect the psychological self*: one's self-concept, identity, self-esteem. Threat to values, beliefs, and ways of life can also give rise to this motive. For some people the experience of threat does not even require an external source; the insecurity, weakness, and incapacity can come from within. Whatever its source, the need to defend the psychological self can be extraordinarily powerful. Often it employs such "internal," psychological means as scapegoating or devaluation of others, which eventually provides a basis for violence against them.

A related goal is to elevate the self. Social comparison, the desire for a favorable comparison of the self to others – in material or psychological well-being, status and power, character and personality – is an important and perhaps universal human motive.[14] Like all human motives, it differs among persons and cultures in its strength and nature.* This desire is more intense when the self-concept is under attack.

---

* Most likely, people can learn to accept inequality with others in skills, character, and so on, and still have a positive self-esteem. What are the minimal requirements for positive self-regard? Can people accept, for example, less intelligence but a positive character in themselves as a basis for positive self-regard? This is an important question for creating a world characterized by the values of caring and connectedness (see Part IV).

Interviews with violent criminals show that many of them have poor self-esteem. Their violence is aimed at protecting their self-image or their image in others' eyes in response to a provocation that is often mild or even imagined.[15] Other criminals are violent because they think a "real man" must be strong and forceful. They seek violent encounters to experience this sense of their maleness and to create an image in others' eyes of a powerfully masculine individual.

4. A sense of *injustice* that arises from unfavourable comparison of one's relative well-being and of the balance between one's efforts and rewards or between one's own or one's group's rights and privileges and those of other people or groups can give rise to resentment, anger, and violence. The experience of injustice motivates aggression of many kinds: revolutions and other social movements, criminal and other violence.[16] In hard times, if others are unaffected, feelings of injustice or unfairness can be especially intense. It is not the actual injustice that is the source of resentment, but the perception of injustice. Those identified as responsible will often be perceived as evil and deserving punishment.

5. A related motivation is to enhance a sense of *personal efficacy* and to gain a feeling of *personal power*. A feeling of inefficacy may result from frustration or it may be a personality characteristic. Aggressive persons are often unsuccessful. For example, aggressive children are often low academic achievers and aggressive adults often did poorly in school as children.[17] Aggressive children tend to be socially unsuccessful, unpopular among their peers.[18] Unable to satisfy their affiliation needs and social goals, they feel powerless. Aggression can give a sense of power or efficacy. In one study, frustrated boys were led to subject others to loud, noxious noise. When the victims denied feeling discomfort, previously aggressive boys turned up the sound, but nonaggressive boys did not.[19] The escalating aggression of some Nazi concentration camp guards in the face of the powerlessness and resulting passivity of victims suggests a desire for efficacy or impact.[20] Over time, the association of efficacy with aggression makes aggressive behavior self-reinforcing.

Clinical experience with a group of incestuous fathers suggests that one of their motives was to gain a feeling of power. These men are weak and ineffectual and have low self-esteem. They often have sexual and emotional problems with sick or rejecting wives and are unable either to take steps to improve their marital situation or to seek sexual and emotional gratification from women outside the home.[21] The capacity to make a daughter into a sexual partner may give them a feeling of power.

Otto Rank and, following him, Ernest Becker proposed an extreme form of the idea that aggression serves a desire for power.[22] Becker maintained that human beings cannot come to terms with death. Killing, including human sacrifice ritualized in some cultures in earlier times, may give the killer a feeling of invulnerability and power over death.

In my view, however, it is the feeling of present insecurity, incomprehension, and lack of control due to cultural background and personality together with life problems that lead people to seek strength and control through the exercise of power over others, including the ultimate power, killing. People who feel valued and significant and who find life comprehensible and their circumstances controllable will not kill out of a need for invulnerability and immortality.

The feeling of vulnerability and the need for aggression to overcome it and the desire for power for its own sake can become persistent characteristics of individuals and groups.

6. Chaos, disorder, and sudden profound changes, especially when accompanied by frustration, threat, and attack, invalidate the conceptions of self and world that serve as guides by which new experience acquires meaning and life gains coherence. (Seymour Epstein has suggested that schizophrenia is an extreme manifestation of the loss of an organizing conception of the self and reality.)[23] The motivation to gain a *renewed comprehension* will be powerful. Ideologies are attractive because they offer renewed comprehension and a renewed self-definition.*

7. In the face of persistent frustrations or threats, an important motive is gaining *hope* for control over events and renewed faith in the future goodness or benevolence of life itself. Ideologies can offer this renewed hope and faith. Being part of a movement to fulfill an ideology offers both hope and a feeling of significance.

8. Humans have a profound need for *connectedness* to others, belongingness, and community. This need coexists with a need for independence and self-sufficiency. Socialization and experience determine the relative importance of these two motives and decide to what extent they are consciously acknowledged and accepted. Under stressful conditions, the desire for belonging grows in intensity, yet is constantly frustrated.

Research shows that after a positive experience (success in a task, material gain through luck, a friendly act by another person, even thinking about positive past experiences) people are more helpful to others. Posi-

---

* Traumatic events – accidents that result in significant harm, rape and other violent attacks, and certain combat experiences – shatter assumptions about the world and one's place in it. The world is seen as less controllable and predictable, less safe, less benevolent.[24] Similar changes in assumptions are likely to follow from severe life problems and social disorganization.

tive experiences diminish self-concern and self-preoccupation and increase attention and sensitivity to others.[25] After negative experiences, helpfulness may be unaffected or may increase, but more often it declines. The effect of the experience depends on its nature and on circumstances. For example, when a child fails in the presence of others on a task, he or she will later be more helpful in their presence, as if to improve his or her tarnished image.[26]

When goals are unfulfilled and people feel frustrated and threatened, it is likely (though not inevitable) that they will become preoccupied with their own needs. When resources are scarce, competition for them increases. As a result, connection to others, community support, and the experience of a shared identity will diminish. Just as importantly, difficult life conditions are often seen as a personal as well as a collective failure that threatens a collective or national self-concept. When the difficulties are severe and persistent, the feeling of identification with the group may lessen.

This need for belonging and community is frustrated just when it is greatest. Shared antagonism to a subgroup of society or an external enemy can create or enhance a sense of community. Erich Fromm's idea of "escape from freedom" in Nazi followers implies both a search for guidance and leadership *and* a desire for attachment and belonging.[27] By giving up the self to a leader and a group, the need for community was fulfilled and a burdensome identity was relinquished for a new group identity.

9. These considerations suggest that the motivation for a *positive social identity* can also be served by joining groups and adopting ideologies. Human beings gain much of their identity from groups and incorporate the systems they are part of into their self-conceptions. That is why changes in society, and in smaller groups such as the family (e.g., divorce) are so wrenching. As the primary group fails economically or loses status and power or moral influence, as it is diminished in its members' eyes, it loses the power to confer a positive social identity.*

---

* The late British psychologist Henry Tajfel and his associates made significant contributions to the understanding of group relations. *Social categorization*, the classification of individuals into different categories (even if arbitrary), results in the perception of similarity among members of one's category (group) and difference from members of other categories. It leads to stereotyping people in categories other than one's own and to discriminating against them. The desire for favorable *social comparison* is strong. People are motivated to positively evaluate not only themselves but also their group and to compare it favorably to other groups. Even when they are arbitrarily assigned to a group, people's self-esteem increases when they are allowed to discriminate against outgroup members. Tajfel and others also stressed the importance of *social identity*, which is the tendency of individuals to perceive and define themselves in terms of broad, "superimposed" social categories.[28] *(cont. p. 43)*

10. The aim of *instrumental aggression* is not to harm but to serve other goals. When goals are persistently frustrated, it becomes more likely that people will try to fulfill them by aggressive means.

11. *Obedience to authority* is another important source of aggression. Stanley Milgram's research demonstrated that many people were willing to obey an experimenter and administer what they believed were life-threatening electric shocks to another person. Each participant acted as a teacher who was supposedly punishing a learner's mistakes. College students at Yale and people living in New Haven administered what they believed to be increasing levels of electric shocks, including extremely intense and dangerous ones, to a person who worked on a task in an adjoining room. They did so simply in response to the demands and insistence of the person in charge of the experiment. A substantial number (62.5 percent) administered the highest levels of shock, even though they could hear the victim's distress and intense complaints. Many did so even when the victim was with them and they had to place his hand on the shock apparatus (30 percent).[29]

Milgram noted that under the influence of authority people can enter an agentic mode. When this happens they no longer evaluate the morality of an action independently, but see themselves as agents carrying out the commands of superiors. However, as I noted in Chapter 2, obedience to authority involves more than the desire to be rewarded and not punished. Often people obey because, starting with shared motives, they join leaders; they identify with them and adopt their views and wishes.

From the perspective of my theory of personal goals, we can say that conflicting moral considerations may not arise when the motive to obey is dominant. As "agents" people will accept the reasons for violence provided by authority, especially if they share with those in authority life problems and culture and therefore also share the motivations underlying violence. One of the followers' motivations may be to receive the guidance of authority. Since human beings tend to strive for goal or motive integration, other motives will join or be integrated with the motive for obedience; for example, Nazi doctors took pride in the professional skills they displayed during inhuman medical experiments conducted in concentration camps.[30]

I use in this book the concept of societal (or cultural or group) self-concept. I stress both its importance for individual identity and that the *content* or nature of societal self-concept strongly affects individual and group behavior and responses to life problems. In difficult times both individual and group self-concepts may no longer provide positive self-evaluation and guidance. They may be intensely defended, or they may become disorganized and weakened, creating an intense need for a new self-definition and a new social identity.

Difficult life conditions and aggression

Difficult life conditions affect both individuals and groups. For example, the loss of World War I and what many saw as a humiliating peace treaty profoundly threatened the Germans' collective self-concept as a strong, superior, proud nation. The war was followed by a revolution and then by a devastating inflation, depression and joblessness, and political chaos and violence. There was a breakdown of sexual and social mores.[31] People felt their physical survival, their ability to support a family, their way of life and values, and their conception of themselves as individuals and as a nation to be profoundly threatened.

There is some formal evidence that difficult life conditions increase violence. In economically difficult times there were more lynchings in the South.[32] Economic hardship (resulting from low cotton prices) was associated with lynchings of black people and to a slight degree with lynchings of white "ingroup" members. In addition, the degree of decline in economic well-being was associated with the frequency of lynchings.[33] Economic problems are associated with an increased rate of murder and other violent crime or, in societies where social taboos against violence are strong, such as Japan, an increased rate of suicide.[34] Associated with higher rates of unemployment are more reports of child abuse.

If difficult life conditions are to result in the mistreatment of groups, a substantial number of people, including a potentially dominant group, must be affected. The problems must be persistent, with cumulative psychological effects. Hitler's rise to power was the result of difficult life conditions, and the Nazi genocide was perpetrated at a time when the fortunes of Germany on the battlefields of World War II took a turn for the worse. In Cambodia, the evacuation of cities and murder of millions of city dwellers occurred after years of civil war, hunger, and misery. Turkey suffered losses of territory, power, and status for many years before and during World War I before murdering the Armenians. In Argentina, severe economic problems and political terrorism preceded the disappearances.

The effect of stress and danger on psychological experience

Scott Peck's account of the My Lai massacre shows how stress and distress, which are among the usual consequences of difficult conditions, affect human behavior.[35]

The life of a soldier in a combat zone is one of chronic stress. . . . The troops of Task Force Barker . . . were at the other end of the world from their homes. The food was poor, the insects thick, the heat enervating, the sleeping quarters uncomfortable. Then there was the danger, usually not as severe as in other wars, yet probably even more stressful in Vietnam because it was so unpredictable. It came in the form of mortar rounds in the night when the soldiers thought they were safe, booby traps tripped on the way to the latrine, mines that blew a solder's legs off as he strolled down a pretty lane. . . . the enemy appeared when and where it was unexpected. (Pp. 220–1)

In the previous month they had achieved no military success. Unable to engage the enemy, they had themselves sustained a number of casualties from mines and booby traps. The province was considered to be a Vietcong stronghold, one in which the civilian population was largely controlled and influenced by the Communist guerrillas. It was generally felt that the civilians aided and abetted the guerillas to such a degree that it was often difficult to distinguish the combatants from the noncombatants. Hence the Americans tended to hate and distrust all Vietnamese in the area. (P. 213)

On the eve of the operation there seemed to be a mood of anticipation; finally they would engage the enemy and succeed in doing what they were there for. (P. 213)

When "Charlie" Company moved into the hamlets of My Lai they discovered not a single combatant. None of the Vietnamese was armed. No one fired on them. They found only unarmed women, children, and old men.

   Some of the things that then happened are unclear. What is clear, however, is that the troops of C Company killed at least somewhere between five and six hundred of those unarmed villagers. . . . These people were killed in a variety of ways. The most large-scale killings occurred in the particular hamlet of My Lai 4. There the first platoon of Charlie Company, under the command of Lieutenant William L. Calley, Jr., herded villagers into groups of twenty to forty or more, who were then slaughtered by rifle fire, machine gun fire, or grenades. (P. 214)

Peck suggested that humans regress under prolonged stress or discomfort; they become more primitive, childish. I believe this happens mainly when basic needs for safety, control, predictability, and self-respect are frustrated. Another response to stress is the mechanism of defense that Robert Jay Lifton called "psychic numbing." When our emotions are overwhelmingly unpleasant or painful, we anesthetize ourselves; soldiers become able to tolerate mangled bodies, and the capacity for horror becomes blunted. While this diminishes suffering, it also makes us insensitive to the suffering of others, especially when the other is defined as different, the member of an outgroup, or an enemy bent on our destruction.

   This analysis applies not only to the stress of soldiers in combat, but also to stress created by difficult life conditions. Starvation, homelessness, and even others' deaths can become less worthy of notice as habituation and psychic numbing diminish our capacity for empathy.

   Victims of mistreatment can reach a point where they welcome another's death or misfortune if it contributes to their own survival or relative well-being. Eli Wiesel says in *Night* that when his own father died in Buchenwald of dysentery, his sorrow was mixed with relief over the lifting of a burden that made his own survival more difficult. Another dramatic example is described in the following statement by a survivor of the Treblinka concentration camp, quoted in Sereny's book *Into That Darkness*. Jewish workers lived on supplies taken while sorting the belongings of incoming "transports," the wagon loads of people brought to the camp to be killed in gas chambers. The survivor talks about a time when, for a while, no transports were arriving.

Things went from bad to worse that month of March....There were no transports....In the storehouses everything had been packed up and shipped – we had never before seen all the space because it had always been so full....You can't imaging what we felt when there was nothing there. You see, the *things* were our justification for being alive. If there were no *things* to administer, why would they let us stay alive? On top of that, we were, for the first time, hungry....It was just about when we had reached the lowest ebb in our morale that, one day towards the end of March, Kurt Franz [a guard] walked into our barracks, a wide grin on his face. "As of tomorrow," he said, "transports will be rolling in again." And do you know what we did? We shouted "Hurrah, hurrah." It seems impossible now. Every time I think of it I die a small death; but it's the truth. That is what we did; and that is where we had got to. And sure enough, the next morning they arrived. We had spent all of the preceding evening in an excited, expectant mood; it meant life – you see, don't you? – safety and life. The fact that it was their death, whoever they were, which meant our life, was no longer relevant.[36]

Sociologists have explained social movements and revolutions in terms of threat to interests. However, participants often represent varied elements of society – the "heterogeneity problem." Thus, members of the lower middle class, who were small merchants and artisans powerfully affected by the financial problems in Germany after World War I, were long regarded as the main supporters of the Nazi movement. The actual evidence indicates, however, greater complexity. A recent analysis argues on the basis of new evidence that the elites voted for Hitler and had a substantial role in bringing him into power.[37] Participation in the French Revolution also came from varied social groups.[38]

Difficult life conditions affect people in many different ways, such as material loss and suffering, diminished social status, and threat to values. In different groups the cultural preconditions for violent reactions are present to different degrees. A larger percentage of Lutherans than Catholics supported the Nazis in Germany. There were probably several reasons for this: for example, a connection between nationalism and Protestantism in Germany and Martin Luther's intense anti-Semitism (see Chapter 9).

Religious groups and groups with conservative values and life-styles will be greatly threatened by societal changes such as the acceptance of homosexuality, feminism, permissive child raising, and drugs. In Latin American countries small rich elites (and their military supporters) are materially threatened by challenges to the status quo. But they also regard their power and privilege as right, natural, and maybe even God-given, they devalue the poor, and they hold a strong anticommunist ideology.

Analyses might specify how different subgroups are affected psychologically by difficult life conditions. This would help us predict which groups will join social movements, including those that lead to genocide. On an individual level, personal characteristics also affect what motives arise and what avenues for satisfying them are acceptable and appealing.

The long-term effects of combat experience

The persistent stress and intense danger that soldiers experience in combat have many long-term effects, as indicated by past work and recent research with Vietnam veterans.

Veterans with a significant long-term stress reaction are diagnosed as suffering from posttraumatic stress disorder. Major symptoms are uncontrollable reexperiencing of the traumatic event(s) (through intrusive recollections, dreams, and in other ways), "numbed responsiveness" to the external world, and denial and avoidance of memories and experiences associated with the traumatic events.

These veterans often lack goals; they have lost a sense of self, identity, meaning, and control. They give the impression of being "empty shells." Other symptoms are easily stimulated anger and rage and sensation-seeking, the need to engage in dangerous activities.[39] They have lost faith in legitimate authority.[40] They no longer believe that the world is a benign, orderly, and controllable place or that they themselves are worthy and that other people are worthwhile to relate to.

Three of the four genocides and mass killings that I will analyze were associated with war, often in multiple ways. In Germany, life problems following World War I contributed to Hitler's rise to power, and the genocide itself began during World War II. Turkey had suffered defeats in wars of liberation; the genocide of the Armenians occurred soon after one such war and during another war, World War I. In Cambodia, the genocide followed an intense civil war. In Argentina the disappearances followed left-wing terrorism and right-wing death squad murders – a civil war on as yet a limited scale.

All wars produce some people with posttraumatic stress disorder. They are likely to be attracted to a movement and leader offering them a sense of significance as well as scapegoats and enemies. Their need for activity and excitement may make the pseudomilitary roles that perpetrators sometimes start with (and later the actual role of perpetrator) appealing.

The effects of traumatic combat stress probably depend partly on the nature of the experiences, partly on personality, and partly on culture, which shapes responses to stress. The feeling in the United States that the Vietnam War was meaningless, a mistake, and even immoral may have shaped and intensified the posttraumatic response of veterans. The loss of World War I, the abdication of the kaiser, and unemployment after the war may have shaped the experience of German veterans in a similar way. Both wars involved movement back and forth over terrain that was won and lost repeatedly; this would heighten the sense of meaninglessness.*[43]

Strategies for coping and goal satisfaction

When the motives that I described earlier arise from difficult life conditions, certain internal, psychological modes of satisfying them may cause aggression.

Devaluation and scapegoating. When there is no aggressor or the aggressor is too powerful or the source of responsibility cannot be identified or the responsibility is one's own (or one's group's), identifying a scapegoat will have "beneficial" psychological effects.[44] A cause is found, and life problems become comprehensible. Known danger is preferable to vague anxiety about an unspecified threat. Finding a scapegoat makes people believe their problems can be predicted and controlled; and it eliminates one's own responsibility, thereby diminishing guilt and enhancing self-esteem.

Devaluation and assigning people to outgroups (seeing a group or its members as "them" rather than "us") are widespread human tendencies that often serve as a basis for scapegoating and a precondition for harmdoing. Devaluation confers a sense of superiority. Poor southern whites who led impoverished, humiliating lives could elevate their self-esteem

---

* Many of the factors contributing to posttraumatic stress disorder are situational. One is poor leadership. Another is uncertainty – in Vietnam, uncertainty whether the Vietnamese were friends or enemies and uncertainty about the aims and strategy of combat missions (see endnote 39). Situational factors seem most important, but personality characteristics associated with posttraumatic stress disorder have also been identified. In a prospective study, low self-esteem in ninth grade was positively related to posttraumatic stress syndrome at the ages of thirty-six to thirty-seven.[41] In another study veterans who were exposed to traumatic events (e.g., in combat) but showed no later symptoms were compared with veterans who suffered from posttraumatic stress.[42] Characteristics of the former group were striving for understanding, consistent attempts to make their experience meaningful, a trust in their own values and judgment, acceptance of fear, and lack of excessive violence. These men were willing to disobey the order of a superior if they felt this was essential for survival.

by a feeling of superiority over blacks; Germans could do the same by feeling superior to Jews. Devaluation and scapegoating also make "retaliation" easier. People who are judged mean or vicious or worthless deserve to suffer. There is also material gain when the property or job of a "wrongdoer" is taken over. Finally, those who scapegoat become an ingroup whose members feel less alone.

Scapegoats are usually selected from groups who are already devalued. Some are chosen for specific occasions, but others are used frequently and repeatedly. In the third century A.D., Tertullian, a Roman as well as Christian, wrote:

> They take the Christians to be the cause of every disaster to the state, of every misfortune to the people. If the Tiber reaches the wall, if the Nile does not reach the fields, if the sky does not move or if the earth does, if there is a famine, or if there is a plague, the cry is at once, "The Christians to the Lions."

Joining groups. Submerging the self in a group can enable a person to relinquish the burdens of unfulfilled goals and a threatened identity and to gain a new identity. It also helps to protect the psychological self and serves the need for connectedness to other human beings.[45] Antagonism to another group intensifies feelings of belonging.

Shared enmity strengthens group identity especially when the ingroup is not greatly endangered by the outgroup. In an experiment two groups of boys in adjoining summer camps were pitted against each other in a series of athletic competitions. One group consistently lost. Their morale plummeted, the group disintegrated, members turned against each other, and their leaders deserted them.[46] To increase cohesion the group must turn against a weaker enemy. Leaders try to select as enemies groups they perceive as weaker, although they often miscalculate, as Pakistan did in its war with India and Hitler and Napoleon did in their wars against Russia.[47] Sometimes past enmity and hatred overcome judgment, as in the case of Cambodian attacks on Vietnam between 1976 and 1979.

When life conditions threaten national self-concept and identity, people need a different group (or improvement in the national self-concept) to provide "positive group distinctiveness," which "serves to protect, enhance, preserve or achieve a positive social identity for members of the group."[48] Religions, cults, political movements, and even social groups that promote new life-styles can fulfill this function. As I have pointed out, scapegoating can accomplish the same end.

The greater the demands a group makes on its members and the more it guides their lives, the more completely the members can relinquish their burdensome identity and assume a group identity. However, submerging oneself in a group makes it difficult to maintain independent judgment of the group's conduct and exert a contrary influence. Deindividuation, a disinhibition of the usual moral constraints on individual action, is a likely consequence. Experiments show that aggressiveness is increased by conditions that weaken a sense of identity or increase anonymity, such as wearing masks.[49]

Adopting ideologies. Adopting an ideology is another solution to difficult life conditions that threaten existence and self-worth. By ideology I mean a system of beliefs and values concerning an ideal social organization and way of life. When traditional ways stop working, an ideology may offer renewed comprehension of the world and give meaning and direction to life. It is useful to distinguish between the *existing culture*, which consists of beliefs, meanings, values, valuations, symbols, myths, and perspectives that are shared largely without awareness, and *ideology*, which I define as a primarily consciously held set of beliefs and values.

Psychological research shows that attitudes and values are related to behavior.[50] Strongly held values give rise to the motivation to act. Attitudes, beliefs, and values will lead to action especially when a person feels competent or the circumstances clearly indicate what action is likely to succeed.[51] Ideology, an interconnected system of beliefs and valuations, can be a powerful source of motivation.

History shows that people will sacrifice themselves to promote ideologies. As I have mentioned, followers of ideologies often identify some people as a hindrance and commit horrifying acts in the name of creating a better world or fulfilling higher ideals. This scapegoating occurs partly because the new social or spiritual order is defined in contrast to an existing order and partly because the ideal way of life is difficult to bring about or the new social system does not fulfill its promise. Examples include the great bloodbath after the French Revolution, the Inquisition and other religious persecutions, as well as genocides and mass killings.

Constructive reactions to life conditions. Responses to difficult life conditions can also be positive and constructive. Like Davitz's children, whose training enabled them to respond to frustration with renewed efforts to reach their goals, so constructive coping efforts by a group can result in positive psychological effects and real improvement in life conditions.[52] Ideologies can be constructive. Different groups can find common goals rather than focus on conflicting goals.[53] Unfortunately, the culture and social organization that would give rise to such constructive responses often do not exist. How to create them is the focus of the last two chapters of the book.

4   Cultural and individual characteristics

The influence of culture

A primary determinant of the response to difficult life conditions is culture and its institutions. Culture helps to determine what motives arise and whether they are fulfilled by turning against subgroups or external enemies.

Culture provides shared explanations and images of the world, shared values and goals, a shared symbolic environment. Through such institutions as the military, schools, and child rearing, it shapes individual personality. Many aspects of culture are *processes* that occur *among* individuals – such as the relative influence of peers versus adults on children.

The correspondence in values between individual and culture is most obvious in simple societies with a single set of dominant values and rules; it is less clear in pluralistic cultures. Moreover, cultural characteristics modify each other. For example, authoritarian child rearing teaches children to be submissive to authority, but also to raise their own children in an authoritarian manner. Depending on other aspects of the culture, this practice can be highly effective or lead to rebelliousness.

Different psychological tendencies predisposing humans to mistreatment of others or prosocial action are present in different cultures and social institutions to different degrees. Unproductive research approaches and excessive initial expectations have reduced interest in the notion of national character. But research has found cultural differences in many domains. For example, Milgram found that individuals conform to a group more in some cultures than in others when they are asked to compare the length of lines in an experiment.[1] The relative influence of peers (as opposed to adults) on children is greater in the United States than it is in the Soviet Union.[2] Abraham Maslow suggested cultural differences in "synergy," the extent to which people fulfill themselves by contributing to the common good as opposed to competitively advancing their own interests.[3] Beatrice Whiting and John Whiting's studies show that cultural

51

differences in child rearing are related to differences in children's altruism and egoism.[4] David McClelland demonstrated differences in achievement imagery in children's stories in different societies and that related differences exist in actual achievement.[5]

Cultural characteristics that contribute to group violence can be surmised from historical and anthropological data, from art and literature, and so on. All cultures possess some of these characteristics. The likelihood of group violence is greatest if a group possesses a constellation of the most essential ones.

Aggressiveness as a persistent behavioral mode

While aggression is an outcome of cultural characteristics and life conditions, aggressiveness can become a habitual way of behaving and even a value. Some people see challenge and provocation everywhere and try to fulfill their goals by aggression.[6] Others will not behave aggressively even under extreme provocation.

It is the same at the group level. For example, among the Mundurucú headhunters of Brazil aggression against other tribes was part of the culture, constantly promoted and reinforced. Potential victims were seen as nonhuman: the very word for a non-Mundurucú means enemy, and warriors spoke of the non-Mundurucú as dangerous animals. Human trophies (heads) conferred high status on a warrior. Males were trained in special skills for hunting enemy tribes. Raids on enemy villages were carefully planned and executed according to well-established patterns.[7] The world was seen as hostile and fighting as necessary for survival.

Sociobiologists argue that there is a genetic disposition to respond with aggression to conditions that threaten survival. Wilson believes that Mundurucú culture itself developed in response to physical conditions that made aggression enhance group survival. "Although solid demographic proof is absent, indirect evidence suggests that numbers of the Mundurucú were (and still are, in a pacified state) limited by the shortage of high quality protein.... When these competitors (e.g., other tribes hunting for game) were decimated by murderous attacks, the Mundurucú share of the forest yield was correspondingly increased."[8] Thus, aggression gave the Mundurucú a "Darwinian edge." Of course, they were not aware of this, the reasons for aggression being richly overlaid by culture, customs, and religion, including the view of non-Mundurucú tribes as "victims by definition."*

---

* There is a great deal of controversy about sociobiological views on the genetic basis of human social behavior,[9] and my own views differ from Wilson's. For example, I regard

Other thinkers have also proposed that human beings are aggressive by nature, often because they were deeply affected by the carnage of war. In the case of Freud, the First World War prompted such reflections. Similar thinking has been based on observations of animals, for example, by the ethologist Lorenz, based on aggression in fish.

Human beings certainly have the *potential* for both altruism and aggression. Possibly we even have a genetic tendency toward aggression when we are threatened, and a tendency to act altruistically toward those who are genetically close to us. But such tendencies are strongly affected by experience and learning, even in animals. For example, when monkeys can obtain food by pressing a lever that also results in shock to another monkey, some will stop pushing the lever and sacrifice the food; they are more likely to do this if they have previously shared a cage with the other animal.[11]

In my view, there are genetic *pre*dispositions toward altruism and aggression, and specific genetic building blocks such as the infants' attachment to caretakers and fear of strangers. These are shaped by socialization and culture into actual dispositions toward kindness and cruelty through exposure to different experiences, such as warmth and intimacy versus rejection or hostility.[12]

In Wilson's analysis Mundurucú culture expresses and serves genetic dispositions evoked by threat to survival. In my view, varied adaptations to life circumstances are possible, but once a culture evolves aggressive characteristics, *aggression can become a way of life*. Cultures can also evolve nonaggressive modes of adaptation, both internally and in relation to other societies (for example, the Semai of Malaysia).[13] This requires a feeling of security, peaceful modes of conflict resolution, or well-regulated social behavior that minimizes conflict, or a combination of these.

We should not expect nonaggressive cultures or individuals to remain so under all conditions. Substantial change in the environment requires new

Mundurucú culture as demonstrating the role of culture in aggression. Sociobiologists' proposals concern the sources of human behavior in the gene pool, in the shared human genetic heritage. Philip Rushton and his associates have suggested that *individual* genetic variation exists in altruism and aggression.[10] Their conclusions are based on self-reports in questionnaires, not direct information about behavior. They found greater similarity between more genetically related individuals (e.g., identical twins in contrast to fraternal twins). It is unlikely that certain genes directly result in more or less aggression or altruism. More likely, genetically based temperamental differences (e.g., in infants' activity levels, intensity of emotion, and social responsiveness) affect the way parents and others relate to infants. This shapes the child's altruistic and aggressive behavior, or, what Rushton and his associates actually measured, verbal self reports related to altruism and to self–other relations. (When reared together, identical twins are also treated more alike than fraternal twins.)

adaptations. At times external conditions put people into the midst of violence. Sometimes persistent nonaggression becomes suicidal.

The peaceful Semai of Malaysia, supposedly ignorant of war and the tasks of soldiers, were lured by promises of rewards into British army units that were fighting communists in the early fifties. When some of their kinsmen were killed, the Semais became fierce. They had strong *social* controls, but not the *personal* capacity to modulate and regulate aggressive feelings and behavior. In the midst of violence, they responded with un-restrained violence. On their return home they reverted to their peaceful ways.[14]

Aggression as a cultural ideal. Some cultures (and individuals) idealize aggression. American television programs and films attest to some ideali-zation. So does the power of organizations such as the National Rifle Association. The Nazis idealized violence. The Bolsheviks considered aggression valuable and necessary. Dzerzhinski, the first head of the Soviet secret police, the Cheka, proclaimed: "We stand for organized terror...terror being absolutely indispensable in current revolutionary conditions."[15]

Past history of use of aggression to deal with conflict. Like individuals, cultures carry blueprints for dealing with problems. Repeated use of ag-gression to deal with conflict makes it acceptable. Aggressive plans and strategies are developed, the aggressor becomes competent in the use of aggression, and renewed aggression is more likely. Thus, a history of aggression makes it more "available."[16]

Cultural self-concept, self-esteem, and world view

As I have pointed out, low self-esteem and a violent and chaotic family background are associated with violent crime.[17] Some violent criminals see threat everywhere and proceed to "defend" themselves or their self-image. Others establish masculinity and strength by seeking physical confrontation and victory.[18]

Self-concept and self-esteem are also important at the societal level in determining the response to frustration and threat. Societal and individual self-concepts need not be the same. Low self-esteem may even intensify the need to compensate by seeing one's group in a positive light. Individ-uals who vary in self-esteem may share a belief in the superiority of their culture, nation, society, or way of life. Most societies are inclined to such ethnocentrism.[19] National self-concept is a complex matter, however.

In times of danger, confidence in existing institutions gives hope and promotes constructive action. Moreover, a positive group identification can help people deal with personal difficulties, especially threats to individual self-esteem.

On the other hand, idealization of one's group may heighten frustration in difficult times. In groups as in individuals, very high self-evaluation often masks self-doubt. Persistent life difficulties may contradict the high self-evaluation and bring self-doubt to the surface. Even if there is no underlying self-doubt, a very high self-evaluation may be associated with limited concern for others. Among individuals, a *moderately* positive self-concept is most strongly associated with sensitivity and responsiveness to other people.[20]

It is not customary to classify nations in terms of self-concept and self-esteem. Nonetheless, parallels to the influence of individual self-concept certainly exist. The components and sources of individual self-esteem are highly complex; those of group or national self-esteem are perhaps even more so.

A familiar aspect of national self-concept is a feeling of deprivation, combined with the belief that one's country deserves more. Often this includes a belief, realistic or paranoid, that other countries or internal enemies are preventing the group from getting its due in material possessions, prestige, or honor. Germany went to war in 1914 to gain the power and advantages that it deserved but others would not yield to it.[21] Later Hitler claimed Germany had the right to more living space (*Lebensraum*). Argentinians too saw their nation as deprived, its potential for wealth, power, and influence unfulfilled.

Both an inflated and a weak self-esteem can enhance threat. When positive self-esteem is strongly tied to power, success, or prestige, difficult life conditions will be especially threatening.

Individual and group world views are beliefs about the way the world works – about the nature of human beings, institutions, and societies. Are others caring or selfish, safe or aggressive? Is aggression normal, or permitted only in extreme cases? Aggression is more likely to occur if it is an acceptable means to fulfill goals, if the world is seen as a dangerous place, and if other groups are regarded as untrustworthy.

Cultural goals and values

Cultures can be characterized by their goals, explicit and implicit.[22] In the United States, for example, according to one analysis, a basic goal is to maintain belief in equality of opportunity.[23] The substantial inequalities of wealth, status, and power are often explained by either hereditary differences in ability or differences in effort. These are genuine influences, but exclusive emphasis on them obscures the extent to which inequality is due to a social organization that enables some people to maintain unearned privileges and limits opportunity for others. One consequence is that people regard themselves as failures when they do not live up to aspirations based on a faith in unlimited opportunity. Another consequence is devaluation of the poor, who are seen as incompetent or lazy, and who may also see themselves this way, which may keep them passive. A contrasting goal, adopted by the Hutterites, for example, is equality of outcome as the basis of social organization.[24]

Some goals are agreed upon by a whole society; others are promoted by conflicting subgroups, who want to influence the whole society. Some goals are internal: health care, freedom from hunger, protection of civil rights, equality under law, and maintenance of certain moral or religious values. Other goals are international; they involve the role of the nation in the world, its relationship to other nations, and its relative power, prestige, and wealth. Nationalism, or the desire to enhance the status, power, or influence of one's country, is a goal more important in some cultures than others. A society's goals include the propagation of a way of life and the creation of a culture and institutions that will socialize the young to maintain it. Long-standing differences among subgroups of a society in values, goals, and ways of life, especially when there are no well-established ways to reconcile differences and resolve conflict, are likely to be seized upon and their significance intensified when life conditions are difficult.

Moral value orientations

Individuals and cultures differ in their concern for others' welfare. A number of writers have distinguished rule-centered and person-centered moral orientations.[25] The focus of a rule-centered morality is norms, conventions, and the maintenance of society. The focus of a person-centered orientation is the well-being of individuals or the group.

On the individual level, there is evidence that certain characteristics, such as the belief in the acceptability of aggression in contrast to anxiety about its use, promote aggressive responses to instigation.[26] But there is little research on the influence of broader value orientations. My students and I exposed individuals to another person who seemed to be in either physical distress from a stomach condition or in psychological distress because a boyfriend had suddenly ended a long-term relationship. Individuals with a strong *prosocial value orientation* – a positive evaluation of human beings, concern about their welfare, and a feeling of personal responsibility for their welfare – helped more.[27] Presumably this person-centered orientation also diminishes the likelihood of aggression.

Lawrence Kohlberg reported that in experiments on obedience to authority, a small number of persons with a stage six (principled) moral orientation were less likely to obey the experimenter and administer the strongest shocks to the learner.[28] When asked to resolve hypothetical moral conflicts, such persons' moral thinking centers on a belief in justice and the sanctity of human life. Using another system to categorize moral thinking, Kohlberg and his associates found that the few people with principled moral reasoning, as well as persons whose reasoning is less advanced but who see themselves as *responsible* for fulfilling important values, tended to act morally in both the obedience study and another morally relevant situation.[29] This type of morality seems similar to prosocial orientation.

Carol Gilligan has drawn a distinction between typical male orientation to morality (based on rules and logic) and female orientation (characterized by caring and responsibility).[30] A prosocial value orientation and a morality of care and responsibility, although not identical, have evident similarities. In our research there were both males and females with strong prosocial orientations. Gilligan later reported that the two moral orientations characterize both sexes, although rule-centered orientation is dominant in males and person-centered in females.[31] In a recent in-depth interview study males and females reported similar values.[32]

Whole societies and their subgroups also differ in moral orientation. The moral orientation of a society sets limits on acceptable conduct and influences the choice of avenues to cope with difficult life conditions. Sparta subordinated individual dignity and freedom to the interests of the state; Athens elevated individual freedom, dignity, human reason, and creativity. The institution of slavery in Athens demonstrates that dominant value orientations need not apply to those outside the boundaries of the ingroup. Indians and blacks in America, Jews in many places, Armenians in Turkey, and those defined as enemies by ideology or other criteria have been traditionally excluded from the domain of dominant moral orientations; otherwise unacceptable acts become acceptable when directed at them.

While moral rules arise to serve human welfare, rules can be reified or held as absolutes, and at times the group rather than the individual is made the focus of their concern. This makes it easier to exclude specific individuals or subgroups from the universe of moral concern. In addition, given the widespread belief in a just world (see Chapter 6), victims will often be seen as deserving their fate.[33]

Moral value orientations are expressed in standards and rules adopted by social groups. Adherence to and deviation from rules have powerful social consequences, but people also obey rules because they have adopted them as their own and believe in them. But group morality can shift and permit harm-doing that was previously inconceivable. It then becomes difficult to maintain a personal morality that deviates from the new group morality. Progressively, personal values will change. Certain groups may be excluded from the realm of humanity, and essential values cease to apply to them. How this happens is discussed in Chapter 6.

Ingroup–outgroup differentiation and devaluation of outgroups

Recent research in psychology has shown that human beings have a tendency to divide the world into "us" and "them." They use seemingly trivial information to create ingroups and outgroups and then discriminate against members of the outgroup. Being told that an aesthetic preference test shows that they prefer the modern painter Klee is sufficient for people to favor others who supposedly also like Klee and discriminate against those who like another modern painter, Kandinsky. Even totally arbitrary and trivial differentiations have such effects.[34]

Once...a group of thirty-two young boys from the suburbs of Bristol, England, had an out-of-the-ordinary experience. It began simply: They sat together in groups of eight and watched dots flash on a screen. Working individually, they were to guess the number of dots that flashed before their eyes. When all of the guessing was done, four of the boys from each octave were taken aside and told that they belonged to a group of people who tend to overestimate in this kind of guessing. The remaining four boys were told that they belonged to a group of people who tend to underestimate. These bogus group categorizations, so seemingly banal and trivial, had important effects on the Bristol boys' subsequent behavior.

After learning that he was either an overestimator or an underestimator, each boy was given the opportunity to decide how a quantity of money should be divided between two other boys. He was told that no one would know who made the decision and that his own earnings would be unaffected by the allocation. About the two others the Bristol boys knew only one thing: that one was an overestimator and the other was an underestimator. It was not much to know, but it was enough: The money was not divided equally. The Bristol boys discriminated in favor of the boy who shared their social category and against the one who did not.[35]

Seemingly, people use available information to divide themselves into an ingroup and an outgroup.[36] Obviously, people group themselves in many ways and can define those who belong to their nation, political party, religion, profession, neighborhood, or local Parent–Teacher Association as "us," and they may consider others who do not belong to their group as different and less worthy. But the ties that bind people to significant ingroups are much stronger than this: deep affective associations, shared understandings, common goals, and the perception of a shared fate. The tendency to form ingroups and ethnocentrism are deeply rooted; they evolve out of genetic predispositions, or "building blocks."

The capacity of infants to form attachment to caretakers is rooted in genetic makeup. Although the quality of attachment varies, only under extreme conditions will infants form none.[37] At the same time they develop attachment, infants also develop stranger anxiety, a fear and/or avoidance of unfamiliar people. This may be a rudimentary source of ingroup–outgroup differentiation. Socialization and experience at this time of life have substantial effects. Infants show less stranger anxiety if they are exposed to a wide variety of people or develop a secure (rather than avoidant or anxious/ambivalent) attachment to caretakers.[38]

Psychologists have long believed that the earliest relationship to the primary caretaker is a prototype for later relationships. Research findings in the last decade show that infants who develop a secure attachment – as indicated by a loving connection with neither undue distress about the caretaker's absence nor anger or avoidance on the caretaker's return – have a closer, more positive, more effective relationship with their peers during the preschool and early school years.[39] This connection to others inherent in secure attachment is an important basis for empathy and caring. Its range may be limited by ingroup–outgroup differentiation; caring may be restricted to those who are "similar," accepted, and valued.

Related sources of ingroup–outgroup differentiation are fear as a common human response to the unusual, unknown, and different and the tendency to like and prefer what is familiar – even among nonsense syllables.[40]

Psychologically, the crux of the matter is that the familiar provides the indispensable basis of our existence. Since existence is good, its accompanying groundwork seems good and desirable. A child's parents, neighborhood, region, nation are given to him – so too his religion, race, and social traditions. To him all these affiliations are taken for granted. Since he is part of them, and they are part of him, they are good.[41]

A further source of ethnocentrism is the fact that the human mind works by categorization. We see and remember objects and people as green or red, tall or short. We would be overwhelmed by uncertainty and anxiety if we approached each person (or event) without using past learning as a guide. Categorization, however, is a basis of stereotypes, exaggerated beliefs about groups that are often negative.

Because of attachment and stranger anxiety, children automatically tend to differentiate between their primary group, the family, and the rest of the world. Socialization may intensify this. Children are often taught to mistrust those outside the family and are often indoctrinated against religious, ethnic, national, or political outsiders. At a very early age they come to evaluate their own nation positively and express stereotypic and negative views of other nations. A nine-year-old Swiss boy, when asked where he learned such opinions as "The French are not very serious,... and it is dirty there," and "Russians always want war," answered: "I don't know. I've heard it....that's what people say."[42]

Having learned such differentiations, people constantly create new ingroup–outgroup distinctions, which are reinforced by feelings of group harmony and other gratifications. One function of warfare may be to redirect aggression away from the ingroup and thereby protect genetically related ingroup members.[43] Leaders also create divisions to rally a dissatisfied population.[44]

The preparation of official or sanctioned torturers and murderers often includes creation of a strong ingroup bond and differentiation from the rest of the world. The Nazi Schutzstaffel (SS) (see Part II) and Greek torturers had rituals of group identification, special nicknames, and a special language.[45]

Just defining people as "them" results in devaluating them.[46] Conversely, devaluation makes it more likely that a person is seen as belonging to an outgroup. Distinctions in race, religion, status, wealth, power, and political views are the main sources of ingroup–outgroup differentiations. They produce stable devaluations: of slaves by slave owners, of the uneducated by the educated.

Sometimes the ingroup devalues most strongly another group that is highly similar: this serves to protect the identity, integrity, and purity of the ingroup. The communist hatred of "revisionist" social democrats was often greater than their hatred for capitalist enemies. Small differences in dogma often resulted in the persecution of religious heretics. The intense anti-Semitism of the early church fathers probably served their need to create an independent identity for Christianity.

How a culture or society shapes its members' evaluation of other people is profoundly important. We rarely harm people we greatly value. When members of an outgroup are highly valued, they are probably regarded as being in a more fundamental sense members of the ingroup. For example, we recognize our shared humanity with the Polish people. We admire their bravery in creating the Solidarity movement and see them as similar to us in their desire for freedom.

Devaluation makes mistreatment likely. In one experiment each participant was to be a teacher and administer electric shocks to a learner who made mistakes on a task. When teachers "overheard" a conversation in which the learner was described as one of a rotten bunch of people,

they administered much stronger electric shocks. Learners described positively received the weakest shocks.[47] Derogatory labels are often used to
create antagonism and prepare people for action against an outgroup. One
writer described the psychological conditions for guilt-free massacre in the
following way:

The most general condition for guilt-free massacre is the denial of humanity to the
victim. You call the victims names like gooks, dinks, niggers, pinkos, and japs. The
more you can get high officials in government to use these names and others like
yellow dwarfs with daggers and rotten apples, the more your success. In addition
you allow no human contact. You prevent travel or you oversee the nature of
contact where travel is allowed. You prevent citizens from going to places like
China, Cuba, and North Vietnam, so that men cannot confront other men. Or on
the homefront, if contact is allowed, or if it cannot be prevented, you indicate that
the contact is not between equals; you talk about the disadvantaged, the
deprived.[48]

Societies differ in their tendency to devalue outgroups. These devaluations may be present in stereotypes or negative images of a group in
literature, art, folklore, theater, television, and shared beliefs. They can
also be expressed in discriminatory social institutions. In general, the
Nazis were able to kill more Jews in those countries where anti-Semitism
and discrimination against Jews were already strong.[49] This was especially the case in countries allied to but not occupied by the Germans. In
countries where Jews were less the objects of social differentiation, the
government was less likely to hand over the Jewish population to the
Nazis.

Sometimes enemy groups are selected or "created" by an emerging
ideology, usually on the basis of cultural devaluation, societal rifts, or
real conflict. In Argentina an anticommunist ideology was used to define
people with liberal views and "leftist" connections as the enemy. In Cambodia their ideology led the Khmer Rouge to kill, starve, or work to death
as many as two million people who were thought either opposed to or incapable of a new way of life. What happened in these cases was a result
of real conflicts of interest and violent confrontation, speedily emerging
devaluation, and overgeneralization in which the definition of the enemy
was extended to include large groups of people.

Sometimes a group is identified for the purpose of assigning blame to it.
Consider the ill-defined "secular humanists," who have been the object of
attack by the Moral Majority and other fundamentalists since the 1970s.
As Leo Wine of Oregon said in a series of radio programs on humanism:

Why are the humanists promoting sexual perversion? Because they want to
create such an obsession with sex among our young people that they will have
no time or interest for spiritual pursuits.... So what do we have? Humanist

obsessions: sex, pornography, marijuana, drugs, self-indulgence, rights without responsibility.

Humanists control America. America is supposed to be a free country, but are we really free?...Now the humanist organizations – ACLU, AHA (American Humanist Association) – control the television, the radio, the newspapers, the Hollywood movies, magazines, porno magazines, and the unions, the Ford Foundation, Rockefeller Foundation....They, 275,000 humanists, have infiltrated until every department of our country is controlled by the humanists.

Humanists will continue leading us toward the chaos of the French Revolution. After all, it is the same philosophy that destroyed France and paved the way for the dictator Napoleon Bonaparte. This time the humanists hope to name their own dictator who will create out of the ashes of our pro-moral republic a humanist utopia, an atheistic, socialistic, amoral humanist society for America and the rest of the world. In fact, their goal is to accomplish that takeover by or before the year 2,000.[50]

Changes in American values and ways of life are a source of confusion and threat to many people. An ancient way of coping with such threat is to find or create a group to blame. Wine's language is like the language Nazis applied to Jews. The Nazis found the Jews; the Moral Majority has *created* the conspiratorial "secular humanists," the enemy within, the source of corruption.

When people are devalued, they may be seen as objects rather than human beings with feelings and suffering like our own. As we shall see, certain culturally accepted ways of raising children diminish their awareness of their own human frailty and therefore make them less likely to appreciate the humanity of others. As a result empathy (the capacity to feel with others) and sympathy (a responsiveness to others' needs and suffering) are undeveloped.

Groups that become the object of mistreatment are seen as unworthy and morally inferior, with many undesirable characteristics. They are also seen as threats, as interfering by their very existence with important ideals, economically exploiting members of the dominant group, and striving for or plotting to gain power, which they will use to harm the dominant group. Identifying them as "evil" deepens the threat and calls moral outrage and the desire to punish evildoers into play.

Pluralistic and monolithic cultures

In a monolithic culture social agents and entities are organized around a single set of goals. In a pluralistic culture, "social agents and entities represent somewhat different expectations, sanctions and rewards for members of the society. These differences generate intergroup conflict which is largely regulated by a set of 'ground rules' (such as constitution) and a common commitment to integrative principles or goals."[51]

Today there are few totally homogeneous societies with common goals and values and lacking all religious, ethnic, or class differences. In a pluralistic society, with a balance of diversity and consensus, greater tolerance for differences among groups of people can be expected. Counterreactions to initial steps along a continuum of destruction are more probable. Democratic societies with different racial and ethnic and religious groups free to express their differences are necessarily pluralistic, especially when these ethnic subcultures enter the mainstream. As a result, children conform less to authority.[52] Moral development is advanced by cultural pluralism, because it requires people to resolve conflicting standards and expectations.

Orientation to authority

Most societies place value on obedience to leaders, institutions, and rules. Some obedience is essential for collective functioning. In some societies, obedience is a major cultural value; child rearing, schools, and other institutions are authoritarian. In other societies (although this is rare) questioning authority might be highly valued.

In the experiments of Milgram, as I noted earlier, certain kinds of moral reasoning reduced obedience, and an authoritarian orientation enhanced it (see the next chapter).[53] If a culture inculcates strong respect for authority and places strong value on obedience,[54] it is less likely that individuals will oppose leaders who scapegoat or advocate violence.

Unconscious motivation – individual and cultural

The unconscious is another source of motivation for harming others. Self-doubt, sexual feelings, anger and the desire to hurt, and even the experience of suffering can become unacceptable to people because of messages from their environment, especially their parents. These desires and feelings cause anxiety and must be defended against. The feelings and related thoughts are repressed, or denied. They become unavailable to consciousness. Later they may be projected onto other people. Anger may be displaced from parents onto people who are acceptable targets of anger. One characteristic of the authoritarian personality is such displacement and projection.[55]

While unconscious processes are recognized, the experimental evidence for the notion of psychological defense, displacement, and projection (originally proposed by psychoanalysts) has remained a subject of debate.[56] Recent research shows individual differences in "defensiveness." Some people are unaware of or deny having a high level of anxiety, but it shows in psychophysiological responses.[57] Others suppress negative emotional memories and emotional experience in general.[58]

People repress anger if they were punished for expressing it. As a vivid example of repression and scapegoating, consider the following case presented by the German psychiatrist Alice Miller:

> I know a woman who never happened to have any contact with a Jew up to the time she joined the Bund Deutscher Mädel, the female equivalent of the Hitler Youth. She had been brought up very strictly. Her parents needed her to help out in the household after her siblings (two brothers and a sister) had left home. For this reason she was not allowed to prepare for a career even though she very much wanted to and even though she had the necessary qualifications. Much later she told me with what enthusiasm she had read about "the crimes of the Jews" in *Mein Kampf* and what a sense of relief it had given her to find out that it was permissible to hate someone so unequivocally. She had never been allowed to envy her siblings openly for being able to pursue their careers. But the Jewish banker to whom her uncle had to pay interest on a loan – he was an exploiter of her poor uncle, with whom she identified. She herself was actually being exploited by her parents and was envious of her siblings, but a well-behaved girl was not permitted to have these feelings. And now, quite unexpectedly, there was such a simple solution: it was all right to hate as much as she wanted; she still remained (and perhaps for this very reason was) her parents' good girl and a useful daughter of the fatherland. Moreover, she could project the "bad" and weak child she had always learned to despise in herself onto the weak and helpless Jews and experience herself as exclusively strong, exclusively pure (Aryan), exclusively good.[59]

Discrepancies between reality and what is valued occur in most cultures.[60] An important motivation for change arises when individuals become aware of such discrepancies.[61] It is thereforee important to look for aspects of the culture that are not acknowledged and are not incorporated into the cultural self-concept, and to analyze how discrepancies are dealt with. Deep-seated hostilities may be maintained by ongoing cultural arrangements that conflict with conscious values. Sometimes social movements arise when discrepancies come to the surface. In America, the civil rights movement of the 1960s arose when discrepancies between long-held ideals and national reality became a powerful motivation for change.

Recent thinking about family systems and the transmission of family patterns across generations helps us expand our understanding of unconscious motivations. Not only explicit family rules but also powerful implicit rules allow the expression of certain feelings and inhibit others.

The influence of sociopolitical organization

Governmental system

The more repressive and dictatorial a government, the more will fear inhibit opposition. Opposition to early steps along a continuum of destruction also decreases when free expression is inhibited, because of a uniform definition of reality: the government propagates its views and no others are heard. (Even in a democratic system, ideology, government information management, and lack of press vigilance may result in a relatively uniform definition of reality; see Chapter 17.) If everyone seems to be thinking the same way, it may stifle doubt or resistance, even inner resistance. Many people report seeing two lines of clearly different length as equal when a number of other people before them report seeing the lines as equal.[62] Social reality can be even more strongly affected by the views of others. The way some people define the meaning of events powerfully influences other bystanders' reactions to emergencies. Even what people regard as sounds of distress and how they react to distress depends on what other people say.[63] A culturally induced respect for authority can join with governmental propaganda and repression in creating uniform views of events. Eichmann noted at his trial that there were no voices raising questions about the Nazi exterminations, nothing to implant doubt.[64]

Authorities also *create* facts. Hitler used the pretext of a Polish attack to invade Poland; actually the attackers were SS members dressed in Polish uniforms. The Gulf of Tonkin incident, used to extend American involvement in Vietnam, may have been intentionally created and falsely reported.

Even in a democratic system leaders are often isolated. Surrounded by a small group of decision makers, they lack direct contact with citizens. Moreover, their power can be enormous even in a system of government purportedly based on checks and balances. Inherent in the leadership role, unfortunately, is a tendency to view people as instruments and devalue opposition. This is more likely when the leader's power is great and his accountability low, and when the leader is guided by a coherent ideology, which offers certainty of goals. Institutions that expose leaders to varied views and increase their accountability may counteract this process (see Chapter 17).

Social institutions

Social institutions affect the likelihood of group mistreatment in several ways.

Discrimination. Discrimination against subgroups combines with cultural images and stereotypes to further ingroup–outgroup distinctions and devaluation. Segregation in housing, movements like the Ku Klux Klan or anti-Semitic political parties in Europe, and discriminatory quotas in education and jobs are among institutions and policies that contribute to this. Discrimination is also served by poverty and persistent differences in social status, together with institutions that limit social mobility.

Organizations capable of carrying out mistreatment. Motivation for mistreating a group is not enough; the capacity to fulfill it must be present. Often the motivation does not even fully arise until there is belief in the capacity to fulfill it.[65] A monolithic central party, a powerful military, and other organized groups loyal to the government are often necessary conditions. A machinery of destruction has to be created.[66] In Germany the SS and prior experience with "euthanasia" provided the instruments and techniques for extermination. In Turkey, Argentina, and elsewhere organized groups either existed or were created.

Institutions creating societal climate. A society's institutions help determine whether its spirit is one of harmony, cooperation, and altruism or one of disharmony, conflict, and harm-doing; for example, compare the English system of voluntary blood donation with the widespread buying and selling of blood in the United States.[67] In schools, emphasis on competition (as opposed to cooperative learning) greatly affects the experience of self and others (Chapter 17). Unfortunately, even cooperative and harmonious institutions may exclude some groups. There is a sharp turn towards group violence when institutions are created or existing institutions assigned the task to harm a subgroup of society. In Germany the Ministry of Propaganda and the SS were such institutions.

In sum, a constellation of characteristics makes a society likely to respond to difficult life conditions in ways that ultimately lead to violence against a subgroup (or another country). All the components need not exist for a society to start along the continuum of destruction; part of a pattern is sufficient. Nevertheless, the absence of a crucial characteristic can inhibit mistreatment or violence or lead to counterreactions that stop its progression. For example, in a pluralistic system, people can speak out against and prevent progress toward genocide.

5   The psychology of perpetrators: individuals and groups

Who become the *direct* perpetrators of violence and the policymakers, and how? It is decision makers who initiate, lead, give orders, and in most cases assume responsibility. Irving Janis found that decision-making groups engage in "groupthink."[1] Members are reluctant to contradict each other. Once an idea has gained any support, especially by the leader, members refrain from criticism or the introduction of new ideas, which limits alternatives.

Groupthink often leads to unintended outcomes. However, genocide and mass killing frequently *fulfill* the decision makers' intentions and goals. In some instances, as in the case of Hitler and the Holocaust, the ideas that led to genocide evolved well before the killers gained power. Inevitably, preexisting beliefs limit the alternatives considered by decision makers. In other instances, as in Cambodia, the genocidal intention evolved during the chaos and turmoil that preceded the genocide.

There has been little direct study of either decision makers or direct perpetrators. Once they lose power, not surprisingly, they tend to avoid scrutiny. Social scientists have rarely approached them. When they are studied, their responses must be "translated," because they need to justify themselves in their own and others' eyes. Indirect approach by the assessment of personality is perhaps a better way to study them.

The Nazis tried at Nuremberg, mostly decision makers, provided such opportunity. Unfortunately, their psychological assessment was based on the questionable hypothesis that they were mentally ill, and used materials such as Rorschach inkblot patterns. Not surprisingly, no mental illness was evident.[2]

In psychological experiments it is possible to study influences that lead people to harm others but difficult to study how people become genocidal *leaders*. The study of real genocidal leaders is also difficult, and their numbers are small. We will focus on followers, which is appropriate because they give power to leaders (together with accepting bystanders). More-

over, the leaders and the followers who become perpetrators appear to
share psychological processes and motivations that lead to genocide.

Certain personal characteristics seem to enter into self-selection by perpetrators. Occupying certain social roles, as a result of self-selection and
personal choice, further shapes personality and attitudes. Although personal characteristics create predispositions, otherwise quite different people may become perpetrators of massacre and genocide by moving along a
continuum of destruction (see next chapter). Social change can diminish
the strength of values and rules that prohibit harm-doing. The perpetrators
may be changed by first passively accepting the mistreatment of victims or
by participating in small, even seemingly innocuous hostile acts. After joining an ideological group, they are under pressure to accept its definition of
what is right.

Psychological research, interviews with criminals, and evidence from
psychotherapy tell us something about situations that lead people to harm
others, the personal characteristics that lead to violence, and the origins
of such personality. These different sources provide a fairly coherent,
although as yet incomplete, picture, supported by a limited number of
studies of perpetrators of torture, genocide, and mass killing. This mosaic
of information suggests that perpetrators often have one or both of two
constellations of characteristics: I will call them *potentially antisocial* and
authority oriented.

A single characteristic, for example, an extreme incapacity for empathy, may be enough, although usually it accompanies other predisposing characteristics. Consider, for example, Suchomel, an SS guard
in Treblinka. In the documentary film *Shoah*, he sings the song that all
Jewish prisoners who were not immediately killed had to learn on their
first day in the camp.

"Looking squarely ahead, brave and joyous,
at the world,
the squads march to work.
All that matters to us now is Treblinka.
It is our destiny.
That's why we've become one with Treblinka
in no time at all.
We know only the word of our Commander,
we know only obedience and duty,
we want to serve, to go on serving,
until a little luck ends it all. Hurray."[3]

Then, he says, "Satisfied. That's unique." He adds with seeming nostalgia
and regret, "No Jew knows that today." He seems blind to what this song
must have meant to Jews. We do not know how much of this incapacity
for empathy is the result of his SS training and guard experience or how

much existed before. Nor do we know whether the incapacity is general or applies only to Jews.

Roles and other social processes as origins of harm-doing

Perpetrators can be ordinary people who have long filled certain *roles* – prison guards, combat soldiers – in which the devaluation of some other people is inherent. If the definition of their role comes to include acts of cruelty, many will adapt. In a study at Stanford, normal college students were randomly assigned to be either "guards" or "prisoners." The prisoners were "stripped naked, skin searched, deloused"; they had to memorize and follow rules restricting their freedom of speech and movement and had to ask permission to do the simplest activities, such as writing letters or going to the toilet.[4]

People so treated must seem inferior not only in power but in their basic humanity. Being in roles that grant power can lead to "us" and "them" separation, devaluation, and cruelty, particularly when the powerless are degraded. Some of those assigned the role of guards became extremely punitive and aggressive. They reacted to a "rebellion" by harassing and intimidating prisoners and putting "ringleaders" into solitary confinement. They made prisoners gather at any time of day or night for the "count," the "duration of which they increased from the original perfunctory ten minutes to seemingly interminable several hours."[5] This re-created a practice used in both Russian labor camps and German concentration camps. Guards who did not themselves engage in such conduct remained passive. The mistreatment became so severe that the experiment had to be discontinued.

Often those who become perpetrators occupy roles that require obedience. In Milgram's research the relationship between the person who administered the shock and the person in authority was transient. The pressures are stronger in prisons, armies, and other hierarchical institutions, systems that stress authority and obedience.

Self-selection and the personality of perpetrators

Even people without significant predispositions may evolve into perpetrators through "us"–"them" differentiation, devaluation, scapegoating, ideology, and submerging themselves in a group. But there is also self-selection and selection by authorities of those who possess at least part of a predisposing pattern, especially when the need for violence is evident from the start.

Scott Peck describes self-selection for the police:

It is only because particular kinds of people want to become policemen that they apply for the job in the first place. A young man of lower-middle-class origins who is both aggressive and conventional, for instance, would be quite likely to seek a position on the force. A shy, intellectual youth would not. The nature of police work...fits the psychological needs of the first young man. He quite naturally gravitates toward it. Should he find during the period of his training and early duty that the work is not satisfying or that he is somehow not compatible with the rank and file of other policemen, he will either resign or be weeded out. The result is that a police force is usually a quite homogeneous group of people who have much in common with each other and who are distinctly different from other types of groups, such as antiwar demonstrators or college English majors.

...the society at large – partly through the self-selection process described – employs specific types of people to perform its specialized roles – as, for instance, it employs aggressive, conventional men to perform its police functions.[6]

Selection by authorities was evident in a study of twenty-five Greek men who became torturers under the military junta that ruled Greece in the 1970s. They were selected as members of the military police and torturers early in their military training because of their total obedience to authority and because they came from fervent anticommunist families who saw leftists as enemies of Greece.[7]

In Nazi Germany, many of the perpetrators – for example, doctors in the "euthanasia" program and the death camps – were selected on the basis of their ideology, their devotion to the Nazi cause.[8] Some Nazis were pressed into the role of killer or into indirect involvement with killing, but even they had joined the movement and the party voluntarily and had advanced in it through their commitment and devotion.[9]

Self-selection may have played a role in the prison study I discussed earlier. The participants were recruited through "ads in city and campus newspapers" and offered fifteen dollars a day to participate in a study of prison life. Not everyone would want to participate in such a study; the personal characteristics of those who answered the advertisements may have been one reason for the intensifying hostility.

Earlier I identified characteristics predisposing societies or individuals to violence. I will briefly summarize those most relevant to individuals.

The potentially antisocial person

Self-concept and world view. A poor or shaky self-image, easily threatened, and a tendency to see the world, other people, or institutions as hostile may cause a constant need for self-defense and elevation of the self. People with such characteristics may be especially sensitive to life problems. A low level of well-being and much frustration and pain – a negative hedonic balance – heighten the desire to enhance the self.[10] Diminishing others raises at least one's *relative* well-being.

Moral values and empathy. A person's values determine his or her orientation to others' welfare. In extreme cases, harming others can become a value in itself. We can call this an antisocial value orientation, the devaluation of human beings and the desire to harm them, whether conscious or unconscious. It makes empathy with victims unlikely.

Moral exclusion. People who devalue other groups will tend to regard moral values as inapplicable to them and exclude their members from the moral realm. An important characteristic of Christians who risked their lives in Nazi-occupied Europe to save Jews was their inclusiveness: "a predisposition to regard all people as equals and to apply similar standards of right and wrong to them."[11]

Competence and a cognitive orientation to aggression. Some people learn strategies of resolving conflict by aggressive means. Research indicates that aggressive behaviors persist from childhood (as early as age eight) into adulthood. Some researchers believe that aggression becomes self-perpetuating because children learn aggressive "scripts" or cognitive schemas, representations of reality that serve as blueprints for aggressive behavior.[12] Fantasies may also fuel aggression.*

People with this constellation of characteristics may be called potentially antisocial. These characteristics can give rise to the motivation to harm or reduce inhibitions against aggression whatever motive it serves, and provide the competencies required for aggression. Aggression becomes a possible avenue to satisfy varied motivations, even a desire for stimulation and excitement.[14]

Lack of self-awareness and self-acceptance. This is part of both the potentially antisocial and the authority-oriented patterns. One effect is difficulty in accepting other people.

Often lack of self-awareness serves a positive self-concept, maintained by rigid defenses, especially denial and projection. Scott Peck regards as "evil" people who must find themselves faultless and blameless and must

---

* It is impossible to identify here all the unusual and even aberrant motivations and personal characteristics that may lead to aggression. However, our discussion might apply even to highly unusual instances of violence. Consider, for example, Dennis Nilsen, an English serial killer. For ten years before his first murder he had had intense fantasies about death. This apparently related to the death, when he was six, of his grandfather, the only person in his life with whom he had a close relationship. In these fantasies death and love joined. The killer, while he functioned quite well, was a solitary man. His fantasies, and the murders, gave him a feeling of connection. After killing someone, he would keep the body with him for a long time, washing and dressing it, "caring" for it.[13]

appear so in others' eyes, but who have an "unacknowledged sense of their own evil nature."[15] As a result they "attack others instead of facing their own failures."[16] I noted in Chapter 3 another reason for scapegoating: the illusion of understanding and control that arises from identifying the cause of one's problem.

Most of us have some difficulty in recognizing and confronting our faults and failures. Greater difficulty contributes more to an antisocial potential, especially under hardship and stress. A person whom Peck regards as evil – someone who in our schema has one strong predisposing characteristic for harming others – may behave in beneficial and helpful ways in ordinary times, as a responsible member of the community, for example, in civic organizations. But when circumstances are complex and threatening and guidance by social rules is unavailable, people who must remain blameless will blame others. When group norms allow violence and even make it socially respectable, such people are likely to engage in conduct that harms others.

Family origins of the potentially antisocial personality

Research identifies certain parental socialization practices related to aggression. Punitiveness (especially frequent physical punishment), rejection of the child, hostility between parents and children (especially boys and their fathers), and violence in the home contribute to boys' aggressiveness.[17] Family disorgaization, the loss of structure and rules, or a coercive, aggressive family system are additional contributors.[18] In a coercive family the child is both the object of hostility and is hostile and aggressive toward others.

These conditions make a child feel hurt and angry, vulnerable and worthless. The home provides a blueprint for human relationships. The child may begin to regard people in general as hostile and dangerous, and view aggression as the best, if not the only, mode of conflict resolution. The child's capacity to fulfill goals by nonaggressive means, and even the development of nonaggressive goals, will be limited.

It is not only physical punitiveness that lessens children's regard for others' welfare. One study by Martin Hoffman indicates that when parents use withdrawal of love as punishment, their children come to focus on conventional rules rather than the needs and welfare of others.[19]

Other research shows that upbringing can also create a predisposition for helping other people. Nurturance and responsiveness by parents contribute to secure attachment in infants, which is the basis of a positive orientation toward others. Reasoning with the child and explaining to the child the consequences of his or her behavior on other people, both negative and positive, are also important. So is firmness in guiding the child to act according to important values and standards, firmness that is flexible, democratic rather than authoritarian, and takes the child's point of view into consideration.[20] These practices contribute to self-esteem and a prosocial value orientation, especially if the parents also guide their children to be helpful and generous in action.[21]

Authority orientation and its sources in the family

Certain people are inclined to obey authority and to act punitively toward people not in authority. This is an aspect of what some psychologists call "authoritarian personalities."[22] Authority-oriented persons prefer hierarchical relationships with a clear delineation of spheres of power. They enjoy obeying authority and enjoy exercising power over those below them. Authoritarian individuals were more obedient than average in Milgram's experiments.*[23]

Certain child-rearing practices produce submissiveness to authority and a tendency to devalue the powerless. These practices usually stress conventional values and make children unwilling to acknowledge in themselves impulses or feelings regarded by society and thus by their parents as un-

---

* The original research on the authoritarian personality by Adorno and associates has been criticized. Although controversy persists, later work together with other data (e.g., research on the SS and on Greek torturers) suggests that at least an *authority* orientation is one predisposition of people who become perpetrators. Some criticisms were that the primary measure of authoritarian personality, the F (fascist) scale, excludes authoritarians of the Left; that the scale simply measures a tendency to say yes to questions; that the initial conception overemphasized maladjustment in authoritarian personalities.

Later research is more sophisticated; it indicates differences in both perception of events and response to them. Authoritarian persons or juries tend to favor greater punishment. Authoritarians are more punitive toward a citizen who killed a policeman at a rock concert if he is negatively described than if he is positively described; "equalitarians" are not affected by information about the character of the defendant. In contrast, authoritarians are unaffected by information about character when the defendant is a policeman, and equalitarians are more punitive toward a policeman who is negatively described. In an experiment where they act as teachers who shock a supposed learner, authoritarians are more punitive toward low-status victims, and equalitarians are more punitive toward high-status victims. More authoritarian persons also have more racist attitudes.

While the research findings have disconfirmed several aspects of the original theory, they do show that people differ in authority orientation and this difference affects the way they relate to ideas as well as people – especially people with differing authority or status. See endnote 22.

desirable—anger, hostility, sexual desire. All human beings have these feelings, and it is destructive to lose awareness of them. People who do not acknowledge these feelings in themselves tend to project them onto others and experience hostility or moral outrage.

Lack of warmth and punitive authoritarian discipline promote this tendency. Alice Miller has shown that historically in Germany (but not only there) children were seen as naturally willful and potentially evil; all means were acceptable, including severe physical punishment, to break the child's will and instill obedience.

When obedience is the highest value, self-guidance becomes impossible. People reared this way look for external guidance. "For how could someone whose inner development has been limited to learning to obey the commands of others be expected to live on his own without experiencing a sudden sense of inner emptiness. Military service provided the best opportunity for him to continue the established pattern of taking orders."[24]

A likely consequence of such treatment, also described in books such as Lloyd DeMause's *The History of Childhood* and Stone's writing on England, is deep hostility toward parents.[25] However, the child is taught that these feelings are unacceptable; expressing them provokes the strongest punishment. The feelings therefore become unconscious; paradoxically, the young child's dependence on the parent becomes especially great, and the need for care and affection especially strong.

But displacement and projection are not the only reason why others are seen as hostile. Parents are prototypes for children, who learn about human beings from their family experience. If parents are punitive, if they make the child suffer, the child will expect and see people in general as hostile, threatening, and dangerous. Children growing up in such families learn the importance of having power and allying themselves with the powerful. As a consequence, they identify with the powerful and are relatively easily turned against the powerless. There is evidence from postwar interviews, from books of child-raising advice, and from other research that these practices were widespread in Germany (see Chapter 8).[26]

Warmth and affection can also be used to limit children's independence, initiative, and deviation from rules. Even obedience generated in an affectionate context can restrict the permissible range of feelings and generate hostility. This is consistent with the research finding that parents who extensively use love withdrawal to indicate disapproval raise conventional children who inhibit their feelings.[27] Affection can be *used*, and it can be part of different patterns of child-rearing practices that modify its meaning and impact.

Most of us have a tendency to respect people with authority or power and follow their lead. As small children, we are all at the mercy of our parents and other adults. We all grow up under the influence of parents, schools, and the state. Most such authorities are in part and at times arbitrary or punitive or threatening.* Most of us continue to carry within us a feeling that avoiding confrontation with and attaining closeness to people in authority will give us security and confer value on us. Because we are often unaware of this feeling, its influence is difficult to control. The extent of this tendency varies with the experience of the child in and out of the home.

The original research identified repression, projection, and hostility as components of the authoritarian personality. These are likely to be, but are not inevitably, part of an "authority orientation," which refers, as I use the term, to a person's tendency to order the world and relate to people according to their position and power in hierarchies. It depends on the total pattern of socialization practices what else becomes part of this orientation.

The origins of destructiveness in personality and in the situation

Our knowledge of personality dispositions and their childhood origins is not specific enough to identify the sources of different types of aggressive behavior: in personal interactions, in criminal violence, in political violence, or in the service of genocide. Circumstances may join with common rudimentary dispositions to shape specific types of hostility and aggression.

There has been much concern about the relative influence of personality as opposed to situation. I believe that the situation – life problems in society and the conditions created by the culture – is highly important. Immediate circumstances – for example, who the perpetrators associate with, what groups they are part of – are also influential. However, these are normally the result of choices people make. When life problems are intense and long-lasting, the relative importance of individual predispositions may decrease: shared cultural dispositions and shared personal characteristics may lead increasing numbers of people to join extreme movements.

The people who participated in Stanley Milgram's studies on obedience to authority did not know what awaited them. Unexpectedly, a person

---

* All states, all organizations, all families have to deal with issues of authority. In the United States child-rearing practices have become less authoritarian. For example, in the 1920s and 1930s Public Health information to parents included the advice that infants be fed on a fixed schedule, rather than on demand (i.e., when the infant is hungry, which is the current recommendation).

standing next to them exerted strong pressure on them to give another person increasingly powerful electric shocks. However, most people who become perpetrators voluntarily join groups that have inclinations they share. Even when a military engages in mass killing, it is unlikely that an average conscript will be called upon to act as a perpetrator; instead, officers select soldiers they judge best suited. In Argentina, conscripts were assigned to guard prisoners but were not called upon to act as torturers or killers.

The fanatic as perpetrator

The personalities of many would-be perpetrators and decision makers predispose them not necessarily to violence but to fanaticism, which in turn can eventually lead to mass killing or genocide. Fanatics are under the influence of a system of beliefs to which they subordinate everything else. They interpret and evaluate reality from the perspective of this system. Any means to fulfill the ideology's overriding goals come to seem acceptable. Other goals, including the interests of the self, are subordinated to or served by working for the movement's goals.

From others' perspective their behavior may seem irrational and self-destructive. For example, Nazis would not use the blood of prisoners of war for transfusions, because some of them might be Jews who would "contaminate" German soliders.[28] Other examples are the Khmer Rouge's massacre of professional and educated people, destruction of industry, and attacks on militarily stronger Vietnam (see Part III), and suicide missions in the Middle East, particularly by Shiites.

The many psychohistorical books about Hitler focus on his pathological personality and its childhood origins. To understand Hitler, however, we must realize that his thoughts and feelings were codified in his ideology and turned into "ideals" and principles. Strong needs, fear or anxiety, and the inability to tolerate uncertainty are likely proclivities for fanaticism. Once personality and circumstances give rise to fanaticism, the commitment to a cause becomes a more immediate influence on behavior than personality.

The ideology usually has roots in the fanatics' culture. This is evident in the case of the three most destructive ideologies that I examine: the Nazi ideology, that of the Pol Pot group, and Turkish ideology. Contemporary Shiite fanaticism also has cultural roots. The Shiites have been a minority for a long time, and assassination of majority leaders and extreme self-sacrifice for their group have characterized their history.[29]

There are two avenues to fanaticism. One is an emotional conversion experience. Substantial relief of physical symptoms can be achieved by intense group religious feelings, as in the miracle cures at Lourdes.[30] The vast theatrical Nazi rallies often had a similar conversion effect. A predisposition – personality, illness, or intense needs produced by life problems – and strong emotion generated in a group context are conducive to conversion. Another path to fanaticism is gradual involvement. As they engage in limited actions in support of a movement, people change. They become ready for greater efforts. Their commitment to the group and its ideals increases, strengthened by the group's rewards (and potential punishments) and by their new identity as members. A progression along a continuum of destruction is an important form of such gradual involvement.

There are also "good fanatics," committed to human welfare rather than to grand, abstract ideals or ideologies. Examples are Oscar Schindler, a German who became obsessed with saving Jewish lives, and Mother Teresa, who is devoting her life to help the poor and sick in India. Some good fanatics cheat and lie and endanger themselves to fulfill their goals. But guided by their concrete goals of protecting the lives and welfare of people, rather than by abstract ideals, they are unlikely to inflict great harm on innocent people as they serve their aims.

Fanatics usually need the support of a group to develop their profound commitment. Even those who *create* extreme ideologies usually require followers, and the followers need support before they abandon themselves to the cause.

Behavior in groups

Belonging to a group makes it easier for people to act in ways that are out of the ordinary. Joining a group enables people to give up a burdensome self and adopt a shared and valued social identity. At the same time they can shed the inhibitions and limitations of individual identity, the formed structure of the self that is limiting even at the best of times, much more so when the self is devalued. Thus, as group members they can open up emotionally. They more easily experience love, connectedness, and caring within the group. Anger and hate toward outsiders can come to the fore, especially when the group's beliefs promote these feelings. And they no longer need to take individual responsiblity for their actions; no one is responsible, or the group is responsible, or the group's leader. Anonymity can lead to the loss of a well-defined separate identity that embodies inhibitions limiting antisocial behavior. Psychological research has shown that wearing a hood increases aggression (as it facilitated aggression by Ku Klux Klan members).[31]

Powerful emotions spread through contagion. It becomes difficult to deviate from group perceptions or values. To deviate in action and risk a break with the group may come to seem impossible. Deviation in thought and feeling alone leads to painful inner conflict and gives rise to defenses that keep the individual faithful. When group norms shift, it is difficult for the individual not to follow.

People predisposed to harm-doing may find membership in certain groups highly satisfying. Hostility toward outgroups becomes desirable; the authoritarian structure is familiar and comfortable; the camaraderie provides a haven in a hostile world.

The subcultures of perpetrators

Groups that perpetrate genocide are usually military or created in a military mold. In Argentina, the mass killings were initiated by military leaders and executed by military personnel. The SS had a military type of organization, with even greater than usual emphasis on loyalty, obedience, and indoctrination in the hatred of enemies. In Cambodia, the rebel troops that won the civil war were the direct perpetrators. Only in Turkey were the direct perpetrators a more mixed group, including the military, the police, common criminals, and some of the population. Groups of perpetrators usually have a well-established authoritarian structure and provide training to strengthen obedience, ingroup ties, and the devaluation of enemies. Members must often pass extreme tests of obedience, fulfilling cruel and senseless orders; they must participate in rituals of group identification, sing songs of hatred, and shoot at targets representing figures identified as the enemy. These features are evident in the training of the SS, the torturers under the Greek military dictatorship, and even the U. S. Marines.[32]

Psychological functioning and individual responsibility

The satisfaction of personal or ideological motivations often conflicts with moral values and principles. How are such conflicts resolved? Do perpetrators consciously make moral choices? How do we judge their responsiblity, especially when they move along the continuum of destruction without reflection or conscious choice? I will explore these questions while examining the conduct of the SS and Nazi doctors in Chapter 10.

6 Steps along a continuum of destruction: perpetrators and bystanders

Once perpetrators begin to harm people, the resulting psychological changes make greater harm-doing probable. However, early public reactions can counteract these changes and inhibit further violence.

Just-world thinking

One psychological consequence of harm-doing is further devaluation of victims. According to the just-world hypothesis, which has received substantial experimental support, people tend to assume that victims have earned their suffering by their actions or character.[1] Perhaps we need to maintain faith that we ourselves will not become innocent victims of circumstance. However, blaming the victim is not universal; some people turn against the perpetrators. For example, a minority of individuals blame the experimenter instead of devaluing a student receiving electric shocks in an experiment.[2] Prior devaluation should make it more likely that victims are blamed.

People believe in a just world with different degrees of conviction.[3] Those whose belief is strong derogate poor people, underprivileged groups, or minorities. Strong belief in a just world is associated with rigid application of social rules and belief in the importance of convention, as opposed to empathy and concern with human welfare.[4] It is ironic and seemingly paradoxical (although not truly paradoxical, because the belief that the world is just is not identical to regarding justice as an ideal or to the desire to promote justice) that the belief that the world is a just place leads people to accept the suffering of others more easily, even of people they themselves harmed.

People do not devalue victims whose innocence is clearly and definitely established.[5] But how often can that be done? How can Jews or blacks, communists or anticommunists be cleared of misdeeds, evil intentions, or faults inherent in their nature, particularly in a climate of prejudice? De-

79

valuation is especially likely if the victims' continued suffering is expected.[6] To feel empathy results in empathic distress. To avoid that, people distance themselves from victims. This can be accomplished by devaluation. Under difficult life conditions, concern about the self also diminishes concern about others' suffering.

Learning by doing and the evolution of extreme destructiveness

The importance of learning by doing became evident to me through studies in which my associates and I induced children to engage in helpful acts and found that afterward they helped and shared more.[7] Children who taught a younger child, wrote letters to hospitalized children, or made toys for poor hospitalized children became more helpful on later occasions than children who spent the same time in activities that were similar in nature but not helpful to others.[8] Examining past research (much of it conducted to test unrelated hypotheses such as the effects of modeling) I found evidence for the same conclusion.[9] The research offers support for the view of some philosophers that morality is learned through moral action. Learning by doing is a basis for developing values, motives, the self concept, and behavioral tendencies.

Even if initially there is some external pressure, it often becomes difficult to experience regular participation in an activity as alien. People begin to see their engagement in the activity as part of themselves. The less force is used, the more this happens. People come to see themselves as agents and begin to consider and elaborate on the reasons for their actions. If there are benefits to others, even imagined ones, they begin to find the activity worthwhile and its beneficiaries more deserving. If there is harm to others, progressively the victims' well-being and even lives will lose value in their eyes. In other words, people observe their own actions and draw inferences, both about those affected by them and about themselves.[10] They attribute to themselves such characteristics as helpfulness or toughness or willingness to harm. Further actions consistent with their changing views of themselves become likely.

Other experiments have explored the "foot in the door" phenomenon.[11] When people are asked for a small favor and comply, they become more likely to agree later to a larger favor than they would if they had been immediately asked for the larger favor. For example, they are more likely to agree to put a large campaign sign on their front lawn if they earlier agreed to put on a small one.

When helping persists for some time, with increasing risk to the helper, the helper's commitment often grows. Rescuers of Jews in Nazi-occupied

Europe often responded first to the need of a friend or acquaintance and then went on to help others, sometimes becoming active in underground railroads. Some who intended to hide a family for only a day or two decided to keep hiding them for years. Still other helpers, such as the Swede Raoul Wallenberg and the German Oscar Schindler, became obsessed with their mission to save lives.

The evolution from indifference to total devotion is clear in the case of Oscar Schindler.[12] He followed the German army into Poland, took over a confiscated factory, and enriched himself, using Jewish slave labor. However, he treated his Jewish laborers as human beings, talked to them, listened to them. He started doing them small favors, then greater ones. Later he established a camp next to his factory to protect his workers from the SS, especially the murderous commander of the nearby concentration camp. He repeatedly endangered his life and sacrificed all his possessions, while saving the lives of twelve hundred Jews.

People also change as they harm others. Many experiments use the "teacher-learner paradigm," in which a "teacher" gives a "learner" electric shocks every time the learner makes an error. Even without any instruction to do so, teachers tend to increase the intensity of the shocks over time.[13] When there is instruction to increase the shock level, in the obedience experiments, the increase is gradual, step by step, so that learning by participation makes obedience easier. Both in these experiments and in real life, repeatedly and increasingly harming others makes it difficult to shift course. Unusual events offer decision points; in the obedience studies many who decided to stop did so when the learner-victim began to protest. However, the pressures of authorities and the system and changes that result from past harm-doing often combine with predispositions to override such opportunities.

Learning by doing is also found in research using verbal reinforcements. One person is instructed to speak either approving or disapproving words in response to certain words used by another person.[14] As time passes, the intensity of both rewarding and punishing verbal reinforcements tends to increase. In addition, the learners are devalued by those who punished them.*

How does harmful behavior become the norm? What internal changes

---

* There was no control or neutral condition, so it is uncertain to what extent rewarding in itself led to a positive evaluation and punishing to a negative evaluation. The change in evaluation did not occur when participants only *role-played* rewarding or punishing another (imagined) person. But even under these conditions, the increase in rewards or punishments occurred.

take place in people? Doing harm to a good person or passively witnessing it is inconsistent with a feeling of responsiblity for the welfare of others and the belief in a just world. Inconsistency troubles us.[15] We minimize it by reducing our concern for the welfare of those we harm or allow to suffer. We devalue them, justify their suffering by their evil nature or by higher ideals. A changed view of the victims, changed attitude toward that suffering, and changed self-concept result.

Hannah Arendt describes a turning point for Eichmann. When he was first exposed to the bodies of massacred Jews, he reacted with revulsion. But "higher ideals" (that is, powerful motives) such as Nazi ideology and loyalty to the führer, as well as a desire to advance his career, led him to ignore his distress and continue with his "work." The distress eventually disappeared.[16] Bruno Bettelheim described the inner struggle of a man who was against the Nazis but had to use the obligatory greeting "Heil Hitler." Even such a limited participation can result in substantial psychological reorganization.[17]

The Greek torturers also learned by participation.[18] First they stood guard outside interrogation and torture cells. Then they witnessed torture and provided help in beating up prisoners. They had to perform these duties satisfactorily before they were given a role as torturers.

Ideological movements and totalitarian systems induce members to participate. Members must follow special rituals and rules; they must join in educational or work activities for building the new society. The more they participate, the more difficult it becomes for them to distance themselves from the system's goals and deviate from its norms of conduct, not only overtly but also internally.

Bystanders also learn and change through passive or semiactive participation. Germans who boycotted Jewish stores or abandoned Jewish friends had to find reasons. The danger of resistance was one reason, but it was not enough to account for the wide-ranging participation and for the actions of the system itself that most Germans came to accept and like. The truly passive also, as a result of not taking any contrary action, come to accept the suffering of victims and the behavior of perpetrators.

Another very important phenomenon is self-persuasion, especially among leaders and decision makers. As they create propaganda or devise plans against victims, they reinforce and further develop their own world view. Psychological research shows that when people are asked to persuade others to a certain point of view, they also convince themselves and change their own views.[19]

Leaders or decision makers are also affected by the consequences of their own actions. Violence instigated by propaganda and official acts reinforces the leaders' views and intentions. In Germany random murders of Jews and looting of Jewish shops made Nazi leaders decide that further official acts against Jews were needed. This may happen even when the acts of violence are instigated by the leaders themselves and intended as justification for their policies.

Compartmentalization and integration

In *1984* George Orwell shows one way complicity evolves. His protagonist, Winston Smith, hates the repressive system of Big Brother, but he occasionally enjoys his work – rewriting history to conform to the current propaganda line. In the middle of Hate Week, the enemy country becomes an ally, and the ally an enemy. All previous history must be rewritten. He and others at the Ministry of Truth work feverishly, day and night, for over a week. "Insofar as he could remember, he was not troubled by the fact that every word he murmured into the speakwrite, every stroke of his ink pencil was a deliberate lie. He was as anxious as everyone else in the Department that the forgery should be perfect."[20]

This kind of compartmentalization enables people to focus and act on goals that conflict with important values. When the discrepancy persists, a splitting of the self can occur that enables people to live with it. Usually, further progression along a continuum will lead to moral exclusion and other changes that lead to a personal integration that allows destructive goals and behavior. Occasionally the split may remain and enlarge.

Dedicated or fanatical perpetrators may come to value killing; there is no inconsistency or need for splitting. However, less fully committed perpetrators must be able to compartmentalize. They may concentrate on the immediate task, ignoring ethics and long-term consequences. Many Nazi doctors focused on medical "achievements" in their cruel experiments.[21] Camp commanders focused on efficiency. Bureaucrats prepared regulations and train schedules for transporting victims. Over time, internal changes will increasingly diminish the need to compartmentalize.

Two psychological developments are of great importance: *a reversal of morality* and *relinquishing a feeling of responsibility* for the welfare of the victims. To a greater or lesser extent, most human beings learn that they are responsible for the life and welfare of others. A feeling of responsibility for others' welfare is central to people helping and not hurting others.[22] Feelings of responsibility are subverted by excluding certain people from the realm of humanity or defining them as dangers to oneself and one's way of life and values. At the extreme, a complete reversal of morality may occur, so that murder becomes a service to humanity. This is well expressed in a conversation described in testimony at Nuremberg by a Nazi who "worked" at Belzec, one of the extermination camps. When asked: "Wouldn't it be more prudent to burn the bodies instead of burying them? Another generation might take a different view of these things," he responded:

"Gentlemen, if there is ever a generation after us so cowardly, so soft, that it would not understand our work as good and necessary, then, gentlemen, National Socialism will have been for nothing. On the contrary we should bury bronze tablets saying that it was we, we who had the courage to carry out this gigantic task!"[23]

The feeling of responsiblity can also be subverted through the assumption of responsibility by leaders. Himmler told the SS that he and the führer would assume all the responsibility for their actions – and that they were discharging a heroic duty requiring tremendous sacrifice.[24] In Argentina, superior officers signed release forms for each kidnapping, which relieved the direct perpetrators of responsibility.[25] In the obedience studies, the experimenter assumed full responsibility for the consequences of shocking the learner. In a variant of this research, participants who had an observer role and were told that they were responsible for the learner's welfare induced the "teachers" to administer weaker shocks.[26] Research on helping in emergencies (for example, when someone falls and is injured or has a sudden asthma attack) shows that a witness is likely to help if circumstances focus responsibility on him or her (for example, he or she is the only person present or has a special competence) or if other people make the witness responsible by instructions or orders. When circumstances diffuse responsiblity, helping is much less probable.[27] Persons with greater ego strength or a greater personal feeling of responsibility for others' welfare are less affected by the presence or passivity of others.[28] The others in this case are strangers. Members of a close-knit group are likely to be more affected by each other.

Specialization and bureaucratization make violence easier, partly by subverting the feeling of responsibility.[29] Peck notes that in conversations with Pentagon officials at the time of the My Lai incident members of each group involved claimed that their role was circumscribed and disclaimed responsibility.[30]

As the destruction process evolves, harming victims can become "normal" behavior. Inhibitions against harming or killing diminish, and extraneous motives can enter: greed, the enjoyment of power, the desire for sex or excitement. This is helped along by the belief that the victims do not matter and deserve to suffer, and even that any form of their suffering furthers the cause the perpetrators serve.

The further the destruction has progressed, the more difficult it is to halt it. Human beings have a tendency to complete what they start. Kurt Lewin described this in terms of a goal gradient: the closer you are to a goal, the stronger the motivation to reach it.[31] Interruption of goal-directed behavior is a source of tension; the closer the goal, the greater the tension. Cognitive consistency theories also present human beings as motivated to reach closure.[32] The further you have progressed toward a goal, the more difficult it is to give up. Combined with personal and societal changes this explains why Germans, while losing the war, diverted substantial resources for the continued killing of Jews. Continued killing may also have served to give the Nazis a feeling of power and invulnerability as their fortunes declined.[33]

A progression of changes in a culture and individuals is usually required for mass killing or genocide. In certain instances – the Armenian genocide, for example – the progression takes place over decades or even centuries and creates a readiness in the culture. In other cases there is a speedy evolution of ideology, personalities, or social conditions that ready people for mass killing.

"Vicarious" rather than direct participation can also contribute to this evolution. Members of Nazi movements outside Germany identified with German Nazis and vicariously participated in their practices.[34] This prepared them for their role as perpetrators when their country was later occupied by or allied itself to Nazi Germany. However, several such countries had themselves enacted anti-Jewish laws, so that learning by direct participation also occurred (see Chapter 11).

Other origins of mistreatment

The model presented here, with its emphasis on the psychological roots of group violence, is not always *fully* applicable. Leaders in nondemocratic states, protecting their power from real or imagined threats, may perpetrate wide-scale violence even when life conditions are not unusually difficult and the group membership of victims is poorly defined. In Stalin's purges the criterion was at first ideological, but people were encouraged to betray others and did so for many reasons, including past enmity and a desire to please the authorities.[35]

The desire for material gain or power can be important. North and South American Indians were killed mainly because others wanted their land. In Paraguay, for example, roads were built into the jungle, greatly increasing land values, and the Ache Indians became "inconvenient."[36] In such cases of "internal colonialization," cultural preconditions include profound devaluation and a history of discrimination – the victims often excluded from participation in society – and at times a history of conflict and mistreatment. In genocides and mass killings that follow decolonialization, as in Burundi and Biafra, deep-seated historical conflicts can come to the fore in the context of profound social–political change. A history of conflict and antagonism fuels a power struggle that ends in genocide.

In these cases and others when mass killing serves to gain wealth or power or to protect entrenched interests, the model is still at least partially applicable. The conflict is fueled by social disorganization and intense devaluation along class or other group lines. Authoritarian systems may limit free exchange. Ideological components (such as anticommunism) may result in a very broad definition of the enemy group.

Relations between a dominant and a subordinate group often remain peaceful until difficult life conditions, social change, or a new ideology intervene. A subordinate group's claims to greater privilege are a threat not only to the material interests of the dominant group, but also to its self-concept and sense of what is right. The established order has usually been elaborately justified by devaluation, an elevated view by the privileged of themselves, and a world view, all fortified by social institutions. Thus the conflict of interests is psychologically enlarged. In countries like Argentina, Guatemala, and El Salvador, anticommunism, belief in free enterprise, and perceived threat to Christianity all have bolstered opposition to social change.

Selection for mass murder may be based not on cultural devaluation, but on a newly evolving or speedily adopted ideology. Usually, the ideology still draws on existing divisions in society. The identification and elimination of class enemies has often been part of established communist practice. In Cambodia, a country traditionally divided between a peasant countryside and cities dominated by a small and partly foreign ruling and commerical class, city dwellers were identified as incapable of contributing to a communist society. Thus, the Cambodian genocide had roots in Cambodian culture and communist ideology.

Leaders' decisions, of course, are also crucial.[37] At times they simply express a leader's personality, motives, or world view. More often the leaders offer devaluation, scapegoating, and murder as ways to deal with persistent life problems and their psychological effects.

The role and power of bystanders

Bystanders, people who witness but are not directly affected by the actions of perpetrators, help shape society by their reactions. If group norms come to tolerate violence, they can become victims. Bystanders are often unaware of, or deny, the significance of events or the consequences of their behavior. Since these events are part of their lifespace, to remain unaware they employ defenses like rationalization and motivated misperception, or avoid information about the victims' suffering.

Bystanders can exert powerful influence. They can define the meaning of events and move others toward empathy or indifference. They can promote values and norms of caring, or by their passivity or participation in the system they can affirm the perpetrators.[38]

Research on helping in emergencies has shown that, when a number of people are present, responsibility is diffused, and each person is less likely to help.[39] Another consequence is what Bibb Latane and John Darley call pluralistic ignorance.[40] People tend to inhibit expressions of feeling in public. In an emergency, the fact that all bystanders are hiding their feelings may lead them all to believe that there is no need for concern and nothing need be done. Hiding reactions is also common when suffering is inflicted by agents of society on members of a minority.

As I have noted, psychological research shows that a single deviation from group behavior can greatly diminish conformity.[41] In emergencies the likelihood of helping greatly increases when one bystander says the situation is serious or tells others to take action.[42] When a society begins to mistreat some of its members, resistance by bystanders, in words and action, will influence others and inhibit the personal changes that would result from passivity.

Even the behavior of governments can be strongly affected by bystanders – individuals, groups, or other governments. Repeatedly when they faced substantial opposition, the Nazis backed away. They did not persist, for example, when Bulgaria (where the people protested in the streets) refused to hand over its Jewish population or when, within Germany, relatives and some institutions protested the killing of the mentally retarded, mentally ill, and others regarded as genetically inferior.[43] Public protest in the United States greatly affected the war in Vietnam. Amnesty International groups have freed political prisoners all over the world simply by writing letters to governments.

A lack of protest can confirm the perpetrators' faith in what they are doing. Hitler saw the lack of response both in Germany and in the outside world to the persecution of Jews as evidence that the whole world wanted what only he had the courage to do. A refusal to cooperate can raise questions in the minds of perpetrators. According to Helen Fein, resistance in Denmark, Italy, and Bulgaria raised doubts in the minds of some Nazi functionaries in those countries.[44] Perpetrators may question not only whether they can get away with it, but also whether what they are doing is right.

Why then are bystanders so often passive and silent? Sometimes silence results from fear, but that is not the whole explanation. Everywhere people tend to accept a definition of reality provided by "experts," their government, or their culture. Lack of divergent views, just-world thinking, and their own participation or passivity change bystanders' perception of self and reality so as to allow and justify cruelty.

Outsiders may also respond little, although they have less to fear. They too are subject to these processes of change. They too are affected by the propaganda or ideology used to justify mistreatment. Before World War II, for example, anti-Semitism increased in many countries.[45] Hitler's propaganda joined with an existing anti-Semitic base and just-world thinking and enabled people in economic trouble to blame Jews.

Ideological conceptions and romantic notions of what is good can mislead us. Very few people, in retrospect, glorify the violence of the Chinese Cultural Revolution. But at the time, some voices in the United States celebrated this "rejuvenation" of the revolution.

Another reason for outside indifference is that governments usually do not see themselves as moral agents obliged to endanger their interests by interfering in the "internal affairs" of other countries. With rare exceptions they protest only when they see their self-interest endangered (see Chapters 16 and 17).

Part II

The Nazi Holocaust

7   Hitler comes to power

Genocide and "insanity"

The Holocaust if often called incomprehensible, partly because of the magnitude of the killings and partly because of the impersonal, techno-logical methods used: the factories of death, which were new in world history. Any genocide might be seen as a form of insanity possessing normal human beings. That people would be gathered in great squares or on street corners, by force or by intrigue – with the promise of resettlement and a better life, or a piece of bread, or simply by threat of force – then herded into freight cars to be transported over hundreds and thousands of miles, taken to a camp and told to undress and go into showerlike chambers, where they were gassed to death, and their bodies burned in huge ovens; millions of people murdered in this way and tens of thousands devoted to the organized killings, in the midst of a losing war in a progres-sively, devastated country – all this seems like madness.

But the people who participated in this mass murder were normal by conventional standards of mental health. Interviews and psychological testing found no evidence of mental illness or psychological dysfunction in the Nuremberg defendants and SS criminals. Large-scale murder and mis-treatment are commonplace in human history. Understanding the sources is our task; labeling it madness does not provide such understanding. In this section, I apply the model offered in Part I to a detailed analysis of the Holocaust, extending it in the process.

Life conditions: loss of war, the Treaty of Versailles, and economic and political chaos

When Germany lost the war in 1918, the peace treaty imposed on it, the Treaty of Versailles, demanded substantial reparation, allowed Germany only a very small army, and took away territories. Germans experienced the loss of war and the treaty as great humiliations, and both were widely seen as the result of betrayal, a "stab in the back" by internal enemies: Red revolutionaries, republicans, Jews. This suited the Germans' collective view of themselves as strong, superior, and militarily powerful. They could not accept the reality, given its discrepancy with their self-concept. A contributing cause was that the military and government had lied about the progress of the war. The collapse seemed sudden and inexplicable. Prussian officers and government leaders could not possibly lie; the legend of the stab in the back was the alternative.

The Treaty of Versailles amputated Alsace-Lorraine on the west and a part of Poland on the east. Under military occupation Germany was humiliated and reduced to the rank of a second rate power. The new liberal regime was opposed on all sides and was openly considered to be a *Judenrepubliq*. For the ultra-conservative circles the burning question arose: How was the sudden cruel defeat and its consequences to be interpreted? The answer was quickly found: by a stab in the back. Accomplices of the Bolsheviks and the Allies, the Jews had fomented an immense plot against the Reich by disorganizing things behind the lines and propagating pacifist ideas. Thus reiterating in his own way the theme of the *Dolchstosslegende*, Marshal Ludendorff wrote: "Those who enjoyed and profited from the War were especially Jews...patriotic cricles felt that the German people, who with weapons in hand, fought for liberty, had been sold out and betrayed by the Jewish people."[1]

As the war ended there was a revolution, the social democrats proclaiming a republic on November 9, 1918. The revolution was relatively bloodless.* In 1922 the French, claiming that they were not receiving reparation shipments on time, occupied the Ruhr, the industrial segment of Germany. Subsequent sabotage and noncooperation by Germans severely reduced industrial output. In part because of the economic difficulties arising from the heavy reparations and the occupation of the Ruhr, severe inflation engulfed Germany, wiping out savings and diminishing livelihoods. While some were unaffected and a few even benefited (e.g., people with mortgages), most Germans suffered greatly. In the late 1920s the worldwide depression also severely affected Germany. By 1932, the year in which the Nazis received more votes than any other party, 7.5 million people were out of work and 17 million, almost a third of the population, were supported "by the dole."[3]

Material deprivation, social disorganization, the feeling of unfair treatment by the victors, and the psychological distress associated with them led to increasing political instability and violence. Many hated the democratic Weimar Republic established after the revolution of 1918–19: some be-

---

* According to some, the orderliness of the revolution was peculiarly German and perhaps a source of its relative failure. A respect for authority manifested itself all along. "Zuckmayer was elected to the soviet because the 'mutineers' felt it essential that they should be led by an officer. The point is characteristic of the whole German revolution. Time and again we shall see revolutionary spirit qualified by an inherent need for order and decorum."[2]

cause of the humiliating Versailles treaty that continued to be in effect; others because of economic conditions or the disorder created by the many political movements and their violence, which the government was unable or unwilling to control; still others because of the threat of communism; and many because they had never made peace with the idea of a democracy, particularly a liberal one. The kaiser's abdication at the end of the war was a tremendous blow to many Germans; the new system conflicted with the value German culture placed on authority and strong leadership. Among the powerful dissatisfied elements were the army and the judiciary.

Life conditions represented a threat to survival. For many Germans, inability to provide for their families was a special dishonor, given their respect for tradition, order, and the family.[4] Their self-respect and social identity – their view of their group – were threatened. Traditional values were challenged by many experiences, such as middle-aged men dancing cheek-to-cheek in nightclubs. Events made it difficult to maintain the world view by which most Germans lived and equally difficult to replace it. The people lacked a predictable future to work for; there was no end in sight.

Although Hitler and his followers greatly contributed to the anarchy and political violence of the later 1920s, they also promised to do away with it. They promised law and order, jobs, and ideals to live by.

A state of virtual anarchy prevails in the streets of Germany. . . . Brown shirts were everywhere in evidence again, and now four private armies, equipped at the very least with jack knives and revolvers, daggers and brass knuckles, were shooting in the squares and rampaging through the towns. Processions and meetings, demonstrations and protest, festivals and funerals, all wore the same face but a different uniform – except that the SS and SA of the Nazis, and the Red Front of the Communists marched more obstreperously, the Sozi Reichsbanner more fatly, the Stahlhelmers more sedately. The Reichswehr, the one legal force, was least in evidence, even though it was in a sense, the private political tool of Hindenburg.[5]

The communists had acquired substantial strength, as Germans were turning to the two extremes. "In 1932. . . between them these two totalitarian parties had an absolute majority in the Reichstag. . . . They were both bitterly opposed to the *System* and without them the system was hamstrung. . . . 'Better Nazi than Red' was an argument which made many turn to Hitler."*[6] In the July 1932 election the Nazis emerged as the largest

---

* Much more could be said about the immense problems in Germany and their immense effects on individual lives. For example, the British and French occupation troops after the war enjoyed humiliating Germans; the unemployment compensation was progressively reduced during the depression, and huge numbers of homeless people lived in tent cities; during several periods there were intense battles in Germany between four private political armies. The decorum of the 1918 revolution had disappeared.

party in the German parliament. After a government led by von Papen and much political maneuvering, in January 1933 Hitler was appointed chancellor; "the city [of Berlin] saw mass hysteria and jubilation without parallel in history."[7]

The guiding motive for the Holocaust: ideology

The Holocaust had many causes, but the original motivation or guiding conception was crucial. Why was this conception accepted by the German people? How was it related to German culture and history?

Hitler laid down the Nazi ideology in his book *Mein Kampf*, dictated to is deputy Rudolf Hess in 1924 while he served a prison sentence following the unsuccessful Nazi putsch in November 1923. In most respects, Hitler acted to fulfill the goals and plans described in *Mein Kampf*. According to Hitler the power of ideals is great. The Nazis had to overcome the views of life and ideals of the "calculating masters of the material Republic." Totalitarian rule and propaganda, once the Nazis were in control, were aimed not only at maintaining power, but also at converting the masses to Nazi ideals.

The core of these ideals was racial purity. According to Hitler, racial principles are fundamental to all life: race is the foundation of all culture. "In this world human culture and civilization are inseparably bound up with the existence of the Aryan. His dying off or his decline would again lower upon this earth the dark veils of a time without culture. The undermining of the existence of human culture by destroying its supporters [e.g., Aryans] appears as the most execrable crime."[8]

The cause of a higher culture "lies exclusively in the existence of a race capable of culture." The Aryans possessed the highest spiritual level. Jews lacked culture and by their very being threatened to destroy the high Aryan culture. "All really significant symptoms of decay of the pre-War period can in the last analysis be reduced to racial causes."[9]

In these long years there was only one who kept up an imperturbable, unflagging fight, and this was the Jew. His Star of David rose higher and higher in proportion as our people's will for self-preservation vanished. Therefore, in August 1914, it was not a people resolved to attack which rushed to the battle-field; no, it was only the last flicker of the national instinct of self-preservation in face of the progressing pacifist-Marxist paralysis of our national body. Since even in these days of destiny, our people did not recognize the inner enemy, all outward resistance was in vain and Providence did not bestow her reward on the victorious sword, but followed the law of eternal retribution.[10]

As part of their plan for world domination the Jews were determined to destroy Germany and the German people. The struggle against Jews served both survival and racial purity. Jews symbolize all evil, but also serve a positive function: by spurring the Aryan to struggle against them, they make him increasingly conscious of his own race.[11] Jews must be destroyed to preserve the higher Aryan culture.

Racial purity was an overriding purpose; it was an obligation to destroy anything that interfered with it, whereas anything that promoted it had to be done. Jews were the most serious threat, but other groups like Gypsies and eastern Europeans were also considered inferior and a threat to racial purity. This was convenient because Hitler intended to provide the German people with Lebensraum (living space) through conquest in the east.

Lebensraum was another central aspect of Hitler's ideology. Aryans, the bearers of superior culture, had a right to a "place in the sun." They had a right to take land from racially inferior people. This aspect of Hitler's ideology was consistent with German nationalism and with the expressed purpose of Germany in fighting World War I. It had strong appeal for many Germans.

Hitler's race theories are sometimes discounted as a cause of his actions. Certainly we often discount politicians' statements of good intentions; apparently this also happens with statements of bad intentions. Before, during, and since the Holocaust some have claimed that Hitler's anti-Semitism was mere demagoguery, intended to gain the support of anti-Semites. The highly influential American psychologist Gordon Allport, author of *The Nature of Prejudice*, wrote in 1954: "Hitler created the Jewish menace not so much to demolish Jews as to cement the Nazi hold over Germany."[12] It is easier to see the generation of hatred and antagonism toward a group as Allport did – "The Macchiavellian trick of creating a common enemy in order to cement an ingroup"[13] – to see it as having a pragmatic purpose that leads to a commonly understood gain, than to see it as being done out of hate or due to commitment to an ideology, seemingly for its own sake.

It is true that anti-Semitism did cement the ingroup and helped it to gain followers – not simply because the Germans were anti-Semitic, but because scapegoating Jews helped Germans deflect feelings of betrayal by their leaders and feelings of personal and collective responsibility for their troubles. The ideology also provided a blueprint for a "better" world and elevated the Germans' greatly threatened view of themselves. The Nazi movement fulfilled the need for connection and for relinquishing a burdensome identity. By the time the extermination of Jews began, the German people were devoted followers of Hitler. By this time the ideology and the progression along a continuum of destruction had lives of their own.

The German historian Meinecke writes as if Hitler had been concerned only about power, rather than ideology.[14] He points out that Hitler's allies, the Japanese, were subhuman – according to National Socialist ideology. This is an oversimplified view. The evidence clearly indicates that Hitler would use and abandon people or countries or strategies in pursuit of his goals; for example, he entered into an alliance with the Soviet Union and then invaded it. His strategy is expressed in the following 1937 response to dissatisfaction with his speed of action against Jews:

The final aim of our whole policy is quite clear for all of us. Always I am concerned only that I do not take any step from which I will perhaps have to retreat, and not to take any step that will harm us. I tell you that I always go to the outermost limits of risk, but never beyond. For this you need to have a nose more or less to smell out: "What can I still do?" Also in a struggle against an enemy. I do not summon an enemy with force to fight, I don't say: "Fight," because I want to fight. Instead I say "I will destroy you!" and now, Wisdom, help me to maneuver you into the corner that you cannot fight back, and then you get the blow right in the heart.[15]

Thus the more successful the Nazi system became, the more it persecuted Jews and others, although many dictatorships become milder as their success and acceptance grow.

In his early public speeches, and especially before the Nazis gained power, Hitler hinted at but did not explicitly state the extremes to which (according to earlier written statements) he was willing to go in his "treatment" of Jews. He knew that many of his potential adherents were not psychologically ready to support such actions or to publicly commit themselves to a group advocating them. Although he underplayed attacks on Jews in the last election campaigns before the Nazis gained power, he did not hide his views.

Five Nazis broke into the hotel room of a young columnist asleep with his aged mother and murdered the man. He was shot, stabbed, and bludgeoned, receiving twenty-nine wounds in all. The five were sentenced to death, reprieved by von Papen, and later released by Hitler. Rosenberg, the Nazi ideologue, wrote this when the sentence was handed down:

Bourgeois justice weighs a single communist, and a Pole at that, against five German war veterans. In this example is mirrored the ideology of the past 150 years, displaying the mistaken substructure of its being. . . . The unacceptability of this attitude explains the world view of National Socialism. It does not believe that one soul is equal to another, one man equal to another. It does not believe in rights as such: it aims to create the German man of strength, its task is to protect the German people, and all justice, all social life, politics and economics must be subordinate to this goal.[16]

How serious Nazi leaders were about their racial views is indicated by the many statements and actions taken to uphold them, sometimes at great cost. Horst von Maltitz wrote and cited the following in *The Evolution of Hitler's Germany*.[17]

"We are a master race which must remember that the lowest German worker is racially and biologically a thousand times more valuable than the population here," said Erich Koch, Reich-Commissioner for the Ukraine, in a speech in Kiev on March 5, 1943. (p. 53)

The policy of utter ruthlessness of the occupation regime naturally resulted in deep hostility, even on the part of those groups of the native population who might otherwise have had some inclination to cooperate or to acquiesce in it, at least for the duration of the war. No one is willing to be stamped subhuman under the terror regime of a self-proclaimed master race. The native hostility immeasurably increased the difficulties of the occupation regime. Moreover, the mistreatment of the Soviet prisoners of war, which soon became known in the Soviet Army, greatly increased the determination of its soldiers never to surrender under any circumstances. More farsighted National Socialists, such as Alfred Rosenberg and even Joseph Goebbels, recognized these disadvantages and dangers, but their objections were useless. To Hitler, Himmler, and countless other national socialist leaders, the importance of asserting themselves as the master race and other ideological racial considerations had unquestioned priority. It was one of many instances in national socialist rule in which ideology took precedence over political and military expediency. (p. 54)

"For reasons of racial hygiene, it is undesirable to use prisoners of war as blood donors for members of the German folk community, because we cannot be sure that no men of mixed Jewish blood among the prisoners would be used for blood donations." (p. 56).

For the improvement of the race, Himmler wanted the SS men to be the breeding bulls: "It must be a matter of course that the most copious breeding should be by this [SS] Order, by this racial elite of the Germanic people. In 20 to 30 years we must really be able to furnish the whole of Europe with its leading class." And Hitler said: "I am firmly determined to station racially valuable military units, such as formations of the *Waffen-SS*, in all areas where the present population is [racially] bad, so as to have them take care of a freshening-up of the blood (Auffrischung des Blutes)." (p. 57)

The killing of Jews and others was highly irrational from any societal perspective, except the ideological one. Even their lesser mistreatment in the 1930s resulted in great losses for Germany in mathematics, in science, and in other realms. The Germans knew this. Hitler said, "If the dismissal of Jewish scientists means the annihilation of contemporary German science then we shall do without science for a few years."[18]

It is an irrelevant question whether Hitler intended to *kill* the Jews from the beginning. Certainly to get rid to them was an obsession with him. Once the Nazis came to power they considered resettlement; we do not know how seriously. Extermination – implied by the word *Ausrottung* used in *Mein Kampf* – may have been considered all along. In a 1922 conversation recorded in the archives of the Institute für Zeitgeschichte, Munich, Hitler said, "As soon as I shall have power, I shall have gallows erected, for example in Munich – Jews will be hanged until the last Jew in Munich is exterminated."[19] Even if he did not seriously intend to do this in 1922, usually intentions do not fully develop without some possibility of their actualization.[20] After Hitler came to power, both the psychological possibility and the machinery of destruction evolved with the progressively greater mistreatment of Jews.

What was the cause of Hitler's personal, deep-seated hatred of Jews? Did it arise from the death of his mother while she was being treated by a Jewish doctor? Was it deep hostility and anger caused by his bad relationship to his father, which found an outlet in anti-Semitism? Was it the virulent anti-Semitism in Vienna while he lived there in his early adulthood?* Did anti-Semitism serve him by elevating his self-esteem and giving a feeling of wholeness to a damaged self? Many attempts at understanding the Holocaust have focused on Hitler's childhood and personal pathology. The predisposition to fanaticism does have roots in childhood and personality, but once a person makes a fanatic commitment to an ideology, knowledge of the ideology, and not his childhood and personality, is the best guide to understanding his behavior. Moreover, as I noted in Part I, we are concerned less with Hitler himself than with the people who came to follow him.

There will always be wild ideas and extreme ideologies. For us the question is how the German people came to follow a leader and a party with such ideas, and how they came to participate in their fulfillment. To understand this, we must consider German culture and its influence during both phases of the genocide: the Nazi rise to power and the progressively greater mistreatment of Jews.

Reasons for Hitler's appeal: a summary

Hitler's ideology had three primary components: (1) racial purity and the racial superiority of Germans, with an especially heavy component of anti-Semitism (and the belief that Germans had to be defended against Jews, who were bent on their destruction); (2) nationalism, an extension of German power and influence, which also promised material well-being expressed in the concept of Lebensraum; and (3) the *Führerprinzip* (leadership principle), which required unquestioning obedience to Hilter.

By accepting the racial theory, which identified them as the pure, Aryan

---

* During his stay in Vienna, while he struggled and failed at various enterprises (e.g., as an artist), Hitler was surrounded by a society soaked in anti-Semitism. It was pervasive in political life and in the atmosphere of the city. It was at this time that he had the "revelation" of the far-reaching destructiveness of Jews. This probably had a number of psychological benefits, including perhaps a feeling of connection to the world around him, not insignificant for a lonely man.

race, the Germans could feel inherently superior to others, as individuals and as a people. Hitler also promised Germans superiority as a nation, which appealed to the strong nationalism and the remnants of militarism that existed in Germany.

Hitler's movement promised to unite two political trends, socialism and nationalism, with the possibility of uniting groups associated with them. Unity was specifically furthered by the notion of *Volk*. Meinecke wrote that "within the Nordic race [i.e., "Aryans"], our own German nation was further especially hallowed and in appearance romanticized by the German idea of *a people* distinguished from other peoples by possessing certain common customs, traditions, and historic past, that is, by the idea of a 'volk' " (a people).[21] The communality of the volk was contrasted with the separateness and competition imposed by capitalism. To a people distressed by inflation, depression, joblessness, and political chaos, togetherness and unity had wide appeal.

The Nazi "people's community" also incorporated an idealized recollection of life in the trenches – comradeship, mutual support, shared danger, equality in the face of a hostile environment. Contrasted with this were the polluters of the economic and national life, especially Jews, socialists, and communists. To combat this pervasive pollution, Germans had to subordinate themselves to the community and give up their individuality.

Hitler promised order and tranquility. The strength and discipline of his followers demonstrated his capacity to deliver. The Nazis provided ideals to live by, guidance, and hope. Finally, Hitler was a charismatic leader to whom Germans could resign their fate, absolving themselves of responsibility for the difficulties of their lives. Following a powerful leader in unity and common cause with others, they could throw off despair.

8   Preconditions for the Holocaust in German culture

Nazi ideology matched basic aspects of German culture; the fit made the extreme ideology acceptable to many Germans. When the Nazis took power, their propaganda and actions further shaped German culture.

No single cultural element can explain genocide. A multiplicity of factors have to coalesce. In the context of intense, persistent life problems, the cultural characteristics that I describe in this chapter made the Germans susceptible to Hitler and the Nazi ideology. An evolution toward destruction followed, without reactions by internal and external bystanders that might have inhibited it.

The devaluation of Jews

One precondition for genocide was widespread anti-Semitism. Political anti-Semitism appeared in a number of European countries in the second half of the nineteenth century. An anti-Semitic party was represented in the German parliament and continually tried to pass anti-Semitic legislation. In 1881 an Anti-Semites Petition was presented to Bismarck, with 225,000 signatures, demanding the "emancipation of the German people from a form of alien domination which it cannot endure for any length of time" and proposing legal steps to restrict the rights of Jews, rights granted under Napoleon in the early nineteenth century.[1] In the late nineteenth and early twentieth centuries, racial dogmas identifying superior and inferior social groups provided a link to the Nazi belief in the racial superiority of Aryans.[2]

Anti-Semitism increased even before Hitler and his party gained national influence. Jews, among others, were blamed for the loss of the war; cultural devaluation led to their selection when a scapegoat was needed. Anti-Semitism was not itself the cause of the Holocaust, but provided an important precondition for it. Devaluation of Jews and discrimination against them had historical sources and acquired a historical continuity.

100

An important source of anti-Semitism was Christian dogma. Jews were regarded as killers of Christ and as unbelievers, doomed to eternal damnation. Their stubborn refusal to be converted and saved was seen as an attack on the Christian religion itself. A central reason for intense early Christian anti-Semitism had to be the need to separate from the old roots of Christianity, in order to create an independent identity.

Girard shows all this in the words of early Christian writers:

A Jewish sect at first, Christianity, under the influence of St. Paul, separated rapidly from the synagogue and engaged in a merciless war with it. The Gospel of John, the last to have been written, is by far the most hostile to the Jews, who were held collectively responsible for the death of Christ. The fall of the temple and the dispersion that followed were interpreted as a divine punishment. As Origen wrote, "We can therefore say with all confidence that the Jews will not regain their former position, because they have committed the most abominable of sins, by hatching this plot against the savior of mankind...it was therefore necessary, that the city where Jesus suffered so be completely destroyed, that the Jewish people be driven from their land, and that others be called upon as the blessed Elect."

...According to the Dayacides, the Jews, as long as they did not renounce their error, must live in a state of eternal disgrace and abasement, therefore proving the veracity of Christianity. The writings of the Byzantine Fathers are particularly hard on them. St. John Chrysostom described them in this way: "Brothel and theatre, the synagogue is also a retreat for brigands and a lair for wild beasts...living by their stomach, mouth always gaping, the Jews do not act any better than pigs and goats, in their lewd grossness and extremes of their gluttony. They only know how to do one thing: stuff themselves and get drunk." As for the no less venerable Gregory of Nysse, he categorized them as "murderers of the Lord, assassins of prophets, rebellious and hateful toward God,...confederates of the devil, race of vipers, informers, calumniators, mentally clouded, pharisaic fermentors, sanhedrin of the devil, cursed, execrable, stoners, enemies of all that is beautiful." These inflamed declarations, fed by popular sentiment, explained the formation of a Byzantine anti-Semitism whose influence made itself felt far and wide in Eastern Europe.[3]

Every Christian child received the teachings about the Jews' profound criminality, inferiority, and sinful nature. This created a constant potential for active hostility.

As attempts at conversion failed, various European countries took action against Jews. Some expelled them. Others restricted them to certain living areas (ghettos) and certain professions. The combination of restrictions and special opportunities led Jews to practice professions that brought further harm to them. Finance and moneylending were devalued by Christians for religious reasons and forbidden by church law. Jews were encouraged to work in commerce, banking, and finance, However, people who became indebted to them often resented the debt and felt that Jews were exploiting them, which further fueled anger and resentment. Rulers at times relieved themselves of debts by expelling Jews. Persecuting Jews, depriving them of rights, and taking away their property diminished economic competition, provided immediate profit, and served as revenge for presumed wrongdoing.*

Jews had different habits, customs, clothing, and external appearance. These differences were partly religious, partly cultural, and partly imposed by authorities. Human beings, as I have noted, fear the different, the unusual, especially when it is prejudged as bad or dangerous. Jews were relatively unaffected by the plague, the Black Death that decimated Europe in 1348, probably because of religious habits of personal hygiene. As a consequence the belief arose that they had caused the plague. Other atrocities were also ascribed to them; it was widely believed that they killed children at Passover to drink their blood.

Finally, Jewish culture encouraged devotion to learning, industriousness, and other characteristics that helped Jews succeed in spite of adverse circumstances. In an atmosphere of prejudice, envy, and resentment, even such positive characteristics as warm, positive family relations and a relatively peaceful life-style were cast in a negative light.

Research shows that existing prejudices and stereotypes determine how the behavior of a group's members is interpreted.[6] Stereotypes are highly resistant to change.[7] Furthermore, they are self-fulfilling prophecies; people who hold stereotypes behave in a way that evokes the stereotyped response.[8]

The very same behavior undergoes a complete change of evaluation in its transition from the ingroup...Abe Lincoln to the out-group Abe Cohen or Abe Kurakawa...Did Lincoln work far into the night? This testifies that he was industrious, resolute, perseverant, and eager to realize his capabilities to the full. Do the out-group Jews or Japanese keep these same hours? This only bears witness to their sweatshop mentality, their ruthless undercutting of American standards, their unfair competitive practices. Is the in-group hero frugal, thrifty, and sparing? Then the out-group victim is stingy, miserly, and penny-pinching.[9]

Anti-Semitism was further encouraged by the writings of Martin Luther, whose influence on German culture was enormous. He began with a positive attitude toward Jews, but turned against them when they refused to be converted. His image of the Jews resembles the Nazi image:

Herewith you can readily see how they understand and obey the fifth commandment of God, namely, that they are thirsty bloodhounds and murderers of all

---

* Direct economic interest was also apparent in the lynching of black people in the South. A black man's lynching sometimes was instigated with a rumor of wrongdoing put in circulation by a white man who had a competing business.[4] The death squads in Guatamala and the kidnappers in Argentina were partly motivated by material gain.[5] When persecution and murder become acceptable, they can be used to fulfill self-interested motives.

Christendom, with full intent, now for more than fourteen hundred years, and indeed they were often burned to death upon the accusation that they had poisoned water and wells, stolen children, and torn and hacked them apart, in order to cool their temper secretly with Christian blood.

It is more than fourteen hundred years since Jerusalem was destroyed, and at this time it is almost three hundred years since we Christians have been tortured and persecuted by the Jews all over the world (as pointed out above), so that we might well complain that they had now captured us and killed us – which is the open truth. Moreover, we do not know to this day which devil has brought them here into our country; we did not look for them in Jerusalem.

Yes, they hold us Christians captive in our country. They let us work in the sweat of our noses, to earn money and property for them, while they sit behind the oven, lazy, let off gas, bake pears, eat, drink, live softly and well from our wealth, sweat, and work. They curse our Lord, to reward us and to thank us. Should not the devil laugh and dance, if he can have such paradise among us Christians, that he may devour through the Jews – his holy ones – that which is ours, and stuff our mouths and noses as reward, mocking and cursing God and man for good measure.[10]

Some speculate that the relative assimilation of Jews in Germany in the late nineteenth and early twentieth centuries contributed to *modern* anti-Semitism.

Modern antisemitism was born not from the great difference between groups but rather from the threat of the absence of differences, the homogenization of Western society and the abolition of the ancient social and legal barriers between Jews and Christians.

Racist passions reach a climax precisely when the psychobiological differences on which they depend no longer exist, having been belied by the facts or reduced to what Freud designates by the term *unheimlich*, the disquieting strangeness, the mysterious unfamiliar. The racist will then rely on a science that has gone astray to justify biologically the charge of "differentness." As Jacques Hassoun has noted: "The usurer now becomes the banker, the rag man now becomes the manager of the high fashion store, the grandson of the rabbi now becomes a scholar in secular matters, all this will occupy the foreground of the scene for the racist."[11]

For those who had Luther's opinion of Jews, remaining separate from them would be a psychological necessity. Separation and control would diminish contamination and danger. Images of contamination and threat were exploited by the Nazis. They adopted nineteenth-century racial dogmas, adapted them, and combined them with the most negative components of the existing image of Jews. Even those Germans who were not consciously anti-Semitic probably picked up enough anti-Semitism from their culture to be susceptible to Nazi propaganda and later to the influence of changing group norms.

The Nazi propaganda about Jews emphasized three broad themes: (1) profound devaluation, (2) threat to racial purity, and (3) threat to German survival. (1) The Jews were pests, parasites, bloodsuckers, low and evil creatures. Jewish doctors harmed their Christian patients; old Jews molested and murdered children; all Jews exploited and abused the rights of Germans. (2) The Jews despoiled Aryan purity. Their very existence threatened contamination and therefore the inherent superiority of Germans, the Aryan race. (3) In an international conspiracy, the Jews plotted to acquire power. This notion, already a theme of anti-Semitism before Hitler, was expanded into the fantasy of a Jewish-Bolshevik conspiracy. First the internal enemy, after the German attack on Russia, Jews were linked to the external enemy. The Jews within Germany had to be eliminated before the external enemy could be defeated.

All this was presented to the German people on radio, in speeches, newspapers, and plays; it became part of standard school education; and it was expressed in laws. The dehumanization of Jews became part of many aspects of group life and an important aspect of the German's self-definition.

Anti-Semitism was part of the deep structure of the German culture and was enlarged by the Nazis. At the start, particular Nazis need not have been more anti-Semitic than other Germans in order to join the movement; given the existence of culturally shared anti-Semitism, or openness to it, intense needs and the satisfactions offered by the Nazi movement could be sufficient motivation. A Columbia sociologist, Theodore Abel, by means of an essay contest collected 581 questionnaires from members of the Nazi Party before 1933. Peter Merkl later used this material to identify characteristics of the early Nazis, for example, different levels of anti-Semitism.[12]

There was an extraordinary amount of prejudice and hatred. The material from about 33 percent of the respondents contained no evidence of anti-Semitism. It may be, as Merkl suggests, that they omitted expressions of prejudice because they anticipated a negative reaction from an American audience. Or it may be that within the Nazi group anti-Semitism was a given, it was the ground of the members' experience, and for some not important to mention. The Abel collection does show, however, that the Nazis who were the most paranoid about the Jews, who were preoccupied by "the Jewish conspiracy," were especially likely to hold Nazi Party, SA (Sturmabteilung), and SS leadership positions.

Self-concept, self-esteem, and national goals

People have not only individual but also collective self-concepts. Their "societal" self-concept includes shared evaluation of their group, myths that transmit the self-concept and ideal self, goals that a people set for themselves, and shared beliefs (e.g., about other groups).[13] It may also include or mask uncertainties, insecurities, and anxieties.

The Germans as a superior people

Germans saw themselves as superior in character, competence, honor, loyalty, devotion to family, and civic organization. Groups tend to think highly of themselves; seemingly the Germans had an extreme positive view of themselves. They regarded German "*Kultur*" – literary, musical, artistic achievement – a further sign of superiority.

In the sixteenth century, *De Germania*, by the Roman historian Tacitus, was rediscovered and read as a celebration of the rough and wild life of the German tribes. Some German intellectuals used it to argue the specialness of the German people and claim the right of the Holy Roman Empire to rule other nations. Early in the nineteenth century Germany was occupied by Napoleon. Afterward, upon the demise of Napoleon, nationalistic feelings intensified.

The *idea of Germanness* became a special source of satisfaction and pride. Johann Gottfried Herder, writing around the time of the French Revolution, wrote of the common quality expressed in the behavior, thinking, values, and goals of people who belong to a nation, "a common ingredient, a Germanness, a Volksgeist that could not be abstracted and defined but represented the individuality of the nation."*[14] Gordon Craig of Stanford University explains the lethargy of the German middle class at a time when democratic revolutions took place in many European countries and in America as the result of their taking refuge in Germanness, "persuading themselves that, since they were imbued by the undying group spirit, they were already in a state of grace."[16] Following the failed revolution of 1848, the political activities of the German middle class were severely restricted, and this may have led them to console themselves further by contemplating the glory of Germanness. Whatever the reason, a set of ideas and images stressing the special quality of Germanness became widespread and highly influential. The Nazis were able to use this, especially the central idea of a volk, to rally the German people.

A related idea was that of a romanticized, superior Aryan race, whose prime representatives were the Germans. This was an aspect of the racial thinking fashionable in Europe in the late nineteenth century. As deve-

---

* Herder emphasized the value of all cultures and probably elevated Germanness because there was no German nation as an entity. Contemporary writers in America refer to Herder's views in stressing the value of ethnicity as a source of cultural diversity and enrichment.[15] In Germany, as the idea of Germanness evolved, it fueled a feeling of specialness.

loped, for example, by Houston Chamberlain, Richard Wagner's son-in-law, it expanded the concept of German superiority and advanced anti-Semitic thought.[17] Chamberlain admired Germans and described Semites (Jews) as enslavers of humanity. Not physical but psychological characteristics defined race. The Nazis later defined Jews by their supposedly inferior culture and habits. Although the Nazis had a physical ideal for Aryans, blond and tall, this nonphysical racial thinking allowed them to regard Germans as superior Aryans in spite of the tremendous variation in their physical characteristics. The physical ideal guided the selection of the SS, regarded as the real "superior stock."

This superior nation was seen as *surrounded and besieged by enemies*.[18] From the ninth to the twelfth century the Holy Roman Empire was powerful, with near hegemony over Europe. This power declined, for many reasons, including the rise of princes who created disunity. By the middle of the fifteenth century Germany had lost many territories, and its borders were constantly threatened. During the Thirty Years War (1618–48), Germany suffered tremendous devastation and a population loss of 35 percent, or seven and a half million people.[19] The settlement that followed the war contributed to its continued division among many states and principalities. The perception of Germany as a "Land in the Middle," threatened from all sides, was realistic. Much later, Napoleon's conquest of Germany and reduction of parts of Germany to the status of satellites resulted in profound feelings of powerlessness.[20] The idealization of the state that followed had to be a defense of a wounded societal self-concept.

Germans continued to have a sense of unfulfilled greatness and present unfairness. The German crown prince said in 1913: "It is only by relying on our good German sword that we can hope to conquer that place in the sun which rightly belongs to us, and which no one will yield to us voluntarily." This suggests the idea of Lebensraum that became so important in Nazi ideology. Such feelings intensified the losses and humiliations that Germans endured during and after the First World War. German militarism and nationalism supported this sense of entitlement. Prussia, which dominated the newly united Germany late in the nineteenth and twentieth century, was a highly militaristic state in which the armed forces were greatly respected. The influence of the military pervaded most aspects of life. Nationalism, which had served to create a united German state, persisted.

German academics and intellectuals strongly supported nationalistic aims. During the shock and uproar created by Germany's violation of Belgian neutrality in 1914, German intellectuals produced a Manifesto to the Civilized World, which denied Germany's war guilt and proclaimed that it would have been suicide not to march through Belgium. They alleged that Allied rather than German war actions were contrary to international law and referred to the "shameful spectacle...of Russian hordes...allied with mongols and Negroes...unleashed against the white race."[21] The manifesto was signed by people like Röntgen, the discoverer of X rays, Max Reinhardt, the pioneer of the modern theater, Paul Ehrlich, the great biochemist, and Engelbert Humperdinck, the composer of the opera *Hansel and Gretel*. It concluded:

Were it not for German militarism, German culture would have been wiped off the face of the earth. That culture, for its own protection, led to militarism since Germany, like no other country, was ravaged by invasion for centuries. The German army and the German people today stand shoulder to shoulder, without regard to education, social position or partisan allegiance.

We cannot wrest from our enemies' hand the venomous weapon of the lie. We can only cry out to the whole world that they bear false witness against us. To you who know us, who have hitherto stood with us in safeguarding mankind's most precious heritage – to you we cry out: Have faith in us! Have faith in us when we say that we shall wage this fight to the very end as a civilized nation, a nation that holds the legacy of Goethe, Beethoven and Kant no less sacred than hearth and home.

In token whereof we pledge our names and our honor![22]

A noted German pacifist, George Friedrich Nicolai, responded with a Manifesto to Europeans calling for a united, peaceful Europe. Only three others were willing to sign this document (one was Albert Einstein), and as a result it was not made public for several years. In 1915, 352 of Germany's most distinguished professors signed a Declaration of Intellectuals saying that it would be reasonable and just for Germany to acquire Belgium, parts of France, the Ukraine, and other territories.[23]

It is hardly surprising, in light of this history, that university professors also rallied to the Nazis. Many proclaimed the greatness of Hitler and swore loyalty to him. Martin Heidegger, the great philosopher, proclaimed that Hitler and the German people were bound by fate and "guided by the inexorability of that spiritual mission that the destiny of the German people forcibly impresses upon its history." The rush of converts to Nazism in the first days of Hitler's rule included many university professors and intellectuals, who excelled in their efforts to "justify the new regime and establish its roots in Germany's history and cultural tradition." A highly distinguished political scientist, Carl Schmitt, devised theories to prove that all of Hitler's actions were justified by a higher morality, which he called "the superiority of the existential situation over mere normality."[24]

How different was all this from ordinary ethnocentrism? It was especially strong and included beliefs in the right to acquire others' territory and to rule others. Moreover, it was systematized in concepts like volk. (This perhaps expresses a German proclivity, a desire for a world view, or *Weltanschauung*.) The elevated German self-concept was especially dangerous when combined with militarism, unfulfilled ambitions, insecurity, and vulnerability. It intensified and shaped reactions to life problems.

Respect for and obedience to authority

A certain degree of obedience to authority is required in all social systems. The view that respect for the state and obedience to authority have characterized Germany to an unusual degree is not a post–World War II phenomenon, a result of so many SS murderers and war criminals claiming that they were following orders.[25] Gordon Craig wrote:

It is not too much to talk of a progressive bureaucratization of Germany in the seventeenth and eighteenth centuries and a concomitant growth among the inhabitants of the German states of habits of deference toward authority that seemed excessive to foreign observers. These last may have had ancient roots – it was a medieval pope who called Germany the *terra obedientiae* – but there is little doubt that they were encouraged by the traumatic effects of the war. The daily presence of death, the constant *Angst* of which Gryphius speaks in his poems, made the survivors willing to submit to any authority that seemed strong enough to prevent a recurrence of those terrors. . . .
  Acceptance of the authority of the prince assumed a willingness to obey the commands of his agents, no matter how petty their position or arrogant their manner. The willingness of Germans to tolerate the most offensive behavior from anyone wearing a uniform or official insignia was something that always surprised Western visitors.[26]

Craig quotes the Württemberg publisher Karl Frederich Moser, who wrote in 1758: "Every nation has its principal motive. In Germany it is obedience; in England, freedom; in Holland, trade; in France, the honor of the King."[27]

One source of this proclivity for obedience, already noted, was the suffering from past wars and people feeling helpless and under siege. Subordination to authorities – the prince, the state – was seen as necessary to deal with external threat or attack. Bureaucratization and militarism also contributed to respect for authority, as they expanded into daily life. In 1781 John Moore described Prussian military life as an early totalitarian system.

The Prussian discipline on a general view is beautiful; in detail it is shocking. . . . if the young recruit shows neglect or remissness, his attention is roused by the officer's cane, which is applied with augmenting energy. . . .
  . . . As to the common men, the leading idea of the Prussian discipline is to reduce them in many respects, to the nature of machines; that they may have no

volition of their own, but be actuated solely by that of their officers; that they may have such a superlative dread of those officers as annihilates all fear of the enemy; and that they may move forwards when ordered, without deeper reasoning or more concern than the firelocks they carry along with them.[28]

Influential German thinkers stressed the the role of the state not as a servant of the people but as an entity to which citizens owed unquestioning obedience. Martin Luther was one outstanding spokesman for the special status and special rights of the state. He viewed it as an organic entity, superior to any individual. Citizens owed unquestioning obedience to all constituted authorities. A Christian captured and sold into slavery by the Turks would not have the right to escape, becasue that would deprive his master of his property.[29] (Alfred Rosenberg's lawyer at Nuremberg claimed that Christian morality required first and foremost obedience to established authorities.)

Fichte and Hegel also viewed the state as a superior organic entity to which the individual owed complete allegiance. "At the time the Anglo-Americans and French were starting to define the state as the servant of the people, Germans were accepting definition of the people as servants of the state."[30] Democratic values, the rights of the individual, were not evolving in Germany.

Both obedience to authority and giving oneself over to a leader had positive value in German culture. Many Germans were shocked and dismayed by the kaiser's abdication in 1918. Following and obeying Hitler became a source of honor and joy, expressed in the testimony of many Nazis before and after the collapse of the Third Reich. The French historian Michelet admiringly wrote in 1831:

There is nothing astonishing if it is in Germany that we see, for the first time a man makes himself belong to another, puts his own hands in the hands of others and [they] swear to die for him. This devotion without interest, without conditions...has made the German race great. That is how the old bands of the Conquerors of the Empire, each one grouped around a leader, founded modern monarchies. They gave their lives to him, to the leader of their choice, they gave him their very glory. In the old Germanic songs, all the exploits of the nation are attributed to several heroes. The leader concentrates in himself the honor of the people of which he becomes the colossal archetype.[31]

Erich Fromm argued that the Germans turned to Hitler to escape personal responsibility for their lives.[32] The need to escape personal responsibility and the concomitant desire for submission to authority would have intensified in the difficult times following World War I.

Authoritarian values also pervaded the most basic of institutions, the family. From varied sources, a picture emerges of a widespread tendency of the German father to be an authoritarian ruler of the family. Some of the evidence for this comes from interviews with Germans after the war, but there are also other important sources.[33] The psychiatrist Alice Miller reviewed the child-rearing advice that German parents received in many publications from the seventeenth to the twentieth century.[34] Children were seen as willful and potentially evil. Their will had to be broken early. Obedience to parents was the highest value and should be sought by any means: manipulation, threats, including the threat of God's punishment or destruction by ill health and severe physical punishment if necessary.

Two representative quotations are the following:

It is quite natural for the child's soul to want to have a will of its own, and things that are not done correctly in the first two years will be difficult to rectify thereafter. One of the advantages of these early years is that then force and compulsion can be used. Over the years children forget everything that happened to them in early childhood. If their wills can be broken at this time, they will never remember afterwards that they had a will, and for this very reason the severity that is required will not have any serious consequences.[35]

Such disobedience amounts to a declaration of war against you. Your son is trying to usurp your authority, and you are justified in answering force with force in order to insure his respect, without which you will be unable to train him. The blows you administer should not be merely playful ones but should convince him that you are his master.[36]

Miller believes that these practices result in a lack of independence in the child, and later, the adult. They also eliminate the psychological freedom necessary to experience one's own feelings. Instead the wishes and commands of others guide the child and later the adult.

It is inconceivable that they were able to express and develop their true feelings as children, for anger and helpless rage, which they were forbidden to display, would have been among these feelings – particularly if these children were beaten, humiliated, lied to, and deceived. What becomes of this forbidden and therefore unexpressed anger? Unfortunately, it does not disappear, but is transformed with time into a more or less conscious hatred directed against either the self or substitute persons, a hatred that will seek to discharge itself in various ways permissible and suitable for an adult.[37]

Authoritarian child rearing has not been restricted to Germany.[38] But it was extreme in Germany and apparently declined there more slowly because of the cultural proclivity for obedience to authority.

Deep feelings of hostility and insecurity result from such childhood treatment. People are seen as dangerous. A strong, independent individual identity does not evolve. The result may be an antisocial value orientation, which has to be carefully controlled, may be largely unconscious, and gains expression only when the group or authorities clearly define permissible objects of hostility.[39] Persons raised in this way may differentiate sharply between outgroups and the ingroup that provides security and self-definition. They also prefer hierarchical systems, with sharp distinctions between people in superior and inferior positions.

Interviews with SS men imprisoned for their participation in mass killings showed that they had unsatisfactory family relations with authoritarian fathers who practiced corporal punishment.[40] Research on a larger group of SS men, which I will discuss in Chapter 10, showed that they were more authoritarian in personality than regular German soliders.[41]

In a postwar study, German preadolescents reported more reluctance than American ones to deviate from adult standards under peer influence. Moreover, they presented themselves as much more obedient to adult rules and guilty about misconduct when a teacher was present while they filled out the questionnaire than they did when alone. In contrast, the presence of a teacher had no effect on American preadolescents.[42] Another postwar study, published in 1980, showed fewer German than American infants (or infants of other nationalities) securely attached to their mothers.[43] Secure attachment appears to be the outgrowth of a loving, comfortable relationship between infant and caretaker and is later associated with effective and satisfying peer relations. These findings probably result from the persistence of authoritarian schools and socialization practices. German mothers allow their children less autonomy than American mothers.[44] German children are more likely to trust authorities and advocate strong leadership than American children.[45]

The life conditions in Germany after World War I would be difficult to bear for any people, but especially for a people who had learned to value and need strong authorities. The sudden inadequacy of their world view and the group's inability to provide security, order, and status profoundly threatened Germans.

The influence of Nietzsche

I have already noted trends in German intellectual thought that contributed to the cultural preconditions for genocide. I will discuss others, especially "biomedical thinking," later. The specific influence of Nietzsche is important: many Nazi beliefs and ideals seem to be highly similar to those expressed by Nietzsche. The following discussion is not a review and evaluation of Nietzsche's thought or the exact meaning of the views he expressed, about which there is disagreement between "tough Nietzscheans" and "tender Nietzscheans."[46] As Nietzsche himself wrote, people can take from a book only what their experience prepares them for; I will focus on ideas that seem to have influenced Hitler and the Nazis.

In Nietzsche's view, there are no givens, no absolutes, whether in human nature or by the dictate of God – who is dead. Nietzsche despised the traditions of the past, especially the beliefs and way of life propagated by Christianity, which in his view elevates what is least desirable in humans – vulnerability, timidity and submission that is paraded as love. Humans define and create themselves. Values are relative; man needs culture and must create it, together with the values the culture is to fulfill. The capacity to generate culture and to produce and impose values distinguishes humans. While producing values and faith in them and commitment to them are themselves central values, Nietzsche does not directly say what is "desirable," what are the right values. Some are implied, however, in his views of human beings, society, and human relations.

The creation of values requires creative, committed, strong men. The clash of cultures is inevitable and each will strive to assert its values in the only possible way, that is, by overcoming others. Wars are inevitable and desirable. All this requires special men (noble men, or supermen), who constitute a small aristocracy. Only they have the requisite qualities.

Nietzsche regarded ordinary human beings as "botched and bungled" and had no objection to their pain and suffering. He did not believe in equality in any respect. True virtue can be characteristic only of the aristocratic minority. Strength of will and the will to power are outstanding virtues. Compassion and weakness are to be combatted. He writes about slave-morality and master-morality. What happens to the mass of people is of no consequence; only what happens to the superior few counts. "The object is to attain the enormous *energy of greatness* which can model the man of the future by means of discipline and also by means of the annihilation of millions of the bungled and botched, and which can yet avoid *going to ruin* at the sight of suffering created hereby, the like of which has never been seen before."[47]

Noble man recognizes duty only to equals, will not spare other people as he acts for his cause, allows himself to be violent and cunning in war, and practices inexorable discipline. He has the capacity for cruelty; almost everything we call "higher culture" is based upon the spiritualizing and intensifying of cruelty.

Bertrand Russell points out that if noble man becomes so as a result of education, it would be difficult to exclude the masses from the advantages for which they are qualified by their potential. Hence, Nietzsche's thinking implies biological superiority, or at least the Nazis could easily interpret it that way. He wrote that "no morality is possible without good birth." Russell also suggests that such a philosophy must arise from fear – a reasonable suggestion in understanding a feeble, sickly professor who admires only strength, all that is military, whose heroes are all conquerors, foremost among them Napoleon. He deals with his own great timidity in relation to women by profoundly devaluing them.

Some of Nietzsche's ideas are contrary to those adopted by the Nazis. He did not believe in the state but in the noble individual; he was not a nationalist and did not admire Germany and was against totalitarianism. Some of the views I described can be interpreted as primarily the advocacy of the overthrow of tradition and of freedom of creation. But ideas are absorbed selectively, and Hitler's needs and his own fears may have been greatly served by Nietzsche's megalomaniacal thoughts. For Hitler, racially pure Aryans became supermen with the highest culture. Given the cultural predisposition – the superior societal self-concept, the preference for authoritarian rule, and German militarism – Nietzsche's ideas could also serve the needs of many Germans suffering from difficult life conditions.

Rationality versus sentimental romanticism

Germans were split between rationality, which was exemplified in problem solving, concern with technological excellence, and authoritarian structures, and irrationality, in the forms of romanticism, emotionality, sentimentality, and mysticism. Kren and Rappaport propose that public behavior was "rational," and private life "irrational."[48] Wagner's operas, with their sentimental advocacy of the supremacy of love and elevation of Teutonic chivalry, represent this private Germanness. Kren and Rappaport suggest that morality was relegated to the emotional and sentimental private world.

This in itself is not unique to Germany: the interests of states are often considered predominant and morality irrelevant to their behavior. In my view, the split between realms in which moral considerations do or do not apply was primarily based on ingroup–outgroup distinctions, ideology, and the perpetrators' experience and evolution in their roles. With regard to the private–public split, probably a spillover from the private to the public was most significant. German romanticism, mysticism, and the tendency to "idealize" made a special contribution to the concepts of volk and Germanness. This allowed preference, desire, and yearning to become a basis of "scientific" racism and public policy.

The psychological effects on German youth of World War I and the postwar period

This is not a cultural precondition but an emergent psychological condition. German fathers left to fight the war; some did not return and others returned defeated, unable to make a living and offer security. Some of their authority was inevitably lost. If they were authoritarian, their authority lacked legitimacy. Young people faced material deprivation and a chaotic world. Some authors argue that these experiences created psychic needs that Hitler offered to satisfy.[49] The psychological effects of difficult life conditions described in Part I would be more intense and wider-ranging in children whose family system was disrupted by the war, with change in family relations and socialization practices.[50] Security needs would increase and the possibility of their fulfillment would decrease. With an authoritarian father whose authority is insecure or illegitimate, the needs for authority may be generated but unfulfilled.

In *The Mass Psychology of Fascism* Wilhelm Reich noted that the Nazis addressed the psychosocial needs of German youth, and the communists did not. The Nazi ideology and world view fit German myths and culture better. Thus, joining them would better satisfy the needs created by the war and later conditions.[51]

Nevertheless, communists and socialists also won substantial support. As I argued in Part I, different subgroups of society have different needs and are differently affected by life problems. The communists offered an ideology aimed at the needs and experience of the working class. Their appeal would have been stronger and broader, in my view, if they had built more on elements of German culture.

Another consequence of the war was an upheaval in values and a loss of legitimate authority. The weak Weimar Republic was besieged from all sides by movements that aimed to overthrow it. Black marketeering and loose sexual morality were supplanting traditional German respect for public order and the family. Young people were not offered moral guidance, although their authoritarian childhoods made their need for it great.

I discussed earlier another important effect of war, posttraumatic stress. Like Vietnam veterans with posttraumatic stress syndrome, many German combat soldiers must have suffered from low self-esteem, loss of meaning, lack of goals, anger and hostility, loss of faith in the benevolence of the world and in legitimate authority, restlessness, and a need for excitement and adventure. Many German veterans were therefore especially sensitive to the promises of the Nazi movement: new meaning, new authority, a feeling of superiority, and targets for hostility. The Abel collection shows that before 1933 veterans made up 53 percent of the Nazi Party membership (with official party statistics showing a somewhat lower percentage).[52]

Youth groups and military groups after World War I

Violence became a way of life for many groups in Germany after World War I. Paramilitary organizations participating in warlike battles served the needs of both veterans and youth. Kren and Rappaport call this way of life "heroic nihilism." It was a bridge to the exaltation of violence by the SA and SS, and part of the evolution toward genocide.

The Freikorps were volunteer military units guided by conservative views and anticommunism. The Wandervögel was a youth movement that began with an emphasis on enjoying nature but eventually became highly nationalistic. The Burschenschaften were student groups that stressed Germanness and volkish views. The Freikorps were in part an outgrowth of such nationalistic and at times violent German youth groups. There were two million young Germans in various youth groups before World War I. It is not surprising, given the life problems and resulting needs, that by 1927 their number was five million. They supplied members to the private political armies (and to the Nazi Party; some party members reported that their youth group joined the party as a group).[53] There are indications here of both cultural continuity and evolution toward the Nazi stormtroopers. Almost two-thirds of the Nazi stormtroopers in the Abel questionnaires who had been youth group members had been involved in violence, either battles in the streets and meeting halls or the organized Freikorps-type violence.

Most of the early Nazi doctors were members of Burschenschaften. The most "unregenerate" Nazi doctor interviewed by Robert Lifton for *Nazi Doctors* followed family tradition and joined a Burschenschaft, then the Freikorps. He described this experience as profoundly important to him, a cementing of the blood of members, a struggle to restore German glory.[54]

9   Nazi rule and steps along the continuum of destruction

Once in power, the Nazis created order, stability, and material well-being. Germans who were not opponents or victims of the system lived increasingly comfortable, satisfied lives under the Nazis until the Second World War began. In my many conversations with Germans who lived through that period, they have talked about Hitler's "mistakes" but have also stressed the good they believe he accomplished. In such conversations Germans seem to go beyond defending their country from the image produced by Nazi wrongdoings and express a positivity based on personal experience. I mentioned in the Preface my discussion with a group of sixty- to seventy-five-year-old Germans. They spontaneously returned again and again to the benefits and satisfactions of the Hitler period, mentioning obvious things like government-created jobs and emotional experiences like sitting around campfires with other young people. A quote from Craig's book *The Germans* well expresses this. In a speech on

April 28, 1939, Hitler had boasted that he had overcome the chaos in Germany, restored order, increased production in all branches of industry, eliminated unemployment, united the German people politically and morally, "destroyed, page by page, that treaty which, in its 448 articles, included the most shameful oppression ever exacted of peoples and human beings," restored to the Reich the provinces lost in 1919, returned to their fatherland millions of unhappy Germans who had been placed under foreign rule, restored the thousand-year-old unity of the German living space, all without shedding blood or inflicting the scourge of war upon his own or other peoples, and all by his own efforts, although, twenty-one years earlier, he had been an unknown worker and soldier. This outburst, Haffner commented, was "nauseating self-adulation," couched in a "laughable style. But *zum Teufel!*, it's all perfectly true – or almost all!...Could people reject Hitler without also giving up everything that he had accomplished, and were not all of his unpleasant characteristics, and his evil deeds as well, mere blemishes compared with his accomplishment?"

...Provided they were not Jews or Communists (a dreadful proviso that they preferred not to think about), most Germans profited materially and psychologically from the first six years of Hitler's rule, and they were quick to point this out when criticism of any kind was leveled against the Leader....but the continuing

116

loyalty of many Germans was a personal one, a willingness to believe, in the face of all the facts, that the man who had done so much for them in his first years could do no wrong and would somehow emerge, victorious and immaculate, to confound his enemies and detractors.[1]

Huge numbers of Germans were enthusiastic about Hitler's rise to power and even more about his subsequent rule. A distinguished American theologian, Professor Littell of Temple University, described how his German church father felt about Hitler.[2] In 1939, this high functionary in the German church, after an impressive array of anti-Jewish actions and one year after the Kristallnacht, described Hitler as God's man for Germany. He praised Hitler for improving the morals of German youth. The youth of Germany drank, smoked, and engaged in debauchery until Hitler came along. He gave them discipline and a sense of purpose. The evil in the Nazi system did not touch this clergyman. His theological anti-Semitism, combined with German cultural anti-Semitism, made it possible for him to ignore the persecution of the Jews. Nazi repression and totalitarianism also left him unaffected.

In the case of the Holocaust, as in some other genocides and mass killings, steps along a continuum of destruction had already been taken in earlier historical periods. Many of the steps against Jews were taken by the church, but acted upon in Germany with special zeal.[3] The Synod of Elvira of 306, for example, forbade intermarriage and sexual relations between Christians and Jews. The Synod of Claremont, in 535, decreed that Jews could not hold public office. The Fourth Lateran Council of 1215 decreed that Jews must mark their clothing with a special badge. Other decrees prohibited Jews from walking on the streets during certain holiday periods and prohibited their obtaining academic degrees (in 1434).[4] Persecution of the Jews was especially harsh in Germany, and this provided a cultural blueprint for the Nazi mistreatment of Jews.[5]

By 1900 German Jews were relatively assimilated, and in spite of increasing anti-Semitism remained so until Hitler came to power. Judging from the social climate in the early twentieth century, one might not have expected intense persecution. However, this view does not take account of the *deep structure* of the culture and the community as described here, which created a persistent potential for scapegoating and persecution.

Increasing mistreatment of Jews

On coming to power in 1933, Hitler immediately moved against the Jews. Jews were dismissed from jobs in government and the military. The first "mild" decrees allowed exceptions, for example, for Jewish war veterans.

Why this slow start? The Nazis may have meant to reward the loyalty of German Jews who fought in the war, as Hilberg suggests.[6] But we must also consider the psychology of perpetrators and bystanders. The Nazis had to move from words to the psychologically more demanding realm of actions. They also had to consider effects on the German population. A process of habituation was necessary, for the Nazis themselves and for the German people.

Dismissal from jobs in all fields followed; many businesses initiated their own dismissals; and after 1938, government rules led the remaining firms to dismiss their Jewish employees. Aryanization, the takeover of Jewish businesses, also proceeded. Jewish businesses were bought by Germans. Various mechanisms were used to limit competition, so that the amount paid to Jews would not be high. Boycotts and limiting supplies began to ruin Jewish businesses and force their sale. In the late 1930s laws were passed forbidding Jews to own businesses. They were allowed only menial and very low paying jobs and were heavily taxed.

Meanwhile, steps were taken to separate Jews from the rest of the population. An elaborate definition of Jewishness based on the number of Jewish ancestors was created. The Nuremberg laws prohibited marriage and sexual relations with Jews. Breaking these laws could result in persecution and severe public humiliation for Aryan Germans. Germans who did not follow these laws and developing mores were labeled – for example, as friends of the Jews (*Judenfreunde*) or as desecrators of the race (*Rassenschänder*), the name for people who had sexual relations with Jews. Jews were forced to wear a yellow Star of David in public and eventually were collected into restricted living areas.

Large numbers of people participated in this process, taking Jewish jobs, boycotting or taking over Jewish businesses, breaking off family contacts and love relations, designing and executing anti-Jewish laws, and disseminating anti-Jewish propaganda. Why did they participate? Fear of Nazis had to be a reason, but the attitude of the population makes this an insufficient explanation. Besides, there was opposition to the Nazi euthanasia program, but not to the persecution of the Jews.*[7] An important reason must have been a *cultural tilt*, an inclination that perpetrators and the ordinary members of society shared as a result of shared culture, and a *societal tilt* as this joined with life conditions and resulted in shared needs

---

* In my discussion with the older group of Germans I had the impression that they thought people would have had reason to fear deviation, but for most of them, including members of their families, the issue never came up, because they did not intend to deviate. Like most Germans, they did not even contemplate ways one might limit cooperation with the Nazis.

and a shared openness or inclination for responding to them in certain potentially destructive ways. Self-interest must also have influenced some: profiting from jobs, from business takeovers. Christians to whom Jews had given their property in an attempt to protect it from the Nazi state would have a stake in actions that made it unnecessary to return the property.

Another source of support for persecution was the desire to be part of the group. Interviews with rescuers of Jews in Nazi Europe show that many were "marginal," separated from the mainstream by religion, background, or experience; this enabled them to reject the system's views about Jews.[*8] For people tied to the group, the cultural devaluation and the climate of hostility generated by the Nazis made passivity or limited participation in action against Jews relatively easy.

Even passivity changes bystanders. But Germans had a semiactive role as they participated in societal actions against Jews. Devaluating Jews even more, regarding them as blameworthy, would make it easier to watch and passively accept their persecution and suffering and one's own involvement. This, together with a changing self-concept, a view of themselves as capable and willing to harm others for "justified" reasons, prepared some people for increasingly active roles as perpetrators. As people participate in harming others, it becomes increasingly difficult to stop and break the continuity. The personal changes make a new vantage point, a new decision, even less likely.

For example, some members of the Berlin Psychoanalytic Institute remained in Berlin after the Nazis assumed power. Self-selection and acceptance of the Nazis probably played a role in who stayed. They passively accepted Nazi influence at the institute and the dismissal of Jewish colleagues. Some of them began to adapt psychoanalytic theory to fit Nazi ideology.[10] Some later participated in the euthanasia killings and even in the extermination of Jews.[11]

Empathy can be affected by simply telling people to take different perspectives when observing what happens to someone else. Observers feel empathy and concern when told to imagine what it is like for someone to experience distress or pain – intense heat or an unpleasant personal

---

* The latest and most extensive study did not report that marginality was a significant characteristic of the rescuers of Jews in Nazi Europe.[9] The difference is partly definitional. The researchers stressed connection and reported the primary motive of many (52 percent) as "normocentric," the desire to fulfill the norms of a significant group they identified with, such as a religious group, a resistance group, family, or friends. However, such groups themselves could be marginal; and once they began to help Jews and thus oppose the Nazis, they distanced themselves from the larger society, which not only in Germany but also elsewhere (e.g., Poland, Hungary) accepted if not supported Nazi persecution of the Jews.

interaction – or to imagine what it would be like to be in that person's place. When observers are told to take a more detached, impersonal view, to simply *observe* what is happening, they feel less empathy and concern.[12]

Differences in perspective can result from external influence or from the enduring characteristics of individuals or whole groups. The greater the differentiation between "us" and "them," the less likely it is that others' fate is observed empathically and that observers will imagine what it is like for "them" to experience distress and suffering. The German people were exposed to extensive propaganda – "evidence" of the Jews' evil nature and the danger they represented to Germany. For example, at a Nazi mass rally in Berlin in August 1935, photographs show two huge signs painted with slogans directed against Jews. One warned German girls and women about Jews; the other was the often-used statement "Die Juden sind unser Unglück" (the Jews are our misfortune). Past anti-Semitism, learning by participation, and propaganda led Germans to see Jews as unworthy of moral considerations or empathy.

When firms began to refuse to pay Jews for holidays (an action they took voluntarily and one of many instances of the population initiating action against Jews before the government demanded it), the courts upheld this action, reasoning that Jews had no "inner tie" to the performance of labor and no loyalty to their employers.[13] Participation in anti-Jewish actions and propaganda reinforced each other. People easily accept propaganda or reasoning that helps them explain or justify their own actions. When children are told about the effects of helpful acts on other children, for example, they are influenced more if they receive the explanation *while* they engage in the helpful acts.[14]

A cycle began in which the population reciprocally influenced Nazi leaders. Increasingly, "unregulated" anti-Jewish actions took place – looting Jewish stores and raping, torturing, and killing Jews. It is impossible to know which of these actions were truly spontaneous and which were ordered or instigated by the state. These actions, even when instigated by them, probably reinforced the leaders' beliefs. In any case, they gave bureaucrats a justification for passing anti-Jewish laws to deal with popular sentiments in a "legal" and orderly way.

The chances of reversing the progression were lessened by lack of contact between Jews and the rest of the population. Social psychologists have shown that although contact between different groups (for example, blacks and whites in America) does not guarantee a loss of prejudice, separation and segregation maintain it.[15] Positive relations that counter a negative image cannot develop.

Progression along the continuum of destruction was also facilitated by

acts that made violence and murder commonplace, for example, the killings of political enemies and the "euthanasia" program (the killing of the
physically handicapped, mentally retarded, and mentally ill Germans). As
the murder of some categories of people becomes acceptable, group norms
change, making violence against others easier as well. This is especially so
when institutions are established for the purpose. In Nazi Germany, the
ideology of race was open-ended. Over time, more and more "genetically
inferior" people were found. After "asocial" prisoners were removed to
concentration camps, the killing of *ugly* prisoners ("outwardly asocial")
was contemplated.[16] "Better-world" ideologies are usually sufficiently loose
or open-ended to allow a broadening of the circle of victims.

The evolution of ideas, actions, and the system: euthanasia and genocide

Human beings are creatures of ideas, which often provide impetus to
action. The continuum of destruction involves a progression of ideas,
feelings, and actions. The Soviet practice of treating political dissidents as
mental patients has a background in such a practice during the Tsarist era,
which served as a cultural blueprint. The theory of schizophrenia developed
by Russian psychiatrists also lends itself to a view of dissidents as mentally ill.[17] Robert Lifton's book on the Nazi doctors and other works show
the significance of ideas and their evolution in the euthanasia program.
Two ideas supportive of the euthanasia program were a vision of *killing as
healing* and the notion of *life unworthy of life*.[18] This biomedical vision and
the scientific racism of the late nineteenth and early twentieth centuries –
as well as German intellectual traditions like Nietzsche's philosophy –
contributed to the Nazi ideology and, eventually, to killing those who were
"genetically inferior."

It began with a concern about eugenics, the vision of improving the race
by improving its gene pool. Sterilization was advocated and limited practice of it was actually instituted in Germany and elsewhere, including the
United States, prior to Nazi rule. "Mercy killing," the killing of physically
or mentally extremely impaired individuals, usually children, was also
advocated, and views on mercy killing were expanded by several German
theorists. Lifton notes a stress on the "integrity of the organic *body* of the
Volk – the collectivity, people, or nation as embodiment of racial-cultural
substance."[19] Robert Proctor shows that in discussions of racial hygiene,
which had a long history but became the official policy of the Nazi government, curing the "folk body" took precedence over healing persons.[20] This

sacrifice of the individual for the group is consistent with German tradition, with the view that the state has superior rights.

One influential writer, Adolf Jost, in a book published in 1895 called *The Right to Death (Das Recht auf den Tod)*, argued that control over the death of the individual ultimately belongs to the state: for the sake of the health of the people and the state, the state has the right to kill. An even more influential book, *The Permission to Destroy Life Unworthy of Life*, was published in 1920 by Karl Binding, a retired professor of law, and Alfred Hoche, a professor of psychiatry. They described large segments of the mentally ill, the feebleminded, and the retarded as unworthy of life: to destroy them was a form of healing. They spoke of "mental death," "human ballast" and "empty shells of human beings." Putting such people to death was an "allowable, useful act." They argued that "a new age will come which, from the standpoint of a higher morality, will no longer heed the demands of an inflated concept of humanity and an overestimation of the value of life as such."[21]

The Nazis adopted, elaborated, and spread such ideas, and the ideas evolved further as they were put into practice in the euthanasia project. Lifton suggests that they also gained support from the prevailing psychiatric attitude toward mental patients: cool, distant, "objective," emphasizing physical forms of therapy. However, as I noted, even some members of the Berlin Psychoanalytic Institute who remained in Germany participated in euthanasia.[22] Individuals with impaired functioning of varied kinds were devalued and their humanity denied. In the framework of the reversal of morality by the Nazis and to a degree the whole society, there was a reversal of medical morality. Killing became a kind of healing – of the nation, the group, the collectivity, the race.

A bureaucracy was established. Questionnaires haphazardly filled out, at times hundreds of them within a few hours, were used to select victims. Overdose of drugs, injections, starvation, and eventually gassing were used. Doctors filled out the questionnaires, made the selections, and did the actual killing, establishing many of the procedures later used in killing Jews. The procedures served both practical and psychological ends. For example, medical leaders of the euthanasia project praised doctors for sacrifices demanded by the killing process; later on Nazi leaders praised the SS killers for the sacrifices and hardships endured in fulfilling their "task."

The medical system was placed in the service of killing. A submissive orientation to authority was even stronger among doctors than in the rest of the German population. Their training and organization were authoritarian and they had a long tradition of seeing themselves as servants of the state. Medical training and practice may have made them believe that they had power over life and therefore the *right to decide* about life and death. The belief in euthanasia and the authority orientation of German doctors created an affinity for the Nazi ideology. The doctors who killed were self-selected or selected by the authorities for their reliability as Nazis.

Systems tend to be self-prepetuating. When a system is well established, members stop questioning its basic assumptions. The relatives of people killed and then the whole population became aware of the killings, and in response to protests by people and institutions, the program was officially terminated. Nevertheless, some killings continued, with the killing of children relatively widespread. Instead of being gassed, they were now starved to death on "special diets" or given drug overdoses. The ideas that justified the killings were unchanged, and the perpetrators were still in their jobs. Nothing happened to eliminate the motivations for the killings or to counteract the personal evolution of the perpetrators. They evidently came to believe in eliminating "genetically inferior" and "incurable" people. Continued killing expressed their investment in this goal and perhaps also provided a form of self-justification.

As I noted, several paths leading to destruction converged. Together they made the extreme destructiveness of genocide possible and, for many of the perpetrators, perhaps even relatively easy (see more about this in the next chapter). The methods of the euthanasia program were directly transferred to the extermination camps, along with the facilities for gassing and many of the personnel, including doctors.

It is important to note that all this took place in a framework of Nazi ideology and a cultural ethos that served it. Ideas and methods were created that moved, in their indirect but far from haphazard way, toward the fulfillment of the ideology. Not only medical doctors but also many other intellectuals, academics, and scientists elaborated a vision that ultimately served genocide. In 1940 Konrad Lorenz, the famous ethologist, wrote:

[I]t must be the duty of racial hygiene to be attentive to a more severe elimination of morally inferior human beings than is the case today....We should literally replace all factors responsible for selection in a natural and free life....In prehistoric times of humanity, selection for endurance, heroism, social usefulness, etc. was made solely by *hostile* outside factors. This role must be assumed by a human organization; otherwise, humanity will, for lack of selective factors, be annihilated by the degenerative phenomena that accompany domestication.[23]

As group consciousness moves in a certain direction, a generative process may emerge that serves this movement.

The power of giving oneself over to a group, an ideal, or a leader

As I have noted, people may find great satisfaction giving themselves over to a group, an ideal, or a leader. Deprivation, distress, a search for solutions, and an environment that creates high levels of excitement and emotional contagion can lead to the abandonment of self, as in the miraculous cures at Lourdes.[24] People attracted to movements (or to contemporary cults and extremist groups) are often people searching for solutions to basic questions about who they are and what life is about, often in response to difficulties in their lives.

The Nazi mass meetings were also occasions for conversion. The Nazi marches, street fights, and rituals both expressed and bred commitment. Proselytizing was an important duty of party members; persuading others also furthers commitment. Feelings of loneliness, vulnerability, failure, and uncertainty gave place to a sense of comfort, comradeship, shared destiny, admiration of a leader, and unquestioned certainty.

Commitment to the group, whether the result of conversion, evolution, or both, gives it great power to guide the interpretation of events, the definition of reality. As I noted, people are powerfully influenced by groups even in their perception of physical reality, which is more objective and verifiable than social reality. Values and "facts" about human beings (such as the evil nature of a minority) are much more subjective. Therefore, conformity is easier to bring about in the social realm. Sometimes people conform to others' definition of the meaning of an event just to avoid conflict or social embarrassment. Extensive research findings indicate that bystanders often *accept* the definition of events offered to them and act accordingly.[25] They may calmly disregard, without apparent conflict, calls for help seemingly arising from serious physical distress once someone says it is not real and does not require attention, or they may respond speedily when spurred on by words or actions of other bystanders.[26]

If this happens even among strangers, the mutual influence of members of an authoritarian group will be even greater. To people who intensely identify with the group or who seek its acceptance (like those who joined the Nazi Party late, after Hitler came to power), deviation from the group in action will seem highly risky, and inner deviation difficult to resolve. An inner alignment reduces conflict. Even though they set the direction, leaders will also be affected by group ideology and group norms and find it increasingly difficult to move in new directions. Giving oneself over to the group and acting in unison with others result in a loss of independent personal identity and individual responsibility and in the loosening of moral constraints.

The role of the totalitarian system

The totalitarian Nazi system was difficult to resist, either physically or psychologically. It used force and propaganda. It indoctrinated children. It induced people to participate in activities that committed them to the Nazi world view: political meetings, youth groups, mating to create "pure Aryan" Germans, the boycott of Jewish stores. Learning by participation resulted in increasing acceptance of and identification with the system. The system offered carrots as well as sticks. Followers could experience both the specialness of being a member of a superior race and the earthly well-being offered to "good" Germans.

Inner resistance was difficult to maintain while outwardly conforming and participating. Families were divided, spouses in conflict, and children set against parents. Children and adolescents in the Hitler youth groups were encouraged to spy on and report their own parents. The human need for consistency made outward conformity lead to inner change. It is difficult to maintain a divided self without support from others. Only within a resistance group or some other support network was it possible for most. The system also set a frame for action. Even Pastor Grueber, whom the court at Nuremberg lauded as one of the just men of the world, worked only to ease the Jews' suffering while accepting the fact of their fate.

Nevertheless, resistance was possible: it stopped the policy of euthanasia, for example. Members of the Catholic church, relatives of victims, and other Germans spoke out. In the summer of 1941, certain groups – lawyers, church authorities – submitted a formal complaint to the government, and in August 1941 the bishop of Münster attacked these killings from his pulpit. After more than a year of rising public clamor and 70,000 to 100,000 dead, the program was discontinued.[27] Few voices, however, were raised against the mistreatment of the Jews.

Perhaps the most profound effect of a successful totalitarian system is the lack of dissenting voices that offer a perspective different from that cultivated by authorities or engender inner conflict or sympathy with victims. Neither German citizens nor leaders were awakened to conflicts between their traditional values and the acts they observed or perpetrated against Jews and others. However, the reactions that stopped the policy of euthanasia suggest that even a totalitarian system is more effective when its actions are consistent with the culture, for example, when it turns against already devalued groups. Perhaps lack of preparation of the population through increasing mistreatment of victims was also a reason for the outcry against euthanasia.

Some writers make it appear that evil and its executors in the totalitarian state are basically different from evil deeds or perpetrators elsewhere. In discussing Arendt's book on the trial of Adolf Eichmann, the man responsible for transporting Jews to killing centers, Bettelheim writes:

This, then is a book about our inability to comprehend fully how modern technology and social organization, when made use of by totalitarianism, can empower a normal, rather mediocre person such as Eichmann to play so crucial a role in the extermination of millions. By the same incongruity, it becomes theoretically possible for a minor civil servant – say a lieutenant colonel, to keep the parallel to Eichmann – to start the extermination of most of us by pressing a button. It is an incongruity between the image of man we still carry – rooted though it is in the humanism of the Renaissance and in the liberal doctrines of the eighteenth century – and the realities of human existence in the middle of our current technological revolution. Had this revolution not permitted us to view the individual as a mere cog in the complex machinery – dispensable, a mere instrument – and the state to use him as such, Eichmann would never have been possible. But neither would the slaughter at Stalingrad, Russia's slave labor camps, the bombing of Hiroshima, or the current planning for nuclear war. It is the contradiction between the incredible power technology has put at our disposal, and the insignificance of the individual compared to it....
  ...this is not the latest chapter in antisemitism but rather one among the first chapters in modern totalitarianism....A more complete understanding of totalitarianism requires that we see Eichmann as basically a mediocrity whose dreadful importance is derived from his more-or-less chance position within the system.[28]

Bettelheim blames modern totalitarianism and technology for the Holocaust. But large-scale murder was not discovered by totalitarian systems, and human beings without special creativity and talent have normally been the instruments of destruction. Those who assembled Christians in ancient Rome to throw them to the lions did not need to possess greatness. In the Middle Ages, priests who identified witches to be burnt had no great vision or intellectual powers that made them and their evil deeds extraordinary. The disappearance and murder of thousands of people in Argentina was perpetrated by an "authoritarian" rather than totalitarian system. The "autogenocide" in Cambodia made limited use of advanced technology.

Evil that arises out of ordinary thinking and is committed by ordinary people is the norm, not the exception. While Hannah Arendt's *views* are consistent with this, her *concept* of the "banality of evil" is misleading: it lessens, or diminishes, evil. It is an expression of wishful thinking, in the same class as the concept of "incomprehensible evil." The latter enhances evil by romanticizing it and giving it mythic proportions; the former diminishes it. Great evil arises out of ordinary psychological processes that evolve, usually with a progression along the continuum of destruction.

What is or is not acceptable to do very much depends, for humans, on the perspective they hold. The most kind or the most brutal actions can appear reasonable and justified to people, depending on their perspective. They can see other humans as trustworthy, wonderful, and infallible – as Hitler was to many Nazis – or as worse than animals, whose killing is not only justified but desirable.

In summary, a number of elements shaped the Germans' perspective: (1) needs and motives arising from difficult life conditions, shaped by cultural preconditions including anti-Semitism and obedience to authority; (2) Nazi ideology and propaganda; (3) intolerance for dissent and lack of voices to remind them of the immorality of their actions; (4) learning by participation; and (5) giving themselves over to a group or system in which many of these elements were dominant. Enjoyment of the good life and admiration of Hitler also contributed. Most Germans, exposed to these influences, evolved a perspective in which the killing of the Jews was acceptable, for many even desirable.* In all of this the *system* was tremendously significant. Being part of a system shapes views, rewards adherence to dominant views, and makes deviation psychologically demanding and difficult. This will be further discussed in connection with the SS.

* Late in my discussion at Trier with the group of sixty- to seventy-five-year-old Germans, I asked them whether they thought the German people had come to support the actions of Hitler and the Nazis against Jews – not the extermination, but what preceded it. After some silence two women expressed their belief that this was the case. The group then went on to other topics. As with a couple other points that raised important questions about the conduct not of the Nazis, but of the German people, after a while someone challenged this view. But several people believed that the German people had accepted the persecution of the Jews and even regarded it as desirable.

10   The SS and the psychology of perpetrators

The SS (Schutzstaffel, security echelon) was the organization that had the major responsibility for the Nazi genocide. SS men were the direct perpetrators. They also operated the bureaucracy that selected, assembled, and transported victims, activities in which many other people were also involved.[1] They were self-selected or selected by the authorities and trained for obedience, violence, and brutality. In its final form, the SS was not only the creation of a larger system but had become a system itself, and it served the purposes of both.

When the proper conditions exist, some human beings become capable of killing others as naturally as if they were animals to be slaughtered, without questioning the act. Some killers may even enjoy it, as they would not enjoy killing animals, because they exercise power over other people or are aware of the victim's suffering, which fulfills their desire to hurt. Even those who willingly kill may feel distress arising from the sight, sound, and smell of dead or dying people, but this does not necessarily make them question the act. Their perspective determines how people perceive and experience what they do and what conclusions they draw from their own emotional upheaval as they commit murder. They may search for "better" methods of killing or convince themselves they are making "sacrifices" for a "higher ideal."[2]

The creation, evolution, and the role of the SS

The SS was created in the winter of 1922–23 as an elite bodyguard for Hitler at political meetings and in street confrontations with the Left. Himmler became the leader of the SS in 1929 when it had 280 members, and he increased their numbers to 30,000 by 1932. By 1942 the SS had 250,000 members. It also commanded about 200,000 auxiliaries, who were members of dissident ethnic groups in Russia (who at least initially saw Germans as their liberators and who were also highly anti-Semitic). They were put to work on the mass killing of Jews.[3]

Himmler elaborated a special code for the SS. The primary criterion for membership was "racial purity": height and physical appearance had to correspond to the Germanic ideal. These criteria were discarded in 1944, when the SS was so desperate for manpower that it tried to attract Europeans from occupied countries and also forcibly inducted Germans and others.

Medieval concepts of loyalty and honor were part of Himmler's code: the SS motto was "My honor is my loyalty." Having been tested by various means, the new member took a ceremonial oath of loyalty: "I swear to you, Adolf Hitler, as Leader and Chancellor of the Reich, loyalty and bravery. I pledge to you and the superiors appointed by you, obedience unto death. So help me God."* Himmler designed other rituals, to create a romantic and mystical atmosphere. The rules demanded complete subordination to the organization. Members had to ask permission for any major decision, including the choice of a wife.

All members of the SS received special training. Haussner, the general in charge of the officer training program that began in 1935, believed in a tough Prussian tradition and a superior aristocracy. The training combined iron-hard discipline and a romantic mystique, including

> ...exercises in total obedience, compulsive attention to detail, dangerous tests of individual courage, and ideological indoctrination – including Himmler's brand of Teutonic elitism as well as standard National Socialist political and racial values. Only after an initial period of testing in this system was the cadet given the privilege of taking the dramatic SS oath of loyalty to Hitler.
> The officers produced by this system were far from being simple-minded robots. Instead, they formed a corps of "true believers" who were effective leaders because, in addition to convictions about their own superiority to other men, they felt a common racial bond with their troops and were imbued with a medieval sense of noblesse oblige toward them. Furthermore, since most of these officers had virtually surrendered their sense of personal identity to Hitler and the SS, they were rarely troubled by any of the personal doubts which can divert men from putting total energy into their work.[4]

Members were eased out if they could not achieve the required discipline and fanatical zeal.

There were many reasons why members of the SS felt special and superior. First, they were selected for being racially "pure" and superior in appearance. Officer candidates in the 1930s had to prove an "Aryan" ancestry dating back to the 1750s. Second, many members were aristocrats or had advanced degrees, including doctorates; both titles of nobility and educational credentials were highly valued in Germany. Although most SS members had only a high school diploma – a more respectable degree in

---

* Obviously, this version was used after Hitler became chancellor.

Germany than in the United States – they could feel that they were in select company. At the same time, the SS had a democratic quality. At least through the mid-1930s men without privileged family background could advance more easily in the SS than in the army.

There were other sources of prestige, honor, and power. The SS was Hitler's private army and Hitler gave it unlimited support and privileges. Late in 1936 it was placed beyond conventional law. The SS were permitted any actions authorized by Hitler or his policies. Internal disputes and conflicts were resolved by its own courts of honor. A propaganda campaign presented the SS to the German people as the elite of Nazi institutions. Distinguished Germans were offered honorary command ranks and the right to wear the SS uniform.

Thus SS members saw themselves as an elite, with common values, common practices, a shared mystique, a sense of camaraderie, and devotion to their organization, ideology, and cause. After a detailed study, Tom Segev concluded that "joining the SS was to become part of an elite, an aristocracy, a religious order, a secret society, a gang, an army and a family all at the same time....At times the SS was something of a mentality, a way of life."[5] An SS veteran who served as a concentration camp commander described the comradeship this way: "We were Germany's best and hardest. Every single one of us dedicated himself to the others. What held us together was an alliance of comradeship. Not even the bond of marriage can be stronger. Comradeship is everything. It gave us the mental and physical strength to do what others were too weak to do."[6] Part of the SS identity involved pride in being able to do especially difficult, but necessary, important deeds – including murder on a large scale.

In place of earlier deprivation, uncertainty, weakness, and threat, membership offered many satisfactions and a strong identity. The SS was a total institution, the center of the lives of its members. Under such circumstances it was extraordinarily difficult to deviate from SS standards of conduct. The more a person's life is centered in a group, the more a person derives identity, self-concept and self-esteem, rewards and satisfactions, conceptions of the right way of life, and ideals from membership, the more difficult it is to deviate and to defy the group. Men who joined the SS after Hitler came to power were shaped not only by personal characteristics (self-selection) and the "socializing" and guiding influence of the organization, but also by a strong need to prove themselves to earlier members who suspected them of opportunism.

At the same time, both the growth and functioning of the SS were complex. For example, there was financial corruption. In principle, all Jewish property belonged to the Reich. In reality, the SS members appropriated some possessions of Jews and others they rounded up. They were also open to bribery. Such practices, common among superiors such as Goering, many have been simply part of the system. Other groups of mass murderers, for example, military units involved in the disappearances in Argentina, were also allowed to "reward" themselves with the property of victims. Bribery in a system where all roads eventually lead to extermination, where it did not matter whether these or those Jews were taken to fill a cattle car going to an extermination camp, need not conflict with the basic policy. Personal enrichment may have been a legitimate reward. In fact, although Himmler issued an order against taking property without authorization, much of what the SS men took for themselves was "authorized" distribution of goods.[7]

Characteristics of SS members

The nature of the tasks the SS performed was a basis of self-selection. Initially created as Hitler's bodyguards, their job was to fight political opponents. They progressively took on the jobs of rounding up people, transporting them to concentration camps, murdering opponents or former comrades, police work, torture, and the administration of concentration camps. Even before the war they enforced boycotts of Jewish stores, destroyed Jewish property, burned buildings, and killed Jews. Some of these duties had to be known to those who volunteered. They had to be willing to do these things. Many probably had a taste for them. In addition to their anti-Semitism and ideology, many apparently enjoyed the violence. Early members especially were probably devoted to Hitler or to the National Socialist ideology; after all, they joined a powerless leader. Those who joined early were usually young. The SS offered them the opportunity to fulfill interests and inclinations for which they had no other outlets. It also served the powerful needs arising from difficult life conditions.*

---

* The Nazi essays collected by Theodore Abel indicate that many members of the Nazi Party before 1933, especially stormtroopers, enjoyed violence already before they joined. Of the 581 respondents 337 were stormtroopers, and probably a large majority were members of the less well trained and less deadly efficient, although violent, SA (see later in this chapter), which was much larger at that time than the SS. In looking at their youthful "postures" Peter Merkl put them into a number of categories. "Politically militarized youth" had a great urge to fight and to march and a desire for good fellowship, but little concern about the movement's ideology (in his classification, 39.9 percent of the stormtroopers but only 6.2 percent of Nazi Party members in general belonged to this category). "Fully politicized youth" were highly ideological and politically oriented, more interested in organizing than fighting (10.3 percent of the stormtroopers, 9.8 percent of party members). "Hostile militants" showed

Studies show that SS members were authoritarian and followed orders without concern about their moral implications or the victims's fate. Interviews after the war with concentration camp commanders showed that many of them were enthusiastic about their role in creating a new order and glad to do whatever was necessary.[9] Rudolf Hoess, the commandant of Auschwitz, presented himself as an idealist in an atuobiography he wrote while waiting to be hanged. He believed that killing millions of Jews was a service to his country.[10] In contrast, Stangl, the commandant of Treblinka, described himself in seventy hours of interviews as a reluctant murderer who wanted to abandon his position but did not have the strength to do so. He came from a family with a highly authoritarian father and a submissive mother, and he had much opportunity to learn by participation. He participated in the euthanasia program and directed the construction of the concentration camp at Sobibor, before he became commandant of Treblinka.[11]

Henry Dicks, a British psychiatrist, interviewed SS officers and men who were serving prison sentences for mass killing.[12] He found that most of them had unhappy childhoods with an authoritarian father who freely used corporal punishment. The interviews showed them as people who committed atrocities with ease when ordered to do so. John Steiner conducted several studies of former members of the SS. As part of one study, he interviewed three hundred, and had fifty of them write or tape-record extensive autobiographies.[13] He also sent questionnaires to former members of both the SS and the German armed forces, which included twenty-one translated items of the American original of the F (fascism) scale, a measure of authoritarianism. Outstanding characteristics of SS members were

intense hostility to certain groups and to societal authority and heavily engaged in violence (12.8 and 7.2 percent, respectively). Authoritarians had an obsession with law and order and were attracted to the leadership cult (4.3 and 6.2 percent). Finally, there were two relatively undifferentiated groups, "prepolitical, parochial, or romantic" (10.2 and 22.2 percent) and "others, including people of no youthful association" (22.5 and 46.4 percent).[8]

This classification is based on limited information that is selective in two senses: first, in that only a small group of Nazis responded to Abel's essay contest, and second, that those who responded necessarily saw fit to provide only certain information. Its nature makes it difficult to judge personality dispositions, such as a potentially antisocial orientation. Nonetheless, Merkl notes an "openness" in the answers to the questionnaires, and they have great value in that they were collected before Hitler came to power and the large-scale Nazi violence.

The last two groups are undifferentiated: their essays suggested no clear categorization. This may be due to lack of information. Or it may be that intense, persistent life problems lead young people without strong personal predisposing characteristics, especially when there are cultural predispositions, to join extreme movements that fit their cultural predispositions. Once they are members, a process of resocialization begins.

1. Attraction to and enjoyment of military or pseudomilitary roles.
2. Mercenary-pragmatic interests: they were attracted by tangible benefits and wanted to improve their lives.
3. Belief in Nazi ideology.
4. A wish to be a professional soldier, which was impossible to fulfill because of the limit placed on the army by the Versailles treaty.

The interviewees often said they were ignorant of the true nature and purpose of the SS. This could be the case with later "tasks" but is not likely with regard to earlier ones, the violent promotion of the Nazi movement.

Many of the early followers said they saw few alternatives to the SS, since they had little training or education that would have helped them secure employment. However, many other Germans were in a similar position during the depression. Those who joined and remained in the SS had to have some special predisposition for the SS role. Moreover, many joined during the economic expansion under Hitler's rule, when other opportunities did exist.

On a questionnaire measuring authoritarianism (conformity and pronounced authoritarian-antidemocratic attitudes) former SS members scored substantially higher than former members of the German armed forces. This may have resulted from self-selection or experience or both. Both SS members and armed forces members shared certain, possibly common, German cultural characteristics: loyalty and honor held in higher esteem than justice; *Mein Kampf* read before 1933; past military or semimilitary activity regarded with satisfaction; and preference for dictatorial or monarchic government. SS members tended to see a great historical threat to German institutions and ideals.[14]

Steiner suggests an explanation of SS violence:

We propose to advance the concept of the "sleeper" who lies dormant until circumstances or specific events will activate him or her and produce behavioral traits not apparent before. Extreme deprivation coupled with powerlessness at one end of the spectrum and the assumption of considerable power, causing elation or ecstatic joy on the other, tend to produce the necessary conditions and thereby passions which can activate the sleeper. As Erich Fromm pointed out, "people with a sadistic character wait for the opportunity to behave sadistically just as people with a loving character wait for the opportunity to express their love." Fromm's findings are supported by this writer's observations of former members of the SS during and after the Third Reich. The shifts occuring in the display of personality characteristics when social conditions change radically is absolutely striking. The sadistic-prone – or authoritarian – character, who may have played a meek or even friendly role under one set of circumstances, may become an absolutely destructive individual in a totalitarian terroristic society in which aggression is rewarded. By contrast, such behavior may be discouraged in a democratic society and therefore less aggression may be expressed.[15]

Steiner's account suggests that self-selection as well as changed circumstances were especially important. The changeability implied by the sleeper concept is a matter of degree. Most persons are sleepers to some degree, inasmuch as they have a violent potential that can be triggered by specific conditions. Only a limited number of SS members were likely to have sleeper characteristics to a high degree. Others had to evolve more. Early joiners had to like or feel comfortable with confrontation and violence and with authoritarian structures and the Nazi ideology: they required less change. To different degrees, changes in their environment – difficult life conditions, membership in the SS, Nazi rule, and changes in Germany – brought forth motivations and aspects of the selves of the SS that previously might have been dormant. This is consistent with the principle that different environments or circumstances activate different motives. The environmental changes, whether self-selected or imposed, also led to new experience, "resocialization," and personal change. Thus, self-selection does not mean that most who joined the SS were ready to become mass murderers as soon as their environment allowed it.

Learning by participation

The SS training required and inculcated extreme willingness to endure danger and submit to authority. Fighting and occasionally killing were demanded from the start.* The training, shared experience, and privileges created a strong group tie. Ordinary rules and prohibitions did not apply to the SS either legally or psychologically. Deindividuation resulting from their group membership and joint actions further broke down moral prohibitions. Ideological indoctrination made killing Jews the fulfillment of a "higher" ideal. Their acts of violence provided constant learning by participation and increased the psychological possibility and ease of greater violence.

---

* The pressure of authority can result in a relatively sudden shift of attitude, as exemplified in the story of a Vietnam veteran (personal communication from Seymour Epstein, who interviewed this veteran). Flying over a group of civilians in a helicopter, he was ordered to fire at them, an order he did not obey. The helicopter circled over the area and again he was ordered to fire, which again he did not do. The officer in charge then threatened him with court-martial, which led him to fire the next time around. He vomited, felt profoundly distressed. The veteran reported that in a fairly short time firing at civilians became like an experience at a target-shooting gallery, and he began to enjoy it. This story also demonstrates what may be a frequent phenomenon: a conversion-type experience in which a final inhibition against killing, in this case of a certain type of victim, is overcome. Prior training and prior steps along the continuum of destruction prepare a person for such "conversion."

In March and April of 1933, tens of thousands of potential "enemies" of the state were rounded up by the SA and SS and placed in concentration camps. Many were indiscriminately murdered. In late 1933 Dachau, where many such murders occurred, was reorganized into a highly efficient facility in which systematic, policy-based brutality was institutionalized, although capricious individual brutality was discouraged. After 1934 the concentration camps were under SS control. The SS also had the lead role in the purge in which the leader of the SA, Röhm, and many other prominent SA leaders were killed. This greatly diminished the influence of the SA, which was a larger, but less well trained, reliable, and loyal Nazi paramilitary organization.

The SS also became responsible for internal security. It operated the secret police, the Gestapo, which was notorious for its reign of terror and torture in Germany and later in the occupied territories. The SS was responsible for party security and intelligence (Sicherheitsdienst, or SD); it also provided concentration camp guards (Death's Head Units) and the general service battalions that later became its military arm, the Waffen SS. Transfers among these units were common, partly to maintain the unity of the organization.

Before the war the SS, together with the SA, enforced boycotts of Jewish business and beat up and occasionally killed Jews. On November 9, 1938, they broke into Jewish homes, killed Jews, deported many Jews to concentration camps, and burned down synagogues and other Jewish institutions. This was the famous Kristallnacht, crystal night, named for the broken glass produced by the night's destruction.

When the war started, small SS units accompanied the army and fought so well that the size of the Waffen SS was greatly expanded. The Waffen SS too participated in civilian massacres and the killing of prisoners. Accompanying the army were special SS detachments or "task forces" (Einsatzgruppen), directed to seize intelligence information and round up troublemakers. They came to be known for swift, brutal action. They murdered the leaders of the Polish people – doctors, intellectuals, lawyers, priests, government officials, teachers. They isolated Jews in ghettos and later transported them to special areas.

Four Einsatzgruppen were created specifically to murder Jews in territories conquered by the advancing German army. These groups received special training, which included further propaganda against Jews. They followed the army, gathered Jews, and shot them, sometimes after they had forced them to dig the trench that was to serve as their grave. During the summer and fall of 1941, about 500,000 Jews were killed.

Killing face to face, the Einsatzgruppen were exposed to the immediate sensory consequences of their acts: tangled naked bodies (including women and children) lying in trenches, the squirming of those not immediately killed. This resulted in nightmares, heavy drinking, nervous breakdowns, and even suicides. Dying and dead bodies are indiscriminate in their humanness: this explains their impact on perpetrators who accepted and even favored the idea of killing Jews.

The Nazis did not begin to question the goal. The process had too much momentum; the idea of turning back did not arise. Their prevailing mind-set led the SS to ask how to do it better, not whether to do it at all. Once a goal is established, a commitment to it develops, and a system is created to fulfill the goal, difficulties need not lead to its abandonment. If anything, the difficulties led to renewed commitment to exterminate the Jews of Europe and get rid of the "problem" forever.

A series of changes in methods followed. First, an SS auxiliary was organized from ethnic groups in Russia, mainly Ukrainians, who were militantly anticommunist and powerfully anti-Semitic.*[16] The Ukraine was the land of pogroms; cultural preconditions were present for Ukrainians to become part of the machinery of mass killing. By the middle of 1942, these SS auxiliaries were heavily engaged in the murder of Jews.[17]

Another innovation was to fill a large van with Jews, route the carbon monoxide exhaust back into the van, and drive it around until everyone inside died. Special units of Jewish prisoners, the Sonderkommando (literally, special command) were forced to unload the bodies. The vans were later replaced by the extermination camps, in which victims were killed in gas chambers disguised as communal bath or shower rooms. This method was used to kill three to four million Jews – the vast majority of those murdered by the Nazis.

At Auschwitz, the largest extermination and forced labor camp, cyanide gas (Zyklon B) was used for efficiency and "humanitarian" reasons – the speedy death of victims. Jews arrived in cattle cars. Many were immediately sent to the gas chambers; Jewish prisoners then removed gold teeth

---

* Education and a profession are sometimes thought to make people less inclined to such destructiveness. Some note with surprise and wonder that the Einsatzgruppen included highly qualified academics, ministerial officials, lawyers, and even a Protestant minister and an opera singer. In contrast, many of the SS auxiliaries were illiterate. People from higher socioeconomic classes may be less likely to engage in criminal murder, both because they can gain advantages by socially acceptable means and because they are more socialized into traditional rules and values. But this would make no difference in an ideologically based mass murder, especially when the fulfillment of psychological needs and "higher ideals" as well as the usual rewards of education and professional life – prestige, recognition, status, money – are offered for participation in repression, murder, and ultimately genocide.

and hair (to be used in mattresses) and burned the bodies in great ovens. Others were selected for forced labor in many enterprises, includng SS-run factories and I.G. Farben, the huge chemical company. They were slowly starved to death on inadequate rations. Some were taken to gas chambers when they weakened. Others simply died. Some were killed in camp hospitals by injections into the heart; some were executed for an infraction of one of the many camp rules. Others died from one of the imaginative Nazi punishments, such as packing many people into a tiny cell without an air supply. Although directed by SS guards and supervised by Nazi doctors, the extermination process itself was now mostly in the hands of the Ukrainian guards, who herded Jews into the gas chambers.

Many of the SS who set up the camps and then remained as personnel were veterans of the euthanasia program and thought of themselves as having special skills or expertise. They could focus their attention on the use of their professional skills. In a public television interview a medical orderly, a transfer from the euthanasia program who had administered deadly injections, described himself as a knowledgeable technician who helped prisoners to a relatively painless death.

The Nazis recognized the importance of making victims seem less than human. Inmates were kept hungry and helpless; they were forced to live in filth and urinate and defecate on themselves. One purpose was to reduce the will to resist by weakening them physically and destroying their former identity and sense of dignity. Another purpose was to diminish the victims and "help" the SS distance themselves from them. Gita Sereny asked Stangl, the commandant of Treblinka: "If they were going to kill them anyway, what was the point of all the humiliation, why the cruelty?" "To condition those who actually had to carry out the policies – to make it possible for them to do what they did" was the answer.[18]

The interweaving and merging of role and person

Given the initial self-selection, the progressive identification with the institution, the evolution of the SS into a system devoted to mass murder in the context of changes in the larger system of Germany, and learning through participation, the psychological condition of many SS members came to fit the role they were to fulfill. They became well adapted to their functions, following the rules and operating procedures and treating their victims as contaminated material to be disposed of.

The "ideal" SS man was not personally brutal and did not enjoy the suffering of victims. He could even treat individual Jews well while serving the machinery of their murder. This level of development is demonstrated by a fictional character, O'Brien, in George Orwell's *1984*. O'Brien, the torturer of Winston Smith, inflicts indescribable pain and terror, but does so in a kindly manner, as if it is a necessary task against his inclination. Dr. Wilhelm Pfonnerstiel, professor of hygiene at the University of Marburg and SS lieutenant colonel, reporting after the war on a wartime visit to the concentration camp at Belzec said: "I wanted to know in particular if the process of exterminating human beings was accompanied by any act of cruelty. I found it especially cruel that death did not set in until 18 minutes had passed."[19] He was also concerned about the welfare of the SS men administering the extermination.

Not all SS members became "perfect." Even in a total organization like the SS, some traveled unique paths. Despite self-selection some had initially greater capacity for empathy for Jews, whereas others had deep-seated hostility or found pleasure in harming people. As a result, what they learned from experience differed. Some SS may have brutalized victims to maintain a dehumanized view of them and their own commitment to murder. Although worse for the victims, this may represent a shakier commitment, a lesser capacity to accept murder as a normal operating procedure. Others were provoked by the victims' helplessness and their lack of response to beatings and humiliations. People who need to experience power over others require a response or they will escalate violence.[20]

In his book *Schindler's List*, Thomas Keneally describes the behavior of Amos Goeth, the commandant of the labor camp (later concentration camp) at Plaszow.*[21] He would come out onto the balcony of his villa in the morning with a rifle and binoculars and scan the campground. When he saw a prisoner doing something that displeased him – pushing a cart too slowly, standing rather than moving, or committing some other unfathomable crime – he would shoot the prisoner. The life of any Jew in contact with him was in constant danger. He beat his Jewish maid mercilessly if he found the slightest speck of dirt or if his soup was not the right temperature. According to the reports of survivors Goeth believed, at least in his sentimental moods, that this Jewish maid, Helen Hirsch, and others who worked for him were "loving servants." This is also attested by the tone of a note asking her to send clothes and reading material when the SS arrested him for black marketeering. This man, who was even more cruel and sadistic than his SS role required, apparently had no capacity to see his behavior from the perspective of others.

---

* This book is a fictionalized account of actual events, based on evidence from many sources, including interviews with former camp inmates and material at Yad Vashem, the Holocaust memorial and museum in Jerusalem.

Research has shown that one type of incestuous father is an authoritarian tyrant who regards his wife and children as chattel. In addition to incest, he physically abuses members of his family.[22] Amos Goeth may have been this kind of person, run amok in a system that has run amok. He was unable to appreciate that his prisoners, these "objects" in his possession, had feelings and needs of their own that did not fit his needs and pre-ferences – a not uncommon human blindness but in this case extreme in degree.

While understanding the perpetrators as individuals is important, an essential truth is that they acted in a system that allowed and encouraged behavior like Goeth's. Jan Karski, a representative of the Polish Civil Directorate, witnessed even more random violence when he infiltrated the Warsaw ghetto in October 1942 to gain first-hand knowledge of the condi-tions he was to report to Allied and Jewish spokesmen in London and the United States. He found everywhere "hunger, misery, the atrocious stench of decomposing bodies, the pitiful moans of dying children, the desperate cries and gasps of a people struggling for life against impossible odds."[23] Once a companion seized his arms and rushed him into a building, to a window:

> "Now you'll see something. The hunt. You would never believe it if you did not see it yourself."
> I looked through the opening. In the middle of the street two boys, dressed in the uniform of the Hitlerjugend, were standing. They wore no caps and their blond hair shone in the sun. With their round, rosy-cheeked faces and their blue eyes they were like images of health and life. They chattered, laughed, pushed each other in spasms of merriment. At that moment, the younger one pulled a gun out of his hip pocket and then I first realized what I was witnessing. His eyes roamed about, seeking something. A target. He was looking for a target with the casual, gay absorption of a boy at a carnival.
> I followed his glance. For the first time I noticed that all the pavements about them were absolutely deserted. Nowhere within the scope of those blue eyes, in no place from which those cheerful, healthy faces could be seen was there a single human being. The gaze of the boy with the gun came to rest on a spot out of my line of vision. He raised his arm and took careful aim. The shot rang out, followed by the noise of breaking glass and then the terrible cry of a man in agony.[24]

In the reciprocal evolution of system and persons, some SS and other Nazis (the Hitlerjugend in Karski's report) came to enjoy their limitless power over other humans. The freedom to completely control others' lives and bodies might give some people a dizzying sense of power or perhaps the experience of both abandonment and strength as in an intense sexual experience. Their background and experience also prepares some people for sadistic pleasure, which develops out of a history of connection be-tween one's own pleasure and others' pain.

One's own advantage or satisfaction can be regularly associated with others' disadvantage or suffering: a bully might forcefully take away toys from other children; rivalry may lead to good feelings when a sibling suffers. Past hurts or feeling diminished can lead people to feel elevated relative to others who suffer. Satisfactions gained from power and from others' suffering can fuse. SS members had many experiences that taught sadism. Coming to enjoy their victims' suffering also had a special function: it could erase doubt and make "work" satisfying. The SS could also feel satifaction from successfully combating "evil."

Keneally offers a glimpse of another individual path.

Poldek Pfefferberg was told about the list by an SS NCO named Hans Schreiber. Schreiber, a young man in his mid-twenties, had as evil a name as any other SS man in Plaszow, but Pfefferberg had become something of a mild favorite of his in that way that was common to relations – throughout the system – between individual prisoners and SS personnel. It had begun one day when Pfefferberg, as a group leader in his barracks, had had responsibility for window cleaning. Schreiber inspected the glass and found a smudge, and began browbeating Poldek in the style that was often a prelude to execution. Pfefferberg lost his temper and told Schreiber that both of them knew the windows were perfectly polished and if Schreiber wanted a reason to shoot him, he ought to do so without any more delay. The outburst had, in a contradictory way, amused Schreiber, who afterward occasionally used to stop Pfefferberg and ask him how he and his wife were, and sometimes even gave Poldek and apple for Mila. In the summer of 1944, Poldek had appealed to him desperately to extricate Mila from a trainload of women being sent from Plaszow to the evil camp at Stutthof on the Baltic. Mila was already in the lines boarding the cattle cars when Schreiber came waving a piece of paper and calling her name. Another time, a Sunday, he turned up drunk at Pfefferberg's barracks and, in front of Poldek and a few other prisoners, began to weep for what he called "the dreadful things" he had done in Plaszow. He intended, he said, to expiate them on the Eastern Front. In the end, he would.[25]

It seems that when Pfefferberg refused to react as a helpless victim, but reacted with an intensity and humanness not fitting the victim role, Schreiber slipped out of the role of executioner. Pfefferberg's anger awoke in Schreiber a human response. That, and his subsequent kindness to Pfefferberg, nurtured in him a consideration for others. One reason for the effectiveness of Oskar Schindler, who saved 1200 Jews, and Raoul Wallenberg, who saved tens of thousands, was that they reacted contrary to the expectations of the SS and Hungarian Nazis.[26] In facing Nazis accustomed to fear and trembling, they acted with self-assurance and authority, sometimes even demanding help in helping Jews.

As the SS became a large, complex, partly bureaucratic elite, more men became members who were not self-selected or selected by authorities for their ability to fulfill task requirements. At one point the whole German equestrian society was incorporated into the SS. Most of these new members became socialized into the SS system. Some late joiners, however, made an incorrect self-selection; they were unaware of some of the requirements of membership or did not anticipate their own reactions to them. These reactions, based perhaps on "inclusive" moral values, inhibited their evolution and resulted in a gap between the role and the person. There were probably few such members in the SS, owing not only to initial self-selection and socialization into the system, but also to dismissal and quitting. Those who did not fit the requirements of SS training, such as extreme obedience and physical courage, were screened out.[27] Those whose values and world view did not fit them for membership could drop out.

A few SS men were relatively humane, at least at times.[28] Prisoners reported that on occasion their lives were saved by SS guards. We can imagine that even very small, causal acts of humanity would have great impact on prisoners searching for humanity in an overwhelmingly cruel, inhumane system.

Only in a very few reported instances was the motivation of a kind SS member clearly to save a Jew. Keneally tells the story of an SS guard who accompanied two children and their fathers from Schindler's camp to Auschwitz and then accompanied three hundred women from Auschwitz back to Schindler's camp, acting in a humane, friendly, helpful manner all the way, at one point even crying in response to their sorrow.[29] All this happened, however, near the end of the war, when the footsteps of the western Allies on one side and the Russians on the other could almost be heard. We do not know to what extent the behavior of this man (and others) was the result of a changed perspective due to changed circumstance that led him to think about his own culpability and to fear retribution.

The extermination camps: Auschwitz

I will use information provided by Robert J. Lifton about Nazi doctors to interpret their psychology as perpetrators in the framework of this book.*[30] These Nazi doctors played an important role at Auschwitz. They selected the many Jews who were to be killed immediately and the few who were to work in the camps. Their cars and ambulances, marked with red crosses, lulled new arrivals at the station of Auschwitz-Birkenau into some feeling of hope and security; the doctors took the gas to the gas chambers and determined the required amount for each gassing, they decided when to

---

* In the account that follows I summarize and recast information provided by Lifton, adding my own interpretations; for example, it is I who infer that the doctors made a speedy adjustment to the camp, suggest motives for the noncommissioned officers' conversations with Hoess, and so on.

open the door to the gas chambers and checked to make sure that those inside were dead. The doctors also selected for killing those who had become useless for work or potentially harmful to the "ecology" of the camp (e.g., a potential source of epidemics); for example, they periodically lined up Jewish prisoners and sent the weak to the gas chambers, making space for stronger new arrivals.

Most of this became practically and psychologically routinized. Whatever initial reservations doctors had, they came to view these activities as "normal duty," as a "regular job." In fact, they fought to retain the right to do the selections, apparently psychologically the most difficult of their jobs, as a sign of their power and status.

A number of the doctors were shocked when they arrived at Auschwitz. I would expect there was less initial shock among doctors at the other extermination camps, because those doctors were transferred from the euthanasia killing centers. Auschwitz was established later and the doctors sent there, not having participated in the euthanasia project,[31] missed steps along the continuum of destruction that would have prepared them.

The initial shock was expressed in conversations – often drunken – with other doctors. The doctors condemned the "filthy" business of the camp, by which they meant not the killings themselves, which they took for granted as necessary, but the overall atmosphere. They were affected by the women and children sent to the gas chambers, the ever-present filth of emaciated, starving inmates, the whole "anus mundi" (the anus of the world) environment, as one Nazi doctor called it.

The expression of such feelings was probably encouraged as part of the initial adjustment. It did not necessarily imply a concern for the victims. German doctors (and other SS men) valued cleanliness, good manners, and good appearance. They were accustomed to using euphemisms and continued to do so in the camp, keeping reality at a distance. The conditions in the camp evoked their discomfort and even disgust. In later years they may have used this discomfort – even to themselves – in self-serving apologias as if it expressed concern about the victims rather than self-concern.

The initial expressions of feeling served many functions. Hoess, the commander of Auschwitz, said that noncommissioned officers "'regularly involved in selections' poured out their heart to him" about the difficulty of their work.[32] They may have sought support or a way to show their devotion (especially because they were told by their superiors that they were doing difficult work requiring great sacrifice). Some may also have sought to transfer responsibility to the commander. If so, it shows that they felt some guilt or apprehension.

The doctors also sought justifications and rationalizations. New doctors were told that gassing saved inmates from suffering, from "croaking in their own shit," and helped them go to heaven in a cloud of gas. They made absurd comparisons, pointing out, for example, that doctors working at the front had to make choices about whom to save and whom to let die. The doctors and presumably other SS members in the camps made a very speedy adjustment. The comments, questions, and doubts stopped soon after arrival. One doctor kept a diary in which there is no mention of difficulty in adjustment after the first few days.

The attention of doctors and other SS men focused on their tasks and on "technical" problems. Their task was to render the killing both effective and "humane." To find "humanitarian [methods in the face of]...general overload of the apparatus – that was the problem."[33] Doctors would discuss for days such questions as "Which is better: to let mothers go with their children to the gas or to select the mothers later by separating them from their children." The issue arose because women criminal capos (camp functionaries drawn from the German criminal population) "found it much less difficult to handle arriving mothers whose children were with them."[34] In the spring and summer of 1944, another practical problem arose when about four hundred thousand Hungarian Jews were brought to Auschwitz. Although the gas chambers had sufficient capacity to kill, the crematoria did not have sufficient capacity to burn all the bodies. Therefore, bodies were also burnt in large trenches. However, naked bodies do not burn well. The whole SS contingent, including the doctors, was preoccupied with finding a good practical solution.

Lifton asks how the Nazi doctors could do what they did and at the same time (some of them) show kindness to inmates, treat prisoners who were pressed into work as doctors with professional courtesy, and go home to be kind husbands and fathers. His answer is that the Auschwitz environment forced them to adapt. They did so by *doubling*. This is a process whereby two opposing selves are created, one of which is responsible for evil. The two selves seem encapsulated, walled off from each other to avoid internal conflict. Auschwitz, the "atrocity-producing situation," created the Auschwitz self. Lifton implies that the Nazi doctors had no choice. "They found themselves [in Auschwitz] in a psychological climate where they were virtually certain to choose evil: they were propelled, that is, towards murder."[35] They adapted to this climate by doubling. Evidence for doubling apparently includes occasional kindness to prisoners and Hoess's account of how noncommissioned officers bared their souls to him.

Doubling is an appealing concept and may accurately describe some perpetrators. It suggests, however, that human beings are incapable of such evil while acting out of their "ordinary" selves. It suggests that the killers acted independently of or contrary to their ordinary selves. But SS doctors sent to Auschwitz were not innocent, uninvolved persons thrown into an extreme environment to which they had to adapt to ensure their own physical and psychological survival. They were ideologically committed Nazis who had undergone substantial resocialization. Their devotion to the Nazi cause and exclusion of Jews from the moral universe prepared them for Auschwitz.

The psychology of perpetrators: individuals and the system

To understand the psychology of perpetrators, we must consider their personality, the forces acting on them, and the system they are part of.* All Germans shared the life problems and culture that gave them a common inclination, a societal tilt, to experience certain needs and to find certain ways of fulfilling them. The earliest Nazis probably had characteristics that intensified these needs and desires – a wish to relinquish a burdensome identity, authority orientation, anti-Semitism – and that made the means of their satisfaction offered by Hilter especially congenial. Doctors in particular may have been attacted to the "biological" aspect of Nazi ideology and its scientific racism.

Once the Nazis came to power, average Germans were led to become semiactive participants. The internal and external forces acting on those who joined the Nazis were even greater. Their experiences resocialized both average Germans and perpetrators. Dramatic changes in the system led to substantial personal changes, which made further change in the system possible. The system required devotion to Nazi ideals. The people, especially Nazis, were to become "autonomously" moral in Durkheim's sense; adopting Nazi values and ideals, they were to pursue them as their own. The world view, ideals, self-definition, and motivational hierarchy of people who joined the Nazis changed substantially over time.

The characteristics and functioning of perpetrators

According to the conception of motivation and action discussed in Part I, human motives can be arranged in a hierarchy. This hierarchy includes personal goals and even unconscious wishes. As a result of their experi-

---

* *Personality* refers to the enduring characteristics of individuals that differentiate them from others. I define personality broadly to include, for example, ideological beliefs, because they are important and usually enduring characteristics.

ences, the motivational hierarchy of the Nazis, and especially the SS, changed substantially. The importance of old motives declined and new motives emerged. Very high in the hierarchy was the desire to fulfill the goals of the Nazi system. Subordinate goals and values included "dealing" with the Jews, "hardness" (dismissal of human feelings for the sake of the cause), and being a good member of the group. Personal advancement was tied to success in working for these group goals. There were also negative goals. For example, the doctors led a privileged life in the "anus mundi" environment of Auschwitz. A transfer would force them to relinquish it and risk being sent to the Russian front. This happened to the only doctor who asked for reassignment.

There are two types of common moral values: a personal, or prosocial, morality focusing on human welfare and a rule-oriented morality stressing obligation, duty, and the necessity of living by rules.[36] The latter was dominant in the authoritarian culture of Germany. The former value was weakened in perpetrators by their experience in the Nazi system and became inapplicable to Jews and other devalued groups.

People do not always act to fulfill goals high in the hierarchy. What goal is actively sought at a particular time also depends on the nature of the environment. The environment may activate – call attention to, call forth, or offer the opportunity to satisfy – goals lower in the hierarchy. Moreover, circumstances may activate several conflicting goals and values. To resolve the conflict, people often use rationalizations and justifications that strengthen one motive or value and weaken the other.

The Nazi system and subsystems such as Auschwitz were strong activators of motives that had already moved high in the hierarchy of the perpetrators. People function best when they can integrate their goals by living and acting in ways that combine the fulfillment of important motives. The Nazi doctors in Auschwitz combined old personal and medical motives with Nazi motives, even when this required denial or other psychological maneuvers. They focused on their professionalism and devoted themselves to improving medical care even while camp inmates were being starved to death and murdered. They performed cruel and often useless experiments on inmates to further "medical knowledge." They preserved their sense of importance and high status by wearing impeccable, elegant uniforms and carrying themselves with dignity.

Behavioral shifts

There was strong overall consistency in the personal motives of the SS and the motives called forth by the camp system.[37] Because certain stimuli were too powerful or an SS member had not been completely resocialized (or both), occasionally a conflicting goal or value was activated. The starving, skeleton-like inmates and the naked bodies of the dead sometimes activated feelings of responsibility. Seeing naked bodies, especially, made it hard to maintain the discrimination between human beings and "subhuman" Jews.

As I noted, motives lower in the hierarchy become active when events or circumstances make them important and offer their fulfillment. Certain stimuli can also break down learned discriminations. This explains some of the seemingly out-of-character behavior of SS men – their occasional human response to Jews. In the example cited earlier, a Jewish prisoner's self-assertiveness activated motivation not usually called forth.

Lifton describes an incident in which an inmate made a request of an especially cruel Nazi doctor, and the request was granted. Apparently the inmate's unusual behavior activated some motivation low in the hierarchy – politeness, correctness in responding to a request, perhaps even compassion. A book of "Hassidic tales" of survival tells the story of a man who hears a familar voice as he progresses to the selection. It is a German neighbor whom he used to greet customarily with a hearty "Good morning, Herr...." Automatically, he blurts out the same greeting, and (perhaps in response) the SS man sends him to the line of those selected for labor instead of gassing.[38] Perhaps a remnant of the old connection had been reawakened in the SS man as well.

I am not suggesting that if all Jews in the camps had behaved in these ways, their fate would necessarily have been better. The predominant motivation to kill and abuse had become too strong by that time. The Nazis would simply have learned better discrimination; an ordinary human action would no longer have brought forth a human response. The overwhelming influence of the system and its consonance with the resocialized motivational system of individuals would have permitted nothing else.

Thus instances of kindness have limited significance. Life was cheap and the SS could grant favors and act kindly without coming into serious conflict with their dominant goals. Their family life is understandable in the same framework: the family environment activated different motives. Complex processes give rise to particular motives and actions. Variations in the behavior of the SS can be understood in the same way as in anyone else's; for example, a driver may ignore a hitchhiker at one time and give him a ride at another time. An already-active motive limits attention or response to the environment.

While splitting of realms can develop into doubling, people tend toward integration. As they evolve, most perpetrators develop unitary selves by changes in their motives, world views, and beliefs and by achieving highly differentiated orientations to different groups of people.

Moral equilibration, choice, and responsibility

I have described a situation in which people who start with varying degrees of predisposition act increasingly destructively, changing along the way and contributing to the evolution of an increasingly destructive system. This does not exclude responsibility. Along the way, there are many opportunities for choice. Unfortunately, choosing often takes place without awareness or conscious deliberation. To make a true choice when facing a conflict between a motive and a moral value that prohibits the actions required a fulfill the motive, a person must be aware of the conflict. Then the person must bring in additonal considerations – further values and norms that tilt the balance in favor of moral restraint (or moral action) or reasons, rationalizations (reasons that would not seem valid to impartial outside observers), and justifications that tilt the balance against moral values. This "work of choosing" places demands on cognitive processing and may involve intense feelings.

But many choices are made without awareness, either preconsciously or unconsciously. All of us have a wide range of moral values and rules at our disposal. Some have been superseded but remain in our repertoire and can be called forth. Some stand side by side, even though they are potentially contradictory. Facing a conflict between a nonmoral motive and a moral value, a person may reduce the conflict by moral equilibration, a shift to a different moral value or principle. For example, the moral principles that prohibit killing or harming other human beings are replaced by the principle of "social good," defined as protection of the German nation from internal subversion and genetic contamination by Jews. Or loyalty and obedience to authority may become the relevant "moral" principles.

Although this can happen consciously, moral equilibration often occurs without awareness: a person automatically selects values and standards that allow the expression of the motive in action. A preconscious or unconscious equilibration circumvents moral conflict. As people progress along a continuum of destruction, moral equilibration becomes more automatic. Moral conflict can still be reawakened by such sights as a heap of dead naked bodies; Eichmann and Himmler both felt sick, overcome. I noted the Nazi doctors' initial shock in Auschwitz. Such emotional and bodily reactions can serve as signals to the self, even in people who have moved to the stage of automatic (and not conscious) moral equilibration. However, by this time Eichmann's, Himmler's, and the Nazi doctors' commitment to the Final Solution and their embeddedness in the Nazi group made a renewal of moral conflict or change in its modes of resolution unlikely.

Individual responsibility

In the progress toward genocide, there were many choice points for each Nazi. The responsibility of individuals is partly a function of the culture and society in which they live. A group can foster psychological and moral differentiation between the group and its members to different degrees. A man raised in the society of Mundurucú headhunters is socialized into behavior that might be judged immoral by outsiders. Many groups require males to kill designated enemies. To the extent a group completely socializes its members into such conduct, we cannot expect them to have a separate perspective or to question its conduct or their own.

But many groups, especially in the modern age, teach their members individual moral responsibility. To the extent that socialization clearly teaches this, it is reasonable to hold people responsible for their moral decisions and actions. However, there is usually ambiguous and conflicting instruction. Loyalty to the group is required and often defined as obedience to its standards and leaders. Loyalty and obedience are even taught as moral values. Part of the tragedy of Germany was that loyalty and obedience were exalted over individual moral responsibility.*

Another requirement for individual responsibility is self-awareness: awareness of one's needs, motives, desires, and psychological processes (see Part IV). For example, devaluation and scapegoating are often nonreflective psychological processes that arise without awareness and make moral equilibration easier. Even absorbing an ideology that helps one to comprehend a chaotic world can be largely nonreflective. Some cultures and modes of socialization enlarge the capacity to bring such nonreflective processes into awareness. German culture and especially German child-rearing practices did not.

Some people develop "processing mechanisms" that enable them to test their psychological reactions and consciously evaluate them in light of their goals, moral values, and beliefs. Such persons are less likely to be pushed and pulled by external forces. Who they are and what they believe and value still define both their initial reactions and how they process them, but

---

* I am stressing the importance of separation and differentiation from the group not to advocate an emphasis on the self and its needs and interests. To fulfill ideals such as concern about other human beings, connection, and community (see Part IV), people must develop strong separate identities so that they are *capable* of standing apart, of independent moral judgment, and if necessary of opposition to the group.

their greater internal flexibility provides them with the opportunity for moral choice.

Even in a society that fosters individual moral responsibility, there is no guarantee that individuals will oppose the group. Resisting is extremely difficult: it requires courage and strong motivation arising from moral values or from empathic caring. The capacity to choose and exercise moral responsibility requires an independent identity (which makes differentiation from the group possible), awareness of psychological processes, and moral values that are "inclusive" (applied to a broad range or all of humanity). Thus, moral responsibility is an ideal. How a society can foster it will be discussed in Part IV.

The completion tendency: killing till the very end

The SS continued killing Jews until the end of the losing war. Most of the Jews of Hungary were killed in the summer of 1944. Adolf Eichmann was still trying to transport Jews out of Hungary when Russian troops were at the gates of Budapest. In the extermination camps, the killings continued until near the end of 1944; then killing facilities were dismantled in an attempt to eradicate evidence. Cruel forced marches of inmates of abandoned camps killed more. Even in the last six months of the war, with the enemy closing in on many fronts, the Germans spent enormous resources on killing Jews. Inertia of the system is a partial but insufficient explanation. Are there others?

As I have noted, Ernest Becker proposed that human being are incapable of accepting their animal nature and its corollary, mortality. Out of the need for immortality much violence arises. The practice of human sacrifice, widespread in ancient times, was an affirmation of godlike power over life and death. As the edifice of superiority the Nazis had built was collapsing over their heads, they reaffirmed their immortality and power by intensified killing.[39]

My similar but less radical explanation is that power gives people a feeling of invulnerability that is especially needed at times of danger. The greatest power over others is the power of life and death. Threatened with the loss of the war, their sense of superiority, and even their lives, many SS men reaffirmed their power and invulnerability by continued killing. They could also find "rational" justifications: to complete the job and eliminate the traces of their actions.

To many SS, the extermination of Jews was a clear, specific embodiment of Nazism. From this perspective, Kurt Lewin's notion of the *goal gradient* is another useful explanation of the feverish murders at the end. According to Lewin, the closer people are to a goal, the more intense their involvement with it and their effort to reach it.[40] The Nazi goal required the abandonment of ordinary human morality. To accomplish it the goal had to acquire great importance and special intensity. The SS went a long way toward fulfilling it, investing not only enormous effort, time, and resources, but also their identity. As Himmler said, they sacrificed much for it. The goal acquired a life of its own, and the motivation to reach it became even greater when, near its achievement, its fulfillment was threatened.

Eichmann remained in Hungary until Budapest fell, continuing his efforts to kill the last large group of surviving Hungarian Jews. He even tried to hunt down individual Jews so that they would not escape. The goal of completing the extermination had supplanted even the elementary need for self-protection, for survival.

11 The behavior and psychology of bystanders and victims

The role of bystanders

The passivity of German bystanders

Germans accepted, supported, and participated in the increasing persecution of Jews. Resistance and public attempts to help were rare. Bystanders too were influenced by difficult life conditions, German culture, and the resulting psychological processes and motives. These gave them a shared societal tilt with perpetrators. Perpetrators probably differed from bystanders in personality and initial values. Some bystanders may have lacked opportunity and were unable to join organizations that became part of the destruction machinery. Some Germans who strongly opposed the Nazis were destroyed by them.

The practice by the Nazi state of "legal" persecution, of creating new laws to disenfranchise and persecute Jews, contributed to the passivity of Germans (and maybe outsiders). Germans value law and order; the new laws helped create new standards of acceptable conduct. They must have helped Germans to distance themselves from the Jews.

The Germans' positive feelings for Hitler also shaped their attitude toward anti-Jewish actions. According to Fritz Heider's balance theory and other theories of cognitive consistency, when attitudes are in imbalance, the motivation will arise to bring them into balance.[1] If a person likes Hitler, given Hitler's hatred of Jews, there is imbalance if that person likes Jews. To create balance, either the attitude toward Hitler or the attitude toward Jews has to change. In Nazi Germany, all the pressures acting on this person would favor Hitler over the Jews.*

* A striking claim by the sixty- to seventy-five-year-old Germans was that they knew nothing about the persecution of the Jews until Kristallnacht, in 1938. (Only one woman clearly acknowledged prior knowledge: she reported that her father, who rented out rooms, was directed by the authorities not to rent to Jews.) In conflict with this claim, some of them

151

Deviation and resistance were dangerous, but not impossible. Some initially refused to comply with boycotts. Over time group norms changed, at least partly because cooperation was so common and resistance so unusual. Hjalmar Schacht, Hitler's economic minister until 1937, exercised some influence by steadily warning against an extreme anti-Jewish policy – apparently because of his fear of repercussions abroad.

In the few known instances where Nazi officials or SS officers expressed disagreement with anti-Jewish actions or refused to participate, nothing happened to them.[2] For example, Sturmbannführer Hartl was not punished when he refused to take over an Einsatzkommando in Russia; Generalkommissar Kuber was not punished when he frustrated a killing operation against German Jews. When a Nazi doctor requested transfer out of the euthanasia program, he was simply reassigned.

Even limited noncompliance by German officials saved lives. Georg Druckner, a high German official in Denmark, warned the Danish authorities about the impending deportation of the Jews and delayed execution of the order, allowing the Danish people to organize the escape of 6,500 Danish Jews to Sweden.[3] As I have noted, protests brought the euthanasia program to an end, at least formally.

Protest, resistance, and noncompliance at an early stage might have been highly effective. Hitler was concerned about popular resistance and feared the churches. Instead, the population often acted against Jews in anticipation of Nazi measures. Businesses often fired Jewish employees even before the laws required it.[4] The monolithic culture and totalitarian system eliminated public discussion and protest that would have called attention to anti-Nazi values and conceptions of reality. A breakdown of uniformity and the expression of contrary views might have influenced bystanders not committed to Nazi ideology.

Bystanders and perpetrators in Nazi Europe

The percentage of the Jewish population killed in different European countries varied greatly. In countries occupied by Germany or allied to it, the behavior of the population, leaders, and institutions (the churches, the government) greatly affected the fate of the Jews. Local resistance

expressed the belief that the German people accepted the anti-Jewish actions. Given the highly public persecution, the perhaps "tentative" awareness might mean false reporting or psychological defense, but probably reflects lack of concern. In the overall context of the period, the fate of the Jews was unimportant to people, especially to youth, and probably barely penetrated awareness.

decreased the effectiveness of steps leading to deportation in territories occupied by Germany (the identification of Jews; stripping them of rights, property, and jobs; and their segregation) and of Germany's success in persuading its allies to deport their Jewish populations.

Some areas the Germans conquered were incorporated into the Greater German Reich. Other areas were to become colonies and their inhabitants to provide labor; these areas had German military or civilian governors who ruled with the help of the SS and army troops; German and SS control was strong and harsh. In other occupied territories, mainly in the west, German authorities relied on existing government institutions and native collaboration. Some countries were German allies; here, the Germans incited anti-Semitism and used persuasion to get governments to deport their Jewish populations – to hand them over to the Germans. Germany invaded several of its allies late in the war, mainly to avoid their desertion, but with the effect that Germany gained direct control.

Helen Fein has shown a direct relationship between prewar anti-Semitism in a country (the existence of anti-Semitic parties and organizations, discriminatory policies, and so on) and the proportion of Jews killed in the country.[5] A related factor was the behavior of local church leaders. Another was the degree of SS control over the population. Some authors argue that SS control (which was often established or increased after 1941) was a primary determinant of the number of Jews killed. When a government in an occupied country was allowed to retain significant internal control through an independent army or police force, the chance of Jewish survival was greater.[6] Fein's work indicates, however, that the degree of preexisting anti-Semitism – and the behavior of church leaders, officials, and members of the population in anti-Semitic countries – affected Jewish fate under most conditions.

Hungary is an example of a country with long-established anti-Semitism. A voluntary ally of Germany in the war, it had introduced legal discrimination against Jews already in 1920. Jews were stripped of equal rights and the entry of Jewish students to universities was limited. Between 1920 and 1938, Jews were excluded from jobs in government, the police, and the schools. They were identified by ancestry in 1938, following the example of Nuremberg laws. The dominant churches – Roman Catholic and Lutheran – both approved this "Jew law," although they attempted to protect converts. The fascist parties received about 45 percent of the popular vote in 1938.[7] During the war, groups of non-Hungarian Jews residing in Hungary were rounded up and massacred. Jewish men were conscripted into forced labor battalions. Hungarians had much opportunity to progress along a continuum of destruction.

To stop Hungary from concluding a separate peace, German troops occupied it in March 1944. Widespread cooperation in Hungary enabled Eichmann, eight SS officers, and forty enlisted men to deport over four hundred thousand Hungarian Jews to Auschwitz in the spring and summer of 1944. In October the Hungarian Nazis, the Arrow Cross, took over the government. Their identification with the German Nazis and thus their vicarious participation in German activities added to their evolution. They brutalized and killed Jews: they lined up and shot groups of them at the river Danube.

In Poland as well anti-Semitism was deep-seated, with many pogroms in 1918 and 1919. After 1935, Poland enacted discriminatory laws. There was widespread support before World War II for Jewish emigration as a solution to Poland's Jewish problem. After the German invasion, the Poles suffered terribly; many in the leadership and educated elite were killed, and many deported for labor in the Third Reich. It is not surprising, however, given the history of anti-Semitism, that this did not lead to the experience of "common fate" and solidarity with Jews. Perhaps also, as Sophie said in William Styron's book *Sophie's Choice*, Poles were glad when the attention of Germans focused on Jews as their victims rather than themselves. Poles helped the Germans supervise the ghettos. Some searched out Jews hidden by other Poles to blackmail them or their rescuers or for the cash offered by the Germans for such information. Members of the right-wing National Armed Forces fought Germans, but also attacked Jewish partisans. The underground Polish Home Army refused to accept Jews and repeatedly refused to help them fight the Germans.[8]

A contrasting example is the resistance of the Danish population and government, including the king, against treating Danish Jews differently from other Danes. Most of the Jewish population there survived. In Italy, a large percentage of Jews survived because officials and citizens sabotaged efforts to hand them over to the Germans.

In Bulgaria, a German ally, the government attempted to deport Jews, but many elements protested: the bishops of the Bulgarian Orthodox church individually and collectively and professional organizations of doctors, lawyers, and writers. A member of parliament introduced a motion against the anti-Jewish policy of the government. Probably in response to these pressures, the king intervened on their behalf. As a result, 82 percent of the Jews survived in the larger Bulgaria that included territories annexed during the war. Bulgaria was ruled by Turkey until 1878 and there were many minorities: Turks, Greeks, Jews, Armenians, and others. There was no sharply drawn differentiation between the Bulgarian ingroup and these outgroups. Anti-Semitism was also limited, perhaps, because Jews did not fill important roles in finance and commerce, which in other places evoked envy and resentment.[9]

In Belgium, the German policy was the same as in other occupied territories: requiring Jews to register, stripping them of their rights, property and jobs, and segregation. Press control, propaganda, the organization of collaborators, and brutal reprisal against resistance promoted these policies. In spite of this, "the Belgian public exhibited an 'aversion' to the acquisition of Jewish real property."[10] The Belgian government in exile declared transfers of such property illegal. The universities and bar associations resisted pressures to exclude Jews. The Belgian cardinal and the queen both protested an order that Jews report for forced labor. (We can contrast this with the behavior of the German public and institutions or even with Vichy France, where the government introduced anti-Jewish legislation before German demands.)

When the Jewish council (see the section entitled The Jewish Councils in this chapter) set up by the Germans delivered call-up orders of forced labor to Jews, the Belgian resistance movement burnt the card file of registered Jews. When this did not stop cooperation, they executed the official in charge of the call-ups. The warnings by the resistance deterred Belgian Jews from reporting, and many were hidden by their Christian countrymen. The Jews joined the popular front resistance movement, creating the Committee for the Defense of Jews. They petitioned and appealed, infiltrated the Jewish council, and acted to help Jews in danger, placing three thousand of the four thousand children who were saved in the country into private homes and institutions disguised as Aryan Belgians. In spite of their high visibility – a large majority of them lived in Antwerp and spoke Yiddish – 53 percent of the 66,707 Belgian Jews survived.[11]

The passivity of the outside world

Foreign institutions and governments did little to deter Germany or save the Jews. There were only a few boycotts. An extremely effective form of Nazi manipulation was the threat of immigration by large numbers of impoverished Jews. In 1938 the Evian Conference, called to discuss the rescue of German Jews, collapsed because nations were unwilling to allow Jewish immigration.

The official SS newspaper, the *Schwarze Korps*, stated explicitly in 1938 that if the world was not yet convinced that the Jews were the scum of the earth, it soon would be when unidentifiable beggars, without nationality, without money, and without passports crossed their frontiers.

A circular letter from the Ministry of Foreign Affairs to all German authorities abroad shortly after the November pogroms of 1938, stated: "The emigration movement of only about 100,000 Jews has already sufficed to awaken the interest of many countries in the Jewish danger.... Germany is very interested in maintaining the dispersal of Jewry... the influx of Jews in all parts of the world invokes the opposition of the native population and thereby forms the best propaganda for the German Jewish policy.... The poorer and therefore more burdensome the immigrating Jew is to the country absorbing him, the stronger the country will react.[12]

In the United States there was strong resistance to immigration, even of refugee children. The number of immigrants actually allowed into the United States during the war years was well below the number that could be admitted without special legislation. The legal quota allowed sixty thousand immigrants a year, but only about six thousand actually got into the United States. An official obstacle course successfully kept them out. As David Wyman has shown, the U.S. State Department and the British did not want to rescue Jews; they did not want to worry about where to put them.[13] The same was true of Canada. The Roosevelt administration did not establish the War Refugee Board until 1944, when threatened by scandal over the administration's inaction. Britain blockaded Palestine to keep out refugees and returned those who were caught. The pope did not speak out and the International Red Cross showed little daring. American Jewish organizations, in part because of their anxiety about the prevailing mood of anti-Semitism in the country, did not press the U.S. government hard enough.

The Nazis, in secret correspondence, used such euphemisms as "solution possibilities" and "special treatment," which limited even their own awareness or facing of what they were doing. The victims themselves used euphemisms, such as "final act of the drama" and "tempting fate" (the fate of being gassed).[14] The bystander could evade awareness of the victims' fate by inattention.

The U.S. press wrote little about the genocide during the war years, even though the facts became known in 1942.* How different might the U.S. response have been if newspapers had reported in huge headlines the incredible fact that millions of people were being gassed in death factories? (See Chapter 17 for a discussion of press self-censorship.)

A request by some Jewish organizations to bomb the gas chambers or

---

* Some have suggested that one reason for the refusal to believe early reports about the killing of Jews was their similarity to reports about German atrocities in World War I. World War I reports were mostly propaganda. However, this is a partial explanation at best, given the very minimal response to the Jews' fate during the preceding years and after their ongoing extermination was conclusively confirmed.

the railroads leading to Auschwitz was not seriously considered.[15] The reasons given were the unavailability of aircraft and the overriding need to bring the war to an end. These justifications were belied by the bombing missions against factories near Auschwitz and flights bringing supplies to surrounded Polish partisans who faced certain annihilation.

How can we explain the conduct of the United States, Britain, Canada, and other countries? Individuals and groups preoccupied by their own immediate needs and pressing goals are inclined to ignore others' need and pain. But resistance to helping began before the war.

One cause was cultural anti-Semitism, rooted in a heritage of Christian anti-Semitism. This was intensified by the worldwide depression. In the United States, workers feared that immigrants would take away scarce jobs from them, and so they scapegoated Jews and other minorities.

A second cause was the perpetrators' ability to increase already existing anti-Semitism. The whole world was exposed to Nazi propaganda representing Jews as evil and bent on world conquest. Serge Moscovici's research suggests that extremely negative statements about groups are not discredited; they can affect basic, general attitudes and beliefs more than moderate statements. His findings imply that people would not immediately accept the content of such statements – for example, that Jews are murderers and seducers of children – but would devalue Jews in a general way in response to them.[16] The 1930s and early 1940s saw a worldwide increase in anti-Semitism. According to public opinion polls, anti-Semitism was at its highest point in the United States between 1938 and 1944.*[17] Fifty-three percent of Americans believed that Jews were different from other people and their behavior should be restricted.[18] In the United States the wildly anti-Semitic radio programs of Father Coughlin were highly popular until it was discovered that he was repeating almost verbatim statements by Goebbels, Hitler's propaganda minister.[19] It was not what he said that was opposed, but that he used the words of a clearly defined enemy.

A third cause of inaction was that the passivity in the course of the increasing mistreament of Jews resulted in changes in people, institutions, and governments. In the end, many people probably had a vague, inarticulate feeling that the Jews somehow deserved what was happening

---

* An interesting example of cooperation with the Nazis was the replacement of two Jewish athletes on the 4 × 400 meter U.S. relay team in the 1936 Olympics in Berlin (*New York Times*, Aug. 10, 1986, p. 95). This was done without any direct pressure by the German organizers. The world's participation in the Olympic Games in Berlin in 1936 was itself a statement of acceptance of Nazi policies.

to them. A final reason for passivity is that states have traditionally not regarded themselves as having moral responsibilities. In Part IV I will discuss the need to change this.

The inaction of other countries and their unwillingness to help Jews confirmed the Nazis in the rightness of what they were doing. "At bottom," Goebbels wrote in his diary in December 13, 1942, "I believe that the English and the Americans are happy that we are exterminating the Jewish riff-raff."[20] Resistance and pressure might have focused the attention of the Nazis on moral values and caused them to worry about the effects of their actions on themselves.

Jewish cooperation, resistance, and psychological experience

Forceful resistance can make the mistreatment and murder of a group both physically and psychologically more difficult. Although Jewish resistance to the Nazis was substantially greater than early reports indicated, it was not strong enough to deter perpetrators. Resistance was also limited by other victims of Nazi Germany and victims of other genocides. Russian prisoners of war did not rebel until nearly the end of the war, even though they were soldiers and even though half of the six million held by the Germans were killed or died of starvation and overwork.[21] Facing overwhelming, brutal force, people follow commands and accept suffering in the hope of saving their lives and the lives of people they love.

Helen Fein classified rulers or masters of a conquered people as oppressors, exploiters, or enemies. Enemies seek not only to debase, oppress, or exploit, but also to destroy. The Jews' definition of the situation was crucial in determining their response: when and where they became aware that the Nazis were enemies, they did attempt to escape and, under certain circumstances, to resist.[22] Resistance required accurate perception of Nazi intentions and a cohesive group. Individual resistance was futile and brought collective retributon: the killing of family members or of large numbers of other Jews.

The Jews survived many centuries of persecution through yielding to their persecutors. Sometimes they even anticipated and fulfilled demands (such as fines) before they were made – in the hope of avoiding greater demands and worse persecution. They believed that if they did not resist, their troubles would blow over; they would be allowed to stay in their homes and retain at least some of their property; in pogroms some would be killed but many would live. In the face of Nazi persecution they initially followed the same blueprint for survival. However, in their history, Jews had faced all three types of threats – oppression, exploitation, and destruction – and responded accordingly. They responded to intensely violent pogroms in Russia by escape. Between 1888 and 1914, 2.5 million of them emigrated to the United States.[23]

The Jewish councils

In medieval Germany, the Jews had been led by Jewish councils (*Judenräte*) made up of respected members of the community. The Nazis reconstituted the Jewish councils and used them to control the Jewish population and help fulfill Nazi goals. What was the degree and nature of "cooperation" by Jewish councils and what was its consequence?

They story of the Jewish councils is complex, and it is still being told. Starting as early as 1939, the existing Jewish leadership and new leadership groups created by the Nazis were turned into Jewish councils in every country the Nazis occupied. First they were to transmit and execute orders. Later, they became instruments of what Hilberg calls the destruction "process" or "machinery": identifying Jews, selecting deportees to fulfill German quotas, and assembling them for transport. They made the Nazis' job easier.

The motivation of council members varied greatly. Many hoped to limit Jewish suffering by maintaining order and effectively executing German orders. Some believed that they might save the people by making the ghettos economically indispensable to the Germans; that they might save people from retribution by suppressing Jewish resistance; that, when they helped in deporting Jews, by sacrificing some people they saved the lives of the rest. Some council members hoped to gain security for themselves and their families. A very few had megalomaniacal ideas, glorying in their power. Many filled the role involuntarily.

Hannah Arendt stressed the cooperation of Jewish leaders.[24] But from the start the Jewish councils varied in cooperation depending on many factors, including the amount of non-Jewish cooperation with the Germans and the degree of local anti-Semitism. The willingness of Jewish leaders to serve was also a response to the conditions and needs of the Jewish population. "Jews in all German occupied states before 1943 were progressively defined, stripped [of their rights and livelihoods], and segregated. . . . [This created] a 'welfare' class. . . needing public assistance to survive. The Judenrat was employed to dispense such assistance."[25]

Even though this endangered them, some Jewish leaders refused service in the councils. Of those who served at the start, a substantial portion did not fully cooperate with German demands (one-third according to Helen Fein, and one-third fully cooperated). Most of those who did not cooperate were killed, were deported and died in the camps, or committed suicide. They were replaced by others more malleable. The elimination and replacement of members of the councils continued, as needed to fulfill SS designs.[26]

Another reason for cooperation was that the SS did everything possible to camouflage the ultimate fate of Jewish victims. Victims were told that they were being deported for resettlement or that the weak would be deported, but the strong would be allowed to stay (or vice versa), using all possible means not only to mislead but also to divide people. Psychological defense mechanisms were essential to make an unbearable situation bearable and contributed to cooperation (see the section on the psychology of victims, pp. 162–5).

Hannah Arendt suggested that organizations within the totalitarian system that compromised with the system became ineffectual in opposing it and ended up helping it.[27] Although cooperation by Jewish councils was in response to strong threat and adverse conditions, past cooperation made it difficult to change: to stop, to cut losses, to give up hope that cooperation will save people. An added block to resistance was that it had only a remote chance of success in saving lives.

The actions and attitudes of the councils influenced the Jewish definition of the situation and diminished resistance. How much did such cooperation contribute to the fate of the Jews? In all places, the Germans attempted to isolate and concentrate Jews. According to Fein, when Jews were segregated, more of them were destroyed; segregation accounted for both Jewish vulnerability and the existence and cooperation of Jewish councils. "In most cases, such councils were imposed in states in which the Jews had already been isolated by the native population, shunned, and/or singled out as targets of attack."[28] As noted, a past history of anti-Semitism and highly developed anti-Semitic movements were associated with cooperation by the state, national leaders, churches, and populations with Nazi aims. Jewish councils were more accommodating when Jews were isolated and abandoned, surrounded by enemies.

Jewish actions

Not only Arendt but also other scholars regard Jewish passivity as a contributor to German success in killing six million Jews. Bettelheim suggests that the response of the German people might have been quite different if it had been necessary to drag each victim down the street or shoot every Jew on the spot; others wonder whether it all might have been different if the Jews of Stetten, the first German Jews to be deported in 1941 to the east, had been unwilling to move, so that they would have had to be bodily dragged from their houses, shouting and screaming.[29] This focus on the victims' passivity may partly be a result of just-world thinking: the victims brought their fate on themselves, not by deserving it but by not fighting back.*

First, we might wonder how different it all might have been if the German population or the rest of the world had shown a strong response – boycotts and other retaliation and threat of punitive action – or had simply expressed outrage in the course of the Jews' increasing mistreatment. Second, our judgment of the victims' behavior will very much depend on our perspective. We can focus on their passivity: "allowing" themselves to be gathered, murdered, or worked to death as slaves. We can focus on their attempts to evade and at times resist the killers and to maintain human dignity in the camps. And we can attempt to understand their psychological experience.

Jews frequently acted when an effective response to the threat was possible. Psychological coping mechanisms, like denial, might have slowed their leaving Germany, but over 60 percent of Jews who lived in Germany in 1933 had left by October 1941, when immigration was forbidden. The same proportion of Austrian Jews fled between the German takeover of Austria in 1938 and October 1941, "exploiting all means – legal and illegal – available. A study of those remaining in Worms in October 1941 indicated that the overwhelming majority had emigration plans and had applied for visas; almost all applied to the United States, which rigidly restricted immigrants."[30] They had nowhere to go.

About three-fourths of Estonian Jews, the only group of Baltic Jews that had an extended period of time between threat to their nation and full occupation, fled to the interior of the Soviet Union in 1941. Dutch Jews did not passively wait to be rounded up. According to a German report of August 3, 1941, only one of five Jews reported when called up, and the rest left their homes and went into hiding.[31] I described some of the actions of the Belgian Jews. Jews extensively participated in resistance movements in occupied territories, often under assumed names so that they would not endanger their families. In many countries, they participated in resistance more than the native population, especially the Zionists, socialists, and communists among them. In some places, strong

---

* Consider the experience of one of my students, which she described in a paper for a course. A man pulled a knife on her and forced her to follow him to a park, where he talked about himself for a while and then raped her. A couple of days later she and her boyfriend were leaving her apartment when, playfully responding to something he did, she held up her fists and said, "Do you want to fight?" He said in response, "Why didn't you fight the other day?"

anti-Semitism made it difficult for Jews to join the resistance. For a Jew to join the Polish underground, he had to lie and pretend to be a non-Jew.[32]

In the Warsaw ghetto, nearly unimaginable suffering due to hunger, disease, isolation, and the slow death of an immense number of people crowded into a small area was followed by the deportation to the death camps of 320,000 Jews between July and September 1942. Left behind were younger people, some of them former Zionists, used for slave labor. Their families had been deported and were therefore not subject to retaliation. Doubts about Nazi intentions were gone. It is under these conditions that the Warsaw uprising began. It was delayed by the refusal of Polish resistance organizations to aid the revolt. The revolt began on April 19, 1943. After four weeks of fighting, the Germans penetrated the bunker of the central command. To destroy the remaining Jews without further losses of their own, they burnt down the ghetto.

In the camps, although there were different modes of adaptation, many prisoners actively engaged with their environment rather than passively succumbing to it. Escape or resistance was made extremely difficult by hunger, brutalization, diminished life drives, extremely low probability of success, and examples of terrible punishment. While relatively rare, there were escapes and uprisings at Treblinka, Auschwitz-Birkenau, and Sobibor. According to many accounts, the prisoners who survived learned to dissemble – for example, to save their strength by not working but appearing to do so. Inmates continued to care for themselves, to try to keep clean.[33] While it varied in the camps how much prisoners competed with each other for scarce resources or maintained solidarity, under conditions that clearly favored the former, bonding and solidarity were frequent.[34]

The psychology of victims

Many influences affected the victims' experience and state of mind. The perception of reality is a construction from "objective" elements, the reality "out-there," and past experience, personality (and the nature of one's group), and current needs. Intense threat or danger can lead to psychological maneuvers, usually automatic, that enter into the construction of reality, their purpose to reduce the experience of threat and anxiety.

Freud proposed the idea of defense mechanisms, the screening or altering of our perception of events in the world and our own thoughts and feelings in order to reduce threat and protect the psychological self.[35] All of us use defense mechanisms, but their use is intensified when there is severe internal conflict or external threat. Especially when people cannot cope with threat by taking action, they will tend to diminish the feeling of threat through unconscious inner processes that alter perception. Denial is one of the more "primitive" defense mechanisms. It means screening out part of reality or making it unreal in our minds. Rationalization is a less extreme defense – interpreting events in ways that fit our needs and purposes. In 1934 the Nazis eliminated the SA, the perpetrators of many of the early attacks on Jews; many Jews almost realistically interpreted this as a sign of a better future.

The denial of an obvious reality is a sign of psychosis. Usually, however, reality or at least its meaning is not so obvious, and differing interpretations are possible. As I noted, the Nazis' own motivation for genocide evolved with increasing mistreatment of Jews. An accurate perception or reality in the Germany of the mid-1930s would have suggested extreme danger, but not impending genocide. However, adding consideration of Hitler's written and spoken words would have made genocide a realistic possibility.

When the Nazis came to power, Jews were uncertain about their fate. Uncertainty creates great anxiety. Thus, they even welcomed the initial laws that "clarified" their status – the Nuremberg laws. According to Hannah Arendt, many Jews continued to cling to the belief that the original program of the National Socialist Party, enunciated in 1920 and never officially abandoned, expressed the Nazis' true intentions.[36] This program contained provisions that in 1920 expressed severe anti-Semitism, but now seemed mild: second-class citizenship for Jews and their exclusion from the civil service and the press.

We do not know the extent that defenses distorted the Jews' perception of reality. Given the progressive increase in persecution, it was possible to see each anti-Jewish measure as the last one. Most likely, defenses delayed the attempts of some Jews to leave Germany and face a new, unfamiliar world and contributed to disbelief of the initial rumors and fragmentary information about the camps and the killings and even of more specific information about the fate of the deported. Such information was so threatening that it had to be kept away from the center of consciousness.

The knowledge that an enemy intends to kill us and there are no effective means to protect ourselves can be unbearable. Belief in a just world, that innocent people do not suffer intense persecution, also entered as a defense. Dutch Jews believed before the war that the German Jews, whom they disliked, must have done something terrible to bring about such persecution.[37] Accounts by concentration camp survivors indicate that even in the camps many could not take in the reality of their situation and kept themselves psychologically removed from it.[38]

The behavior of bystanders contributed to despair and hopelessness.* In Germany, where Jews regarded themselves fully German, they felt deeply betrayed. Isolated in many countries, abandoned and without support, often persecuted by their own countrymen, facing a brutal enemy who did everything to weaken life drives and inhibit Jews from uniting, they had to feel utterly helpless. People rarely act if they believe that their action will have no effect in reaching a desired goal. A goal itself – escape, resistance, or revenge – does not usually arise without some hope that it can be fulfilled.

In animals as well as humans, the inability to protect oneself leads to a state of helplessness – for example, dogs stop attempting to avoid or escape electric shocks if they have been repeatedly unsuccessful. Many studies show that humans also learn to give up unsuccessful efforts and become passive and depressed.[39]

The psychological state and behavior of victims was also affected by the German practice of collective retribution. In 1942, five Germans were killed in Berlin by a group of Jewish communists. In retaliation, the Gestapo executed 250 Jews, deported another 250, and threatened to kill 250 more for every German killed in the future.[40] In 1941, Jewish action groups killed a member of the Defense Troop created by the fascistic National Society and Movement of the Netherland. The Germans arrested 425 Jewish men, deported them to Mathausen, tortured them, and worked them to death.[41]

All along the Jews were deprived of individuality, treated as an anonymous mass. I have pointed out that deindividuation freed perpetrators from moral constraints. But the effect of the loss of individual identity in a

---

* The story of a woman born in Austria is consistent with many of the themes in this chapter. Now a Canadian citizen, she was fifteen years old at the time of the Anschluss, the German takeover of Austria in 1938. She and her family felt well-regarded and well-treated members of the community. Immediately upon the German entry they became nonpersons. Schoolmates stopped talking to her. Austria had a history of intense anti-Semitism, which, as conditions changed, immediately came to the fore. (We can contrast this with the Danes' loyalty to Jews after they were occupied by the Germans.)

Her family, especially her father, refused to believe that the Nazi actions were aimed at all Jews, innocent Jews. When they witnessed the Gestapo taking away a neighbor's son, her father thought that he must have done something terrible. Even as he himself was arrested, he claimed it had to be a mistake.

After he was released, a shadow of his former proud self, and the family accepted the reality of their situation, they had no place to go. No country was willing to accept them. Ultimately, they succeeded in getting to Palestine. (I am grateful to Michael Shandler, who made available to me an interview of his mother, taped for a documentary.)

group depends on the context. It can ease killing or it can lead to passively marching to a gas chamber.*

When Jews had support or opportunities, for example, allies in the native population, they became active in evasion, escape, and resistance. Certain conditions, as in the Warsaw ghetto, fostered unity and group action. But conditions were mostly conducive to passivity. Many Jews must have progressed along a continuum of victimization and abandoned themselves to the currents that invariably led to destruction.

The power of heroic bystanders

Many lines of evidence indicate the tremendous potential of bystanders to influence events: in emergencies, the words and actions of witnesses affect others' definition of the situation and response; the population brought the euthanasia policy to an end in Germany; different attitudes and behavior by local populations and their leaders in European countries resulted in Jewish death or survival.

The extraordinary power of bystanders was apparent in the village of Le Chambon. The inhabitants of this Huguenot village in Vichy France saved several thousand Jews, most of them children, despite a penalty of deportation or death for sheltering Jews. They were led by their pastor, Andre Trocme, who had a firm belief in nonviolence and the sanctity of life. Their willingness to sacrifice themselves had great impact even on would-be perpetrators, such as the police and the military. It became common for strange voices to call on the telephone in the presbytery to tell of an impending raid. This enabled the inhabitants to send the refugees they were harboring into the nearby forests.

> As the Resistance in Le Chambon developed, a curious phenomenon was taking place there: many of the Vichy police were being "converted" (as Trocme puts it in his notes) to helping the Chambonnais and their Jews. Even as the official policy of the Vichy toward Le Chambon and the Jews was hardening, *individuals* among the police and the bureaucrats of Vichy were more and more frequently resisting their orders to catch or hurt people who had done no visible harm to anyone. They found themselves helping those who were trying to save these innocent, driven creatures. Caring was infectious.[42]

When the doctor Le Forester was accused, tried, and executed as an example to the villagers, his deeds and the words he spoke at his trial

---

* This point is illustrated by the famous story of the dancer who was recognized by a Nazi officer in the line leading to the gas chamber and told to dance. As she danced, she grabbed the officer's gun and shot him. By becoming a dancer again she had regained her identity and capacity to resist.

influenced a German officer, Major Smelling, who persuaded Colonel
Metzger, the head of the infamous Farber Legion of the SS, not to move
against the village.

I heard the words of Dr. Le Forester, who was a Christian and explained to me
very clearly why you were all disobeying our orders in Le Chambon. I believed
that your doctor was sincere. I am a good Catholic, you understand, and I can
grasp these things.... Well, Colonel Metzger was a hard one, and he kept on
insisting that we move in on Le Chambon. But I kept telling him to wait. I told
Metzger that this kind to resistance had nothing to do with violence, nothing to
do with anything we could destroy with violence. With all my personal and military
power I opposed sending his legion into Le Chambon.[43]

What is the psychological basis of this kind of influence? Helpful bystanders provide a different definition of reality. They break the uniformity of views and call attention to values disregarded by perpetrators and
passive bystanders. They affirm the humanity of the victims. If they themselves are not devalued by perpetrators, they set a standard and also invoke
a deep-seated human desire to be well regarded by others.

Heroic rescuers

Some people risked their own lives to save Jews and others persecuted by
the Nazis. Among the bleak memories of the Holocaust, their actions offer
hope for the future. Some of these rescuers and the rescued have been
interviewed, either in the 1960s or recently.[44] The interviews show that
many of them had parents with strong moral concerns that they transmitted
to their children. As a result, these rescuers were motivated both by a
desire to fulfill moral and humanitarian values and by dislike of the Nazi
system. Many valued caring or felt empathy for those who suffer. Other
rescuers responded to the plight of one victim, often a friend or an acquaintance, and then continued to help others. In some instances a person
began to help after witnessing the murder or brutal treatment of a Jew,
or the Jews' evident suffering. One person repeatedly noticed a group of
ragtag Jewish children on his street. He was aware that they could be arrested and taken away anytime. A characteristic of many rescuers was
"inclusiveness," the tendency to apply caring, moral values and standards of right and wrong to people in different social, ethnic, or religious
groups.[45]

Some rescuers had already shown in their earlier lives that they were
unusually fearless, self-confident, and adventurous. Personal goal theory
suggests that adventurousness may have been a contributing motive for
resistance against the Nazis.[46] Oscar Schindler and Raoul Wallenberg

were both men of action who gained satisfaction from exercising their skills and personal power in confrontation with the Nazis.

Another reported characteristic of some rescuers was marginality: being a member of a minority religion (Huguenot in the case of Le Chambon), being new to the community, having a parent from another country, or some other source of social separateness that allowed a different perspective and reduced fear of risking one's relationship with the majority group.[47] Many rescuers, however, were closely tied to some group. Samuel and Pearl Oliner, in a major study of rescuers, found many rescuers "normocentric," or norm-centered, characterized by a "feeling of obligation to a special reference group with whom the actor identified and whose explicit and implicit values he feels obliged to obey."[48] The reference groups included religious, political, and resistance groups, family or friends. Sometimes these rescuers helped when authorities in the group (e.g., priests or resistance leaders) or other members directed, persuaded, or in other ways influenced them. At other times, they responded when events called forth their internalized group norms. The position taken by their group or implied by its norms led these rescuers to deviate from the majority.

This type of motivation was frequent and is highly significant, especially when a large social group supports it, as in the case of Belgium. Social defense networks developed and helping became the norm. However, such motivation can be unreliable. Individual helpers do not necessarily care about the fate of the victims, but are guided by the stance of the group or its leaders. Resistance groups and local church groups sometimes influenced their members to help, but some priests and church authorities (e.g., in Poland) urged their flocks to support Nazi policies of extermination, and some resistance groups killed Jews.[49]

The Oliners found that most rescuers in their study, not only normocentric ones, felt connected to other human beings, whether family, a group, or people in general. In contrast, the passive, nonhelping bystanders, members of a comparison group they interviewed, tended to be disconnected. Repeated helping by most rescuers, over long periods of time, must have strengthened their experience of connection. Seventy percent of the rescuers first helped in response to a request, by either the person in need or an intermediary. Most of them continued to help. According to personal goal theory, motives for helping become active in response to activating conditions. Requests might have led rescuers to appreciate the mortal danger of Jews or called forth important values or exerted pressure.

As I have mentioned, in many instances there was an evolution of commitment to help by steps along a continuum of benevolence. People who agreed to hide some Jews briefly went on to care for them for years. A person who responded to the need of a friend continued by helping strangers.

The evolution of Oscar Schindler was dramatic.[50] He was a German born in Czechoslovakia who, although not a committed Nazi, became a member of the Nazi Party. An opportunist, he followed the German army into Poland in 1939, took over a confiscated Jewish factory, and proceeded to enrich himself with Jewish slave labor.

But contrary to others in this position, in many ways he treated Jews who worked for him like human beings. He indulged in small acts of kindness and consideration, followed by more significant acts. To protect his Jewish slave laborers from the dangers of their brutal camp, he created his own camp. He began to endanger his own life in order to help and continued to help even after he was arrested and released. As the Russians approached, he moved the laborers to his hometown in Czechoslovakia and set up a factory that produced nothing but served as camouflage to protect the Jews. Eventually, he sacrificed all his possessions while saving the lives of twelve hundred Jews.

Schindler's intense sympathy for Jews was evidenced in many acts, one of which stands out because it was so uncharacteristic of this elegant dandy and bon vivant. Once when he visited his "friend," Amos Goeth, the commandant of the camp at Plaszow, a train filled with Jews was standing by in the burning sun. Terrible sounds of distress and pain emanated from it. Schindler grabbed a nearby hose and started to water down the wagons, to the tolerant amusement of the SS guards.

Raoul Wallenberg was a Swede, a citizen of a country that was neutral in the Second World War.[51] His example shows the multiplicity of experiences and influences that at times join in leading to extreme altruism. He had a Hungarian business partner whose relatives were in immediate danger. He knew the relatives from business trips to Hungary, so he had a personal connection to people in need. His familiarity with Hungary also gave him some competence. While working in Palestine, he had seen refugees arriving from Hitler's Germany; this direct contact with victims must have contributed to his concern and caring. He was asked to go to Hungary by representatives of the American War Refugee Board; this request may have helped to define for him what was right and activate important values. Finally, Wallenberg was one-sixteenth Jewish.

Wallenberg was a member of a poor branch of an influential Swedish family. He had wide experience in work and travel under the guidance of his diplomat grandfather. At one point, his grandfather urged him to join the family bank, but he refused. Later his grandfather died, his connection to the family was weakened, and when he changed his mind, he was not allowed to join the bank. His work as a partner in an export-import firm was less than fulfilling for him. Because he was not fully involved in pursuing a goal important to him, he was more open to other goals; the request was more likely to activate a desire or obligation to help.

In Hungary he started to help by creating a document, impressive from the bureaucratic standpoint but of questionable validity, that gave thousands protection. He threatened, bribed, and cajoled high-level Hungarian officials. He personally intervened in many ways that required great courage, exposing himself to assassination attempts and the guns of Nazi guards. He showed great courage and self-confidence in dealing with Nazi officials, including Eichmann. His sense of invulnerability may have been inspired by his aristocratic background. Wallenberg and Schindler developed total commitment to saving Jewish lives. These men may be regarded as "good fanatics," people with an overriding commitment to a goal to which they subordinated all others. Their aim was not to improve "humanity" but to help human beings.

In conditions of extreme danger, people need support to evolve and maintain the motivation to help. As they begin to help, they also begin to create their own environment, their own context. They build connections to a community that supports them. Schindler was supported by the people he helped and also by outside contacts he made through his actions in behalf of Jews. For example, a delegation of Hungarian Jews asked him to come to Hungary to convince the skeptical Jewish community there of the existence of the camps and killing operations. This had to reinforce and support his identity as an ally, a helper of Jews; acceding to the request contributed to his evolution. As I wrote elsewhere, many rescuers were connected to "an elaborate network of people, required for the practical aspects of helping, but in my view also essential in giving emotional support and confirmation."[52]

Because the potential power of bystanders is great, so is their obligation, an obligation only occasionally fulfilled. How can we enlarge compassion, the awareness of responsibility for other lives, and the feeling of obligation to act? These questions are considered in Part IV.[53]

Part III

Other genocides and mass killings

In this section I examine three more cases of genocide and mass killing: the Armenian genocide, the "autogenocide" in Cambodia, and the disappearances in Argentina. The description and analysis will be detailed enough, I hope, to show that the conception presented in Part I promotes the understanding of a broad range of such tragic and horrible events. I briefly describe difficult life conditions, cultural preconditions, and steps along the continuum of destruction. This will enable the reader to judge the extent to which the influences I posited in Part I were present in these genocides and mass killings as well as in the Holocaust.

12   The Turkish genocide of the Armenians

Historical (life) conditions

When the First World War began, the Ottoman Empire had been losing power and territories for more than a hundred years. Once a great military power that ruled over many countries, it was called the Sick Man of Europe by Czar Nicholas of Russia in the middle of the nineteenth century. In 1877–78 it lost a war against Russia, and Russia annexed parts of Turkish Armenia. Turkey lost additional territories in the Balkan wars, between 1911 and 1913.

Turkey was also commercially and industrially backward and dominated in these realms by other nations. In 1875 the Ottoman Empire went bankrupt. A Public Debt Administration was set up by the great powers with representatives of Britain, France, Germany, Italy, Austria, and Turkey to control Turkey's finances, and 12 to 15 percent of Turkey's revenues were ceded to this organization.[1]

Within Turkey, commerce, trade, and finance were largely in the hands of foreigners or of non-Muslim minorities such as Greeks, Armenians, and Jews.[2] "Capitulations," which were extraterritorial agreements between the Ottoman Empire and foreign nations, granted judicial and economic privileges to foreigners. Partly because of the Islamic belief that law is derived from religion, so that only believers can participate in it, and partly for other cultural and historical reasons, foreigners were judged and protected by their own laws. They were exempt from all taxes except export and import duties, which had ceilings specified by capitulations. Foreign products flooded into Turkey, inhibiting industrial development.[3]

The Ottoman Empire continued to repress its many minorities. Reforms announced in 1839 and 1856 that would have provided rights to all citizens and others promised later (partly under foreign pressure) were not carried out. A constitutional government was created in 1876 but dissolved in 1878 by Sultan Abdul Hamid. A long reign of repression and terror followed.

173

Foreign powers continuously exerted influence on Turkey, military and political. Russia was consistently belligerent, partly because it wanted to acquire Turkish territories and reduce Turkish power. England's prime concern was the containment of Russia. Western powers and Russia were also interested in protecting the rights of Christian minorities in Turkey, but realpolitik usually won out. In exchange for promises of reform, England supported Turkey in its conflicts with Russia. After Russia's victory in the war of 1877–78, England intervened to shape a treaty that would minimize Russia's gains. The promises of reform remained unfulfilled.

In 1908 a revolution compelled Abdul Hamid to restore constitutional government. In 1909 the revolutionaries, who called themselves the Committe of Union and Progress but who were also known as the Young Turks, gained complete power. Initially, the revolution was widely welcomed. The Young Turks promised universal rights, freedom, and equality. However, political disorder, internal upheavals, internal violence, especially against Armenians, and losing wars continued. There was a counter-revolution and interventions by the military, but the Young Turks retained power.[4] Three months after their revolution, on October 5, 1908, Bulgaria proclaimed complete independence, and in the Balkan wars, between 1911 and 1913, the Ottoman Empire lost Greece. By 1913 it was effectively eliminated from Europe.

Probably to a large degree as a result of these conditions, an ideology of Pan-Turkism, or Turanism, became dominant, its aim to enhance the power of the Ottoman Empire and to purify the nation, making it Turkish in language, customs, and religion. The Young Turks abandoned the alliance with England in response to political and material support from Germany. In the hope of regaining lost territories or conquering new ones, the Ottoman Empire entered the First World War on the side of Germany. Immediately, it suffered heavy losses to a massive Russian invasion. Although it also won a victory over the British at Gallipoli, the possibility of its losing the war at this early point was real.

Before the war, poverty, hunger, disease, an influx of refugees from lost territories and their conflicts with minorities added to life problems. The loss of provinces in Europe caused substantial migration of Muslims into Turkey, especially Anatolia. After the war of 1877–78 more than a million people moved into Turkey.[5] There was conflict between the newly arriving Muslims and Armenians living in the territories that they had moved into. After the revolution strife between Armenians and Young Turks further contributed to political instability and violence.

The people experienced much hardship. Agricultural methods were primitive, and the yield was poor. Peasants had difficulty paying their taxes and lived in many areas in houses without sanitation, "without hope or ambition."[6] The peasants had feudal obligations to landlords and were forced to serve in the army, where they were poorly fed, rarely paid, and kept in active service beyond the legal period.[7] Cholera epidemics continued until the end of the century.[8] Eighteen percent of the Muslim population in Anatolia died during World War I, from starvation and disease as well as fighting. Two-thirds of the dead were civilians.[9]

These were the circumstances in which the genocide of the Armenians began in 1915. The loss of power, prestige, and influence as a nation and the tremendous life problems within Turkey had to result in powerful feelings of frustration and threat in both the people and the leaders and to give rise to the needs and motives that lead a group to turn against a subgroup of society.

Cultural preconditions

The devaluation of minorities and Christians. Devaluation of the Armenians had several sources. First, the Ottomans devalued and mistreated all their subject peoples. According to Toynbee, the concept of *rajah* (cattle) was applied to them.[10] In 1922 the *Encyclopedia Britannica* described the status of non-Muslims in Turkey the following way:

The non-Mussulman subjects of the Sultan had indeed early been reduced to such a condition of servitude that the idea of their being placed on a footing of equality with their Mussulman rulers seemed unthinkable. Preserved merely as taxpayers necessary to supply the funds for the maintenance of the dominant and military class, according to a foreign observer in 1571, they had been so degraded and oppressed that they dared not look a Turk in the face. Their only value was from a fiscal point of view, and in times of fanaticism or when anti-foreign sentiment ran high even this was held of little account, so that more than once they very nearly became the victims of a general and state-ordered massacre.[11]

Although this statement may have been affected by the genocide of the Armenians, earlier sources are consistent with it.

Subject status and religion coincided. The treatment of non-Muslims was based on the Koran and Ottoman culture. The Koran has many passages prescribing the correct relationship between Muslims and "infidels." The legal rights of *Dimmis* (non-Muslims) were restricted. A Dimmi was allowed to give testimony in court, but the testimony was not weighted as heavily as a Muslim's. When the two testimonies conflicted, the Dimmi's was disregarded.[12] A Muslim who killed a Dimmi would not receive a death penalty; a Dimmi who killed a Muslim would. A male Dimmi could not marry a female Muslim, but a male Muslim could marry a female

Dimmi. For a long time Christians were forbidden to own guns or ride horses; the possession of a gun was a serious crime.[13] They had to pay extra taxes and board migratory Kurdsmen, who beat their hosts, raped their daughters, and looted their property.[14] The Armenians in particular were constant prey. At international conferences they repeatedly requested protection from the violence of Kurds and Circassians.

Religious and cultural devaluation of Christian minorities was thus maintained and strengthened by discrimination and constant mistreatment. After the Balkan wars the Armenians were the only large Christian minority left, a potential target for scapegoating and violence.

Orientation to authority. The Ottoman regime was theocratic. Islam ruled the masses, whose deep respect for authority had a partly religious basis. The sultan was both a worldly and a spiritual leader.[15] The society was still feudal and hierarchical. In 1896 Muray Bey, expressing the views of the Young Turks, held that the population's crime was blind obedience to authorities, although obedience in general is a virtue.[16] In the Young Turk revolution, officers of the army gained the support of common soldiers partly because of unquestioning military obedience and partly by claiming that the sultan was in the hands of bad advisors.[17]

The Ottoman Empire was a monolithic society in which Islam and the Ottoman Turkish values, culture, and power structure held sway. Despite the many ethnic groups and religions, true pluralism did not exist. In 1856–57, a committee of Armenians attempted to redefine the Armenians' rights and responsibilities. Ottoman authorities rejected this and rewrote the Armenian constitution so that it reaffirmed subservience; for example, the election of the Armenian patriarch and of political and religious councils had to be approved by the sultan.[18]

The removal of the sultan and other political changes and upheavals must have added to the many-faceted life problems and intensified the people's need for authority, for a positive self-concept, and a world view that offered guidance and hope.

Steps along the continuum of destruction

Devaluation and increasing mistreatment. In some ways the Turkish image of the Armenians was strikingly similar to the German image of Jews. The two minoritiers had a similar status in society and had developed in similar ways over centuries of persecution. Because of their religious beliefs and a tradition of militarism, the Turks devalued and avoided commerce, finance, and other middle-class occupations. These as well as low- and middle-level administrative positions were open to the Armenians.[19] Foreigners preferred minority group members as trading partners because of their better education, shared religion, and contacts with Europeans. The Armenians were hardworking, capable, and intelligent. Many were successful, and some became wealthy. They became essential for the maintenance of the country. The result was the two-sided devaluation familiar from our discussion of German attitudes toward Jews: Armenians were seen as of low character, as cunning and treacherous, and as parasites, exploiters who plotted against Turks.

Aside from their "unofficial" victimization by Kurds and Circassians, Armenians were also subject to violence directly inspired by the authorities, which intensified under Abdul Hamid. In 1894–96, special troops composed mainly of Kurds, the Hamidaya, massacred over two hundred thousand Armenians in the midst of an apparently approving population.

Abraham Hartunian, an Armenian pastor, who survived both the killings of 1894–96 and the genocide of 1915–16, wrote of the earlier killings:

On Sunday morning, November 3, 1895, the church bells were silent. The churches and schools, desecrated and plundered, lay in ruins. Pastors, priests, choristers, teachers, leaders, all were no more. The Armenian houses, robbed and empty, were as caves. Fifteen hundred men had been slaughtered, and those left alive were wounded and paralyzed. Girls were in the shame of their rape....

On Thursday, November 7, the fifth day of our imprisonment, we were taken out and driven to the courtyard of a large inn. As we moved along in a file under guard, a crowd of Turkish women on the edge of the road, mocking and cursing us like frenzied maenads, screeched the unique convulsive shrill of the zelgid, the ancient battle cry of the women of Islam–the exultant lu-lu-lulu filled with the concentrated hate of the centuries.[20]

Under the Young Turks massacres of the Armenians continued. In Adana in the spring of 1909, about thirty thousand Armenians were killed. Administrative and military officials did not try to stop the massacre, and some of the troops fired on the Armenians. While the Young Turks probably did not initiate the killings, they let the two principal officials of Adana off with light sentences.[21] Dr. Chambers, the director of the American Missionaries at Adana, wrote in a message to London:

A frightful massacre began on April 14; it subsided on the 16th, but it is continued in the suburbs. The following week an organized effort was made to bring help to 15,000 sufferers. The massacre began all over again furiously on the 25 of April, the soldiers and the bashibozouk (irregulars) began a terrible volley of firearms on the Armenian school where around 2,500 persons had taken refuge. Then the building caught fire and when the refugees tried to save themselves by running outside they were fired upon; many perished in the flames. The destructive fire continued until Tuesday morning. Four churches and the adjacent schools were burned as well as hundreds of homes in the most populated quarters of the city.[22]

Armenian "provocation"

Some writers claimed that the genocide was a response to Armenian provocation, to the great threat the Armenians presented to Turkey and the Committee of Union and Progress.[23] The Armenians increasingly resisted repression and violence against them and demanded greater rights and more autonomy. From the middle of the nineteenth century, they repeatedly turned to foreign powers for protection. Russia helped other subject peoples, such as the Bulgarians, in their fight for independence, and its 1877 military action was at least partly on the instigation of Armenians. The Turkish government constantly feared that foreign powers would intervene on behalf of the Armenians or use the Armenians as an excuse for their designs on Turkey. The Armenians were closely linked to Russia (much hated by the Turks as the ancient and current enemy) by their Greek Orthodox religion and, after the Russian conquest of parts of Armenia, by the large population of Armenians in Russia. It was thus easy to associate the loss of power and humiliation by foreigners with the Armenians inside Turkey.

The Armenians attempted to gain increased rights as well as protection as conflicts between them and displaced Muslims moving into Turkey intensified. They organized and formed societies. The government-directed killings in 1894–96 arose partly from the sultan's fear of the "Armenian peril," a result of Armenian "agitation," protests, and demonstrations.[24] Occasional refusal to pay taxes, for what to the Armenians seemed justifiable reasons, also incited anger. One of the events leading up to the massacre of Armenians at Sassoon in 1893 was refusal to pay taxes; they claimed the Kurds forced them to pay and could not pay a second time.[25]

Armenian acts designed to call attention to their plight also resulted in violence. At the time of the large-scale killings under Abdul Hamid, in 1896, a group of Armenians seized the Ottoman Bank in Constantinople and held it until they were guaranteed free passage to Europe. More Armer in massacres followed in Constantinople.[26] Once an intensely negative image of a group develops, its acts of self-assertion or defense will be regarded as evidence of hostility and evil nature.

In 1876 the Young Turk movement sought the cooperation of the Armenians against their common enemy, the sultan, for the "good of the fatherland." The appeal was rejected, and the Young Turks interpreted this as evidence of Armenian aspirations "apart from the welfare of Turkey," which pushed them to "criminal resolution."[27] The role of outside powers was a persistent issue for the Young Turks. Ahmed Riza of the

Young Turks complained that the Turks suffered too under Abdul Hamid, but had no foreign protectors. At the 1902 Congress of Ottoman Liberals, the Armenian delegates and Ahmed Riza's Young Turks were at odds, especially about outside powers ensuring the rights of minorities in the Ottoman Empire.[28]

The conflict continued after the Young Turks came to power and was intensified by the refusal of the Armenian Revolutionary Federation at its meeting in 1914 to organize an insurrection in Russian Armenia if a war was declared. In a book edited by Arnold Toynbee, *The Treatment of the Armenians in the Ottoman Empire, 1915–1916*, this is described as follows:

> At the beginning of the European war, the Dashnaktzoutioun' party met in congress at Erzeroum in order to decide on the attitude to be observed by the Party. As soon as they heard of this congress, the Young Turks sent their representatives to Erzeroum to propose that the Party should declare its intention of aiding and defending Turkey, by organizing an insurrection in the Caucasus in the event of a declaration of war between Turkey and Russia. According to the project of the Young Turks, the Armenians were to pledge themselves to form legions of volunteers and to send them to the Caucasus with Turkish propagandists, to prepare the way there for insurrection.... The Erzeroum Congress refused these proposals, and advised the Young Turks not to hurl themselves into the European conflagration – a dangerous adventure which would lead Turkey to ruin.[29]

In postwar Turkish writings, the Armenians are described as instruments of foreign agitation, tools of the European powers, an avenue for their mingling in the internal affairs of Turkey and for pursuing their designs on the empire.

Did the Armenians represent a dangerous internal enemy? There was some violence by Armenians against Turks in the early part of the First World War, its extent a matter of dispute. According to Turkish writers, as the war started, invading Russian Armenian troops were joined by Turkish Armenian volunteers, killing Turks, with estimates as high as 150,000 to less than 40,000 killed. Apparently, the source of some of these estimates was the unreliable and repeatedly revised claims of the Ottoman government, for example, claims presented to their German allies.[30] Non-Turkish sources claim that participation by Turkish Armenians was very limited. They also claim that uprisings by Turkish Armenians were attempts at self-defense as the genocide began.[31]

An uprising at Van in April 1915 was the immediate justification for the deportations that started in May 1915. The nature of this uprising is also in dispute. Armenian writers minimize its scope. Missakian, for example, claims that it was only a defense of the Armenian quarter of the city when it was attacked by Turkish troops; Turkish troops had massacred Armenians in outlying villages, and the deportations had already started in Cilicia before the fighting broke out in Van.[32] Richard Hovannisian, a leading historian of the genocide, also sees the uprising as defensive. It started after three leaders of the Armenian community were killed and refugees from surrounding villages were coming into Van (personal communication).

Gurun, a Turkish writer, claims that Armenians seized Van and delivered it to the Russians.[33] Turkish writers claim Armenians endangered Turkey through acts of sabotage, defection, spying, and mass uprisings. Their actions made it necessary to deport them "from the neighborhood of the front and from the vicinity of railroads and lines of communications."[34] There was no genocide. Lives were lost during the deportations as were Turkish lives in the war, but much fewer than the number claimed by Armenians.

Justin McCarthy makes singular claims. There was a civil war. "Large elements of the Muslim population in the Kars region of the Russian Empire aided the Ottomans whenever possible, and Armenian activities at the rear of the Ottoman army were a factor in Ottoman defeats."[35]

Other non-Turkish accounts make the claim of a civil war untenable. There were some Turkish Armenian attacks on Turks, but the Armenians gave only limited aid to the Russians and perhaps only after the atrocities against them had begun.

It is certainly possible that the Turks believed that the Armenians represented a serious threat to them. They had long mistrusted Armenians. Armenian males in the army were placed in unarmed batallions – although perhaps already in preparation for genocide. The Armenian unwillingness to cooperate with Turkish designs, however unreasonable they were from an Armenian point of view, conflicted with the evolving ideology and goals of Turkish leaders and what they saw as their long-established right to rule. This occurred when the war was already being lost and the empire was near collapse. Armenian actions before the war threatened nationalistic aspirations; those during the war perhaps generated a belief that the Armenians threatened Turkey's existence.

To sum up, the Armenians were victims of a progression of increasing destructiveness. They were devalued because of their religion and inferior status as a subject people. They were resented because of their financial, commercial, and administrative success. They provoked hostility by their attempts to protect themselves and to gain greater rights and autonomy, and in the end by acts of violence against Turks. Their religion, commercial involvements, and attempts to gain outside support linked them to foreign powers, especially Russia. Armenians were subject to many forms of discrimination, brutality, and murder on increasing scales.

The evolution of Young Turk ideology

The Young Turks began as liberals who promised equality regardless of religion or ethnic background. They favored religious tolerance and freedom of religious practice, self-government in education, and the right of all to private property. Colleges and schools were to be opened to Christians. The word *rajah*, or cattle, used to designate Christians, was to the removed from all public documents.[36]

From the start, however, there was a strong nationalistic element in the Young Turks' movement and a nationalistic component in their ideology. Young Turks wanted to restore the glory of the Ottoman Empire. They hoped to forge a new nationalism that would include other ethnic groups. In 1908 Enver Bey, a Young Turk leader, declared, "We are all equal, we glory in being Ottomans."[37] Ahmed Riza, whose outlook came to dominate the policies of the Young Turks, was a strong nationalist who believed that subject nationalities should be made into good Turks. After the outbreak of the Balkan wars, the Young Turks organized the Committee for National Defense. Its purpose was to encourage popular support for the war effort, substituting national identity for the old Ottoman or Islamic identity.[38]

From the start, despite their liberalism, the Young Turks were insistent on Muslim and Turkish supremacy. They feared non-Muslim supremacy in parliament and manipulated elections to ensure a Muslim majority. They believed, probably correctly, that only the Muslim element would work to maintain the empire's integrity.[39] To ensure their dominance the Young Turks were ready to use power ruthlessly. According to some, they brutalized political life. They successfully mobilized the people, held mass meetings, and organized effective boycotts of foreign goods.[40]

The Congress of the Committee for Union and Progress met in Saloniki in October 1911 and proclaimed a nationalistic pan-Islamic program. "The sole reign of the Turkish race and the construction of the Empire on a purely Islamic basis" became the program of the government according to the German doctor Johannes Lepsius, president of the German-Armenian Society.

Sooner or later the total Islamization of all Turkish subjects must be accomplished, but it is clear that this can never be achieved by verbal persuasion, therefore the power of arms must be resorted to. The character of the Empire will have to be Mohammedan, and respect for Mohammedan institutions and traditions is to be enforced. Other nations must be denied the right to organize because decentralization and self-government would constitute treason against the Turkish Empire. The nationalities will become a negligible quantity. They could keep their religion, but not their language. The proliferation of the Turkish language would be a principal means to secure Mohammedan predominance and to assimilate the remaining elements.[41]

New visions set new goals: the creation of a single pure and homogeneous Turkic culture and an empire that would unite all the Turkic peoples, a worthy successor to the late Ottoman Empire.[42] The Young Turks feared that the Armenians might succeed in creating an independent state in eastern Anatolia, which would form a barrier between the Ottoman Turks and Turkic people to the east and destroy the possibility of the new empire.[43] Greater Turkishness, a national-cultural purity, and the creation of a new empire were to reestablish a feeling of unity and positive identity in Turks, including the Young Turk leaders themselves.

The machinery of destruction

As in Germany, preparations that initially served other purposes later came to function as part of the machinery of genocide. The Young Turks set up a party apparatus whose leaders in the Armenian regions became organizers of the genocide. The genocide was under the control of the Interior Ministry, led by Talat, and its subsidiaries, the Directorate of Public Security, the Istanbul police, and the Deportation Service, as well as the provincial gendarmerie. Turkish refugees from emancipated Balkan countries were also active. At the time of the genocide, a special organization was created to massacre the Armenians deported in convoys. It consisted of jailed criminals who were freed, organized into detachments, and placed, together with other suitable groups such as Kurds, in the path of Armenians on the deportation march.[44] Executive officers of cities were instructed to evacuate Armenians along designated routes, guarded by military police.

The genocide

A group of political activists had gained power in Turkey. Within a few years their hopes and visions were profoundly frustrated by losses of wars and territories and by all the hardships and internal conflicts inside Turkey, including Armenian opposition and actions. In response to these conditions, their nationalistic ideology became more extreme. The Young Turks could at least in part deal with their intense frustrations, with the experience of threat and attack, and the resulting needs and motives by turning against the Armenians, one of the few enemies they could defeat. Genocide was not intrinsically tied to ideology, as it was in Germany. But it was a way – maybe the only one available at the time – to fulfill both ideological goals and emotional needs.

The Turkish population adopted the nationalistic fervor, and shared with its leaders the complex of motives and lack of prohibitions that I have previously described as reasons why a society turns against a subgroup. Those selected to perpetrate the genocide were willing, and the rest of society gave its support. A telegram to Jemal Bey, a delegate at Adana, said that it was the duty of all to realize the noble project of "wiping out of existence the Armenians who have for centuries been constituting a barrier to the Empire's progress in civilization."[45] As in the Holocaust, the killings were meant to realize a "higher" value.

It is known that specific orders for genocide were given by the government. The evidence comes from telegrams captured by the British and from accounts by foreign observers, including a detailed account by the U.S. ambassador to Turkey, Henry Morgenthau.[46] A frequently quoted "memoir" was published in London in 1920 by Naim Bey, the chief secretary of the Aleppo committee in charge of deported Armenians.*[48] Another memoir, by Merlanzade Rifat, a Young Turk on the committee's Central Board, described the meeting at which the extermination policy was decided.[49] Rifat's account shows that the leadership meant to revitalize Turkey by purging it of non-Turkish nationalities, especially Armenians. The war provided the opportunity to exterminate them.

The Naim-Andonian documents outline a "radical solution" to the lingering Turko-Armenian conflict. They contain no reference to the wartime conduct of the Armenian populations, but refer to "the humiliations and bitterness of the past."[50] Morgenthau notes that Talat referred to the policy as the result of prolonged and careful deliberation. The documents show secret orders from various ministers. All Armenians were to be killed and

---

* In recent years questions have been raised about the authenticity of the Naim "memoirs" – in reality not memoirs but fifty-two pieces purported to be documents, two letters, and fifty decoded cipher telegrams, with Naim's annotations explaining the individual items. There are also interspersed comments by Aram Andonian, the Armenian who received the material from Naim and compiled it. Vakahn Dadrian examines the question of forgery and the factual errors contained in the documents but concludes that the errors can be explained and the material can be authenticated in many ways. Their validity is supported by the official and mostly secret reports of German and Austrian diplomats to their government, allied to Ottoman Turkey; by information that surfaced at the time of Turkish court-martial proceedings in 1919–20 that tried Young Turk leaders for their conduct of the war and the policy of extermination; by the German consul at Aleppo, Rossler, whose district was in the center of events described in the documents and who read the French translation and judged the documents seemingly genuine. While they are important, these documents are only one source of information about the genocide in Turkey.[47]

the responsibility fully assumed by the government. The designated officials are assured that they will not be held accountable. Officials who stall are threatened with sanctions. Some telegrams exhort functionaries to show no mercy to women, children, or the sick and to dispose of Armenian orphans who were retained by Muslim families.[51]

First the leaders of the Armenians and the men in the labor battalions were killed.[52] Then the rest were marched into the desert without supplies. Many died along the way, and many were killed. Armin T. Wegner, a German eyewitness, wrote to President Wilson:

"And so they drove the whole people – men, women, hoary elders, children, expectant mothers and dumb sucklings – into the Arabic desert, with no other object than to let them starve to death."

"...They drove the people, after depriving them of their leaders and spokesmen, out of the towns at all hours of the day and night, half-naked, straight out of their beds; plundered their houses, burned the villages, destroyed the churches or turned them into mosques, carried off the cattle, seized the vehicles, snatched the bread out of the mouths of their victims, tore the clothes from off their backs, the gold from their hair. Officials – military officers, soldiers, shepherds – vied with one another in their wild orgy of blood, dragging out of the schools delicate orphan girls to serve their bestial lusts, beat with cudgels dying women or women close on childbirth who could scarcely drag themselves along, until the women fell down on the road and died....

"Parties which on their departure from the homeland of High Armenia consisted of thousands, numbered on their arrival in the outskirts of Aleppo only a few hundred, while the fields were strewed with swollen, blackened corpses...."

"Even before the gates of Aleppo they were not allowed to rest...the shrunken parties were ceaselessly driven barefooted, hundreds of miles under the burning sun, through stony defiles, over pathless steppes, enfeebled by fever and other maladies, through semi-tropical marshes, into the wilderness of desolation. Here they died – slain by Kurds, robbed by gendarmes, shot, hanged, poisoned, frozen, parched with thirst, starved."

"...I have seen maddened deportees eating as food their own clothes and shoes – women cooking the bodies of their new-born babes."[53]

Like the German Holocaust, the genocide was self-destructive. Turkey deprived itself of a large portion of its professional and administrative class. Resources badly needed for war were diverted. Killing and removing Armenians resulted in a lack of support personnel that made the 1916 Russian invasion of Turkish Armenia easier. Count Metternich, a German official, noted that the Turkish government seemed almost bent on losing the war.[54]

The role of bystanders

In 1876 Turkey put down a Bulgarian revolt with indiscriminate massacres. In England there was a strong public reaction led by Gladstone, then in the Opposition. He said that the evidence of atrocities "makes the responsibility of silence...too great to be borne."

An old servant of the Crown and State, I entreat my countrymen, upon whom far more than perhaps any other people of Europe it depends, to require, and to insist, that our Government, which has been working in one direction, shall work in the other, and shall apply all its vigour and concur with the other states of Europe in obtaining the extinction of the Turkish executive power in Bulgaria; let the Turks carry away their abuses in the only possible manner, namely by carrying themselves off.[55]

However, Great Britain's policymakers feared Czarist Russia and therefore courted Turkey.[56] Realpolitik won out over moral or humane considerations. British (and world) indignation was not brought to bear on Turkey.

European nations also passively accepted the great massacres under Abdul Hamid. At the time of the massacres Kaiser Wilhelm of Germany visited Constantinople, publicly embracing the sultan. Massacres of Russian Armenians during the Russian revolution of 1905 also made killing Armenians more acceptable. The German atrocities in Belgium early in the war had a similar effect.

During the war Turkey was heavily dependent on Germany, which gave it tacit support in suppressing Armenian opposition. Count Ernst von Reventlow wrote in the *Deutcher Tageszeitung*:

If the Porte considers it necessary that Armenian insurrections and other goings on should be crushed by every means available, so as to exclude all possibility of their repetition, then that is no "murder" and "atrocity" but simply measures of a justifiable and necessary kind.[57]

Germany was the only nation in a position to exert influence on Turkey, but the German government never responded to invitations by the United States and other governments to cooperate in efforts to end the genocide. In the view of one Armenian writer:

It is clear that, whoever commanded the atrocities, the Germans never made a motion to countermand them, when they could have stopped it at the start by a single word...by entering the war, Turkey placed herself entirely in Germany's power. She is dependent on Germany for munitions of war and leadership in battle, for the preservation of her existence at the present and for its continuance in the future, should Germany succeed in preserving it now. The German Government had but to pronounce the veto, and it would have been obeyed; and the central authorities at Berlin could have ensured its being obeyed through their local agents on the spot. For ever since 1895, Germany has been assiduously extending the network of her consular service over all the Asiatic provinces of the Ottoman Empire. In every administrative centre throughout those districts where massacres and deportations have occurred – in Anatolia, Cilicia, and Armenia proper – there is a German consul; and the prestige of these consuls is unbounded.

They are the agents of a friendly power, the only power that offers Turkey her friendship with no moral conditions attached.[58]

The capacity of Germany to halt the genocide is probably overestimated here. Once an intense motivation to kill becomes dominant and gains expression in action, suppressing it is not easy. But Germany did not try.[59]

Ulrich Trumpener argues that German diplomats and military officials had little capacity to influence the internal policies of Turkey, whether to promote German financial and economic interests or with regard to the treatment of the Armenians.[60] But he also indicates that Germany, intent on keeping the Turkish army fighting, was reluctant to do anything "drastic" about the atrocities. The German ambassador refused to consider extending German protection to the Armenians. As it became evident that the extermination was in progress, the ambassador informed his government, which took no action and sent him no policy directive. His own protests of actions against Armenians not "dictated by military reasons" were ignored by the Ottoman government.[61] The German government showed no concern about the victims, but did show an interest in preparing a defense against possible charges of complicity.

In the early stages the Germans did believe that there was an Armenian insurrection. Later they realized the true nature of events but continued to use insurrection as a justification. The German ambassador in Washington, once the atrocities became difficult to deny, defended them on the grounds that "the Armenians were disloyal and secretly aided Russia."[62]

Just-world thinking, the devaluation of victims, fear of alienating their ally and a tendency to adopt its attitude, a focus on their own concerns in the midst of the war, and perhaps their own attitudes toward minorities all contributed to German passivity. An article in the *Frankfurter Zeitung* in October 9, 1915, reveals part of the German attitude.

"The Armenian...enjoys, through his higher intellect and superior commercial ability, a constant business advantage in trade, tax-farming, banking, and commission-agency over the heavy-footed Turk, and so accumulates money in his pocket, while the Turk grows poor. That is why the Armenian is the best-hated man in the East – in many cases not unjustly, though a generalization would be unfair.[63]

Dr. Johannes Lepsius went to Armenia to see, to protest, and also to aid Armenians, which was not allowed by the Ottoman government. Upon his return to Germany, his description of events in Turkey was criticized as exaggerated, even by liberal politicians.

Germany's behavior with respect to Turkey during the First World War may have been one element that paved the way for the Holocaust. The Armenian genocide helped shape German attitudes toward violence against "internal enemies." The quiet acceptance by the rest of the world also contributed. Even after Turkey lost the war, and despite new massacres of Armenians in 1922, little was done to punish Turkey or individual Turks. Hitler could later jsutifiably say, "Who remembers now the massacres of the Armenians?"*[64]

* After the military trials, Turkey reversed course and has ever since denied the atrocities. The reasons for this probably include psychological defenses (denial in the psychological sense, rationalizations, and justifications), fear of Armenian claims for reparations, and the unrealistic fear of an Armenian attempt to establish an independent state. Such denial is potentially very harmful. A society not facing up to atrocities it committed and not dealing with its own inhumanity is likely to continue or repeat such actions. In Turkey, interference with the cultural life of the Armenians, discrimination, and economic pressure have continued. Complicity by others contributes to the possibility of denial: for example, the U.S. State Department, apparently influenced by U.S. national interests in Turkey, decided in 1982 that the evidence of the Turkish genocide or atrocities was unclear. Later, Congress reasserted the earlier U.S. view recognizing that a genocide had taken place.[65]

13 Cambodia: genocide to create a better world

The killing of perhaps two million people in Cambodia was an example of human cruelty perpetrated to fulfill a vision of a better world. God made the Jews wander in the wilderness for forty years so that only a new generation, with souls uncontaminated by slavery in Egypt, would reach the promised land. The Cambodian communist leaders did not have the patience of God. They set out to create a radically new society immediately. Anyone bound to the old ways by their former status or present behavior was to die, to make this better world possible. In the resulting climate of violence and suspicion, many of the communists themselves were killed.

Historical (life) conditions

One popular view depicted Cambodia as a jungle paradise, filled with peaceful, gentle people, until the civil war that brought the Khmer Rouge into power. In this view the people were poor but contented; their Buddhism was a source of their inner peace, and the land was bountiful. Not only French colonials, but even the Cambodian elite saw the Cambodian peasantry this way. It was an image actively propagated by the Cambodian leader Prince Norodom Sihanouk after the country gained independence from the French in 1954.

For Sihanouk and others this image may have served to fend off discontent. While there were elements of truth in it, it was far from accurate or complete. For centuries Cambodia had been invaded and at times brutally ruled by outsiders – for example, by the Vietnamese in the first part of the nineteenth century. It was ruled by the French (through a protectorate) from 1863 to 1954. The peasants had always been heavily taxed.[1] After independence their economic condition deteriorated until the civil war started in 1970.

Cambodian peasants: economic conditions, uprising, reprisals

After World War II there was a population explosion. The acreage of arable land declined and the number of large landholdings grew.[2] While

188

a few had more land, many had less. After independence, many peasants were forced off their land and drifted into the cities, rootless and destitute.[3] The number of rich peasants grew from about 6 percent to 14 percent of the population; they rented land to the landless poor. The number of peasants in debt increased, with annual interest rates as high as 100 percent to 200 percent. Much of this indebtedness was to Vietnamese and Chinese who owned commercial institutions.[4]

The shrinkage of average landholdings combined with the increase in population led to food shortages and a general decline in living standards. Food prices rose about 350 percent from 1950 to 1970. A peasant uprising began in 1967–68 in the Samlaut region, and disturbances later spread to cities and other provinces. The immediate cause of the uprising may have been government land expropriations for a sugar refinery; aggressive tax collecting; or an influx of Khmer refugees from the war in Vietnam settled by the government on land the peasants regarded as communal property.[5]

Peasants in Samlaut killed two members of a tax-collecting detachment, attacked a garrison, and carried away its arms. Prime Minister Lon Nol, the leader of the government in the absence of the head of state, Sihanouk, responded by sending the national police to pacify the region, mainly by killing peasants. Two communists then in the government, Khieu Samphan and Hou Youn, were accused by the returning Sihanouk of complicity with the uprising and went underground. It was widely believed that the government had murdered them and fifteen thousand people demonstrated in Phnom Penh.

The next day Sihanouk declared a state of emergency. Army troops assisted by local peasants armed with clubs combed areas of the uprising to crush actual and potential unrest. In a 1972 interview Sihanouk said that he had "read somewhere that 10,000 died" at this time, but insisted that his intervention had restored peace and order.[6]

The uprising indicated, and together with the harsh reprisals enlarged, the growing cleavage between the government and the people. It led Khieu Samphan and Hou Youn to give up their attempt to work within the system. They were associates of Pol Pot and members of the group that later became the architect of genocide.

Political instability and violence

Prince Sihanouk, Cambodia's king under French colonial rule, demoted himself so that he could participate in party politics after independence, and ruled until 1970. He came to believe in the 1960s that ultimately the communists would rule most of Southeast Asia. He followed policies that may have been pragmatic under the confused conditions in Southeast Asia, but seemed opportunistic and inconsistent. He brutally repressed communist activities within Cambodia, but offered some support to communists outside Cambodia. He first permitted the North Vietnamese and Vietcong to use sanctuaries in the border regions of Cambodia, but later tried to curb their activities and their use of Cambodia as a supply route. He both protested against the U.S. bombing of Cambodia and secretly asked for U.S. bombing of North Vietnamese troops in Cambodia.*[7]

Sihanouk's vacillating policies alienated elements of the ruling class, especially his indulgence of the Vietnamese, Cambodia's ancient enemies, which was even objectionable to many Cambodian communists. Mainly because of his compromises with the Vietnamese communists, he was overthrown in 1970 by the general and then prime minister Lon Nol. After that, the conflict with the communists turned into a full civil war.

Government corruption was rampant during this conflict. Food sent by the United States was sold by corrupt officials on the black market. Arms sent by the United States were sold by corrupt officers to the Khmer Rouge. This was consistent with Cambodian cultural experience; a high political position was seen as an opportunity to sell privileges.[8] As the population fled from violence in the countryside and Khmer Rouge occupation, the population of Phnom Penh increased from six hundred thousand to nearly three million. Starvation was widespread; medicine and other essentials were totally inadequate.

The Khmer Rouge started the guerrilla war in 1968, at about the same time U.S. bombing began. Between 1970 and 1973, the United States dropped three times the tonnage of bombs on Cambodia that it had dropped on Japan during all of World War II. The bombing began in the border areas that served as a sanctuary for Vietnamese fighting in Vietnam, but was extended to the increasingly large areas under the control of Cambodian communists.[9] In 1973, much of the bombing occurred in the most heavily populated areas of the country. This sustained, intense bombing killed many thousands of people, disrupted communities, and created many refugees. It had profound effects on the people's feelings about their

---

* Sihanouk vacillated in his relationship to the United States; for example, at times he accepted, at other times rejected, aid. This is understandable because he had great need of U.S. economic help but also justifiably mistrusted the U.S. government. Sihanouk was convinced, correctly, that the United States had backed a plot to overthrow him in 1959. He immediately blamed the United States for the November 1963 assassination of Diem, the leader of South Vietnam; he condemned the act as criminal and rejected all U.S. aid to Cambodia.

government, whose ally was the perpetrator. Communist recruitment became easier.

Meanwhile, in 1970, the U.S. and South Vietnamese armies invaded Cambodia, pushing the North Vietnamese and their Khmer Rouge allies further into the interior. Lon Nol, especially after he gained power, expounded a nationalistic, racist view of Khmer superority, intensely hostile to Vietnam.[10] His government instigated punitive actions against Vietnamese living in Cambodia. They were murdered, raped, their properties seized. The invading South Vietnamese army countered Lon Nol's policies by confiscating Khmer property, which they gave to victimized Vietnamese families.[11]

The fighting between government troops and the growing army of the Khmer Rouge spread all over the country. In the increasingly large area occupied by the Khmer Rouge, the lives of the people were completely disrupted. Some were killed or forced into reeducation camps. Others were driven out of their villages to start new lives elsewhere, as part of the communist program of radical change. The social structure was profoundly changed, and many traditional practices were prohibited. The actions of the communists in at least parts of the occupied areas presaged their later policies, even the mass killings. The combination of terror and rewards for prescribed behavior resulted in substantial compliance. Until they gained final control, the communists balanced force with maintaining certain traditions and playing on the people's loyalties.

In sum, life conditions in Cambodia were increasingly difficult before 1970, and difficulties intensified greatly after 1970. Because of the historical role of the ruler and his own long rule, Sihanouk's ouster had great psychological impact on Cambodian peasants, especially when combined with loss of homes and livelihood, social disorganization, and constant violence. The results were, as usual, feelings of hostility and needs for defense of the physical and psychological self, renewed comprehension of reality, guidance, and connection to others. All this prepared Cambodian peasants to accept the Khmer Rouge and subordinate themselves to new leaders.

The Khmer Rouge rule and autogenocide

On April 17, 1975, the Khmer Rouge occupied Phnom Penh. According to some reports they were greeted warmly by a population tired of war.[12] They proceeded to evacuate the city, killing on the spot some who did not follow orders and driving others from their homes and even from hospital beds. Many died on the way out of the city. With three million people leaving at once, congestion was tremendous and progress very slow. Food was in short supply and temperatures in the 100s. People had to drink from roadside puddles, wells, and rivers, which were contaminated by corpses and excrement. They died of starvation, dehydration, and illness.[13]

There were several reasons for the evacuation of the cities. One was fear and suspicion of enemies, who were believed to be everywhere, threatening the rather small Khmer Army (party membership was only fourteen thousand people).[14] In addition, the Khmer Rouge considered the cities evil. Some classes of city people, especially military officers, were regarded as traitors and were killed. Professionals and intellectuals were also regarded as enemies. Although there was no plan to kill all such people, many were killed; only those survived who faithfully and completely followed the rules, dictates, and ideals of the new society.

People sent to the country had to work with their own hands in the fields. These "new" people were not granted even the few privileges of the "old" people, the original peasants who were at first allowed to retain their land and animals. The new people were allowed no private property and had to work extremely hard, ten hours a day and often added hours at night, with limited food rations. Many of them starved. There was enough food in the forest for sustenance but the new people were forbidden to supplement their meager diets by foraging. Disease was rampant; medical care poor. In 1976, an estimated 80 percent of the population suffered from malaria.

With little or no experience of farming and entirely without help, the new people were to establish communities, under the most stringent rules. Even if villages emptied by the war were near the places where they were sent to settle, they were forced to start from scratch. At times the area proved unproductive and they had to move and start all over again.[15]

After they evacuated Phnom Penh and other cities, the communists began exterminating the officers of Lon Nol's army. Many were instructed to put on their dress uniforms, ostensibly to greet Prince Sihanouk returning to Cambodia. Driven by trucks to the countryside, they were ordered to disembark and killed by machine-gun fire or marched into mine fields. At first sporadically but later more systematically, the Khmer Rouge also killed teachers, doctors, technicians, and intellectuals, individually or in groups. "Traitors" were executed by a blow from an axe handle to the back of the neck. Family members were forced to watch as their husbands, sons, and daughters were killed. They killed Buddhist monks and, guided by nationalism, members of ethnic minorities. People who deviated from communist rules or showed evidence of city ways might be executed.

Discipline, however, was extremely strict, and minor infractions could be punished with extreme severity. The most important criterion of survivability was to adopt entirely the demeanor of a poor peasant; and a former city intellectual who would not be bothered if he acted like a peasant and worked hard, might well be executed if he showed the least hint of his former class superiority.[16]

Killings also occurred in reeducation and interrogation centers. In the infamous Tuol Sleng, many communist government, party, and military personnel were tortured and killed – victims of purification and power struggles. They were forced to write and rewrite elaborate confessions before they were killed. Records suggest that about twenty thousand people were killed at Tuol Sleng.

Expressions of love, courting, sex before marriage, and adultery were strictly forbidden. Childen "educated" by the government spied on their parents and neighbors. The system broke up the extended family; it is uncertain whether it intended to break up and destroy nuclear families.[17]

The most common estimate is that nearly two million people were killed or died from starvation and disease under communist rule. The aim was to kill all actual or potential enemies, everyone who could not adopt the world view and way of life required in the new state. Some of the killing was seemingly casual, perhaps intended to terrorize the population and stifle resistance. Later, executions for transgressing rules became the normal operating procedure in certain places.

Ideological bias and reports and views of atrocities

Some of the reactions to events in Cambodia were guided by ideology. In an early report, Hildebrand and Porter describe the evacuation of Phnom Penh as necessary because of hunger and overcrowding. They present a positive image of the new regime and discount unfavorable news.[18] They also blame the United States for starvation in Phnom Penh before the Khmer Rouge conquest and for conditions in Cambodia in general. (They are partly right; apart from military intervention and bombing, the United States had supplied military aid but not food while Phnom Penh was starving.) Hildebrand and Porter uncritically celebrate "Democratic Kampuchea."

Michael Vickery provides valuable information and insights despite his bias in favor of communist revolution.[19] He discusses what he regards as the prejudiced nature of most early reports about the system and its atrocities. He notes specific inaccuracies of many kinds; for example, the evacuation of Phnom Penh may have been less hurried and more humane than at first reported, and not all doctors, intellectuals, and skilled workers were killed. Vickery blames inaccurate reporting on ideological bias and sensation-seeking and on the fact that refugees in Thailand, who were the only available source of information, were largely people with a stake in the overthrown system. Vickery argues that these people could not be trusted and, in the process, shifts the blame to the victims. He writes:

These were the people – spoiled, pretentious, contentious, status-conscious at worst, or at best simply soft, intriguing, addicted to city comforts and despising peasant life – who faced the communist exodus order on 17 April 1975. For them the mere fact of leaving an urban existence with its foreign orientation and un-realistic expectations to return to the land would have been a horror, and a horror compounded by their position on the receiving end of orders issued by illiterate peasants. On the whole they cared little or nothing for the problems of the "other half" of their countrymen, and would have been quite content to have all the rural rebels bombed away by American planes. Even having seen the damage done to the country during the war they seem to exclude it from their thoughts, almost never mention it unless asked, and then seem astonished that anyone would take interest in what happened in the rural areas before they arrived there in 1975.[20]

Only in passing does Vickery report, in a footnote, that most of these "city people" were in fact recent refugees from the countryside, former pea-sants. Moreover, being "soft," "spoiled," or "intriguing" hardly justifies murder. Despite his bias, Vickery's account of the nature and extent of atrocities is very similar to other accounts.

However, he points out variations in the level of atrocities in different provinces, under the rule of different leaders, and at different times. For example, after the initial killings, murders and executions became rare in 1975 and 1976, and then commonplace in 1977 and 1978. These variations were associated with struggles among the leadership. Pol Pot and his group were highly influential in the central government from the start, but the leadership in some of the provinces opposed them. Pol Pot lost his position as prime minister from June to October 1975, and the regime was milder during that time. After that, his faction consolidated its power and the severity of the system increased.

Ideology, world view, and the aims of the Khmer Rouge

The major tenets of the Khmer Rouge ideology were to create a society organized around the soil, a peasant society in which life was to be com-munal. Neither private property, knowledge, nor pleasures were to dif-ferentiate people or separate the individual from the community. Social leveling was one aim of the evacuation of cities. Life was to be simple and ascetic. Everyone was to have the status of a simple peasant.

Policies and actions expressing the ideology and world view of the Pol Pot group, other than those already described, included the establishment of communal dining and the elimination of education, except for early pri-mary grade schooling in some areas. The young received ideological indoctrination. The communists also tried to establish a purely barter economy. People were supposed to despise wealth and money. Upon their victory in Phnom Penh, the communist troops destroyed money.

Technology was mistrusted and destroyed, except for some factories producing goods deemed absolutely essential, mainly for agriculture. Strong nationalism and an emphasis on national self-reliance were part of the ideology. One reason for this emphasis was mistrust. The Pol Pot group mistrusted everyone: the people, especially the "new" people; communists with a background or beliefs different from their own; and other countries, especially Vietnam. Their suspicion and fear were one reason for the killings. Those killed after October 1976 included many old-time communists, especially those who spent periods of time in Hanoi and were suspected of Vietnamese sympathies.

The scope of intended change was enormous. "Its designs penetrated beyond the reorganization of political and economic institutions, social relations and kinship systems, and into the very seat of human consciousness itself. This was genuine totalitarianism . . . .The aim was to transform the grammar of thought within the culture."[21] The sources of this fanatical ideology were (1) certain characteristics of Cambodian culture, (2) personal experiences of Pol Pot and his associates, (3) ideas within the communist movement and the example of communist states, and (4) changes that resulted from learning by doing and from the political and social consequences of the Pol Pot group's actions.

The genocidal ideology was created by a small group of people. Given the assumption stated early in the book that there will often be some individuals who evolve deviant and destructive ideologies, important questions are how did they gain followers and how did their followers become the perpetrators of their genocidal ideals?

Cultural preconditions: the roots of ideology and genocide

The Cambodian genocide had many cultural and historical roots or building blocks. This is especially so if we look far enough back in time. David Chandler described substantial continuity from the sixteenth to the nineteenth century in many Cambodian practices and customs, such as clothing, ceremonies, and the worship of the king.[22] In spite of nineteenth- and twentieth-century societal upheavals, many of these cultural elements persisted.

Class divisions, urban–rural rift, and slavery. Cambodia was a country with deep class divisions. The king was an object of devotion for the people. However, the country was actually ruled by a rich oligarchy that controlled the land and taxed the peasants. The aristocracy expressed its devaluation of the common people by using such names for specific individuals as "stinking brute," "detestable," and "dog."[23] A related division was the rift between cities and countryside. In many regions the peasantry was isolated, hostile to everything urban, and in certain areas restless and dissatisfied long before 1970.[24]

The cities were small; Phnom Penh, the largest, had substantially fewer than one hundred thousand inhabitants at the end of World War II. To the peasants, city dwellers were officials who enforced rules, landlords who controlled the land, and owners of financial and commercial enterprises (often foreigners) to whom the peasants were indebted. The results of long-term resentment can be seen in the practice under Pol Pot of having people turn up "the palm of the hand – roughened, it saved – if not it was death."[25] Vickery reports that he heard a similar story in 1962 from an urban schoolteacher who was stopped by Issarak while traveling on a bus in 1952. The Issarak ("free") were anti-French groups and antiroyalist freedom fighters active between 1946 and 1954. He survived only because he sat in the back and security forces arrived before the Issarak reached him. The others with smooth palms were taken away. The violence preceding 1975 – the U.S. bombing, the invasion, and the revolutionary war – affected the countryside most, and this intensified peasant hostility toward city dwellers.

The treatment of the new people under Pol Pot had specific cultural origins as well. They were treated as slaves, without any rights. Slavery had a long history in Cambodia. According to the report of a Chinese envoy in 1296–97, the majority of the people in Angkor, the capital city of the Angkor empire, were slaves. There were three classes of slaves, one of them hereditary. Six hundred years later, in the 1850s, the French discovered the Angkor complex and found a prosperous Buddhist monastery tended by over a thousand hereditary slaves. The French attempted to eliminate slavery in the second half of the nineteenth century, but at first found the institution so deeply rooted that they allowed it to continue. It was outlawed only at the beginning of this century.[26] In addition to its other uses, slavery was regarded as a means of civilizing people such as "wild" mountain tribes.

The new people were forced to work the land and to build elaborate irrigation systems. The Cambodian kings too had used forced labor in extensive building programs, which often included irrigation systems and reservoirs. David Chandler notes that the only feature of Cambodian life singled out for praise by the Pol Pot system was the mobilization of the people by King Jayavarman VII, late in the twelfth century, to build temples, hospitals (maintanence and food supplied by slaves), reservoirs, and rest houses for travelers. Like the Khmer Rouge, this king stated as a central motive for his policies compassion for the people and the desire to deliver them from pain. Forcing hundreds of thousands of people to build his structures could serve compassion in his mind because building a city and temples to honor the Buddha "assured workers of less suffering and greater happiness – but in another life."[27]

Thus class divisions and the urban–rural rift were sources of devaluation of the wealthy and educated that helped the Khmer Rouge gain followers, and the Cambodian history of slavery and forced labor provided a cultural blueprint for their policies.

Orientation to authority. The authoritarian-hierarchical character of Cambodian society was probably one source of the totalitarian system created by the Pol Pot regime. A Portuguese missionary who was in Cambodia in 1556 wrote that the people

dare do nothing of themselves, nor accept anything new without leave of the king, which is why Christians cannot be made without the king's approval. And if some of my readers should say that they could be converted without the king knowing it, to this I answer that the people of the country is of such a nature, that nothing is done that the king knoweth not; and anybody, be he ever so simple may speak with the king, wherefore everyone seeketh news to carry unto him, to have an occasion for to speak with him; whereby without the king's good will nothing can be done.[28]

Ever since the great empire of Angkor (ninth to fourteenth century), the king had been elevated to the rank of a god. The tremendous temples of Angkor Wat served the cult of the divine king.[29] Although the actual power of the king diminished greatly under the French protectorate, his symbolic power probably increased. As the French eliminated princely offices, the king became the sole center of the nation. The people repeatedly demonstrated their tremendous devotion to him during French rule. Disrespect shown to the king by the French was one cause of an uprising that occurred in 1884. In January 1916 dissatisfied peasants came to Phnom Penh to petition the king or merely to see and talk to him, until thirty thousand of them were in the capital.[30]

The king's authority over the aristocracy resided in his capacity to assign titles, roles in the government, and authority over land cultivated by the peasants that entitled them to a share of the crop. Wealth was not inherited; it was returned to the king when the owner died. Possessions, land, and rank were all held at the king's pleasure. Offenses against the king were strictly punished, for example, by stripping the offender of his possessions. The authority of the king over the peasants was also maintained by superstitions, such as the belief that he controlled rainfall. The role of the king in Cambodian society provided a cultural blueprint for absolute authority and made it easier for people to accept the absolute authority of the Khmer Rouge.

Sihanouk became king in 1941. After the country gained independence, he abdicated, was elected prime minister, and continued to rule. For the common people he continued to fulfill the role of king, providing a source of authority and guidance, representing a way of life, and helping them maintain a world view and an understanding of the world and their own place in it. The peasantry's devotion to him was great. Under the difficult conditions of life the need for such a figure would have intensified.

Socialization in the home and schools stressed authority. Until recently Cambodian schoolchildren memorized a collection of informal laws, the *chbab*, which clearly delineated conduct. Social status determined conduct; for example, the status of a speaker in relation to the person addressed determined the mode of address.

The ideology of antagonism toward Vietnam. Among the Khmer Rouge's many irrational policies, the most self-destructive was its provocation of Vietnam, such as border attacks in which soldiers raided inside Vietnam, a country with ten times Cambodia's population and a powerful army.

Hatred of the Vietnamese had a long history and was shared by people across the political spectrum, except for communists who worked with the Vietnamese after World War II. Although the Pol Pot group also worked with Vietnamese communists until about 1973, for them it was only a marriage of convenience. Once they gained power most members of the party who had been associated with Vietnam were killed.

There was a long history of conflict between Cambodia and Vietnam. In the 1620s the Vietnamese moved south to the Mekong Delta (now part of southern Vietnam), pushing back the Khmer people living there. Subsequently, Vietnam invaded Cambodia and supported dissenting elements within Cambodia. In the 1830s and 1840s the Vietnamese occupied Cambodia, substituting Vietnamese for Cambodian provincial administration. They ruled brutally, desecrated pagodas, persecuted monks, and rendered the royal family powerless. Osborne wrote in 1969: "It is difficult to exaggerate the searing effect of the Vietnamese occupation. . . . the Vietnamese struck at the vital roots of the Khmer state."[31]

He described Vietnam and Cambodia as two cultures in irreconcilable conflict. In the 1860s the Cambodian king, Ang Duong, asking for French help, referred to the Vietnamese as traditional enemies. The main reason

Cambodia accepted the French protectorate was a wish to be protected from Vietnam. One reason for Sihanouk's overthrow was his apparent support for Vietnam in the war. Upon gaining power Lon Nol expressed intense anti-Vietnamese sentiments, insisting that the Vietnamese were racially inferior to Cambodians. His rise to power was followed by murderous attacks on Vietnamese in Cambodia. In 1970 Pol Pot described Vietnam as the traditional enemy.

Cultural devaluation can be directed at another nation as well as a subgroup of society. An ideology of antagonism (see Chapter 16) may evolve, a way of thinking that represents the other (accurately or inaccurately) as an extreme threat and gives rise to the motivation to diminish or overcome or even exterminate the other. Such an ideology of antagonism motivated the actions of the Khmer Rouge toward Vietnam.

Cultural self-concept. The Khmer Rouge had a sense of superiority, combined with underlying feelings of inferiority and vulnerability. This arose from a combination of long past glory, recent history, and present circumstances.

Cambodia had once been a great and powerful empire. Angkor was rich and had conquered large territories. According to some writers its wealth was due to highly advanced agricultural techniques, especially irrigation systems that increased rice-growing capacity.[32] A symbol of this past greatness was Angkor Wat, a magnificent complex of temples and other buildings. The French enlarged the memory of past greatness by beginning the restoration of Angkor Wat and writing the history of the empire that created it. According to one writer, "By the time their work was halted in the 1960s, the French had proved the Khmers ranked with the Romans and Greeks as unrivaled artists and innovators of the ancient world."[33] Each of Cambodia's four national flags since 1970 "has featured a stylized representation of Ankor Wat's three towers."[34]

Pol Pot (or Saloth Sar as he was originally known) and his associates were strong nationalists from the start, and this may have gained them support early in the civil war.[35] Their identification with the past greatness of Cambodia, combined with their success in the war against the United States, the giant, may have led them to believe that Cambodia could bring about a total transformation without any external support. With proper guidance, they thought, the people could accomplish anything. That the past greatness of Cambodia was rooted in agriculture probably contributed to their nearly complete reliance on agriculture in creating the new Cambodia.

On the other hand, for several centuries, Cambodia had been dependent on external powers and suffering at their hands. This, together with mistrust of all outsiders and many Cambodians, made the Khmer Rouge feel weak and vulnerable. The small size of their army added to their insecurity. Their divided identity, their lack of integration of feelings of strength and weakness, interfered with a realistic assessment of themselves and their circumstances. This was one cause of their violent and self-defeating policies, including constant purges of communists.

A tradition of violence in Cambodia. Chou Ta-Kuan described the brutal penal system of Angkor in the thirteenth century. People convicted of serious crimes were buried alive; lesser crimes were punished by the amputation of toes, fingers, and arms. When a new king was proclaimed, all his brothers were mutilated. At the beginning of large construction projects Khmers of low status were ritually decapitated. People believed they could gain power by cutting off parts of another person's body – genitals, organs, or head.[36]

The Issarak, the anti-French freedom fighters, were also extremely violent. Bun Chan Mol was the political leader of a group carrying out executions in the 1940s. He wrote in his 1973 book, *Charit Khmer* (Khmer mores), that he left the Issarak in 1949 because he could not restrain the brutality of his men, their gratuitous use of torture, and their pleasure in violence.[37] They were suspicious of everyone, including their leaders. Banditry was also long practiced in Cambodia, sometimes the Issarak a cover for it.

Referring to David Chandler's dissertation on life in nineteenth-century Cambodia, Vickery writes:

Patterns of extreme violence against people defined as enemies, however arbitrarily, have very long roots in Cambodia. As a scholar specializing in 19th-century Cambodia has expressed it: "it is difficult to overstress the atmosphere of physical danger and the currents of insecurity and random violence that run through the chronicles and, obviously through so much of Cambodian life in this period. The chronicles are filled with references to public executions, ambushes, torture, village-burnings and forced emigrations." Although fighting was localized and forces small, "invaders and defenders destroyed the villages they fought for and the landscapes they moved across." "Prisoners were tortured and killed...as a matter of course."[38]

David Chandler also stated, in testimony before a subcommittee of the U.S. House of Representatives, that the "frequency of locally-led rebellions in the nineteenth century – against the Thai, the Vietnamese, the French and local officials suggests that Cambodian peasants were not as peaceable as their own mythology, reinforced by the French, would lead us to believe."[39]

Violence by various rebel groups continued in rural areas during the 1940s, 1950s, and 1960s. The Khmer Rouge moved from politics to guerrilla war in 1968. The Sihanouk government's actions during the Samlaut peasant rebellion I have already described. One scholar on Cambodia, Ben Kiernan, writes:

During 1968 in Kompong Cham, the Provincial Governor Nhiem Thein organized witch-hunts for suspected Communists. According to a witness, provincial officials were ordered to take part in beating innocent peasants to death. According to another witness, in Prey Totoeng (a village in Hu Nim's former electoral district) two young children accused of being messengers for the guerrillas had their heads sawn off with palm fronds. Also in 1968, 40 schoolteachers accused of subversive activities were, on Sihanouk's orders, bound hand and foot and thrown from a cliff at Bokor in Kampot.[40]

Kiernan further notes that in a May 1968 speech Sihanouk described what happened to captured communists thus: "I...had them roasted. When you roast a duck you normally eat it. But when we roasted these fellows, we had to feed them to the vultures. We had to do so to ensure our society."[41] Communist violence, which became rampant in occupied territories after 1970, was also increasing: in mid-1969, communists publicly executed government-appointed officials in five villages.

Vickery points out that peasant revolutions have often been extremely violent and cites the examples of Spain, Russia, and Vietnam.[42] He means to show that the excesses of Pol Pot were results of a Cambodian tradition of violence and "poor-peasant" frustration, rather than Marxism-Leninism.[43] However, the ideology of Marxism-Leninism and some of the practices of communist countries also contributed: they influenced Cambodian communist ideology and offered models for action. These models included Stalin's brutal collectivization of the peasantry and his later purges, the early Yugoslav purges, and the excesses of the Cultural Revolution in China.

Experiential and intellectual sources of ideology and fanaticism

Out of these cultural roots, combined with personal experience, members of the Pol Pot group developed their destructive ideology. For example, their deep-seated view of Vietnam as hereditary enemy may have been confirmed when Vietnam, in the late 1960s, not wanting to antagonize Sihanouk, refused material help to the Cambodian communists. In fact, when the Cambodian communists began to arm themselves in 1967–68, North Vietnam discouraged them. This was frequently cited after 1975 as evidence of North Vietnamese ill will. Although the Vietnamese provided essential military help after Lon Nol came to power, the past was not forgotten. The hatred of North Vietnam grew with the Paris peace accord of January 27, 1973, which ended the war between the United States and North Vietnam. The Khmer communists saw it as a sellout and refused to be part of it. The U.S. bombers, called off Vietnamese targets, concentrated their bombing on the Khmer communists. The Khmer Rouge ordered the Vietcong and Vietminh out of the country.

There were other reasons for mistrust of all outsiders, even communists. In order to maintain friendly relations with Sihanouk, China provided his government with military equipment that was used against the Khmer Rouge. Even the Soviet Union sold Sihanouk arms. It seemed that the whole world, communists and imperialists, were enemies of the Khmer Rouge. In addition, Pol Pot and his associates were victims of brutal repression by the supposedly democratic government of Sihanouk's Cambodia. Being forced to live in the forests was traditionally regarded as a disgrace, and this may have been another source of frustration and anger.[44]

The Khmer Rouge ideology also had intellectual sources, some of which are traced by Craig Etcheson.[45] The writings of Marx, Lenin, Stalin, Lin Piao, and Mao Tse-tung had led the Pol Pot group to accept the need for a communist revolution. Lenin and others convinced them that a vanguard party could create a revolution that "leaped" the stage of mature capitalism originally described by Marx as a prerequisite for communist revolution. Mao persuaded them that a people's war was necessary to crush such "national-democratic" structures of oppression as police, courts, labor unions, myths, and religion. Soviet writings convinced them that socialism could evolve in one country before the emergence of a unified global communism.

All members of the central group led by Pol Pot had been students in Paris together and members of the Stalinist French Communist Party and communist study groups. They continued to work together, which created many opportunities to influence each other and evolve a coherent ideology. Etcheson argues that they must have been influenced by the thinking of French revolutionaries. Robespierre led the Reign of Terror with the maxim that a revolution has no constant laws but must adjust to changing circumstances. A group of radical leftists who called themselves the Conspiracy of Equals published a manifesto in 1796 asserting the principle that the revolutionary end justifies all means. The ideology of the Pol Pot groups seems to have contained all these ideas, although their sources are necessarily conjectural.

Vickery points to a source closer to home, the thinking of Son Ngoc

Thanh.[46] This complex man was an anticolonialist enemy of the French, a collaborator of the Japanese during their brief occupation of Cambodia, and probably a CIA collaborator while he was opposing Sihanouk from the forests of Cambodia. He was the first modern anti-French nationalist, a left-leaning political thinker and leader of efforts to modernize and democratize Cambodia. He spoke of developing the people's will to serve the nation without concern for personal interest and rank, suppressing moral evils, eliminating oppression, and using the land fully.

Utopian thinking was another influence. Vickery writes:

DK Cambodia first of all bears unmistakable similarities to a Utopia as, for example, envisaged by Thomas More: the rigidly egalitarian communism, identical clothes and houses, the latter of which are changed regularly; identical fixed working hours, mass lectures, communal farms and communal dining halls, shifting of children out of families, strict rules on sexual morality, no money, and contempt for gold....

In the real world, Utopian features have often been combined with violence; and the particularly violent aspects of the DK revolution manifest echoes of Bakunin's anarchist program: "universal revolution, simultaneously social, philosophical, economic and political, so that of the present order of things...not a stone will be left standing"; "death to rulers, exploiters and guardians of all kinds, we seek to destroy all states and all churches along with their institutions and laws." Along with that the youth were to abandon universities, academies, schools, "and go among the people," and were advised to "not bother at this moment with learning," for "the people know themselves, and better than we do, what they need." All "means of social existence" were to be concentrated in the hands of "Our Committee" [Angka Loeu] with physical labor proclaimed compulsory for everyone, the alternatives being work or death. As in Utopia all property would be communal and communal eating and sleeping the norm.[47]

Vickery also points to the examples of certain other revolutions. Yugoslavia too had an indigenous communist movement with indigenous leaders who tried to limit outside influence. The Yugoslav communists too acted violently against former enemies and had ambitions for great, immediate change. Pol Pot visited Yugoslavia in 1950, a seemingly incongruous act for a Stalinist given Yugoslavia's rejection of Soviet influence. The Great Leap Forward in China in 1958–60 could also serve as a model. In its ideology the peasant masses were the source of true revolution, backwardness was an advantage for the success of revolution, and it was necessary to eliminate differences between town and country, peasant and worker, mental activity and manual labor. The Great Leap Forward also built huge irrigation and water conservation projects, with masses of peasants performing labor under military discipline.[48] Others have argued that the Chinese Cultural Revolution also had influence.[49]

Some early elements of the ideology were also apparent in doctoral dissertations by the Pol Pot group in France. Hou Youn, the intellectual

founder of the revolution, argued in his 1955 thesis that peasant masses
are the real creators of a nation's wealth.[50] In his later writing he states,
"Our purpose is to transform and develop the rural economy based on
establishing the peasant as the key to the organization of production."[51]
Khieu Samphan's 1959 thesis held that only by ending its dependency on
the outside world could Cambodia develop into an industrial society.[52]
The nationalism of the Pol Pot (then still Saloth Sar) group was also apparent very early. For example, they denounced the king in an open letter
in 1952, complaining (incorrectly) that he had renounced territorial claims
to former Cambodian possessions.

From ideas of others and examples of other countries, from their own
cultural background and their personal experiences, the Pol Pot group
evolved a coherent ideology and believed that by fulfilling it they would
create an ideal Cambodian society. This ideology was the primary guide
to genocidal practices.

Gaining followers: the tools of revolution and genocide

The turmoil in Cambodia gave rise to many of the motivations that arise
under difficult life conditions. Given the economic problems and decline
in living standards, the bombing and war that ravaged the country, there
had to be strong motivation for defense of the physical self. Political instability and violence, the loss of Sihanouk in 1970, physical dislocation,
and social chaos also gave the Khmer peasants a deep need to protect their
identity and to find new authority and guidance. With their customary ways
of life destroyed, they needed a new world view. The communists threatened their lives for noncompliance and offered rewards for compliance,
including the fulfillment of these needs.

Three major influences on the peasants stand out. First, the overthrow
of Sihanouk and his call for an uprising in support of the communists. Before 1968 the communists did not have sufficient support to win a war.[53]
Sihanouk's call on the peasants to support the Khmer Rouge may have
been decisive. The rebels used Sihanouk skillfully. He became head of
the government in exile (established May 5, 1970) and thus, in name, the
leader of the revolution. He was occasionally presented to the people. In
actuality, he spent most of his time in Peking, and all real authority was
in the hands of the Khmer Rouge.

Second, the U.S. bombing "destabilized" the peasants and turned them
against the Lon Nol government. They believed it was done at the request
of the government, which they already regarded as corrupt and indifferent
to their welfare. (In actuality, Cambodian officials constantly submitted

vigorous protests to the United Nations before 1971.)[54] The U.S. bombing also had another effect. There were many communist factions, and initially members of the Pol Pot group were not in the highest leadership positions. Although their cold-blooded determination might have brought them to power anyway, the bombing radicalized the peasants and made it easier for this radical group to gain their support. The bombing also further radicalized Pol Pot and his group. Finally, U.S. bombs helped them in a more direct way. In 1973, in the first major independent offensive by the Khmer Rouge military (without the North Vietnamese army), the battalion of the Pol Pot faction held back while the others were decimated by a terrible pounding from the U.S. Air Force. When U.S. air power was withdrawn in August 15, 1973, the Pol Pot faction was dominant.[55]

The third major influence on the peasants was exerted by the communists. They destroyed the traditional structures of life in territories they occupied, creating total dependence on themselves. They executed some and terrorized all, broke up extended families, forced peasants to move to new villages, and drove people from worksite to worksite under constant supervision. They erased many of the traditions in the occupied territories between 1970 and 1975 and many more after the victory in 1975. All this increased disorientation and susceptibility to the communist movement.

Ith Sarin, a school inspector who joined the communists and then abandoned them and wrote a book about them, wrote that the communists understood and worked to enlarge the peasants' deep dissatisfaction with the corruption, arrogance, cruelty, and incompetence of the Phnom Penh government.[56] Having enhanced the needs created by difficult life conditions, the communists offered ways to fulfill them. In place of the authority of the king, they offered the authority of Angka Loeu (the "organization," their central authority). They linked some of the traditions and myths of the culture to the new system. While they changed the village administrative system, they maintained and even strengthened certain traditional elements such as communal ownership and communal work. During the civil war, while they acted with severity and enforced discipline, they also worked together with the people, while maintaining a modest demeanor.[57] They offered a movement and ideology that could provide connection, comprehension, and even inspiration, and they propagated it through an extensive program of political education. Like other totalitarian systems, they used songs to unite and energize people. They used myths and traditions to gain support, but once victorious, they vanquished the king and the vestiges of the old culture.

The communists paid special attention to youth, creating youth groups as early as 1962. Young people have a less fully formed identity, and their minds are more open to new ideals. Armies like young soldiers because they are easier to mold and have a sense of invulnerability that makes them worry less about dying. They have a need to separate from parents and old traditions (although this depends on the culture), but they also need emotional security. An authoritarian system that proclaims higher ideals and provides membership in a group can fulfill deep needs for youth, especially in the midst of societal turmoil, and gain their commitment. Plato's dictum in the *Republic* for those seeking to build the perfect city was a psychologically sound recipe for exerting influence: "Taking over their children, they will rear them – far away from those dispositions they have now from their parents – in their own manners and laws."

Many Khmer Rouge fighters were very young; some were children. There are reports of children who killed their parents. How did they come to this? The breakdown of social structures, including the family itself, affected children and adolescents especially strongly. Starting in 1970, parents lost the power to support and protect their children or give them a sense of belonging, especially in communist-occupied areas. Young people could gain this feeling of protection and belonging from the Khmer Rouge, as well as a sense of power from wielding a gun. Some were so successful at extinguishing all former ties while adopting a new group identity that they were able to kill their parents.

The role of specific individuals

A small number of individuals had an essential role in bringing about the genocide: Khieu Samphan, Hu Nim, Son Sen, Ieng Sary, Ieng Thirith, Koy Thuon, Pol Pot, and Hou Youn (who was himself murdered soon after the 1975 victory). Do specific characteristics of these individuals help to explain the genocide? Certainly they were different from Cambodians who were not sent to study in Paris and who did not become members of the Communist party and devote their lives to politics and revolutionary activities. A few of them went into the government; for example, Khieu Samphan was at one point Sihanouk's secretary of state for commerce. Others started to organize the revolutionary force in the jungles and the countryside, where they were later joined by Khieu Samphan, Hou Youn, and a third member of the group, Hu Nim. Although I discussed their ideological and experiential evolution, we do not know enough about them as people to identify what childhood experiences and personal characteristics prepared or predisposed them for their genocidal ideology and cold-blooded determination.

We have anecdotal information, which is of limited value. Barron and Paul write that in the context of their values and beliefs, apparently all were principled, honest, brave, and almost puritannical.[58] Both Pol Pot and Ieng Sary have been described by some as friendly and even gentle.[59] We get a different view of Pol Pot through an outburst during a study group meeting of communist students in Paris. He attacked Hou Youn's more democratic views: "It is I who will direct the revolutionary organization. I will become the secretary general. I will hold the dossiers, I will control the ministries, and I will see to it that there is no deviation from the line fixed by the central committee in the interests of the people."[60]

Khieu Samphan was described by a contemporary who attended school with him in both Cambodia and France as sickly, quiet, and passive. He was ridiculed and teased by classmates and did not defend himself. He was sexually impotent.[61] At one point while he was in public office, security agents stripped him naked in the street, photographed him, and showed the photograph in government circles.

Of somewhat more value is the information that Pol Pot and Ieng Sary managed to get scholarships to study in Paris without an elite background and, in the case of Pol Pot, in spite of a mediocre academic record. University education was the privilege of the aristocracy, and they must have received their scholarships through connections, by clever maneuvering. Gaining this privilege, studying in Paris, associating there with Cambodians of aristocratic background, and participating in public activities in the Cambodian and the larger community appeared to give them "a sense of being chosen, of being part of a vanguard of the capable-informed – an attitude they never abandoned."[62]

The evolution of Pol Pot and his associates as persons and as a group and the evolution of their ideas led to the ideology that was the blueprint for genocide. They shared a framework and provided each other with support. Much study is required before we shall come to understand the childhood and later experiences that create a propensity to join or lead extreme movements. In the last part of the book we shall consider individual characteristics that prevent the acceptance or creation of destructive ideologies and the origins of these characteristics in socialization and experience.

One other person had great influence: Prince Sihanouk. His policies while ruling Cambodia have been viewed both as pragmatic and as opportunistic. He probably wanted a democratic capitalism in a neutral Cambodia. To protect neutrality, he attempted to balance the influence of the Western and Communist blocs. After his overthrow he did everything he could to regain power. Having fought the communists, he now joined them and continued to support them even after he saw that they were using him.[63] His actions were not principled; his aim seems to have been to regain an important political role. This, presumably, led him to enter again into an alliance with the Khmer Rouge to recapture Cambodia after the Khmer Rouge were driven from the country by Vietnam.

Steps along the continuum of destruction

Starting in the mid-1960s, antigovernment violence and government violence followed each other with increasing intensity. During the civil war, there was the U.S. bombing, the invasion, and the communist violence against populations in the territories they occupied. The civil war was fought with great fury, and atrocities were committed on both sides. Government soldiers were known to disfigure captured Khmer Rouge soldiers or behead them, cut them open, and eat their livers.[64]

Instead of increasing violence inflicted by one group on another, Cambodia saw an increasing cycle of reciprocal violence between warring factions. As a result of the turmoil during their formative years, communist guidance, and their own experience in fighting, violence against "enemies" became integral to the identities of the young Khmer Rouge fighters.

The role of bystanders

There were few bystanders, internal or external, who could have exerted influence in Cambodia. As their power grew, the members of the Pol Pot group killed anyone who did not cooperate. China had continuing friendly relations with Cambodia and was the only country in a position to exert influence, but it did not. In the end, the North Vietnamese invasion stopped the killings.

The United States had no power to change Cambodian policies once the Pol Pot group took power. U.S. actions did a great deal to "destabilize" Cambodia. The 1970 invasion might be justified by the North Vietnamese use of Cambodia as a sanctuary, but it is difficult to see any justification for the extensive bombardment of heavily populated areas just because they were in the hands of the communists.

Within the United States we have institutions that protect human and civil rights. In contrast, neither the United States nor other nations have institutions concerned with actions by their governments against the citizens of other countries. Leaders have no direct accountability in this realm. International institutions have little power and therefore little influence.

Lacking accountability, leaders are often guided by ideology, prejudice, and broad (and often unexamined) notions of national interest.

Cambodia also offers another lesson in the careless use of American power. The United States entered, destroyed lives, changed the circumstances, and, when the ship sank, left. Congress ordered President Nixon to stop the bombing on August 15, 1973. Under congressional pressures President Ford terminated the airlift that was bringing supplies to Phnom Penh as the city was near collapse, on April 14, 1975.

To be an effective bystanders, the United States must maintain friendly relations with other countries. To maintain our ability to exert influence, we must respect others' independence and right to choose their ways of life. And we must intervene only when human considerations make this imperative (see Minimalism in the Relations of Nations in Chapter 16).

Another issue is the behavior of the United States and the world toward Pol Pot and his fellow leaders of "Democratic Cambodia" after their fall from power. The United States and China insisted that the Pol Pot government was the legitimate representative of Cambodia in the United Nations. It was regarded as preferable to the current government of Cambodia created by the Vietnamese. Ever since, the United States and China have supported groups fighting against the Vietnam-backed government. China has been supplying the Khmer Rouge with arms. In 1982 rebel groups led by Son Sann, a former prime minister of Cambodia, and Sihanouk officially joined in a common cause with the Khmer Rouge.

As Vietnam plans to withdraw from Cambodia, it is a real danger that the Khmer Rouge will regain power. It is the militarily strongest rebel group. Its actions, including its brutal treatment of Cambodians in refugee camps located in Thailand just outside Cambodia, demonstrate its essential continuity.

The United States has been exerting pressure on Vietnam to withdraw as a condition for normalizing relations between the two countries, without making prior efforts to stop the Khmer Rouge from regaining power. What values guided this U.S. policy? Was it the abstract ideal of freedom or national self-determination, which prevailed over valuing the lives the Khmer Rouge would be likely to destroy? Was it hostility toward Vietnam due to our military defeat by them? Was it antagonism toward the Soviet Union, the supporter of Vietnam?

As the Vietnamese withdrawal promised for September 1989 nears, fast-moving events offer hope that the Soviets and Chinese will agree on a policy, that the current government of Cambodia will join forces with the ever-present Prince Sihanouk, and that the Khmer Rouge will be stopped from regaining power.

14 The disappearances: mass killing in Argentina

Historical (life) conditions

In 1930, the Argentine military overthrew the elected president. A long period of political and social instability followed. From then until 1976 only two presidents completed six-year terms; one was Juan Perón, from 1946 to 1952. All other elected governments were deposed in military coups. There were

institutional crises, the establishment of irregular or de facto governments, an internal state of war, state of siege and Martial law, attempts at totalitarian or joint rule, changes in the organization of State powers, an abrupt increase in terrorist violence by the extreme left and the extreme right, as a means of armed conflict.[1]

Economic difficulties

The same years saw recurrent economic crises, large disparities in wealth, a decline in workers' living standards after 1955, and substantial inflation in the years preceding the military takeover of 1976. Perón was one of the leaders of a military coup in 1943 and became president in 1946. His rule ended with a military coup in 1955. Perón enacted legislation that aimed at social justice and the redistribution of income and he attempted to strengthen the national economy and "national bourgeoisie" (that is the middle class in contrast to the small ruling elite) through government subsides to national industries. At first, combined with increased demand for Argentine argicultural products, this improved economic conditions for large segments of the country.[2] However, from the mid-1950s on, the Argentine economy was in a "continuing state of crises and stagnation."[3] Some believe that these economic problems resulted from Perón's actions. According to Ronald Dworkin he "created a cult of personality, particularly among workers, by lavish spending that exhausted the huge financial surplus Argentina amassed during the Second World War. He also created a police state, using informers and torturers. . . . Perón's (1946–1955) administration prepared the way for the terror described in Nunca Mas."*4

Early in the century, Argentines saw their country as cultured and powerful and having great promise, with substantial economic resources. At the end of the Second World War it seemed economically strong, but a precipitous decline followed. In 1945 it was fourth in the world in gold reserves; by 1964 it was twenty-eighth. Its per capita exports were sixth in the world in 1913, thirtieth in 1964; its per capita exports actually declined during that time.[5] Rampaging inflation had reached 700 percent by 1976 under Isabel Perón. Economic output was not growing but diminishing.

Political conflict and violence

The division between Left and Right became deeper and deeper. Conflicts had long existed between the wealthy oligarchy and the military on the one hand (with the military itself divided) and the working classes and elements of the middle class on the other hand. The military was antagonistic to Perón because he reduced its influence and offered too much to the working class and its unions. The military also blamed Perón for economic decline and corruption.

Perhaps the most direct cause of Perón's ouster was his conflict with the Catholic church, which had a high status in Argentina guaranteed by the constitution. Both president and vice-president had to be Catholic. Perón strongly attacked the church in response to its opposition to a youth movement created by him. The military and others with strong Catholic and nationalist ties or deep respect for tradition turned against Perón.[6]

After Perón's exile, the military excluded the powerful Peronist movement from the political process. This made it difficult for the remaining parties to rule effectively. Some of Perón's followers moved to the Left, proclaimed "armed struggle," and began committing terrorist acts. Perón encouraged them from his exile in Spain.

For most of the postwar era, either the military ruled directly or military men were elected as presidents and ruled with military support. Repression and the exclusion of the people from the political process also contributed to instability. Heavy-handed intervention in the universities

---

* After the demise of the military dictatorship, Raul Alfonsin, the democratically elected president of Argentina, appointed a national commission on the disappeared. The published part of their report, *Nunca Mas* (never again), describes in detail the methods of abduction, torture, and murder used by the military and the nature and functioning of important social institutions of the society under the dictatorship. This is a document of great importance and provides data to test the explanations I offer here.

and repression under General Ongania (who took power in 1966) helped to radicalize youth.[7]

In the relatively brief intervals of genuine civilian rule, military plotting and the instability it generated continued. Crises ensued when the military disagreed with government policies. The inclinations and desires of the military had to be carefully considered by any government if it was to survive. Moreover, civilian political factions sought influence not through elections but by gaining the military's favor. Civilian governments came to rely on the military to govern. For example, Arturo Frondizi, elected in 1958, the first nonmilitary president since 1943, used the military to put down strikes and had military courts pass sentences on workers who refused to return to their jobs.[8]

Supported by the extremes of both Left and Right, Perón came back to power in 1973. From exile he had encouraged leftist violence, but now, facing continued leftist terrorist activity, he sided with the Right and joined in the persecution of the Left. Argentina was in a state of virtual civil war. Leftists kidnapped and publicly executed high-ranking political and military leaders and attacked and bombed broadcasting stations and military posts.[9] Extremists of the Right, including police and military personnel, formed death squads and killed leftists.

The difficult life conditions evoked the motivations that I have described as sources of destructiveness. People felt threatened physically and psychologically. The reaction of military men was especially strong, because their personal and group self-concept, role in society, world view, and ideology were intensely threatened by economic decline, political violence, and social disorganization.

Cultural preconditions

The role of the military in public life

Argentina gained independence in 1816. After that there were incessant wars among various caudillos (strongmen) in the interior, and until about 1870, fierce battles were fought between centralists, who advocated a centralized state, and federalists, who preferred a flexible federation.[10] In the nineteenth century the country was ruled by an oligarchy of landowners. In the twentieth century political reforms resulted in a highly pluralistic many-party system. But none of the parties had enough power to rule. Groups outside the party system, especially unions and the army, increasingly exerted direct influence. The military regarded political instability as both an obligation to correct and an opportunity. It increasingly assumed the role of the dominant party.[11]

A guide to political parties of South America states:

1930 (the overthrow of President Yrigoyen) marked the end of a period of Army indifference to political life which lasted three quarters of a century, and the collapse of the system for electing civilian governments. It is a curious fact that the Army's progressive elimination of the political parties has taken place almost without a struggle; political leaders have of course openly condemned the military coups but the lack of anything more than a verbal reaction gives rise to the suspicion that most of them have accepted these interventions with equanimity, if not relief.[12]

When life conditions are complex and difficult, submitting to an authority that offers a vision can satisfy important needs and goals. The military, although unable to stabilize the country economically or politically, had become the big brother in Argentina. Much of the population and political leadership relied on it, and the rest accepted its dominance.

The military came to see itself as the savior of the nation. The colonels who took power in 1943, for example, "were intent on ruling directly, on the premise that whatever benefited the armed forces would also benefit the country."[13] Perón originally gained influence through the support of right-wing nationalist officers with fascist views. Although he later acted to reduce the influence of the military, he continued to believe in "the tutelary role of the army as custodian of the supreme values of the nation embodied in Hispanic cultural tradition."[14]

A 1966 publication by the secretary of war on the operation of civil affairs states that the tasks of the army include supervision, evaluation of civil authorities, including judges, and offering guidance to them. It also describes the conditions under which civil authority is to be replaced.[15] This document, prepared to guide the military in establishing its rule after the coup of 1966, indicates the extent to which the military was willing to assume dominance over civilian structures.

The military saw the nation as a living entity, occupying territory in which it lives, gains strength, and expands. Their views were somewhat akin to German ideas about the special nature of the state; individual interests and rights had to submit to the greater good of the country. Substantial segments of the military had a "corporate" view of society: all in it are together, joined. Individual rights did not have a strong tradition in Argentina. All this contributed to the military's paternalistic view of its relationship to society. Because the military created the policy of disappearances and was the primary agent of torture and killings, we must come to further understand its nature.

The self-concept and ideology of the military

In a 1970 publication Robert Potash described the self-concept and ideology of the Argentine military.[16] His views are highly consistent with those offered after the disappearances. Argentine military officers saw themselves as heirs to a heroic tradition established in the wars of independence. Self-sacrifice, devotion, and duty were emphasized. The military vocation is like a priesthood; the permanent officer has mystical and passionate dedication. All members of the command corps were graduates of military academies whose rigorous curricula were designed to promote character, honor, and pride.[17] They chose a branch of service early, and it became a lifetime association. The indoctrination of officers became well established under Perón. Potash quotes a recent statement about the purpose of training: "A purely technical-professional efficiency has no meaning if it is not based on deep convictions, and on full faith in the values that are defended and *in the success of the ideological struggle that divides the world*" (italics mine).[18]

A strong sense of corporate identity developed. Army officers saw themselves as members of a unique elite organization; they often felt contempt for civilians and especially politicians.[19] They had little faith in democracy and regarded political parties as unnecessary.

Army officers (and the society in general) regarded Argentina as a nation set apart from the rest of Latin America by its historic role in liberating other countries during the wars of independence, by its natural wealth, size, cultural advancement, and by what they saw as a racially superior population of primary European descent. The country's steep decline greatly threatened their self-concept: as individuals, soldiers, and nationalists.[20]

The threat was enhanced by other aspects of their self-image, view of their role in Argentine life, and ideology. First, as Potash noted in 1970, strong anticommunism had become a major factor in their thinking on both domestic annd international politics since 1930. They showed admiration for the German military and strong fascist sentiments during World War II. Argentine sympathies were primarily with Nazi Germany in that war. The military overthrew the government in 1943 partly to preserve Argentine neutrality. Argentina broke diplomatic relations with Germany and Japan only in 1944, when the outcome of the war was evident, to avoid isolation and retaliation after the war.

Anticommunism was strengthened by Castro's success in Cuba, especially after he dissolved the Cuban army and executed many officers. Increasingly close relations with the U.S. military contributed to anticommunism. The United States trained Argentine army officers and provided antiinsurgency training in the fight against the internal enemy. President Frondizi was ousted in 1962 after a campaign in which the military depicted him as a communist.

The anticommunism of the Argentine officers was strengthened by their commitment to Roman Catholicism.[21] While not all officers were devout, they saw themselves as defenders of the church, especially of Christian ideals. An intense anticommunism, representing a world view, an ideology, and even a self-definition, developed among the Argentine military. Potash notes prophetically in his 1970 publication that some high officials recognized the dangers of unreflective communism that does not differentiate between reformers and revolutionaries.

The military were traditionally viewed as the state's instrument for defending sovereignty and maintaining domestic order. After World War II this view changed, in complex ways. According to some authors the Argentine military hoped to become a continental or even a world power and aspired to rule the Antarctic and South Atlantic. Books written by civilians promoted the idea of the "manifest destiny of the Argentine people" – the country's influence stretching beyond its boundaries – which supported the military's world view.[22] Yet the military had few opportunities for war and there was little threat from other nations. Despite continuing border disputes with Chile, war against either Chile or Brazil, past and potential enemies, was highly unlikely for geographic and political reasons.[23] Other neighbors were friendly or weak or both. Lacking opportunities for self-defense or conquest, the army sought a new rationale for its existence in fighting against revolution, defending the nation and Christian civilization against communism.

The political instability, turmoil, and terrorism in Argentina (to which the military substantially contributed) greatly threatened the military's view of itself as protector of the nation's traditions, well-being, and public order. The military came to see it as their primary role to protect the state from subversion by alien forces and ideas, preserve essential Argentine values, and maintain internal purity.

The military attacked all who might possibly, even in the remotest way, be or become the enemy. This overgeneralization in the selection of victims occurred partly because of their view that all the forces that might change traditional values and the status quo were subversive, partly because of the nature of the terrorist activity. In one instance, for example, the house of General Cardozo, the chief of the Federal Police, was blown up by a bomb left under his bed by a school friend of his daughter while she was a guest in the house.[24] It seemed that anyone might be a terrorist.

Edwardo Crawley offers a view of the Argentine military consistent with my perspective on the psychology of perpetrators. In his view, when the police proved unable to control terrorism and the military took up the task, its self-respect demanded that the guerrillas' status should be enhanced.

So the guerrilas became *demonized*. The few thousand armed fighters began to be portrayed as merely the tip of the iceberg, which consisted not only of the "surface" organizations of the left, but of a vast subversive conspiracy which, according to the military, had already taken hold of every aspect of life in Argentina. There was the "ideological subversion" that pervaded the universities, the press, the arts, some professions like psychiatry and sociology; there was the "economic subversion" detectable in the adoption of policies aimed at destroying the national economy; there was the infiltration of the state apparatus, and an orchestrated campaign to destroy the family and morals, to falsify history and corrode all traditional values.[25]

A 1980 government publication on Terrorism in Argentina provides insight into the mind of the military. Behind the terrorism the military saw foreign Marxist influence. Argentina had been targeted for destruction by its enemies, the communists, whose "ideology of death" had come to dominate all domains of national life: education, the economy, justice, culture, and labor. In different appendixes, the infiltration in each realm is described in detail. For example, the following refers to preelementary and elementary schools.

Subversive operations were carried out by biased teachers who, because of their pupils' age, easily influenced their minds' sensibility. The instruction was direct, using informal talks and readings of prejudiced books published to that effect. Using children's literature, terrorism tried to convey the kind of message which would stimulate children, and make room for self-education, based on freedom and the search for "alternatives."[26]

The schools, instead of instructing children in their parents' values, inculcated "self-development" and rebelliousness in an attempt to destroy the family.

These views are similar, in their image of an enemy threatening both essential identity and survival, to the ideologies guiding the perpetrators in other genocides and mass killings. In the Argentine case, enhancing the enemy made difficult life conditions and social upheavals more understandable. The military blamed civilian politicians for all failures of society, but given its dominance in Argentine society, it required additional psychological maneuvers to avoid feeling responsible. It was the pervasiveness of the enemy that explained the failure of the military as the nation's guardian.

Crawley's analysis also highlights the fact that for the first time in many years, the military felt needed in the fight against a real enemy – "someone who made sense of the long years of training, the military mystique, the long sacrificial years of barrack boredom; someone who enabled the professional soldier to test his own mettle, his skills, his self abnegation and patriotism."[27]

Following the example of its Brazilian counterpart, the Argentine military adopted a

sweeping doctrine of national security....In its essentials, the national security doctrine regards domestic political struggles as an expression of a basic East–West conflict and sees Marxist penetration and insurgency as an all-prevading presence of a new type of enemy fighting a new type of war. Civilians are also warriors, ideas a different form of weapon.[28]

The ideology was directly expressed in many statements by military leaders. For example, as reported in April 29, 1976, in the newspaper *La Razon*, the head of the Fourteenth Regiment of the Airborne Infantry, Lieutenant Colonel Jorge Eduardo Gorleri, had this to say to journalists who were invited as witnesses to the public burning of books by Marxist authors or by those with a similar philosophy: [We] "are going to burn 'pernicious literature which affects our intellect and our Christian way of being...and ultimately our most traditional ideals, encapsulated in the words God, Country and Home.'"[29]

In sum, the officers' fascist inclinations, their preference for centralized bureaucratic rule, their elevation of the nation over the individual, their loyalty to religious traditions, their nationalism, militarism, and strong anticommunism, and the needs aroused by societal problems led them to devalue not only terrorists, but broad segments of the community. They were supported in this by the dominant culture of Argentina, which stressed Christian values, a sene of unfulfilled greatness, and anticommunism, and by the Argentine people, who suffered under the persistent life problems and shared a societal tilt with them. In 1976 the majority welcomed the military takeover and initially accepted and justified the repression and violence that followed.

Steps along the continuum of destruction

Some of the historical material presented in the section on life conditions is relevant here as well. Military takeovers and repressive military dictatorships had become commonplace in Argentina. As I noted, Perón created a police state and began using informers and torturers.[30] After his overthrow political arrests and torture of political prisoners recurred. The student riots in Cordoba in 1969 and the repression that followed were a turning point toward persistent repression and confrontation.[31] Suspending individual rights and press freedom reduced the free expression of diverse views.

The Marxist-Leninist People's Revolutionary Party and a group of left-wing Peronistas who called themselves the Montoneros engaged in hit-and-run assaults, bombings, and attacks on political offices, broadcasting stations, and even military installations.[32] They killed about six hundred military officers, government officials, business executives, and even labor leaders. In turn right-wing terrorist bands, including army and police groups, were killing left-wing leaders. There was an increasing cycle of violence. The Alianza Anticommnista Argentina, formed in 1974, even murdered priests suspected of left-wing sympathies.[33]

This cycle of violence made ever greater violence seem necessary and acceptable. It contributed to the evolution of the military's ideology, its perception of extreme threat, and its extreme devaluation of all opponents. The result was the arrest, torture, and murder of real and supposed enemies, and even of persons who happened to be in a house from which a supposed subversive was kidnapped.

The military itself evolved over time in ways that made it psychologically easier for them first to assume total power and later to do anything they deemed right. According to Robert Potash only a minority of the army took part in the military takeover in 1930, while others regarded it as contrary to the military's professional role and some officers refused to join. But a precedent was set that would "inspire a series of plots over the next decade and facilitate a more broadly based movement next time."[34] The military repeatedly assumed power with substantial impunity. Participation in an unsuccessful rebellion might interrupt an officer's career, but amnesties usually allowed full restitution. The Supreme Court came to accept military rebellion as a legitimate source of power; military coups were regarded as establishing de facto governments, rather than as acts of treason.[35]

Anticommunist activity abroad also increased readiness for further violence. During the 1962 missile crisis the Argentine navy participated in the blockade of Cuba. In 1965 the army offered to participate in the Dominican occupation by the United States. The example of the military in nearby Chile, Uruguay, Bolivia, and Brazil also contributed to the evolution along the continuum of destruction. In these countries military dictatorships used anticommunism to justify their brutal rule. The Brazilian army was reported to have crucified some political prisoners in 1969.[36] The Argentine military acted jointly with other repressive governments to suppress dissent. Uruguayans, Paraguayans, Bolivians, and Chileans who had been granted political asylum or had fled to Argentina to avoid persecution were kidnapped, tortured, and killed in joint operations.[37]

Changing institutions

In 1974 the government of Isabel Perón declared a state of siege and suspended constitutional rights. In 1975 a decree ordered the police to help the army eliminate subversion in Tucumán Province. A second decree set up an internal security council to direct all armed and police forces in fighting against subversion. A third decree placed the provincial police under the council's authority and directed military and police to "annihilate the activities" of all subversive elements.[38] Although the wording is ambiguous, the last decree seemingly requires killing without due process of the law.

Upon taking power in 1976 the military junta adopted the Statute for the Process of National Reorganization. It issued communiqués and enacted special laws further suspending basic rights and justifying subsequent actions. Following established precedent, it replaced many officials at the highest levels of the judiciary, for example, the Supreme Court, the attorney general, the Provincial High Courts. All members of the judiciary were suspended; the judges, some reappointed but many newly appointed, had to swear to uphold the articles and objectives of the Process of National Reorganization. Over the next few years, as disappearances progressed, changes in laws and court procedures weakened individual rights. The habeas corpus law was enfeebled (and disregarded anyway) and the right to leave the country was often denied. The judicial process became almost inoperative as a means of appeal.[39] Such changes in norms, practices, and institutions, as I have pointed out, are both products and means of resocialization.

The machinery of destruction

The machinery of destruction was readily available in the military, which had been growing since before World War II. The number of soldiers and the quantity and quality of arms increased greatly. The military became an increasingly autonomous system that produced its supplies in its own factories. Admission to military academies, although partly based on ability, was limited to Catholics after 1930. Germany had helped train and organize the armed forces. Argentine officers were sent to Germany to study. The Staff College, which opened around 1900, was directed and some of the training in it was provided by German officers. German advisors remained with the army until 1940. The result was an institution that resembled the Prussian army.[40] Even more than in most armies there was emphasis on discipline and obedience within a hierarchical command systems.[41] The German influence partly explains the Argentine military's inclinations toward Nazi Germany in World War II. The attitudes and practices of the military were further shaped by training by the United States in the fight against subversion.[42]

The mass killings

Upon assuming power, the military proceeded with extreme ruthlessness to kidnap, torture, and in most cases kill not only suspected leftist terrorists but also anyone who in their minds was politically liberal or left-leaning or seemed to care for the welfare and rights of poor people, and even people who were accidentally associated with intended victims – for example, happened to be in the same home when the victim was kidnapped. In the end they also tortured and killed for a variety of purely personal motives.

The abductions, tortures, and murders were committed with the help of three major paramilitary forces. The organization was loose, but with leadership from the highest authorities in the military. Each branch of the military and local units enjoyed broad discretion in deciding the fate of captured persons.

As early as 1975, the military established secret detention centers – in army barracks, old prisons, and police stations. It is at these centers, starting in 1976, that torture and sometimes killings took place.[43]

The military's practices were guided by the attitude expressed in the Institutional Act of June 18, 1976. The junta assumed the "'power and responsibility to consider actions of those individuals who have injured the national interest,' on grounds as generic as, 'failure to observe basic moral principles in the exercise of public, political, or union offices or activities that involve the public interests.'"[44]

While the junta's defense was that it had been forced to fight a "dirty war" in which certain "excesses" and "errors" had been unavoidable, the pattern of repression followed far more closely the statement of Buenos Aires Governor, General Iberico Saint-Jean, at the time of the military takeover: "First we kill all the subversives; then...their sympathizers; then...those who remain indifferent; and finally we kill the timid."[45]

As Ernesto Sabato wrote in his proloque to *Nunca Mas*:

All sectors fell into the net: trade union leaders fighting for better wages; youngsters in student unions; journalists who did not support the regime; psychologists and sociologists simply for belonging to suspicious professions; young pacifists, nuns and priests who had taken the teachings of Christ to shanty areas; the friends of these people too, and the friends of friends, plus others whose names were given out of motives of personal vengeance, or by the kidnapped under torture.[46]

Nunca Mas clearly shows that there was a plan: procedures of the perpetrators varied in many details but clearly were based on a shared design.

Some leftist guerrillas were killed when found or killed in the course of fighting, but most of the "disappeared" were abducted by groups of armed men in civilian clothes who drove in unmarked cars to the homes of victims, blindfolded them, and took them away. The kidnappers usually maintained that they were acting under military authority.

When a victim was sought out in his or her home at night, armed units would surround the block and force their way in, terrorizing parents and children, who were often gagged and forced to watch. They would seize the persons they had come for, beat them mercilessly, hood them, then drag them off to their cars or trucks, while the rest of the unit almost invariably ransacked the house and looted everything that could be carried.[47]

Usually the gang of kidnappers arranged a "green light," or a free zone of operations, by calling the local police beforehand. They sometimes came in small numbers, but sometimes in huge force with helicopters hovering over the victims' homes. They looted (sometimes on another day) and at times destroyed the home of the abducted person.

When witnesses attempted to report kidnappings to local police, they were usually told that the police were unable to intervene. Victims were rarely informed about reasons for their arrest. When relatives tried to obtain information about the whereabouts of victims, from the police or through the courts using writs of habeas corpus, the authorities usually claimed that the person was not in detention.

The blindfolded or hooded victims were placed on the floor of the back seat of the car and taken to the military establishments, prisons, or police barracks used as secret detention centers. Here they were kept under horrible conditions. Constantly blindfolded, they were totally disoriented and helpless. They received starvation rations in a manner designed to contribute to their degradation and helplessness. For example, they would be given soup on a flat plate, with a fork. They were repeatedly tortured and interrogated for as long as weeks, months, and in some cases even years. One purpose of this was to force confessions and get the names of other "subversives."

Electric prods were applied to all parts of the body; victims' heads were immersed in water while covered by a cloth; they were beaten with fists, rubber, and metal; put into pens with vicious dogs until they were almost dismembered; put into a sack with a cat. There were mock and genuine executions in front of other prisoners and relatives. Pregnant women were also subjected to torture, resulting in miscarriages and sometimes death.[48]

In most of this book, I have discussed the mistreatment and murder without providing a vivid picture of the suffering. I hoped this would allow a more careful analysis of the psychology and culture of perpetrators. However, this suffering and the perpetrators' will to inflict it are the core of our concern. *Nunca Mas* quotes the testimony of victims extensively; I present some fragments here:

Everything happened very quickly. From the moment they took me out of the car to the beginning of the first electric shock session took less time than I am taking to tell it. For days they applied electric shocks to my gums, nipples, genitals, abdomen, and ears. . . .

Then they began to beat me systematically and rhythmically with wooden sticks on my back, the backs of my thighs, my calves, the soles of my feet. At first the pain was dreadful. Then it became unbearable. The agonizing pain returned a short while after they finished hitting me. It was made still worse when they tore off my shirt, which had stuck to the wounds, in order to take me off for a fresh electric session. This continued for several days, alternating the two tortures. Sometimes they did both at the same time. . . .

In between torture sessions they left me hanging by my arms from hooks fixed in the wall of the cell were they had thrown me.

Sometimes they put me on the torture table and stretched me out, tying my hands and feet to a machine which I can't describe since I never saw it, but which gave me the feeling that they were going to tear my body apart.[49]

Afterwards they beat me with sticks and a hammer which they used to smash my fingers whenever my hands were on the floor. They undressed me and tied my hands and feet to a bed frame they called a "grill." For what must have been an hour they applied electric current to the most sensitive parts of my body: genitals, hips, knees, neck and gums.[50]

I was arrested on 15 October 1976 by an army unit, which surrounded and raided my mother's house, where I was living. Jorge Armando Gonzalez was arrested with me. We were tied up and blindfolded, then I was suspended from a tree with my hands tied behind me and beaten from noon until evening. I could hear my mother's screams as she begged them not to kill me. I could also hear them hitting Gonzalez. At one stage they filled a container with water, hung him up by the feet and submerged him head first. That was repeated several times.[51]

Women were interrogated in the same manner. They were stripped naked, laid down on the bed, and the torture session would begin. With women, they would insert the wire (to give electric shocks) in the vagina and then apply it to the breasts, which caused great pain. Many would menstruate in midtorture.[52]

Even in a murderous system, the devaluation of victims and the violence inflicted on them can vary in degree. Consistent with the military's ideology and prejudices, communists and Jews were the most horribly treated. Examples are provided by Amnesty International:

On approximately November 1978, an active member of the Argentine Communist Party aged about 40 was kidnapped. . . . Several officers and junior officers tortured him savagely. . . . In the words of a special task force officer: "We killed him before the order came from above (i.e., from superior officers) that we were to let him go without touching him."[53]

And about the torture of Jews:

> The situation of these prisoners was particularly difficult....From the moment
> they were kidnapped until they were included in a transfer they were systematically
> tortured. Some of them were made to kneel in front of pictures of Hitler and Mus-
> solini, to renounce their origins and humiliate themselves.... In the words of a
> Federal police officer nicknamed "Padre," "In here, some people are mercenaries
> and others aren't; but we are all fascists."[54]

Jews were made to shout "I love Hitler"; they had swastikas painted on
their backs; they were especially humiliated in many ways.

> All kinds of torture would be applied to Jews, especially one which was extremely
> sadistic and cruel: "the rectoscope," which consisted of inserting a tube into the
> victim's anus, or into a women's vagina, then letting a rat into the tube. The rodent
> would try to get out by gnawing at the victims internal organs.[55]

Christian teachings about Jews and Christian anti-Semitism were influential in Argentina as well as Germany. Nazi propaganda and practices,
which increased anti-Semitism worldwide, had especially strong effects on
the Argentine military. The fascist inclination of military leaders had long
been evident: some of them provided their troops with fascist and Nazi
reading materials.[56]

Prisoners for whom their captors had no further use were usually
"transferred" – strangled, dynamited, or shot, sometimes after being
forced to dig their own graves. Their killing was sometimes made to appear as a shootout between guerrillas and security forces, but there is
overwhelming evidence that this was a deception. Many prisoners were
injected with sedatives and dropped into the ocean from helicopters.[57]
Prisoners allowed to survive were often left to be "found" by an army or
police unit, officially imprisoned, charged, and, because there was no
evidence against them, released.

The selection of victims: ideology, self-interest, caprice

Individuals were defined as subversives or enemies of the state if they
showed the slightest sign of either liberalism or concern for the poor.
For example, people were abducted and houses destroyed in March 1976
after residents of a housing area demonstrated to get legal recognition as
a housing community. Two years later again several people were kidnapped when a mass was called to celebrate the freeing of a woman abducted in 1976.[58] Others were kidnapped because of their association
with social welfare institutions. Still others because prisoners who were
tortured gave their names to gain some reprieve, or by mistake because of

similarities in names. Military conscripts suspected of leftist sympathies disappeared.

Prisoners were tortured in response to world events that upset perpetrators.

We would be beaten up and tortured for the slightest transgression of certain rules of the detention camp....Any event related to repression outside the pozo, the death of a soldier, a gun battle, a politically significant act, events occurring in other parts of the world such as the advances of the Sandinista revolution, constituted a motive or pretext for intensifying the repression.[59]

Pregnant women, while usually tortured, were often allowed to live until they delivered the baby. Often the perpetrators then gave the baby to childless military or other ideologically reliable couples who would raise the baby with the right world view. It is a curious comment on ideological fanaticism that apparently the Montonero guerrillas engaged in a similar practice. When members were killed, they refused to release their children to grandparents, who might raise them with the wrong ideology.[60]

Although the military claimed to be defending Christianity, priests, nuns, and seminarians were among those kidnapped, tortured, and killed. The following gives a clue to the motives of the perpetrators:

The person who was interrogating me lost patience, and became angry, saying, "You are not a guerilla, you don't believe in violence, but don't you realize that when you go to live (in the shanty towns) with your culture, you are joining people, joining poor people, and to unite with poor people is subversion....the only error you have committed was that you interpreted doctrine in a too literal way. Christ spoke of the poor, but when he spoke of the poor he spoke of the poor in spirit and you interpreted this in a literal way and went to live, literally, with poor people. In Argentina those who are poor in the spirit are the rich and in the future you must spend your time helping the rich, who are those who really need spiritual help." (Testimony of the priest Orlando Virgilio Yorio)[61]

How can we explain this contradiction? First, Christianity was only part of the ideology. It was more important to eliminate subversives. Second, the definition of *subversives* was inexact, the line between ingroup and outgroup poorly drawn. Varied elements of society were concerned with social change, the welfare of the workers or the poor, or held liberal ideas. The military believed that an international terrorist conspiracy had infiltrated most aspects of the nation's life. As a result, the ideological net was broadly drawn. Third, the Christianity of the military had been modified to fit in with other strands of the ideology – anticommunism, nationalism, and hatred of social change.

To understand ideologically based violence it is important to notice how abstract ideals guide conduct. A vision of an ideal communal state of affairs can be divorced from the welfare of individuals. Thus, Christian ideals can exist without respect for individual priests and nuns; an ideal of humanity can be divorced from the value of specific human lives.

But not all the killing was ideological, and not all victims were subversives even in the minds of the perpetrators. *Nunca Mas* describes cases in which the *primary* motivation was robbery. Wealthy victims were abducted simply to collect ransom or to loot their property. Originally this may have been justified as part of the war against subversion, but once violence becomes normal practice additional, totally self-serving motives for it can come into play, including greed, sex, or sadism. According to a book by two BBC reporters, "at the height of the terror . . . bored junior officers in the murder squads roamed the streets in their Falcons, looking only for pretty girls to take back to camp to torture, rape and kill."[62]

The reports of victims show the enjoyment of torture by some perpetrators and casual, callous brutality. Torturers would suddenly shift from casual conversation among themselves to a brutal assault on a victim. *Nunca Mas* indicates that the torturers' behavior was planned. The victims were disoriented as a result of blindfolding, hunger, and psychological and physical torture. The torturers succeeded in their likely purpose: to make "casual," but at least in part planned, brutality seemingly spontaneous and therefore unpredictable. It is known that other torturers, for example, in Algeria, have also shown such seeming caprice.[63]

Occasionally a perpetrator was actually "punished" for officially unsanctioned brutality. *Nunca Mas* reports the case of a guard who raped a pregnant woman. He was arrested, held for ten days, and then reinstated.[64]

The psychology of direct perpetrators

As steps along the continuum of destruction continue, the intensity of violence increases, casual torture and the enjoyment of torture become more common, probably more acceptable, and the victim group expands. This occurred even in historical periods when torture was part of the legal process: at first used to extract evidence or confessions from low-status defendants, it was eventually used on high-status defendants and even witnesses.[65]

We can distinguish between decision makers and direct perpetrators. Decision makers were guided by ideology and their need for defense against threats mainly to their self-image and world view, as discussed earlier in this chapter. Self-interest and maintaining privilege were also involved. However, to the extent the military leaders were protecting their status and position, they did so as part of a belief system and world view in

which their long-held elite status had become their inalienable, "natural"
right.

The direct perpetrators had more mixed motives. Obedience to authority was involved. According to Amnesty International, superior
officers signed release forms for kidnappings.[66] This relieved direct perpetrators of responsibility and thus made abduction, torture, and murder
easier. The navy high command gave open support to the Task Force that
carried out abduction and torture.

Admiral Massera delivered an inaugural address to the appointed officers, which
concluded with the exhortation to "react to the enemy with utmost violence and
without hesitating over the means employed." Massera also took part in the first
secret operations of the Task Force under the pseudonym "Black" or "Zero" to
demonstrate his commitment to the task assigned to his officers.[67]

Direct perpetrators were also exposed to a different progression along
the continuum of destruction, through their experience with victims. Their
ideological and identity-related motive became integrated with other personal motives (e.g., power, stimulus seeking, sadism). People function
better when their different motives join and support each other, especially
if they have to overcome personal inhibitions or social prohibitions.

Over time, their respect for human life had to diminish. The many types
of victims made it difficult to differentiate between more and less worthy
human beings. It became acceptable to torture and murder teenage girls,
nuns, and pregnant women. Learning by doing stifled the torturers' feelings of empathy and concern. They had come to see themselves as absolute rulers over the victims' well-being and life, not subject to normal
human constraints. They often talked to the victims about this absolute
godlike power and the victims' total dependence on them; as they did this,
they strengthened their own belief in it.

At this stage, whatever "higher morality" may have been the initial
motive, ideological purity is lost. Violence can result from a desire for
money, sex, or pleasure. What in this context must be regarded as "base"
human motives are integrated with the "higher ideals" provided by leaders.

The kidnappers, torturers, and killers were regular members of the
military and paramilitary units. Conscripts were kept on the fringes of the
secret detention centers. There is some information about the types of
military and paramilitary units from which perpetrators with different
functions were drawn.[68] Guards and torturers were usually not the same
individuals. Self-selection, selection by superiors, and training probably
all contributed to the creation of torturers. It makes sense from the standpoint of the theory of learning by doing that guards, as *Nunca Mas* reports,
at times showed concern for prisoners and other signs of humanity, while

torturers did not. A very small percentage of prisoners consented to become part of the "task force" of perpetrators, the "mini-staff."

Whoever designed the system had an intuitive sense of the psychology of perpetrators and aimed at diminishing all constraints on their behavior. The prisoners were identified only by numbers.[69] As in Nazi Germany, euphemisms were used. The torture chamber was the "intensive therapy room." A person about to be killed was sometimes said to have "gotten his ticket." Those who were to be killed were "tranferees." Prisoners were blindfolded, not only to disorient them and protect perpetrators from recognition, but I believe also to give perpetrators a feeling of total un-accountability and reduce restraint. Perpetrators usually referred to each other by pseudonyms in the presence of victims.

The role of bystanders

Internal bystanders

When the military assumed power, many welcomed it, including the Nobel Prize–winning writer Jorge Luis Borges.[70] The coup promised deliverance from difficult life conditions, political violence, and social disorganization, in a society accustomed to military takeovers.*

Most major social institutions collaborated with the military. The judiciary accepted military denials of knowledge about persons whom relatives tried to free by habeas corpus. As *Nunca Mas* notes, not a single judge visited any place where relatives claimed that their loved ones were held captive. According to a deposition by one abducted and tortured person:

> The judge was totally passive, though I was a wreck. Two guards had to support me as I walked and my face was disfigured. . . . It seems that Judge Carizze approved of the methods used, as he convicted me despite all I said. Some day these

---

* In mid-April 1987, in response to a rebellion by a military unit, President Alfonsin called on the population to show support for his government. Hundreds of thousands of people assembled and demonstrated, expressing intense hostility to the military. As the *Guardian*, a London newspaper, noted on April 20, 1987, "Bitter and rowdy mass protests against military regimes have been held in Argentina, but usually at the end rather than before the beginning of a (military) regime." The behavior of the people as internal bystanders helped Alfonsin defeat the military threat. Unfortunately, Alfonsin also made concessions to the military by introducing a Due Obedience bill, which argues that junior officers were coerced by their superiors and should be absolved of human rights crimes. Although this might have been, or he might have regarded it as, the only way to save his government, Alfonsin's capitulation reduced the effects of his other efforts to limit the role of the military in political life.

judges will have to explain why they took declarations from people completely out of their minds and went to police premises to do it.[71]

All active opposition was eliminated. The free press, labor unions, the right to strike, the rights to a fair trial and due process, and other civil liberties were suspended. As soon as the military came to power, it issued communiqués threatening up to ten years of prison for journalists who transmit information that might demean or subvert the activities of the army. The press, with a few exceptions, accepted censorship and did not report the disappearances. The population kept quiet; essential institutions were silent or cooperated, expressing (or at least allowing the appearance of) a uniformity of views and of support for the military.

Argentinians shared the difficult life conditions, and many of them shared the cultural orientation of the military and the resulting motivation for stability, order, and purification. It is difficult to explain the cooperation of the clergy in any other way. The church officially condemned the methods used by the military but was otherwise silent. Moreover, individual priests are reported to have been present at secret detention centers, even during torture.

The very methods used by the military must have impressed on the population the importance of their cause and the necessity of extraordinary measures: helicopters hovering over buildings from which citizens were taken, tanks surrounding and destroying the homes of supposed subversives. The military said they were doing it all for the sake of Argentina's children, and the nation joined in or accepted it.

The military also "bought off" the middle class with policies that improved its material condition, for example, monetary policies (subsidizing the rate of exchange) that enhanced its international purchasing power. However, overvaluation of the currency increased foreign imports and drove down domestic production. A recession followed, with a drop of purchasing power, and by 1981–82 the middle class was disillusioned.[72]

Savage repression also helped to keep the population docile. For example, midwives who told relatives about a child born in captivity to an abducted woman later disappeared. Defense lawyers who were identified as subversives or tried to act on behalf of disappeared persons were assassinated or kidnapped and tortured. The fate of 109 lawyers is still unknown. Others avoided this fate by going into exile.

Mothers of the Plaza del Mayo

The example of the Mothers of the Plaza del Mayo shows that opposition was possible. The mothers of disappeared persons began to march every

Thursday in the Plaza del Mayo, wearing white scarves, with the names of their children and the dates of their disappearance. There were attempts to silence them. The group was infiltrated and three of its member were kidnapped. The military also began to kidnap their relatives. Despite terrible struggles with their consciences over this, the mothers continued to gather and demonstrate.[73] In the end they exerted great influence by calling the attention of the people of Argentina and the world to the disappearances.

One of the leaders of the Mothers was at first completely inactive. She spent every day waiting by the phone to hear about her son. Her daughter and daugher-in-law went to court, trying in vain to use habeas corpus. One day someone said to to the mother, "You are the mother, you have the power, they can't treat you as they treat your daughter." This had great impact on her. She started to haunt government offices. There she met other women, joined them, and they moved out to the plaza. Nonviolently, with dignity and courage, they pursued their aim.[74]

Their power arose partly from their status as mothers, a highly respected role in Argentine society, partly from their courage. Their solidarity made it possible to continue in spite of the dangers. Moreover, they evolved, learning by doing. From concern about their children, they moved to concern about all the disappeared and then a more universal interest in human rights, an expansion of concern to all humanity. The evolution of heroism and of what I have called "good fanaticism" is apparent here.

External bystanders

Many external influences contributed to the mass killing. I mentioned the shared ideology and examples of other South American countries and the common cause of their governments with the Argentine military during the mass killings. The rest of the world had tolerated torture and murder in South America for years, confirming for the Argentine military at least its acceptability, if not its rightness.*

The United States had no role in creating the policy of disappearances, but its anticommunist zeal helped foster the ideology, institutions, and practices that became the cultural preconditions for mass killing. At the time of President Johnson's inauguration, Defense Secretary McNamara told the U.S. Congress:

---

* I am not suggesting military intervention as a means of influence, but policies that respond to the disregard by a nation of essential values. For an extended discussion see the section on Minimalism in the Relations of Nations in Chapter 16.

The primary objective in Latin America is to aid, whenever necessary, the continual growth of the military and paramilitary forces, so that together with the police and other security forces, they may provide the necessary internal security.[75]

Even during the disappearances, some countries withheld criticism, especially the Soviet Union and Eastern European countries: "The representative of the USSR even asked the UN 'not to put to the Human Rights Commission any denunciation of Argentina' adding that 'new things are happening there with the takeover of power by a new government' (he was referring to the Presidency of General Roberto E. Viola who had been the Army Chief of Staff during the cruelest years of the dictatorship)."[76] Other nations condemned the disappearances, but did nothing more. When some French nuns disappeared, the French government attempted to gain their release. Promises were made, but they never reappeared. Human rights organizations protested, and the Inter-American Commission of Human Rights of the Organization of American States made a visit in Argentina. However, without the tangible support of nations, such organizations have limited influence, especially once mass killings have begun. By the time the machinery of destruction is in operation, the capacity of bystanders to influence the perpetrators has greatly weakened. The potential for influence is greatest at early stages – in the case of Argentina, during earlier military takeovers characterized by repression and violence.

One of the few exceptions to worldwide indifference was the Carter administration's strong, vocal policy of support for human rights in South America and elsewhere. The U.S. Embassy was one of the few sources of support for the persecuted; the U.S. government intervened on behalf of individuals and also to halt the policy of disappearances in general. In South America Carter's human rights policy was credited with an easing of repression. In contrast, it evoked skepticism in the American press.

Conclusions

The culture of the Argentine military and historical conditions created in part by the military gave rise to mass killings. Military self-concept, world view, ideology, and goals, the steps along a continuum of repression over decades, and the machinery of destruction inherent in the military were important contributors. The influential position of the military in Argentine society, both the ceding of rights to them and powerful segments of the population sharing their values, ideology, and goals, was also important. These predisposing characteristics joined with economic crises and political violence to create instability, chaos, and fear. The stifling of pluralism and political repression by the military also contributed. Internal and external bystanders contributed to the evolution of the cultural preconditions or even supported the mass killings.

Their failure in dealing with the economy and the increasing international attention given to their brutality eroded support for the military. Their inclusive definition of victims put many people in danger and further eroded support. After 1979 there were few disappearances. Many of the more obvious targets had already been kidnapped. However, given the seemingly self-perpetuating and frequently expanding nature of such group violence, new targets might have been found if the Argentine people and the world community had not become hostile. In April 1982, the military attacked and occupied the Malvinas, or Falklands, a small group of offshore islands ruled by England but claimed by Argentina, probably in the hope of fanning the patriotism of the masses. To their surprise, England sent a fleet, which defeated the Argentine army and retook the islands. The debacle brought down the military government and put an end to the disappearances. The present democratically elected government in Argentina, by prosecuting at least some of the perpetrators, may have contributed to a world in which governments will not torture and murder their own people.

15 Summary and conclusions: the societal and psychological origins of genocide and other atrocities

In this chapter I will discuss the extent to which the conception of genocide presented in Part I is confirmed or disconfirmed by the four instances described. What modifications and extensions of it are required? Can genocide be predicted? I will also discuss the psychology of perpetrators and bystanders in analyzing other atrocities, such as torture.

A comparison of the four instances

The model is substantially confirmed in all four instances, although elements vary. Table 2 provides a summary.

Difficult life conditions

In all four instances, life problems were great, although they differed in magnitude and kind. Inflation and deteriorating economic conditions existed in Germany before Hitler came to power, in Argentina, and in Cambodia, and Turkey suffered from persistent poverty. Violence was a common precursor. One common scenario was as follows: economic problems intensified by inequalities in their impact (in Argentina, in Cambodia, and to some degree in Germany), often occurring together with social and political changes, led to intense political conflict and violence (Argentina, Germany) or civil war (Cambodia). In Argentina there was much internal political violence; in the other three instances the genocides took place either during a war (Turkey, Germany) or right after a civil war (Cambodia). In the case of the Holocaust, difficult life conditions contributed by bringing a destructive movement to power. The violence of World War II then intensified the motivation for genocide and reduced inhibitions.

"Difficult life conditions" is an abstraction. Its realities include homelessness, loss of individuality in a mass of needy humanity or standing

232

Table 2. *Cultural preconditions and progressions in four genocides or mass killings*

Cultural preconditions and evolution	Nazi Germany	Turkey	Argentina	Cambodia
I. Cultural self-concept, goals, and values	Combination of superiority (right to rule others) and feeling threatened and insecure; nationalism, desire to expand and to rule	Uncertainty and insecurity arising from loss of power territories, and status; nationalism, desire to regain power and status	Belief in Argentina's empire and of invasions by neighbors; goals of self-determination and nationalism	Memories of old Angkor empire and of invasions by neighbors: goals of self-determination and nationalism
II. Devaluation of subgroups	Long history of anti-Semitism, anti-Semitism embedded in culture and political life	Long history of devaluation and mistreatment of Armenians	Increasing division between Left and Right; strong devaluation of communists and of anyone working for social change	Increasing division between Left and Right; historical separation between town and country
III. Orientation to authority	Strong culture of obedience to authority, authoritarian parenting	Very hierarchical society	Within military, who were the planners and agents, strong obedience to authority	Among Khmer Rouge, very strong orientation to authority; traditionally, strongly hierarchical society, worship of king, feudallike system
IV. Monolithic (including totalitarian) vs. pluralistic culture	Monolithic-totalitarian	Monolithic; for centuries preceding genocide authoritarian-repressive	Within military, monolithic; at the time of the mass killings, military dictatorship	Among Khmer Rouge, monolithic-totalitarian
V. Ideology (emerging or adopted)	Strong Nazi ideology, ideology the guiding force leading to genocide (racial theory, living space, leadership principle)	Pan-Turkism or Turanism (Turkish nationalism, idea of new empire)	National security doctrine, strong anticommunism, religious ideals	Strong ideology of leadership group; ideology the guiding force leading to "autogenocide," "ideology of antagonism" to Vietnam
Steps along the continuum of destruction	Increasing mistreatment of Jews by Nazis – past history of mistreatment; increasing levels of violence (eugenics program)	Increasing mistreatment of Armenians over an extended period, including large-scale mass killings	Increasingly violent repression by the military in previous takeovers; leftist terrorism; increasing cycle of violence between Left and Right	Increasing cycle of violence preceding and during the civil war; high level of communist violence against people starting after 1970

in line for a job, fear for one's life and one's family, the oppressive anxiety of an uncontrollable and unpredictable future, and the disconnection among people who have lost their bearing in the world. Persistent difficulties of life give rise to the complex of motives described in Part I (see Chapter 2, Table 1). In future analyses classification systems and assessment techniques may be developed to specify in more detail which life problems are the most important precursors of mass killing and genocide.

Cultural preconditions

The cultural preconditions summarized in Table 2 were present to a substantial degree in all instances. Some of them were most evident in the subsystem responsible for the genocide – the Nazis and SS in Germany, the military in Argentina, the Khmer Rouge in Cambodia. However, there were similar inclinations in the larger society as well. In Germany and Argentina at least, the groups that became the perpetrators were accepted and even admired by the majority of the populations.

The SS was a highly authoritarian, dominance-oriented system, and Germany a strongly authoritarian society. The military in Argentina was also highly authoritarian, as was the Khmer Rouge in Cambodia. Turkey was also a hierarchial, authoritarian society, although the subsystem responsible for genocide was less clearly delineated.

Cultural self-concept is the most complex of the cultural preconditions. It involves high self-esteem, a sense of entitlement, and underlying insecurity. The setbacks of Argentina and Germany and their belief in unfulfilled greatness,* the Cambodian memory of past glory contrasted with present misery and humiliation, and Turkey's steady loss of power and influence – all produced societies especially devastated by life problems because of their self-concept. A more detailed specification of the relevant components of the self-concepts and a more formal assessment of the degree to which these characterize various groups are tasks for the future.

Devaluation of the groups that became the victims was always evident. In Germany and Turkey its primary source was deep-seated cultural devaluation, subsequently enlarged by ideology. In Cambodia and Argentina the main source was ideology, built on societal divisions. Again, a system of classification and assessment of the components of devaluation would be useful.

Ideology was important in all four instances. There were both nationali-

---

* It is possible that the Germans saw themselves as having achieved greatness between 1871 and 1914, which was followed by decline.

stic ideologies, glorifying the nation, its purity, and greatness, and better-world ideologies, providing a vision of the world and of a type of society meant to improve life for all who follow. Usually, the guiding ideology combined these two. In Turkey the stress was on nationalism, in Cambodia on a better world. In Germany and Argentina the two were wholly intertwined.

In monolithic societies the group is more susceptible to a narrow ideology and a highly specific blueprint for society. In a pluralistic society people are exposed to varied values and beliefs and various ways of resolving conflicts; this makes it unlikely that a single cultural blueprint will be accepted and held with certainty. However, this issue is complex. Life problems and social disorganization may produce an apparent pluralism. The Weimar Republic that preceded Nazi rule was seemingly pluralistic in many ways. However, this "pluralism" bordered on chaos and the collapse of tradition. The underlying, powerful authoritarian cultural tendencies and the desire for order were only temporarily overshadowed by it. It intensified the needs evoked by life problems. Once the Nazis came to power they reestablished a highly monolithic culture and political system.

Ideology was important in all four instances. There were both nationalistic ideologies, glorifying the nation, its purity, and greatness, and better-ciety, and a multiplicity of possibilities and identities. Tolerance is greater, and counterreactions to steps along the continuum of destruction are more likely. Pluralism in the larger society offers bystanders an independent perspective. It allows them to exert influence with less danger of ostracism and without having to fear for their lives. Inevitably, there will be potentially destructive elements in any pluralistic society. Even so, pluralism, with its ferment, is more beneficial than a monolithic culture or totalitarian society that limits prespective, prescribes a mode of existence, and insists on its brand of goodness and purity. The only "absolute" in a society should be respect for human rights, including the basic material needs of people, and civil rights.

As I have repeatedly stressed, even when the destruction of a group serves privilege, the perpetrators' motivation is usually broader than self-interest. The privileged come to see their privilege as in the natural order of things, and the social arrangements that maintain it as just. Ferdinand Marcos of the Philippines probably believed a statement that he made during the election campaign that led to his downfall: "God is with us. God knows that to protect the Filipino people (we) must win."[1]

Movements and ideologies often arise in response to injustice and cruelty. Victims of injustice and cruelty and their sympathizers need a vision of a better society or a better world to create and maintain the motivation to act. In the face of repression or tyranny, violence is sometimes the only means for change. The violence of the Argentine guerrillas and the Khmer Rouge began in attempts to improve genuinely unjust social conditions. But the danger inherent in a violent movement is great. When such a movement develops a sharply delineated abstract blueprint, with a total commitment to an ideology and sharp differentiation between the worthy "us" and the evil "them," its destructive potential will be great. Any means become acceptable in the name of "saving" one's nation or humanity or creating justice. The lives of real people become unimportant.

Leaders and followers

All along I stressed the importance of followers. The four cases I have discussed also show the crucial importance of leaders. They shape the progression of events and make the decision to kill whole groups of people. Leaders have choice. In no instance did the steps along the continuum of destruction make the final step of genocide or mass killing inevitable. However, usually at some point few avenues except mass killing remain available to fulfill motives of great importance to leaders, their followers, and the population as a whole.

The relationship between leaders and followers in genocide or mass killing is not primarily a case of obedience to authority in the classic sense elucidated by the experiments of Stanley Milgram. Followers are not simply "agents" and their psychology "agentic." Usually, followers *join* the leaders, and the direct perpetrators often unite with them in a highly authoritarian subsystem of society. Many of the followers freely join the group – many members of the Nazi Party and SS and officers in the Argentine military did. The Turkish leaders demanded cooperation by military, police, and administrative officers, but there is little indication that they had to overcome much reluctance. In Cambodia some members of the Khmer Rouge were inducted by force. Probably little continuing force was required to maintain their participation in genocide.

In a tightly operating system such as the Khmer Rouge or the SS, members are shaped by the system and adopt its goals. Pressure to conform is inherent in the system. Identification with the group gives it great power over members. Coercion is normally not required. Often the beliefs, values, and aims of the whole group evolve together. Given their shared culture, shared difficulties of life, and similar evolution along a continuum of destruction, the motivation for destruction develops in both leaders and followers (and even in bystanders).

The psychology and motives of perpetrators

A complex of motives discussed in Parts I and II is the starting point for genocide (see Chapter 2, Table 1); motives evolve further with steps along the continuum of destruction.

Motives of control and comprehension are important all along. Scapegoating, subordinating the self to authorities, joining a movement and adopting an ideology, assuming power over others through dominance and violence can all provide people with feelings of comprehension, control, and power. Some of these also satisfy the need for connection and support. Fear of the victims who are the designated enemy is important. It may have a realistic component, but the victims' power or evil intentions are usually exaggerated. Although the fear is in part culturally and ideologically induced, it is also a defensive process whereby anxieties about life problems are projected onto a convenient target. Fear of an identifiable object is more bearable than unspecified anxieties. Anger, hostility, and hate that arise from frustration, threat, and attack of many kinds are focused on a culturally or ideologically selected scapegoat. Over time, the boundaries of this group enlarge and frequently more people are assigned to the victim group. Both leaders and followers invest themselves in an ideology or movement that comes to define their core identity. This helps to integrate and organize the followers' motives, greatly contributing to their sense of wholeness and well-being.

The psychological processes of groups

Psychological processes in groups may have different meanings from those of individuals. If an individual blames members of a minority group for his problems and his beliefs are not shared, he will be seen as paranoid rather than visionary. Individual solutions to frustration, threat, or incomprehension may include individual violence, psychotherapy, or a new religious faith. Only shared problems, motives, and "solutions" will lead a group to turn against another. Eric Hoffer has suggested that "a rising mass movement attracts and holds a following not by its doctrines and promises, but by the refuge it offers from the anxieties, barrenness and meaninglessness of individual existence."[2] I agree that joining mass movements fulfills important personal needs, but in part it does so by providing doctrines and promises that offer hope, a vision, and a sense of significance.

Membership in a group changes people. The change is greater in groups that exert more control over members and require more total commitment, more extreme actions, or greater sacrifice.[3] Individual goals are supplanted by or integrated with group goals. The desire to achieve, loyalty, self-sacrifice, and the inclination for violence are invested into serving the group and its ideology. The enjoyment of violence and the breaking of social rules become acceptable in the service of the group. Not all personal goals can be integrated with group purpose. Some must be relinquished. After an initial commitment, sacrifice or suffering for the sake of the group can increase commitment.

Characteristic psychological processes operate in groups. The boundaries of the self are weakened. The "I" becomes embedded, enveloped, and defined by the "we." This makes emotional contagion easier, a form of empathy that I have called "empathic joining."[4] It exists even among animals; for example, it causes the spread of fear and the propensity for flight in herd animals.[5] In human groups the speedy spread of feelings can lead to lynchings or mob violence. Emotional contagion is both a means of mutual influence and a source of satisfaction for group members.

The members' perception of reality is shaped by their shared belief system and the support they receive from each other.* Thus, members of the John Birch Society could interpret the killing of sixty-seven peaceful demonstrators in South Africa in 1960 as necessary self-defense by the police against a mob of "frenzied savages."[7] Intense group beliefs are intensely defended by denial, selective perception, selective exposure to information, and other methods.

Steps along the continuum of destruction

As I have noted, individuals and groups change along many dimensions. Many influences contribute to change. Aside from those already discussed, there is evidence from research that children are more likely to learn helpfulness through participation in helping acts if they are also given *reasons* for helping, for example, if they are told of its benefits.[8] Explanations and information even help people deal with pain.[9] Propaganda, a type of information and explanation, is an important tool in the hands of perpetrators and an important force moving people along the continuum of destruction.

---

* The importance of the group in defining the "right" behavior is evident from reports about Vietnam veterans. The killing of civilians was widespread in Vietnam, partly as a consequence of the bombing and partly due to the belief that many civilians supported the Vietcong. Soldiers who did not go along, for example, those who withheld fire at My Lai, reported wondering whether something was wrong with them. Leaders often set the stage for atrocities in Vietnam by instituting body counts and search-and-destroy missions and by silence in the face of rumored atrocities.[6]

Further study is needed to specify and quantify the dimensions of change in individuals and groups that lead to group violence. A classification scheme might also specify the social institutions involved in varying forms of mistreatment and their evolution.

Historical hindsight about steps along the contiuum of destruction is not enough. As individuals and societies we must learn to foresee the potentials at an early stage. We must not allow small evil to pass until great evil triumphs.

The obligation of bystanders

People do not see themselves as bystanders (or perpetrators). They notice some events but not others. They process some events they notice while actively removing themselves from others.* How they respond depends on their motives, values, and aims. Frequently, they are inhibited by fear. But frequently they are so resocialized that they do not oppose, even in their hearts, the perpetrators' aims. This has great "therapeutic" value, because it eliminates or short-circuits guilt, sympathetic distress, and fear. At times, the bystanders' aims include protecting victims or helping people in need. Do witnesses to the mistreatment of other people have an obligation to act?

All groups teach values, some of which have an imperative quality to which members are held strictly accountable. But societies do not normally require or expect their members to endanger their lives or sacrifice themselves for the persecuted, especially for people defined as enemies of their own society. We do know, however, that victims are often innocent. We should hold up the ideal of effort and sacrifice in behalf of people in extreme need or danger. At times this requires great courage – an important component of moral character.†

To avoid the catastrophes of group violence, people often need to act

---

* In an experiment my students and I conducted in the early 1970s, we observed as passersby saw a person collapsing on the street. Some people, after a single but unmistakable glance, turned their heads and moved on without looking again, as if to avoid any further processing of the event they had witnessed. A few of them turned away when they reached the first corner, apparently in order to escape.[10]

† The courage needed is not necessarily a willingness to put one's life on the line. It may be the courage to oppose the group and endanger one's status or career. Many army leaders in Vietnam reported after the war that they disliked search-and-destroy operations and the policy of using body counts as an index of success. In a 1974 survey "almost 70 percent of the army generals who led the war in Vietnam were uncertain what the objectives of that combat were...and 61 percent believed that body counts, kill ratios...were inflated and invalid." They seem to have kept quiet, according to researchers, because their careers were at stake.[11]

at an early stage, which requires a feeling of responsibility and often the social and moral courage to deviate, but normally not physical courage. Living in highly interdependent social groups, the well-being of all requires that people feel responsible for the welfare of others. We can expect people to engage with the world as responsible actors in shaping their immediate circumstances as well as the broader social order. We can expect them to see themselves as agents of human welfare, the welfare of others as well as their own.

In sum, we can expect that people will observe and make efforts to inhibit the mistreatment of members of their society – or of human beings anywhere. Thus, bystanders do have obligations. For these obligations to be fulfilled, certain social conditions must be created, and members of society must be socialized in certain ways (I will discuss this in Part IV). In the meantime, we must educate people about the "bystander role": the insidious effects and moral meaning of passivity and the psychological processes by which people distance themselves from those in need.

More and less central origins of genocide

What is the relative importance of various factors in the origin of genocide?

Cultural characteristics and life conditions act jointly. Difficult life conditions are unlikely, by themselves, to lead to genocide. Certain cultural characteristics are more central than others. Devaluation is highly central. Real pluralism prevents the development of broad support for harming the victims. Genocide is unlikely in a society with a moderately positive cultural self-concept; a positive evaluation and relatively equal treatment of subgroups; pluralistic culture and social organization; and the absence of a firm, authoritarian blueprint for a better society or better world. Unfortunately, most societies have at least some of the predisposing characteristics and therefore some propensity for group violence.

A strong pattern of predisposing characteristics may be enough by itself to make a group turn against another group, guided by motives that need not arise from life problems, such as the desire for economic gain or even images of the glory of war (see next chapter). In the Americas desire for land and economic expansion caused the mass killing of Indians, who were excluded from the pluralistic process.* Moreover, some life problems will

The emotional difficulty of opposing the group must also have been important. Arguing against group policies should be respected and *rewarded*, but groups in general and the military in particular are disinclined to do this.

* It would be worthwhile to examine whether times of especially intense violence against Indians were also periods of economic hardship or other life problems.

inevitably arise in any society as a result of technological or other changes.

As I noted in Chapter 1, for many reasons the frequency of mass killing and attempts at genocide have been great since World War II. Extensive worldwide communication allows learning by example. Modeling influences many types of behavior, including aggression. The first airplane hijacking was immediately and repeatedly imitated.[12] Knowledge about the Holocaust and other mass killings and about torture and terrorism has a cumulative impact. Such violence represents worldwide steps along a continuum of destruction. Furthermore, the threat of nuclear destruction may diminish the seeming magnitude of "lesser" violence. Such interconnected change can lead to a worldwide lessening of moral concern and an increase in the ease of killing. We must take steps to counteract this process.

Predicting genocide and mass killing

The model I have outlined may help us identify societies likely to commit mass killing or genocide.* I shall briefly consider, as a demonstration, the potential of the United States for genocide.

U.S. culture includes a sense of superiority, even a belief in the right to dominate others (or at least to bring to them the "right" values and ways of life), and there is also an underlying insecurity about worth, moral goodness, and, recently even about competence, a dangerous combination. The individualism of American culture is a double-edged sword.[13] On the one hand, it makes people likely to speak out and avoid blindly following leaders. On the other hand, people standing alone may intensely feel the need for connection and support in difficult times. This makes them vulnerable to such movements as survivalist groups, the Ku Klux Klan, or extreme fundamentalism.

* This model may also help us identify effective ways for bystanders to intervene. For example, in South Africa, actions that destroy the economy without producing other changes might make life more difficult and thereby increase the probability of genocide. Therefore, boycotts and divestment ought to be accompanied by other efforts, which must be based on understanding of the cultural self-concept, world views, and values of South African whites. Those who have friendly relations with South Africa should constantly communicate the values and beliefs that make them object to South African policies. They should point to positive values that white South Africans hold but do not apply to the black population. Bystander nations might create commissions to develop conceptions of just social and political organization in South Africa, taking into account the need of the white population to maintain not only security but self-respect while they relinquish their unjust and, late in the twentieth century, unrealistic superior position. Such conceptions might then guide international policies toward South Africa (see also the next chapter).

Devaluation and discrimination still exist in the United States but have been diminishing. There is some cultural awareness that negative images often are not representations of reality but expressions of prejudice. This is an important and difficult advance. Efforts to expose and eliminate stereotypes and negative images have to some degree been institutionalized in laws. In all this there has been continuous progress for decades, with only occasional backlash. But the joblessness and poverty of previously devalued groups, the result of many forces, provide a renewed basis for devaluation.

Respect for and obedience to authority are moderate, which creates less potential for mass killing. Society is pluralistic, both culturally and procedurally. Self-censorship by the media (see Chapter 17) makes it somewhat difficult for certain views to gain an audience and somewhat limits pluralism. Still, extremely varied groups have been accepted in the open forum of society. It seems progressively less likely that certain groups will have neither access to the pluralistic process nor the opportunity to define their rights. This is not a simple, linear process: the poor, homosexuals (especially in the era of AIDS), and Hispanics are emerging targets of devaluation. However, devaluation in the United States generates contrary processes; this demonstrates a relatively healthy pluralistic system.

Pluralism, freedom, and respect for the individual limit the potential influence of destructive ideologies within the United States. Valuing freedom and pluralism, as well as capitalism, and a past history of antagonism toward the Soviet Union created an intense anticommunism. This, in combination with an elevated self-concept and with the role of a great power, has led to an "ideology of antagonism" toward the Soviet Union. All these characteristics have also led to a disregard for the human rights and well-being of people in certain nations, which is related to a recurrent policy of support for violent, repressive, but capitalist, governments, coupled with hostility to governments inclined toward communism.

Finally, the United States has a history of aggressiveness, both on the individual level and between racial groups. Aggression against blacks and Indians arose from deep-seated devaluation, exclusion, and economic motives. Substantial inequalities between groups provide a potential for political and intergroup violence. An increase in economic problems could intensify feelings of injustice, and the resulting anger would increase the potential for violence.

In sum, despite some predisposing elements, the total cultural pattern for genocide or mass killings does not seem to exist in the United States. (Much more detailed and formal analyses are possible, using the conception I have outlined.) But for a full picture we must also consider the nature of life conditions and their contribution to a genocidal potential. The United States has experienced moderately difficult life conditions and undergone social upheaval in the last twenty-five years, with effects that have further contributed to social disorganization. There was the civil rights movement, a struggle for cultural and societal change, with sit-ins and demonstrations and resulting in police brutality and violence. There were the assassinations of leaders. There was the Vietnam War, with the loss of life, the protests, the emergence of a youth movement, profound political conflict, and after-effects such as posttraumatic stress in veterans, economic problems, and threats to and changes in societal self-concept, world views, and culture. There has been rapid technological change.

There have been profound changes in social mores and practices: the acceptability and frequency of divorce and abortion, changes in sexual practices, and widespread drug use. Even though some of these changes, like the movement to create equality for women, are inherently positive, they have contributed to the existence of one-parent families, which in turn have led to problems in the socialization of children.

Although there has been increased concern with social justice, there has been an increase in poverty, homelessness, and unemployment among the youth, especially black youth, with bleak prospects for the uneducated poor. Movements like the Moral Majority and white supremacist groups have come to serve the needs that have been created by all this upheaval, in turn contributing to divisions in society.

Pluralism, values and institutions that stress procedural justice, the positive social currents that I have described, and positive political currents such as improved relations with the Soviet Union make me confident that we will pass through this period without extreme destructiveness. But to decrease the violent potential in the United States we must strive to fulfill constructively the basic needs that have arisen from these upheavals and that are strengthened by the nature of our societal self-concept. This requires crosscutting relations (see Chapter 17) to create positive connections among subgroups of society, efforts to create a sense of community, and different segments of society working together to fulfill the basic needs and provide decent and dignified conditions of life for all citizens. It requires societal ideals that stress joining (rather than exclusion), an expansion of the boundaries of "us."

My analysis also suggests ways to prevent group violence. In the *short run* we can diagnose predispositions. We can identify the motivations of groups and the destructive potential in the ways they attempt to fulfill them. We can try to make individuals and nations aware of their power and obligations as bystanders. A more permanent decline in the probability of group violence requires changes in individual personalities, in culture and social organization, and in the international system. I will discuss these in Part IV of the book.

The psychology of torture and torturers

As I have noted from time to time, the psychology of perpetrators presented in this book applies to torturers. Torture has been used for many purposes. Among these are eliciting information, forcing an admission of guilt, intimidating political adversaries, and establishing one's power and the superiority of one's group. In China and in medieval Europe torture was part of the legal process.[14] Sometimes the scale of torture is limited, and sometimes (as in Germany, Cambodia, and Argentina) it accompanies mass killing or genocide. Although torture is more frequent in nondemocratic societies, it has also been practiced by democracies, both at home and in their colonial role; for example, the French used torture in Algeria extensively. Currently, torture is used in many countries.

When torture occurs on a limited scale or is performed by colonizers in a colonized country, it does not require broad societal processes, and torturers need not have psychological processes and motivations that are part of a more general societal psychology. In many ways, however, the psychology of the torturer resembles that of perpetrators of mass killing and genocide.

"Us"–"them" differentiation, the devaluation of victims, and just-world thinking (and other processes of moral exclusion that distance the self from victims), as well as a better-world ideology, often characterize torturers. Victims of torture are often seen as a threat to the ingroup. Perpetrators are self-selected or selected by people in authority. Their characteristics include obedience to authority, membership in trusted groups, and belief in the group ideology. Some may have an antisocial value orientation. A capacity and willingness to harm others is required and enjoyment of it is useful (although the torturer should not enjoy it *too* much, because he is there to do a job). Learning by participation contributes to the psychological evolution of torturers.

When torture is not part of a broad societal process, obedience to authority becomes more important. The group or its leaders must find the "right" persons to use as perpetrators, must further shape them, and at times must exert strong influence to gain obedience, especially in the early stages. The study of torturers has been limited, but it does seem that a mixture of self-selection and selection by personality, learning by doing, shaping, and "educating" is involved. In the case of the Greek torturers, special procedures were used to produce blind obedience. However, this might be unnecessary in groups with well-established hierarchical systems. For example, the relatively sudden onset of large-scale torture in Argentina suggests that the military personnel, who were the perpetrators, did not need special training in obedience. Military training itself aims to produce obedience. The motivations of many who later became torturers had evolved and their inhibitions had declined in the course of the increasing violence between left-wing terrorists and right-wing death squads partly composed of military personnel.*[15]

* A flexible use of the conception I have presented can provide a framework for understanding many types of harmdoing – for example, father-daughter incest. With all forms of harmdoing we need to identify what motivates the perpetrators, how their inhibitions are lost, and what blocks them from other ways of fulfilling motives.

In addition to cultural and subcultural characteristics (like devaluation of women, rules about ways of relating and sexual relations between men and women, tolerance for incest or sexual abuse) the culture of the family must be considered. This is largely the result of the parents' past experience, their "blueprints" from their families of origin. Difficult life conditions in the society can generate intense needs; added to this are the conditions of life in the family. Within incestuous families emotional disconnection and withdrawal by the wife are common.

Individual characteristics assume special importance. In one type of incestuous family the man is insecure and has strong needs for being cared for, for emotional security, and for feelings of control. These needs had been satisfied by his wife, but her emotional and sexual withdrawal powerfully activate them. The evolution toward incest begins when a "parentified" daughter replaces the withdrawn mother, initially in physical caretaking (preparing food, etc.), then in providing emotional closeness. Ultimately, the father violates the parent-child boundary. His insecurity prevents him from seeking the satisfaction of his needs outside the family.

Another type of perpetrator clearly devalues women, and considers his wife and children his property, to do with as he pleases. In such cases physical violence is likely to accompany incest. In both types of incest some perpetrators use fantastic justifications or forms of moral equilibration: that it is good to teach the child about sex, or that incest protects the daughter from wild sex outside the home.

The mother is frequently a passive bystander. At least in the first type of incest she may (unconsciously) defend herself from awareness of it, partly because not being burdened by her family is one of her important needs. When the perpetrator is of the second type, fear may contribute to her passivity. Occasionally mothers join fathers or stepfathers as accomplices or coperpetrators.

Incest usually has a profound impact on the victim. In her own home, where she should be most secure, she is victimized by one parent and abandoned (not helped) by the rest of her family.

Part IV

Further extensions: the roots of war and the creation of caring and nonaggressive persons and societies

16   The cultural and psychological origins of war

Many of the psychological reactions, motives, and needs that give rise to genocide can be a source of war as well. Difficult life conditions and their psychological consequences combined with cultural preconditions can lead to the selection of another nation as the enemy rather than a subgroup of society.

War has other sources as well, of course, among them the relationship between a nation and one or more other nations and, more generally, the quality and mood of the international order. However, relations among nations are themselves shaped by their cultures, which join with "real" conflicts of interest and other conditions to generate the psychological reactions that are often the main cause of war.

Motivations for war

Like genocide, war may be an attempt to fulfill motivations that arise from difficult life conditions and cultural preconditions – the need to defend or elevate the personal and societal self-concept, the need for connectedness, the need for a renewed comprehension of reality.* Other motivations are power, wealth, and national or personal glory. In addition to occupying territory or gaining physical dominance, conquest may involve getting others to adopt one's ideals and values. Conflicts of interest – conflict over territory or competition in trade – can also give rise to hostility and war. Insecurity and fear of attack are obvious sources of hostility and at times of "preventive" attack. Such fear may be realistic, as in the case of Poland facing Nazi Germany, or exaggerated. Feelings of injustice, deprivation, or suffering attributed to the actions of other nations can also be powerful sources of hostility.

* In discussing war (and peace) I will consider past realities and future possibilities, using U.S.–Soviet relations as an example of conflict and antagonism.

249

Injured honor and the need to defend it (what Ralph White calls macho pride) are another important source of antagonism.[1] But cultural and psychological factors determine what is insulting, what causes embarrassment or shame, and what is regarded as weakness or failure that must be balanced by the assertion of strength.

Like genocide, war is often the outcome of steps along a continuum of antagonism. Hostile acts by one party or acts of self-defense that are perceived as hostile cause retaliation, which evokes more intense hostility. A progression of mutual retaliation may start with small acts that escalate. Morton Deutsch calls this cycle of negative reciprocity the "malignant social process."[2] As hostility increases, nations may operate in a *conflict mode*. Each wants to impose loss on the other to gain relative advantage, even if this does not realistically serve security or other aspects of the national interest. One frequent antecedent of the conflict mode is a history of antagonism between neighboring states.

Cultural preconditions for war

The ideology of antagonism

Often what participants see as genuine conflict of interest or threat from another country is the result of "us"–"them" differentiation, negative evaluation and mistrust, or a societal self-concept.

The wars between India and Pakistan (1947–49, 1965, and 1971) are good examples.[3] Free from British rule, the two became separate nations because of the mutual distrust, devaluation, and fear of Moslems and Hindus. The leader of the Moslem League, Mohammed Ali Jinnah, explained his insistence on separate states this way:

How can you even dream of Hindu–Moslem unity? Everything pulls us apart: We have no intermarriages. We have not the same calendar. The Moslems believe in a single God, and the Hindus are idolatrous. Like the Christians, the Moslems believe in an equalitarian society, whereas the Hindus maintain their iniquitous system of castes and leave heartlessly fifty million Untouchables to their tragic fate, at the bottom of the social ladder.[4]

The wars were fought partly for disputed territories, but mutual devaluation and mistrust were central causes. Devaluation led to miscalculations. In 1971, belief in their inherent superiority led the Pakistanis to initiate war, despite their great numerical inferiority. They suffered a decisive defeat. According to John Stoessinger, even the Pakistani leader's, Yahya Kahn's, traditional views on the sexes influenced his decision to attack: he was unable to believe that a nation led by a woman (Indira Gandhi) could defeat him.[5]

Conflicts will arise, and real conflict will be magnified, as we respond not to the issues at hand or the people on the other side, but to the stereotypes and negative images that we hold. An ideology of antagonism may evolve out of differences in values, beliefs, and ways of life, devaluation, and a past history of antagonism. It encodes the negative evaluation and identifies the other as a threat to the well-being, security, and even survival of one's group. It may lead to a belief that superiority is required for security and a wish to diminish, subdue, and in extreme cases exterminate this enemy.

An ideology of antagonism is an "other-conception" in some ways comparable to a self-conception. The group's own past actions will contribute to the formation of its ideology of antagonism. For example, U.S. participation in an international force attempting to overthrow the young Russian communist state in 1919 probably helped to shape the ideology of antagonism toward the Soviet Union.

Another source of an ideology of antagonism is better-world thinking. For example, Marxist-Leninist ideology devalued the beliefs, values, lifestyles, and social and ecomonic arrangements of capitalist countries. Its view that workers were repressed and exploited in them could incite moral indignation. To create a better world, capitalism was to be eliminated. Moreover, it was a hostile force that required constant vigilance and self-defense. Intense anticommunism qualifies as a parallel better-world ideology.

An ideology of antagonism provides a powerful tool in explaining the other's actions, guiding one's own actions, and justifying aggressive acts. It makes it difficult to realistically evaluate the other's actions and intentions and to draw proper distinctions; for example, to follow a policy that aims to lighten the repressive nature of the Soviet system, while at the same time acts on the shared goal of diminishing the threat of nuclear war. It also further reduces a nation's normally weak inclination to see itself as other nations see it; for example, to consider how the Soviet Union might have perceived repeated U.S. buildup of arms.

Societal self-concept and national goals

A society's self-concept of superiority or of self-doubt or their combination is important in giving rise to war-generating motives. A societal self-concept often designates the territories that are part of a nation and may include some that the nation has not possessed for centuries. The Jews have prayed for two thousand years for their return to Jerusalem. Hungary joined Germany in World War II partly in the hope of regaining territories lost in World War I. The Palestinians see themselves as a people defined by the land of which they were dispossessed. The Falklands war was fought, as were many others, for land of extremely limited value that Argentina regards as part of its territory.

One focus of the nation's account of its history may be the wounds others inflicted by taking and holding lost territory. A nation's identity, like the identities of individuals, is often defined by past hurt, pain, or injury. According to Isaiah Berlin, the "infliction of a wound on the collective feelings of society, or at least on its spiritual leaders, may be a necessary condition for the birth of nationalism."[6] These conditions tend to create both a shaky self-esteem and nationalism, which is the desire to protect and enhance the nation economically and to maintain or increase its power, prestige, and purity.

A national self-concept often includes a view of the "right" relationship to other nations. The self-concept of the United States seems to include the right to dominate Central America. Policies that maintained the arms race may have been partly due on the American side to a national self-concept of superiority over the Russians, which made parity in arms unacceptable. (Obviously, in this dangerous nuclear age, superiority of arms also diminishes fear.) Leaders and citizens often refer to the United States as the "best country in the world." This is in part an exaggeration of a universal tendency toward ethnocentrism, in part a reflection of real accomplishments, and in part an outgrowth of the U.S. role as a superpower and defender of the free world from communism. Whatever its source, for the United States as well as other nations, a balanced view of the self would serve as a better guide in relations with others.

Nationalism, belonging, and the self-concept

Nations have a tremendous capacity to enlist the loyalty and self-sacrifice of their citizens, especially in conflicts with other nations. Belonging to groups is of profound significance for human beings. It fulfills deep needs and provides satisfactions inherent in connection. It provides a feeling of security. It is essential in defining the self: as a member of a family, a profession, a religious group, voluntary associations, a nation. Individual identity is defined and the self gains value and significance through identification with groups and the connection to others that membership provides. Group support – whether it is a group of fellow concentration camp victims or companions working for a shared cause – contributes to survival even under the worst conditions.[7] It can make life hopeful and satisfying.

The importance of the group arises partly from a genetic proclivity, a sociotropic inclination, and partly from the experience of the child while growing up in a group unit.[8] As we grow older at least part of the initial connection to a small unit such as the family or clan is replaced by connection to a larger unit, the nation. The less is the need for connection and belonging fulfilled in the family and other small groups, the greater will the need be for larger groups. In many places in the modern age the extended family has disappeared, the nuclear family has loosened its hold, and the clan and the tribe have lost their significance. As John Mack notes, the intense commitment to these smaller groupings has often been transferred to the nation.[9] This identification is enlarged by the capacity to generalize and expand the group boundaries, which is encouraged by the state through the use of symbols, education, and other means.

Belonging to a group has a destructive potential if the members stop questioning its beliefs, values, ideals, policies, and actions. But not belonging results in physical and emotional vulnerability. Most people cannot stand emotionally alone and be effective, well-functioning human beings.

It is possible, however, to have a strong bond to the group without giving up individual identity. If the integrity of the self is maintained, discrepancy between one's own values and those of the group can be noticed and faced. Independent judgment and deviation from the group become possible. This is easier in groups that do not severely punish nonconformity. Moreover, people who are connected to varied, smaller communities and have varied group identities can shift perspective more and free themselves more of their embeddedness in a particular group. Critical loyalty – deviation from current group beliefs and practices in the service of the ultimate integrity and well-being of the group and in the service of human welfare – becomes easier.

The relationship to the *other*, to outsiders, is partly a function of the self-concept. If groups do not have valid ways of defining themselves on the basis of their past history, tradition, values, and customs, they will have to define their identity by contrast to outside groups. Psychoanalytic thinking suggests that groups, like individuals, project unacceptable aspects of themselves onto others. Pinderhughes posits an urge to join or come together in groups and an urge to differentiate from the self and repudiate. Those who are repudiated become "bad"; they possess the rejected and renounced parts of the self, which remains pure and "good."[10]

The tendency to maintain a view of the good self (group, nation) by making others bad should be strongest in groups whose self-image is least accurate. The more a group has succeeded in encoding most aspects of its experience into its self-concept, and the more this self-concept is realistic and moderately positive, the less likely that it will give rise to nationalism as an important goal. There will be less need to protect and enhance the nation by "purifying" it or by enlarging its territory or power.

National self-examination is important, but difficult.* It is even more difficult for nations than for individuals to see and accept imperfections in themselves, to discover their denied and unacknowledged parts, as well as to see others without distortion and become aware of their own impact on others. Members of the community of nations have an obligation to be active bystanders who act as mirrors in which other nations can see themselves. The words and acts of friendly nations are more likely to be accepted, but showing critical loyalty to friends requires both courage and tact.

National security and related ideologies

An ideology of national security is another important source of national policy. In the Southern Cone of South America, ideologies of national security led to the widespread murder of supposed internal enemies. The ideology depicted subversion aimed against a country's government, economic order, way of life, religion, and values. Internal enemies were supposedly supported by communist nations. Drastic policies were justified as necessary for national security, even survival.

Richard Barnet has proposed that the ideology of the national security state also characterizes the United States. The search for national security has become pervasive in this "Century of Total War." That peace depends on preparation for war was thought to be a lesson of the Hitler era and of the appearance of Soviet totalitarianism on the march after World War II.[11] A permanent arms race is justified by the image of the Enemy.† In

---

* The group of sixty- to seventy-five-year-old Germans in Trier showed intense involvement in our discussion. After nearly four hours, only one had left; I had to stop the discussion because of other obligations. My impression was that many in the group had never had this kind of discussion before. As a result, they had only very partially restructured or reorganized their original experience in light of the full knowledge about the Hitler era that later became available to them.

The group of students had also failed to work through the past and integrate it with the present. Most of the students had little historical knowledge about the details of the Hitler era and even less "personal knowledge" handed down to them by the older generation. National self-awareness requires processes of exploration within the society.

† The *image of the enemy* has become a widely used concept. In my view, while images of the enemy are important in maintaining and enhancing hostility, they are just one component of a broader ideology of antagonism. Moreover, it is important to identify the roots of enmity and hence of enemy images – a central goal of this book.

Barnet's view, the ideology of the national security state "distorts the meaning of security by defining it primarily in military terms."[12] Such an ideology is built on specific ideologies of antagonism, or a view of the world and of other nations as hostile. It exists in the Soviet Union as well, which has been devastated by many enemies in its history, with about twenty million people killed during World War II.

When national security becomes an ideology, nations stop testing the reality of danger. Attempts to gain security by nonmilitary means are relinquished. A conflict mode of relating to "antagonists" becomes nearly inevitable. Within the nation the flow of information is limited and there is less open discussion of facts and policies.

World views that contribute to war

Many have believed that war is glorious both in itself and in its consequences. We continue to glorify past wars: the companionship, the bravery, the worthy cause, the honor it brings the nation. Great military leaders, like Alexander, are celebrated, even if conquest was their only purpose. Napoleon is a French national hero, in spite of the destruction he wrought. To create loyalty to the group and to communicate its values and ideals, most nations extol their military triumphs in their schools.[13]

William James eloquently described the good qualities brought forth by military service and war: persistence, strength, bravery, spirit of adventure, devotion to community, and discipline in the service of a just cause. Without war these admirable human qualities might be lost. Human beings would know only drudgery, boredom, weakness, and uninventive participation in unappealing labor. James believed that special effort was required to preserve the good qualities brought to life by military service and war. He proposed community service as a moral equivalent to war.[14]

The glorification of war persists in the age of nuclear weapons. Human thought patterns do not abruptly change with the evolution of new technology and new realities. Freeman Dyson wrote that some people "believe that nuclear war is not fundamentally different from other kinds of war and that the old fashioned military virtues, preparedness, endurance and discipline, will enable us to survive it."[15]

Traditional thinking about human nature, morality, and war also contributes to a proclivity for war. "Realist" thinking and just-war theory are widely influential.[16] Realist thinking from Hobbes and Machiavelli on assumes that human beings are self-seeking. They try to fulfill their aims regardless of the harm to others, using "instrumental calculation" and force. Both individuals and nations are untrustworthy; force is necessary to maintain civic virtue. Just-war thinking specifies what makes a war accept-able. It must be fought against enemy forces, not unarmed civilians, and for self-defense, not conquest. However, one cannot always wait until an enemy actually strikes. It is necessary to prepare for war when others have hostile intentions, and at times one must strike first to avoid mortal danger.[17] Because others' intentions and actions are judged not only on the basis of "objective reality," of actual conditions, but on the basis of a world view and other cultural preconditions, miscalculations are highly probable.

Both general world views and specific beliefs affect relations among nations. According to Richard Ned Lebow the Argentine leaders decided to attack the Falklands on the belief that if you throw out a colonial power in the year 1982, it cannot return. In contrast, the English response was partly dictated by their experience with Hitler and the resulting view that if you appease dictators, they will never stop.[18]

Pluralistic versus monolithic societies

Heterogeneity in society is essential for diminishing the chance of war as well as genocide. Unfortunately, pluralism is vulnerable in international relations, even if it exists within a society. The existence of diverse values and ethnic and religious subgroups may lead to a yearning for a larger unity and the belief that citizens and subgroups must overcome differences in facing external threat.

In addition, there are usually no institutions to restrain hostile acts against another nation, as there are internal institutions in a pluralistic society to restrain discrimination and the mistreatment of subgroups. There are no procedural rights that protect other nations, or watchdog groups that would speak out in favor of the other side. Those who do speak out may have to face the wrath of the rest of society. Even a democratic nation is therefore highly vulnerable to manipulation by leaders who create incidents or produce false information, as in the U.S. attack on Libya or the Gulf of Tonkin incident that Lyndon Johnson used to intensify the Vietnam War. The result is patriotic fervor, a uniform definition of events, and lack of critical analysis.

Leadership

Leaders have great power to shape relations between nations, but they are also the products of their societies. Characteristics of the culture and social organization – or at least the culture and organization of a powerful subgroup – shape their thinking and define their range of possibilities.

Unfortunately, some of the cultural preconditions for war are present in most countries.

The leaders' power is enlarged by their capacity to initiate a cycle of hostility. Citizens rarely criticize hostile acts of their own country (especially if they are effectively justified by leaders), but they are aroused to patriotic fervor by hostile acts against their country, even merely retaliatory ones. By generating hostile acts from others, leaders can create psychological readiness for war.

The process of leadership may also produce faulty decision making, such as groupthink.[19] Cultural characteristics may contribute not only to motivations for war but also to faulty decision making. For example, leaders may underestimate an opponent on the basis of devaluative stereotypes, or the culture may produce authoritarian leadership that limits the consideration of options. But faulty decision making accounts for only a small part of the process that leads to war. Given hostile intentions, effective decison making can be more destructive.

The power of leaders to diminish hostility is also great. Sadat's trip to Jerusalem and Nixon's trip to China are examples. Such acts may require great courage when they break with an already predominant orientation in the group, as Sadat's fate demonstrated. Although they can produce a drastic temporary change in perspective, further action is required for lasting change. Less dramatic actions by leaders can also be starting points for change in relations. For change to persist, the cultural elements that underlie conflict must change over time. Beginning steps are crucial, however, in initiating a cycle of positive reciprocity and crosscutting relations (see Chapter 18). A new Soviet rhetoric and new policies initiated by Mikhail Gorbachev and a changed rhetoric by Ronald Reagan, partly a response but probably also a result of societal processes including the peace movement, appear to have started such a cycle between the United States and the Soviet Union.

The national interest

Rarely is there a formal specification of what a nation's citizens and leaders regard as the essential national interest. Hitler is an exception: in *Mein Kampf* he agreed with German leaders before the First World War that the national interest required the conquest of new territories.

According to Hans Morgenthau, interest is best defined as power.[20] Sufficient power to balance others' power is essential to give a state the capacity to protect its interests. The tradition of political realism, of which Morgenthau's writings have been perhaps the most influential contemporary expression, regards international politics as a struggle for power, a contest among sovereign states. However, power ought to be regarded as a means toward an end. Stanley Hoffman suggests that "one ought to start with a definition of those ends and calculate the amount of power needed to reach them"[21] Selecting and specifying goals are essential in defining the national interest.

In the United States, after World War II, national interest came to include protecting the free world from communism. This meant containment of the Soviet army, keeping communists out of power everywhere in the world, and strengthening and spreading institutions that maintain capitalist democracy. At first, this seemed reasonable, but it developed into a rigid ideology of antagonism and a conflict mode of relating and made everything that happened in the world seem to be part of the struggle with communism.

To reduce the dangers of war, nations need a definition of national interest that differentiates essential goals from desirable ones. Several components of national interest can be identified: the capacity of each state to fulfill its internal goals; the security required for this and for survival; relations with other states that maximize the benefit of one's own. These interests can be interpreted in widely varying ways. How a nation maximizes its benefits depends, for example, on whether it desires peace and cooperation more than power and dominance. It depends on whether its world view makes peaceful cooperation seem possible.

Minimalism in the relations of nations

In the long run it is possible to create changes in individuals, cultures, social organizations, and the systems of relations among nations that will reduce group violence. Until then, we must strive to further minimalism in order to make genocide and war less likely. This means (1) a limited definition of national interest as a guide to foreign policy, (2) foreign policies toward other nations guided in part by the extent they fulfill essential, "minimal" values, and (3) the practice by nations of "persistent minimalism" in their relations.

Minimalism requires that nations respect the human rights of their own citizens, their right to life and freedom from abuse by authorities. Less imperative but also important is respect for civil rights. Nations must also respect the security and legitimate interests of other nations. Minimalism is antithetical to expansionist ideologies or an expansionist nationalism. Minimalism also requires that nations act as responsible, active bystanders. By influencing one another, so that each acts on the basis of the "essential" values, nations can both serve their own interests and fulfill their obligation as members of the community of nations. Apart from its focus on essential values, minimalism allows heterogeneity in political and economic systems.

The above principles should be expressed in the practice of persistent minimalism, which relies on the power of bystanders. Nations should be unwilling to accept a nation's mistreatment of its citizens. They should protest and, if necessary, limit trade, aid, and cultural exchange to stop the mistreatment. Only as a last resort should nations break their relations with an offending nation, since they can exert more influence in the context of ongoing relations. Nations should respond to other nations' positive actions (and minimalist practices) by expanding relations. The more nations practice persistent minimalism, the more stable the world order will be. Great powers such as the United States have a special obligation, because they are especially influential.

Experience shows that minimalist practice by nations and international groups can have powerful influence. International pressure, including pressure by human rights organizations and the policies of the Carter administration, helped to reduce torture in South American countries. For a long time it had little effect on the Soviet practice of diagnosing and treating dissidents as mentally ill.[22] But there was inconsistency in opposition and pressure. For example, the International Medical Association was extremely slow to condemn the Soviet practice.[23] This applied to Iran: it had been pressured by some nations to stop its war with Iraq, while receiving arms and support from other nations. Unequivocal minimalist practice by nations and organizations, which is extremely rare, is likely to have great influence on state violence at home or abroad. The earlier such influence is exerted, the greater its chance of effectiveness.*

Toward positive reciprocity

An important source of war is the perception either of the need for self-defense or that a conflict cannot be peacefully resolved. People must become aware of individual and group processes that cause biased perception and must learn to test perceptions and create strategies to resolve conflict peacefully.

Reciprocity, for example, is a profound law of human relations, so universal that some sociobiologists argue it is part of our genetic makeup.

---

* The vision of minimalist practice may seem idealistic. However, ideals are essential in the creation of new realities. Minimalist practice and the evolution toward positive connections among nations described in Chapter 18 can progress together and reinforce each other.

We harm those who have harmed us and help those who have helped us. Thus a friendly initiative directed at a supposed adversary may lead to better relations on both the individual and the international level, especially when the power of adversaries is balanced.[24] This is one way to test the intentions of a supposed enemy.

Positive reciprocity is unlikely when ideologies of antagonism and a conflict mode are dominant. First, to initiate positive action requires some trust that the other will reciprocate in kind. Second, to reciprocate a positive act, the actor's intention must be judged benevolent. The greater the mistrust between parties, the less is it possible to test another's intention by unilateral positive acts. Research shows that individuals, at least, will not reciprocate a kind act if they see its motivation as selfish (including the desire to gain benefits by inducing reciprocation.)[25] Correspondingly, they will retaliate less or not at all if they perceive a harm-doer as having acted thoughtlessly or the harm as an unintended by-product of some action.[26] Alternatively, parties may justify their unwillingness to reciprocate positive acts by expressing mistrust, when the real reason is that their true motives conflict with the positive acts required to reciprocate. Mistrust was the stated reason for the U.S. refusal to stop testing in response to the Soviet suspension of nuclear tests in the mid-1980s; the United States claimed that the Soviet Union stopped only after a long series of tests that gave it an advantage.

To change a malignant mode of relating, nations must begin a process of positive reciprocity starting from the most basic level. They must move from diplomatic contact, to tourism and cultural exchanges, to cooperation in joint enterprises, to mutual help. Over time, motivations that support conflict should diminish, and the desire for cooperation and peace should increase.

Having identified the cultural preconditions for war (and genocide), we must evolve cultures without them. In the next two chapters I discuss an agenda for creating nonaggressive, cooperative, and caring individuals and social groups. Cultural changes together with planetary interrelatedness in economies, in communication, and in facing the nuclear threat may create readiness for an international system that functions as a world community.

17 The nature of groups: security, power, justice, and positive connection

What characteristics of cultures and individuals and what social arrangements and relations among nations are required for caring, connectedness, and nonaggression among subgroups of societies and among nations to become both strongly held values and realities of life? How might we promote them?

Social change requires highly committed people, guided by ideals. Since abstract ideals can become destructive, these ideals must remain connected to the welfare of individual human beings. There are many examples of the influence of such commitment. A group of abolitionists in the first half of the nineteenth century greatly influenced attitudes toward slavery. Their ideals conflicted with the practice of slavery and the beliefs and values of much of society.[1] By clearly expressing their ideas and bravely suffering abuse, they impressed other Americans with their character, and ultimately the virtue of their cause. More recently civil rights activists have had a similar impact. Many rescuers of Jews in Nazi-occupied Europe became highly committed, and some influenced even perpetrators.

Serge Moscovici's research suggests that by expressing and enacting values to which they are committed, a minority can affect the attitudes of the majority. If their beliefs and values are extreme relative to those of the majority, substantial change can still occur, although at first mainly in basic orientations (e.g., blacks are also human beings) rather than attitudes and values that directly guide behavior.[2] The research on bystanders and the real-life examples I described also show that people can powerfully influence others.

In working to diminish group violence, and especially the nuclear threat, people often focus on short-term goals. Arms control and crisis resolution procedures are realistic goals. However, a lasting decrease in the likelihood of war or genocide requires deeper changes in consciousness and perspective, in personalities, culture, and institutions. Such changes require long-term goals and a vision of the road leading to them.

261

Theories of social change abound, but our knowledge of how to bring it about is limited. Actions often have unintended effects. But some movements for change are successful. Perhaps sensitivity to existing realities must be added to a focus on the desired outcome to foresee the pyschological and social consequences of a course of action.

The United States is the place I know best. Whatever its imperfections, the democratic nature of U.S. culture and society makes change possible. Given the power and influence of the United States, its practices and policies can greatly affect international relations and influence the internal practices of other countries, for the worse or for the better. For all these reasons, I will use the United States as the main example in discussing an agenda for change. However, the discussion applies to other nations as well.

Assumptions about human nature and the nature of societies

Does human nature or the nature of social groups limit the possibility of cooperative, caring, nonviolent relations? As I have noted, some philosophers, social thinkers, and psychologists assume that humans are good by nature, others that they are selfish, uncaring, or aggressive. I have stressed my view that human beings have genetic potentials for both altruism and aggression, which evolve through socialization and experience.

Theorists have also discussed the nature of groups and the implications of human nature for group behavior. Andrew Schmookler, in *The Parable of the Tribes*, offers "selection for power" as a central evolutionary concept. He says that social selection is not random, like biological selection; its main principle is power. It is likely to "discard those who revere nature in favor of those willing to exploit it. The warlike may eliminate the pacifist; the ambitious the content...modern industrialized powers will sweep away archaic cultures." Given the unprecedented capacity for growth developed by civilized society, "a Hobbesian struggle for power among societies became inevitable." In Schmookler's view, the "problem of power is inevitable in human societies....Inequalities of power lead inevitably to corruption, and human affairs tend naturally to create inequalities of power."[3] In the long run competitive strivings inevitably dominate over cooperative ones.

Reinhold Niebuhr, in his 1932 classic *Moral Man and Immoral Society*, argues that there is a "basic difference between the morality of individuals and the morality of collectives, whether races, classes or nations."[4] Collectives have a brutal character. In groups egoism and self-interest resist all moral or inclusive social interest.

Our contemporary culture fails to realize the power, extent and persistence of group egoism in human relations. It may be possible, though it is never easy, to establish just relations between individuals within a group by moral and rational suasion and accommodation. In inter-group relations this is practically an impossibility. The relations between groups must therefore always be predominantly political rather than ethical, that is, they will be determined by the proportion of power which each group possesses at least as much as by any rational and moral appraisal of the comparative needs and claims of each group.[5]

Even the individual's capacity for altruism is subverted by the group. The ethical paradox of patriotism is that it "transmutes individual unselfishness into national egotism. . . . The unqualified character of this devotion is the very basis of the nation's power and of the freedom to use power without moral restraint." Critical loyalty to the group is very difficult to achieve, and the group frowns upon it. Another source of support for the group is that individuals try to fulfill egoistic needs and elevate themselves through the nation. Still, unity even within nations is difficult to achieve, partly because privileged groups are concerned with their own self-interest, not the interest of the whole nation. "National unity of action can be achieved only upon such projects as are either initiated by the self interest of dominant groups, in control of the government, or supported by the popular emotions and hysterias which from time to time run through a nation."[6]

This is a highly pessimistic view. The history of the twentieth century may make it seem realistic. Niebuhr criticizes social scientists for unrealistic belief in the possibility of radical change by "reorganization of values" or by socializing the young. However, it may be Niebuhr's assumptions that are incorrect.

Life arrangements vary greatly. The evolution of societies can lead to more or less differentiation among members and more or less justice. India is currently struggling to eliminate the pervasive differences institutionalized in the caste system. In the United States tremendous changes in race relations have resulted from the civil rights movement. Slavery, once common in many regions of the world, has essentially disappeared. Some once warlike nations, for example, Denmark and Sweden, have had harmonious internal and external relations for many years. Although the struggle for power and wealth and a forceful defense of privilege are often dominant in the behavior of both individuals and groups, the desire to create just and caring societies appears again and again, and not only among those who lack privilege.

An alternative view of individual and group potentials

Individuals' and societies' assumptions about human nature and the nature of groups will significantly shape their realities. Our assumptions determine how we perceive others' actions. Seeing the world and human beings as hostile, we may perceive ambiguous acts as threatneing and friendly acts of individuals or groups as devious and manipulative. Perceiving others' actions as hostile we act to defend ourselves. We escape or aggress. Others' reactions to our actions confirm our original assumption. Through a cycle, which is often a vicious cycle but can instead be a benevolent one, we create and maintain our realities.

There are basic human needs for material and psychological security, for a positive view of the self and of one's group, for a world view that offers comprehension. The experience of insecurity arises not only from actual threat but from the very fact of otherness. Since establishment of an identity as an individual and member of a group is both inevitable and desirable, the potential for feeling threatened and for devaluing others is always present. Since human societies and individual relations are rarely static, especially in the modern age, the needs and motives that arise from change are also ever present. Schmookler in his *Parable of the Tribes* suggests that if among neighboring groups one begins to arm, the others will be threatened and will have to follow suit. However, as much of this book suggests, the experience of threat can arise from psychological and societal sources, without real external threat.

Power offers protection against attack. It also assures persons and groups that they can fulfill their basic needs. Are the motives for power and dominance and wealth basic and fixed, or are they strong because they ensure security and the fulfillment of other important needs? Can they be replaced or superseded?

Abraham Maslow offered a conception of a universal hierarchy of human needs, from safety, the most basic need, to esteem, creativity, and self-actualization.[7] Maslow's "higher" needs seem more like important potentials that may or may not evolve as a function of experience. Although the exact nature of an individual's hierarchy is certainly affected by nurture and not only by our shared genetic makeup, the need for safety or security is basic. A related need is efficacy and control, the capacity to influence events. This need is greater if the environment is perceived as hostile. Even if actual control is limited, the illusion of control is essential.[8] Power and dominance and wealth and privilege offer the reality or illusion of security and control.

Humans are malleable. Given insecurity in childhood and authoritarian child rearing, the need for security, power, and control can become profound motives, persisting through life. In a benevolent environment, however, the needlike quality of security, its imperative force, may be lost. This is true of collectivities as well as individuals. Deep individual connections to others and the experience of benevolent persons and institutions result in feelings of safety and trust. Connection and community offer deep satisfaction and can become valued and even dominant in the hierarchy of motives. As heroic self-sacrifice proves, the values of community, caring, and connection can supersede the need for security. Moreover, in a benevolent environment both individuals and groups can acquire confidence in their ability to gain security and fulfill essential motives through connection and cooperation.

To this end society must offer the opportunity to fulfill human potentials as well as basic needs. For example, part of the human potential is striving for spirituality or transcendence, a seeking that goes beyond the material and visible and beyond the boundaries of the self. Transcendence can be sought through human connection and community. The more a society offers opportunities for transcendence by positive means, the less likely that it will be sought in destructive movements.

Even in the most benevolent society, the experience of frustration is inevitable. All of us suffer from external constraints, limitations in our abilities, or inner conflicts. All suffer injustice at times. All suffer the pain of separation or loss and experience threats to the psychological self. How people respond to this depends on past experience and present circumstance. Their response is more constructive if they trust their own capacities and the world. People can even take frustration as a positive challenge and proceed with constructive efforts to fulfill blocked goals – or relatively painlessly relinquish goals that are not in their power to fulfill.

Trust within a group does not necessarily lead to good relations with other groups. Trust and connectedness arise from "proximal" experiences. Members of different groups usually have no such direct, proximal ties. Trust must evolve through a history of contact, cooperation, and friendly relations.

Without it groups need power to feel secure and power often comes to be valued for its own sake. The "selection" of leaders contributes to this. Those who seek and succeed in achieving leadership tend to have stronger motivation for power than other group members. Because power strengthens feelings of security within the group (and possibly fulfills an ideal self-concept), leaders who successfully use or enhance the group's power please members and strengthen their own leadership position. All this is not inevitable, and I will later discuss ways to strengthen the values of connection and cooperation between groups.

Relations between the individual and the group

Individuals often give up autonomy, responsibility, and decision making to their group and leaders. The group often helps people fulfill hopes and desires that they cannot fulfill in their individual existence. It hones desires for self-aggrandizement and its fulfillment through the group, partly because this enhances loyalty. Social identity often embodies hopes, desires, and ideals different from individual goals and identity. In addition, giving the self over to the group can diminish a burdensome identity and give people an oceanic feeling of connectedness, of breaking out of the confines of the individual self.

Can the relationship between individuals and the group change? It is important that people acquire a critical consciousness, the ability to see their group's imperfections as well as strengths. Then their loyalty to the group may be expressed in attempts to improve it, rather than insistence on its virtues. Such critical loyalty may seem incompatible with the aim of strengthening the group as a community, but it is not. In well-functioning families the members can express their own needs and beliefs without rebellion, and conflicts can be resolved. The same can happen in larger groups. Close ties can provide the security to oppose potentially destructive ideas and practices. The group may come to regard such opposition not as disloyalty but as service to itself.

Important societal issues

Social justice and life problems

The awareness of injustice motivates people to seek justice, and sometimes also to take revenge. However, conditions that would be defined as cruelly unjust at one time are accepted as fair at another time. Besides, just-world thinking and other psychological processes may make both victims and bystanders see unjust suffering as fair or deserved. Depending on the culture and traditions of a society, what is regarded as the "right" input (contribution) and outcome (reward) of different parties greatly varies. If the culture regards inequality as natural and right, if the work expected of the less powerful is not unbearable, if their basic needs for food and shelter are met, and if the culturally accepted standards for their treatment do not permit excessive cruelty and the powerful party abides by them, the experience of injustice may never arise.

In times of severe and persistent life problems, the poor are often most affected. If they suffer greatly while others still seem to thrive, they are likely to feel a sense of injustice. Dislocation by rapid technological and social change may have a similar effect.

In all our instances of genocide and mass killing, disparities in the suffering of different groups under difficult life conditions were significant. In Germany, between the two world wars millions suffered great deprivation while some lived ostentatiously and well; Hitler used this to fan the dissatisfaction of the masses. He also fanned anti-Semitism by claiming that Jews profited from the suffering of Germans. In Argentina with its very rich elite and many poor, the decline in living standards severely affected many people but not the wealthy elite. This contributed to the violence of leftist groups, which provoked the military. In Cambodia the cities swelled with people who had lost their land or could not live off it, while corruption and profiteering were rampant.

Societies need institutions, both government agencies and citizen groups, that deal with the material and psychological effects of difficult life conditions and mitigate inequality in misfortune. Such institutions must offer material help, for example, through adjustments in welfare policies or through work programs like those in the United States during the depression. Added taxes on the rich may be needed to equalize the burden. Institutions are also needed to reduce isolation and to enhance feelings of community. The experience of shared suffering contributes to feelings of community and minimizes the psychological impact of material difficulties.

When facing adversity, people have a strong urge to protect their own privilege and resources, but their separateness makes them lonely and scared. As the bombing of London by the Germans in World War II and the Hungarian revolution of 1956 showed, people are greatly strengthened when they face adversity together. Joined in a fight for survival, they can feel strong, even joyful, under the worst of circumstances. Trusting enough in a better future to share their resources with others can make them feel strong and contented. Can societies help people come together in such ways?

Creating a society of enablement

Enablement is one important avenue to social justice. The experience of enablement and the capacity to choose and fulfill "reasonable" goals go a long way toward increasing personal satisfaction and the perception of justice. The "culture of poverty," "underclass" mentality, and disordered and chaotic family backgrounds greatly impair enablement. Children from such backgrounds do not develop faith in their capacity to shape their lives. They cannot take advantage of education and other opportunities, or they lack the values and motivation to learn or work hard. They have no stake in the community and therefore no concern for the communal good. On the other hand, stable families with their basic needs fulfilled have a stake in society and a belief in the possibilities it offers.

Programs such as Head Start, a government-sponsored preschool enrichment program for disadvantaged children that proved successful in preparing them for the schools, offer one avenue to enablement. Children do better in these programs when the parents are also involved. Parents who participate may come to value education more and learn modes of interaction with their children that enrich the children's experience and improve their skills and self-esteem.

Social justice requires that some people accept less materially. This means finding contentment and satisfaction less in material wealth and more in connection and community. People must be more willing to devote themselves to improving the welfare of others and more interested in the intrinsic values of excellence, creation, and cooperation, as well as aesthetic and other nonmaterial pursuits. Satisfying connections among individuals and communities can evolve into deeply held values and increasingly become realities of life.

Individualism and community

In the United States an ethic of individualism is a potential barrier to feelings of connection and responsibility to others. Bellah and his associates, writing about contemporary American values and mores, note that individual freedom is interpreted as freedom from restraint. They identify two dominant forms of individualism: economic and expressive. Americans have long valued the pursuit of economic gain and have come to value the pursuit of knowing, developing, and enjoying the self and its potentials. As they found in their interviews, expressive individualism can be narcissistic, or self-centered. People can selfishly cultivate themselves and believe that they have no responsibility even for their spouse or children.[9]

Alternatively, people can see self-actualization *in relationship to* other people, as part of a community. In my view Carl Rogers and Abraham Maslow, the psychologists regarded as fathers of the current cultural movement of expressive individualism, believed this. Maslow found that the people he regarded as advanced in self-actualization were also willing to act for the common good.[10] Rogers said that as people in therapy accept and love themselves more, they also accept and love others more. Maslow also believed that "uncovering" therapy leads to more caring and even that this was probably evidence that human nature is basically good.[11]

People who fully develop and harmoniously integrate their capacities, values, and goals will be connected to others. The full evolution of the self, the full use of the human potential, requires relationships and the development of deep connections and community – as well as the capacity for separateness.

Along with an ethic of individualism there is widespread volunteerism in the United States.[12] People collect money for the United Way, volunteer in hospitals, help with youth activities, and join to work for political causes. Still, the overall sense of community is limited. Subgroups have strong feelings of differentness, and many Americans are isolated. Individualism accounts for this in part, but the complex technological society we live in and the traditional U.S. pattern of mobility are also important. Americans move more than people in most other highly industrial societies. An analysis reported in the 1960s found that the average American moved about fourteen times in life, the average Briton about eight times, the average Japanese about five times. In other countries populated by immigrants, such as Australia and Canada, the rate of moving is similar to that of the United States.[13]

Our experience of connection and community shape who we are, how we experience other people, and how we bear the stresses of both ordinary and extraordinary events. For example, in Korea, prisoners of war were "brainwashed": through isolation (e.g., solitary confinement for long periods) and extreme psychological pressures, their captors tried to get them to confess to crimes by their military and government and to endorse the communist system. Amitai Etzioni writes that American prisoners of war were more susceptible than prisoners from other counties.[14] For example, thirty-eight out of fifty-nine air force men " 'confessed' to non-existent U.S. bacteriological attacks on Korea" and many collaborated with their communist captors. In contrast, almost all Turkish prisoners withstood the pressure of isolation. According to military investigators, they "stuck together as a group and resisted as a group."

When a Turk got sick, the rest nursed him back to health. If a sick Turk was ordered to the hospital two well Turks went along. They ministered to him hand and foot while he was there, and when he was discharged, brought him back to the compound in their arms. They shared their clothing and their food equally.[15]

In contrast, many Americans thought of themselves "not as a group bound by common ties and loyalties, but as isolated individuals."

Individualism has advantages as well as disadvantages. Young American children are less affected by the presence of teachers, for example in subscribing to standards of good conduct on questionnaires, than children in other cultures.[16] Perhaps in "normal" times Americans are more able to preserve their own views and resist authority.* Without support by connection to others, however, one's views may collapse under the pressure of difficult life conditions.

We must strive for an ideal of individuals with strong, independent identities who are also supported by their connections to others and rootedness in a community. Connectedness that extends beyond one's group to all human beings is an important building block of a world in which groups turn toward, not against, each other.

The accountability of leaders

The lack of accountability and the limited perspective of leaders are problems even in a democracy. A leader is usually advised and guided by a small group of persons who have the same values and views as the leader. The processes of decision making in groups further limit a leader's perspective.[17] Following the Bay of Pigs fiasco (the attempted invasion of Cuba by CIA-trained Cuban exiles), President Kennedy wondered how he could have been so ignorant. Apparently, in the course of lengthy deliberations, two facts that most members of the group knew were never discussed. First, the invaders would face an enemy that had a 140:1 numerical superiority. Second, CIA investigation showed that the Cuban people would not rise up to support the invaders. The decision to invade had been made, so nobody brought forth this information. Human beings cannot commit themselves to a course to action while contemplating information that makes it unreasonable; such information may submerge in their consciousness and disappear from working memory.

Great power is another danger. Power and the leadership role easily lead to a belief in special knowledge and the devaluation of those who dare to oppose. Leaders may come to believe that they have the right to use whatever means are necessary to achieve their desired ends.

---

* One reason Oliver North struck such a chord in the American people may be Americans' ambivalent relationship to authority. In his testimony at the Iran–Contra congressional hearings North showed disrespect for members of congress and lectured them on a number of topics including patriotism, while professing deep respect for and obedience to the president. Respect for authority combined with a realistic sense of its limitations and imperfections makes a nation less vulnerable to excesses that might arise from a strong authority orientation.

For all these reasons, it is essential to decrease the insulation of leaders and increase their accountability. One way to achieve this would be to increase direct contact between leaders, especially the president, and the public, in ways that are conducive to dialogue. Leaders might be obliged to attend town meetings or other comparable public gatherings on a regular basis to answer questions and hear varied views. Exposure to a broad range of views and the need to talk to a broad range of people in settings that are not "managed" (like news conferences) would require leaders to seriously think about perspectives different from their own and the human consequences of their policies.

Freedom, pluralism, and self-censorship

Freedom requires the free flow of information that makes people aware of discrepancies between their ideals and existing realities. Awareness of such discrepancies led to the civil rights movement. A BBC television program depicting the famine in Ethiopia produced an outpouring of help. The visions of blood and suffering in Vietnam on the daily television news were important impetus to the antiwar movement. Seeing the homeless freezing on the streets of New York City can mobilize movement for change.

Without free public discourse a uniformity of views can be imposed on the population. Barry Goldwater, a political conservative, showed the spirit of pluralism when he spoke out against the Moral Majority's attempt to censor television and against Jesse Helms's attempt to deny the courts the authority to rule on cases involving the separation of church and state in public schools.[18] Censorship and intimidation of the media are one mark of a repressive system. Government "disinformation" (falsehoods intended to affect international or domestic conditions) also deprives the people of a fair knowledge of reality on which to base their judgments.

"Self-censorship" by the media (biased and selective reporting) has the same effect, and it is widespread. A well-documented example was the reporting of the extermination of Jews during World War II. Reports in American newspapers were rare and mostly buried inside the papers. America's response would certainly have been different had the horrendous story screamed at the people from the front page. When Franco ruled Spain, the editors of *Time* magazine rejected a report on Spanish communists because "it made the communists look too good."[19] In 1963, their reporters from Vietnam submitted an article that depicted a losing war. The article was rejected and replaced by one that stressed, among other things, improved fighting by government troops.[20] Nuclear alerts because of computer malfunction are frequent, and some proceed to the last stage before launch, but stories about them are reported in small articles inside newspapers. The attitude of the population toward the huge nuclear arsenal might have changed and the pressure for disarmament might have intensified if lead articles had called attention to this situation.

Social systems use "propaganda of integration" to promote citizen support.[21] The media tend to report in ways that support and maintain the system, sometimes consciously, at other times not. One reason is that editors and newspaper and television reporters share with their audience dominant cultural perspectives or biases. Like almost everyone else in the United States, when the Vietnam War started, they saw not a freedom fight or a civil war, but dominoes falling.

The suppliers of information and opinion may also fear straying too far from culturally dominant views because it would mean breaking with the group and might result in social sanctions: disapproval, criticism, loss of readers. Reporters may incur problems with their editors if their point of view is "radical," even if this is expressed simply in their choice of facts to report. After all, facts acquire significance by their meaning, which derives from the perspective of the reporter – and the reader or viewer. Adherence to currently dominant views often occurs automatically, as a result of shared views and a natural tendency to conform. However, a conscious choice to avoid controversy may explain such things as the problems citizens' groups had in 1984–88 when they tried to get films about Central America on television. Editors and reporters may also want to "protect" the people and not cause panic or social discord. It is clear, however, that such protection is selectively employed.

The value systems dominant in organs of the media are known to reporters and influence their reporting.[22] In a pluralistic society different orientations can counterbalance each other, but dominant values and views tend to result in overall biases, limiting the picture of reality.

The economic factor is also a subtle and potentially destructive influence. This is a complex issue; the independence of the media requires financial independence. But if, in pursuit of money, the media create a climate of sensationalism, that climate will in turn require the media to be sensationalistic. A television report on black–Jewish contacts aimed at improving relations concluded with a picture of Farrakhan, the virulently anti-Semitic black leader; this added drama, but counteracted the point of the news it was reporting.

Finally, even in a free society, powerful government pressure can influence reporting. Some of this pressure is direct. The FBI in the late 1960s pressured Columbia Records and other companies to stop advertising in underground newspapers that opposed the Vietnam War.[23] As a result, many of these newspapers went bankrupt. Subtler pressure is produced by government requests to underplay, not report, or report in a particular way certain events – or simply by knowledge of what the government would prefer. This power of government has many sources, including its ability to regulate access to news.

Self-censorship may be an intentional decision, a barely conscious bias, or an unconscious screening of reality. This cognitive screening can involve "dissociation," the keeping out of consciousness aspects of life or reality that do not fit cultural self-conception and values. For example, members of the media probably screened out clues about atrocities in Vietnam before My Lai because they were discrepant from Americans' views of themselves. Because the screening and the resulting dissociation are shared by the group, the distortions are difficult to detect. Attempts to call awareness to it will generate hostility. It is essential to promote public discussion that enhances awareness of self-censorship and its sources. One way to correct cognitive screening is to take seriously the voices of those who claim to point to a reality we do not see, even if they present an unpleasant image of us.

Self-censorship can work in many directions. Conservatives have claimed that the media have a liberal bias. This is debatable. In the mid-1980s there have been reports of atrocities by the Contras in Nicaragua. Especially because the United States was directly involved, "objective" reporting would have included pictures on television and in the papers of the aftermath of brutal Contra attacks on civilians. Such reporting did not occur. Whatever political orientation is its main victim, self-censorship impedes the natural processes of a free society.

18   The creation and evolution of caring, connection, and nonaggression

Changing cultures and the relations between societies

Crosscutting relations and superordinate goals

As I have noted, human beings tend to create "us" – "them" differentiations and stereotypes. Constrasting ourselves with others is a way to define the self. We see our values and way of life as natural and good and easily see others who diverge as bad. By preadolescence even trivial differences in clothing, musical preference, appearance, or behavior may cause substantial devaluation.

Crosscutting relations (a term proposed by Morton Deutsch) among subgroups of society and between nations can overcome these tendencies.[1] To evolve an appreciation of alikeness and a feeling of connectedness, members of subgroups of society must live together, work together, play together; their children must go to school together. Members of different nations must also work and play together. Social psychologists found in the 1950s that given existing prejudice, it was not enough for blacks and whites simply to live near each other. To reduce prejudice requires positive contact. Later, as schools were integrated, minority children continued to do less well academically and had poor self-esteem. Cooperative learning procedures, which led to extensive interaction on an equal footing, increased the prosocial behavior of all children and the academic achievement and self-esteem of minority children. Real interaction in a framework of equality is essential for people to come to know and accept each other.

Ideally, people will join in the pursuit of shared goals. "Superordinate goals" are goals that are shared by individuals or groups and that are higher in the hierarchy than other potentially conflicting goals.[2] Such goals express and further generate shared values and ideals. For example, in the civil rights movement in the United States, whites and blacks joined. In many other grass-roots movements in the United States diverse groups of

274

people work together.* Economic well-being, protection of the environment, the creation of community, and working against nuclear destruction may become shared, superordinate goals.

We can begin in a small way. For example, in 1985 in Amherst, Massachusetts, old and young residents, members of the local police, and university professors and students joined to build a playground at one of the local elementary schools. For four days they worked, talked, and ate together. Those present were transported by the experience. People who came on the first day to work a four-hour shift remained until the end. A shared goal provided an opportunity and the permission to be part of a community. Similar events have occurred in other towns of the Northeast, under the direction of the same architect.

An outgrowth of this community action was a larger-scale collaborative effort at the nearby campus of the University of Massachusetts. The graduating class of 1985 cleaned, repaired, and painted one floor of the library building. The project was initiated by the director of the university's physical plant, who had participated in building the playground. In the fall of 1986, students, faculty, administrators, staff members, and some Amherst residents, under the leadership of volunteers from the physical plant, repaired and repainted in four days the remaining 23 floors of the huge library. I believe this joint effort greatly improved cohesion within subgroups, such as students and faculty from the same department who participated together, improved ties across group lines, and generated a greater feeling of community.

Groups must have some trust in each other to adopt superordinate goals. Moreover, the strength of existing group identities and previous successes in achieving joint goals affect the extent to which intergroup cooperation reduces conflict and results in positive ties.[3] However, joint goals can be wisely selected, starting with less demanding ones.

Preparation for interaction can increase acceptance of the other group's values and perspective on life and acceptance of differences in everyday customs and behaviors that, even when they have little practical significance, have great emotional impact. Differences in culture can be a source of irritation, conflict, and mutual devaluation. People have different nonverbal cues or degrees of openness and emotional expressiveness, different rules of interpersonal relations and different work habits, beliefs, and

* There are exceptions, however. The peace movement in the United States includes few blacks. For black people, concern about nuclear war may be overshadowed by immediate economic and social problems. Until their basic material and psychological needs are met, individuals and groups may be less inclined to concern themselves with the evolution of caring and nonaggression in general, unless they can see in it hope for themselves.

values. Preparatory education in diversity and actual contact with different groups from an early age can make intergroup relations satisfying rather than frustrating.*

Learning by doing and steps along a continuum of benevolence

Starting with common everyday acts and moving on to acts requiring greater sacrifice while producing greater benefits, helping others can lead to genuine concern and a feeling of responsibility for people. To reduce the probability of genocide and war, helping must be inclusive, across group lines, so that the evolving values of caring and connection ultimately include all human beings.

We devalue those we harm and value those we help. As we come to value more highly the people we help and experience the satisfactions in-

---

* As I have noted, physical proximity alone does not increase acceptance. For example, foreign students' evaluation of their host nation may become more negative over time. However, they start out with highly positive evaluations and perhaps unrealistic hopes and expectations. It may also be that evaluations turn more negative if the students experience no crosscutting relations or close contact. American students evaluated the French less positively after a year-long stay. They usually lived in apartments with other Americans. In contrast, American students in Germany maintained more of their initial positive evaluation of Germans. They lived in student dormitories with German students and reported greater ease in establishing contact with both students and nonstudents.[4]

While contact is important to reduce negative beliefs, not all contact improves group relations. Certain conditions contribute to "positive exposure": equal-status contact between the members of interacting groups; cooperation between them to fulfill shared goals; intimate rather than casual contact; and authorities or the social climate approving of and supporting the intergroup contact.[5] Other research shows that information about another group that prepares people for contact can improve the effects of contact. When casual contact (e.g., between Israeli tourists and Egyptians) reinforces the existing stereotypes, preparatory information can reduce the negative effects.[6] In addition to information that stresses the positive characteristics of the other group or explains the roots of "negative" characteristics in their cultural history, communication that brings to the fore their shared humanity and personalizes them (perhaps through the "stories" of real individuals) may be of great value.

That contact alone is insufficient to create positive relations but can strengthen devaluation was demonstrated in the real (rather than romanticized) history of the evacuation of children from London in World War II.[7] The children removed from the city were mostly poor, inner-city children. Their hosts in the countryside were all well-to-do. In spite of their initial desire to be helpful, without being prepared for the experience many reacted with aversion to these verminous children with poor habits of hygiene, cockney accents, and often religions different from their own, some of them Jewish. Given pronounced class differences and prejudice, many hosts became hostile and schemed to get rid of the children. Many went home.

herent in helping, we also come to see ourselves as more caring and help-ful. One of our goals must be to create societies in which there is the widest possible participation in doing for others.

We need to greatly expand the opportunities of both children and adults to act on others' behalf. We could provide children with the opportunity to visit sick children in hospitals (contrary to current hospital policies), to help older people, and to collect and send needed items to people in other countries. Both schools and community organizations could establish such projects and guide children to participate in them.* My experience with a number of relevant experiments suggests that children would willingly do a great deal in others' behalf, given the proper opportunity, guidance, and some choice, so that their activities fit their inclinations.

Adults must also help others if they are to guide children and must themselves develop more the values of caring and connection. As I noted, many Americans are involved in volunteer activities.[9] In England volunte-ering to donate blood is widely practiced.[10] We ought to create wide-ranging opportunities for service to others and promote the spirit that leads people to use them, including cooperative activities in which we receive less than our partners. Cooperation connects people. Research with young children has shown that when they work cooperatively rather than com-petitively, with joint rewards, they like one another and children outside the group better.[11]

Business people and engineers can give up some profits to train unskilled youth. Many people could "adopt" teenage mothers (or fathers) and help them learn what infants require for healthy development. The helpers could impart skills and awareness of the infants' needs and at the same time provide the mothers with desperately needed emotional support. Although concern with societal problems like unemployed youth and teenage parent-ing has long existed, the motivation to help might increase if people realized that, as they promote humanitarian ideals like greater justice and improved quality of life for many, their actions also contribute to a long-

---

* In Metro High School in St. Louis, doing for others is an integral part of education. Its 250 selected students (65% black, 35% white) are required to work as volunteers in the com-munity. In 1983, the service requirement was sixty hours a year at a nonprofit agency within the city of St. Louis. According to Ernest Boyer, and students receive "far more than they give." "One young man with longish hair, tight and faded blue jeans, and a street-wise expression on his face spoke movingly of what he learned while working on the 'graveyard shift' (12 midnight to 7 a.m.) in the emergency room of a medical center: 'I learned a lot this past summer. I learned how to deal with my own feelings. I learned how to cry. That was a big step. When a little three-year-old girl goes into seizures and they found out she had meningitis and died that morning, you learn to feel for people.'"[8]

term evolution of caring and nonaggression. This makes such concerns relevant also to peace activists and human rights advocates.

How we help others is crucial. Helping can be divisive if helpers use it, perhaps unconsciously, as a means to elevate themselves over the people they help. Welfare recipients in the United States often feel diminished, powerless.[12] We must strive to treat recipients of both government and private help with respect, as full members of the community. Only this way will helpers (and recipients) experience the connection to others that helping can promote.

Creating positive connections between groups

Much of the preceding as well as following discussion applies to relationships between both subgroups of societies and nations. Positive reciprocity, crosscutting relations, superordinate goals, and unilateral and mutual help are all important. Daniel Patrick Moynihan, starting with Freud's dictum that anatomy is destiny, adds that social structure is destiny as well.[13] Anatomy is less destiny than Freud thought; social structure more than we usually recognize. Change in individuals, unless it leads to changes in culture and social structure, will remain unstable and will not spread. Changes in individuals and societal institutions must be followed by changes in international structures.

Uri Bronfenbrenner, a U.S. psychologist who has studied the socialization of children in the Soviet Union, noted the mutual devaluation in the United States and the Soviet Union. The two societies' attitudes toward each other were mirror images. While he was in the Soviet Union, his views of the country and its people were positive. A few weeks after coming home and after talking to people in the United States, he began to doubt his own experience.[14] For change to persist and spread, groups need a *minimum mass* – of people sharing an attitude, of the culture expressing it, and of the institutions embodying it.

A first step is expanding contact between nations. Without real human contact, tourism has limited value. Tourists are likely to interpret the behavior of foreigners according to stereotypes, and strong devaluative stereotypes tend to be self-fulfilling. Real contact is important for the beginnings of positive connection.

Crosscutting relations that bring people from different groups to work and play together are also essential. Educational, cultural, and scientific exchanges between nations can provide such contact. Joint projects are a further step. Joint manufacturing and joint work in technology and science create positive ties and increase the cost of aggression. The world is already moving in this direction. The United States produces movies cooperatively with many countries; Japanese and American manufacturers work together, even build plants together.

Service by people as volunteers in each others' countries – a kind of mutual peace corps – would be a vehicle for both crosscutting relations and the learning of benevolence. If people in one country do not have technical skills to impart to another, they can make other contributions. They can teach about their own culture: their art, their values, their perspective on reality.

Cooperation should progress from small projects to highly significant ones, such as the development of new energy sources, AIDS research, and the exploration of space. All such projects represent potentially significant superordinate goals. An overarching superordinate goal would be an international economic and political order in which all countries have significant stake. Third world countries need aid in development from industrial countries, to create connection and diminish the chance of international conflict. Superordinate goals have already been thrust upon nations: dealing with the nuclear threat and environmental destruction.

The processes and practices that I have described can build trust and the valuing of connection, produce a redefinition of national interest in minimalist terms, and lead members of the international community to regard it as an obligation to be active bystanders. Comparable practices can focus on creating caring and connection among subgroups of societies.

Some progress toward international institutions has been made in recent years, although not along the lines discussed above. A large and increasing number of binational and multinational treaties have been concluded. Multinational corporations, although they tend to be exploitive in their present form (of the resources and populations of countries where they operate), have the potential to function as collaborative enterprises that embody superordinate goals and establish crosscutting relations among citizens of different countries.

Positive socialization: parenting, the family, and schools

All along I have discussed the importance of how we raise children. Certain experiences children have in their interaction with others shape their dispositions for antagonism or for caring and connection. They contribute to their prosocial orientation, empathy, positive self-esteem, and a sense of security, which are the sources of both benevolence and the capacity to act in one's own behalf. The positive socialization practices that contribute to the development of these characteristics include affection;

responsiveness to the child's needs; and reasoning with the child, explaining rules both for the home and for the outside world and the impact of the child's actions or inaction on others.[15] Parents also need to focus responsibility on the child for others' welfare: their siblings, pets, and, when appropriate, people outside the family. Parents must exercise reasonable control and make sure that the child adheres to moral and social standards they regard as essential. They need to use "natural socialization," guiding the child to participate in worthwhile activities, including helping. Substantial learning and change result from participation rather than from direct tuition or reward and punishment.[16] Finally, parents themselves must show concern for others.

Children so raised will be both caring and "enabled," capable of using the opportunities society offers for education and achievement. If parents allow the child increasing autonomy, if families are reasonably democratic, and if they allow the expression (and thus the experience) of the full range of human emotions, children are also likely to gain the self-awareness, emotional independence, and security required for independent judgment and critical loyalty.

At least minimally supportive social conditions are also required, that is, reasonably secure and ordered life circumstances. The benevolence and care that are necessary for positive socialization may be impossible for parents who cannot fulfill their basic needs for food, shelter, stability, and psychological support. Minimal social justice is therefore necessary.

Families are systems, with varying rules. Some families do not allow the expression of sadness or pain, feelings that are inevitable. Others do not even allow joy to be expressed. The practice of diagnosing family systems would help families see themselves and the systems they have created. Being made aware of research showing that children respond well to positive parenting from birth on could change assumptions that contribute to physical punishment and other destructive practices.[17] Education about children and child-rearing techniques, possibly starting before birth, can provide parents with feelings of expertise and control and increase their affection and benevolence toward their children.[18] Social scientists and interested citizens can provide an important service by systematically disseminating such information, which now reaches the public in a haphazard manner.

The schools can also make an important contribution. Beyond teaching skills and substantive knowledge, schools inevitably shape children's personalities. Teachers, like parents, should employ positive discipline practices. The schools should not be authoritarian systems, but democratic ones in which children learn the capacity for responsible decision making. It is important to introduce cooperative learning procedures in which children work together, teach each other, and coordinate their activities. Such programs improve academic performance and self-esteem in minority children and increase prosocial behavior toward peers and the capacity to cooperate in all children.[19] The schools can guide children to participate in prosocial behavior outside the school and provide them with opportunities to assume responsibility and be helpful to others within the school. By guiding children to concern themselves with the world around them and contribute to the social good, the schools (and parents) can help children become socially responsible citizens.

By their rules, schools help determine whether children interact with each other aggressively or cooperatively, and thereby the behavioral skills and tendencies they develop. This is highly important, because the child's socialization becomes self-socialization: the child's behavior shapes others' behavior toward the child, and the child's responses to others create the cycle of interaction that further shapes the child's personality, motives, and world view.[20]

Schools can teach about diversity and commonality. George Orwell, in *Homage to Catalonia*, described his profound change in attitude toward the enemy when during the Spanish Civil War he saw from his trench an enemy soldier pull down his pants and relieve himself. Schools (and universities) can teach their students about differences in customs, ways of life, and values of people in different groups and their shared humanity and shared needs and yearnings. To accomplish this, it helps to move beyond abstractions and concretize and particularize human beings.

By helping students enter the framework of other cultures, schools can let them see how cultures and subcultures evolved differently because of different circumstances and different choices. By coming to see cultures as modes of adaptation and to appreciate the functions of different customs, especially if this is combined with a wide range of personal experience, students may come to accept quite varied ways of life.

Finally, parents, schools, and universities can teach children to recognize in themselves and others the psychological processes that lead to destructive acts. To realize that seeing others as of lesser value or blaming them might represent devaluation and scapegoating is significant progress. Further progress is achieved by learning to catch oneself devaluing others or deflecting self-blame to others and by acquiring the capacity to become an observer not only of others' but of one's own psychological processes.

Avenues for change

Social change requires highly committed citizens. Groups of citizens can set for themselves such goals as building playgrounds, renovating neglected neighborhoods, or helping the homeless, as well as cultural or business ventures with members of other groups or nations. They can spread information and ideas. We need a vision of long-term change and specific, small ways in which people can contribute. Most people will do nothing unless they lose the feeling of powerlessness through the understanding that small changes are not only important in themselves but part of an evolutionary process.

Language and ideas

Ideas can be destructive or prepare us for caring and benevolence. Negative realities like dangers to the environment, scarcity of resources, the threat of nuclear winter, and the state of the world economy all suggest our inescapable global interdependence.

Language shapes experience. Those who destroy often use euphemisms. The language of nuclear policy creates illusions: by referring to shields, umbrellas, deterrence, and "defense," it implies a security that does not exist.[21] A language true to reality will motivate people to join in efforts to eliminate the potential of nuclear destruction. Presenting to people the realities of torture and atrocities will motivate them to work against their practice.

Writers, artists, the media, leaders, all citizens

Books, films, and other cultural products sometimes have substantial influence on whole societies. The films *Dr. Strangelove* and *The Day After* shaped and mobilized the public spirit. A BBC television report on starvation in Ethiopia resulted in a worldwide effort to help. The novel (and film) *Gentlemen's Agreement* brought anti-Semitism to the public awareness in the United States. Artists, writers, reporters, and others who work in the public domain can make powerful contributions to social change. We must engage them and discuss with them the individual and cultural bases of violence and benevolence and their potential to shape public awareness and influence policy.

National leaders have tremendous potential to shape attitudes and lead people to action. John F. Kennedy, in creating the Peace Corps, inspired a generation of Americans. Those committed to positive change should engage politicians and other influential public figures in an exchange of ideas about the origins of antagonism and positive connection.

A vision of the future, ideals that are rooted in the welfare of individual human beings rather than in abstract designs for improving "humanity," small and intermediate goals along the way, commitment, and the courage to express ideas in words and actions – all are essential to fulfill an agenda for a world of nonaggression, cooperation, caring, and human connection.

Notes

Preface

1. Staub, E. (1978–79). *Positive social behavior and morality*. Vol. 1, *Social and personal influences*; Vol. 2, *Socialization and development*. New York: Academic Press.
2. Marton, K. (1982). *Wallenberg*. New York: Ballantine Books.
3. Staub, E. (1985). The psychology of perpetrators and bystanders. *Political Psychology, 6,* 61–86.

Chapter 1

1. Bettelheim, B. (1986). Their specialty was murder. Review of Robert J. Lifton's "The Nazi doctors." *New York Times Book Review*. October 5.
2. Kuper, L. (1981). *Genocide: Its political use in the twentieth century*. New Haven & London: Yale University Press.
3. Ibid., p. 23.
4. Ibid., p. 28.
5. Ibid., p. 28.
6. Ibid., p. 19.
7. On the political identification of groups for torture (and mass killing) see also:
   Staub, E. (1987). The psychology of torture and torturers. Paper presented at a symposium on torture at the American Psychological Association meetings, New York. Also in P. Suedfeld (Ed.). (In press). *Psychology and torture*. Washington, D. C.: Hemisphere Publishing Co.
8. Hilberg, R. (1961). *The destruction of European Jews*. Chicago: Quadrangle Books.
   Davidowicz, L. S. (1975). *The war against the Jews: 1933–1945*. New York: Holt, Rinehart & Winston.
9. Davidowicz, *War against the Jews*.
   Des Pres, T. (1976). *The survivor: An anatomy of life in the death camps*. Oxford: Oxford University Press.
   Hilberg, *Destruction*.
10. Toynbee, A. J. (Ed.). (1916). *The treatment of the Armenians in the Ottoman Empire, 1915–1916*. London: His Majesty's Stationery Office.
11. Morgenthau, H., Sr. (1918). *Ambassador Morgenthau's story*. New York: Doubleday.
12. Etcheson, G. (1984). *The rise and demise of democratic Kampuchea, 1942–1981*. Boulder: Westview Press.
    Becker, E. (1986). *When the war was over: The voices of Cambodia's revolution and its people*. New York: Simon & Schuster.

284

13. Amnesty International Report. (1980). *Testimony on secret detention camps in Argentina.* London: Amnesty International Publications.

   Argentine National Commission. (1986). *Nunca Mas: The report of the Argentine National Commission on the disappeared.* New York: Farrar, Straus, Giroux.

14. Rubinstein, R. L. (1975). *The cunning of history.* New York: Harper & Row.

Chapter 2

1. Berlin, I. (1979). Nationalism: Past neglect and present power. *Partisan Review, 46.*

   Mack, J. (1983). Nationalism and the self. *Psychohistory Review, 2,* nos. 2–3, 47–69.

2. Dimont, M. I. (1962). *Jews, God and history.* New York: New American Library.

   Po-chia Hsia, R. (1988). The myth of ritual murder: Jews and magic in Reformation Germany. New Haven: Yale Univeristy Press.

3. Craig, G. A. (1982). *The Germans.* New York: New American Library.

4. Staub, E. (1978). *Positive social behavior and morality.* Vol. 1, *Social and personal influences.* New York: Academic Press.

   Idem. (1980). Social and prosocial behavior: Personal and situational influences and their interactions. In E. Staub (Ed.), *Personality: Basic aspects and current research.* Englewood Cliffs, N.J.: Prentice-Hall.

   Idem. (1984). Steps toward a comprehensive theory of moral conduct: Goal orientation, social behavior, kindness and cruelty. In J. L. Gewirtz & W. M. Kurtines (Eds.), *Morality, moral behavior, and moral development.* New York: Wiley-Interscience.

   Idem. (1986). A conception of the determinants and development of altruism and aggression: Motives, the self, and the environment. In C. Zahn-Waxler, E. M. Cummings, & R. Iannotti (Eds.), *Altruism and aggression: Social and biological origins.* New York: Cambridge University Press.

   Idem. (Forthcoming). *Social behavior and moral conduct: A personal goal theory account of altruism and aggression.* Century Series. Englewood Cliffs, N. J.: Prentice-Hall.

5. Craig, *The Germans.*

6. Wilson, E. O. (1978). *On human nature.* New York: Bantam Books.

7. Peters, E. (1985). *Torture.* New York & Oxford: Basil Blackwell.

8. Ainsworth, M. D. S. (1979). Infant-mother attachment. *American Psychologist, 34,* 932–7.

9. Sroufe, L. A. (1979). The coherence of individual development: Early care, attachment and subsequent developmental issues. *American Psychologist, 34,* 834–42.

   Bertherton, I., & Waters, E. (Eds.). (1985). *Growing points of attachment theory and research.* Monographs of the Society of Research in Child Development, vol. 34, nos. 1–2. Chicago: University of Chicago Press.

10. Bertherton and Waters, *Growing points.*

    Shaffer, D. R. (1979). *Social and personality development.* Monterey, Calif: Brooks-Cole.

11. Sroufe, Coherence of individual development.

12. Niebuhr, R. [1932] (1960). *Moral man and immoral society: A study in ethics and politics.* Reprint. New York: Charles Scribner's Sons.

13. There is much evidence for this from the observation of group behavior, and there is also evidence from psychological research:

    Wallach, M. A., Kogan, N., & Bem, D. J. (1962). Group influences on individual risk taking. *Journal of Abnormal and Social Psychology, 65,* 75–86.

    Latane, B., & Darley, J. M. (1970). *The unresponsive bystander: Why doesn't he help?* New York: Appleton Century Crofts.

Mynatt, C., & Sherman, S. J. (1975). Responsibility attribution in groups and individuals: A direct test of the diffusion of responsibility hypothesis. *Journal of Personality and Social Psychology, 32,* 1111–18.

14. Campbell, D. T. (1965). Ethnocentric and other altruistic motives. In D. Levine (Ed.), *Nebraska symposium on motivation.* Lincoln: University of Nebraska Press.
15. Hilberg, R. (1961). *The destruction of the European Jews.* Chicago: Quadrangle Books.
16. Peck, M. S. (1983). *People of the lie: The hope of healing human evil.* New York: Simon & Schuster.
17. Arendt, H. (1963). *Eichmann in Jerusalem: A report on the banality of evil.* New York: Viking Press.

    Hilberg, *Destruction.*
18. Milgram, S. (1974). *Obedience to authority: An experimental view.* New York: Harper & Row.

    Sabini, J., & Silver, M. (1982). *Moralities of everyday life.* New York: Oxford University Press, Chap. 4.
19. Fromm, E. (1965). *Escape from freedom.* New York: Avon Books.
20. Miller, A. (1983). *For your own good: Hidden cruelty in child-rearing and the roots of violence.* New York: Farrar, Straus, Giroux.
21. Kren, G. M., & Rappoport, L. (1980). *The Holocaust and the crisis of human behavior.* New York: Holmes & Meier Publishers.
22. Erikson, E. H. (1950). *Childhood and society.* New York: Norton, Chap. 9.
23. Charny, I. W. (1982). *How can we commit the unthinkable? Genocide: The human cancer.* Boulder: Westview Press.
24. There has been a multitude of psychohistorical studies of Hitler. Some prominent ones are:

    Binion, R. (1976). *Hitler among the Germans.* New York: Elsevier.

    Waite, G. L. (1977). *The psychopathic God: Adolf Hitler.* New York: Basic Books. For reviews, see:

    Carr, W. (1978). *Hitler: A study in personality and politics.* London: Edward Arnold.

    Kren & Rappoport, *Holocaust.*
25. Berghahn, V. R. (August 2, 1987). Hitler's buddies. *New York Times Book Review.*

    Abraham, D. (1987). *The collapse of the Weimar Republic.* New York: Holmes & Meier.
26. Staub, Social and prosocial behavior.

    Idem, A conception.

    Idem, *Social behavior and moral conduct.*
27. Dekmejian, R. H. (1986). Determinants of genocide: Armenians and Jews as case studies. In R. G. Hovannisian (Ed.), *The Armenian genocide: A perspective.* New Brunswick, N. J.: Transaction Books.
28. Hartt, B. (1987). The etiology of genocides. In I. Walliman and M. N. Dobkowski (Eds.), *Genocide and the modern age.* New York: Greenwood Press, p. 43.

Chapter 3

1. Averill, J. R. (1982). *Anger and aggression: An essay on emotion.* New York: Springer-Verlag.

   Baron, R. A. (1977). *Human aggression.* New York: Plenum Press.

   Berkowitz, L. (1962). *Aggression: A social psychological analysis.* New York: McGraw-Hill.
2. Baron, *Human aggression.*
3. Ibid.

4. Wilson, E. O. (1975). *Sociobiology: The new synthesis*. Cambridge: Belknap Press of Harvard University.

Idem. (1978). *On human nature*. New York: Bantam Books.

5. For genetic potential see:

Staub, E. (1978). *Positive social behavior and morality*. Vol. 1, *Social and personal influences*. New York: Academic Press.

For genetic predisposition see:

Hoffman, M. L. (1981). Is altruism part of human behavior? *Journal of Personality and Social Psychology, 40*, 121–37.

6. Baron, *Human aggression*.

Averill, *Anger and aggression*.

7. Averill, *Anger and aggression*.

Krebs, D. L., & Miller, D. T. (1985). Altruism and aggression. In G. Lindzey & E. Aronson (Eds.), *Handbook of social psychology*. Vol. 2, *Special fields and applications*. 3d ed. New York: Random House.

Mallick, S. K., & McCandless, B. R. (1966). A study of catharsis of aggression. *Journal of Personality and Social Psychology, 4*, 591–6.

Pastore, N. (1952). The role of arbitrariness in the frustration-aggression hypothesis. *Journal of Abnormal and Social Psychology, 47*, 728–31.

Staub, E. (1971). The learning and unlearning of aggression: The role of anxiety, empathy, efficacy and prosocial values. In J. Singer (Ed.), *The control of aggression and violence: Cognitive and physiological factors*. New York: Academic Press.

8. Staub, *Positive social behavior*, vol. 1.

Idem. (1980). Social and prosocial behavior: Personal and situational influences and their interactions. In E. Staub (Ed.), *Personality: Basic aspects and current research*. Englewood Cliffs, N. J.: Prentice-Hall.

Idem. (1984). Steps toward a comprehensive theory of moral conduct: Goal orientation, social behavior, kindness and cruelty. In J. L. Gewirtz & W. M. Kurtines (Eds.), *Morality, moral behavior, and moral development*. New York: Wiley-Interscience.

Idem. (1986). A conception of the determinants and development of altruism and aggression: Motives, the self, and the environment. In C. Zahn-Waxler, E. M. Cummings, & R. Iannotti (Eds.), *Altruism and aggression: Social and biological origins*. New York: Cambridge University Press.

Idem. (Forthcoming). *Social behavior and moral conduct: A personal goal theory account of altruism and aggression*. Century Series. Englewood Cliffs, N. J.: Prentice-Hall.

9. See endnote 8.

10. Staub, *Positive social behavior*, vol. 1.

Idem, Social and prosocial behavior.

Durkheim, E. (1961). *Moral education*. New York: Free Press.

Hoffman, M. L. (1970). Conscience, personality, and socialization technique. *Human Development, 13*, 90–126.

Gilligan, C. (1982). *In a different voice: Psychological theory and women's development*. Cambridge: Harvard University Press.

Gilligan, C. (1984). Remapping the moral domain in personality research and assessment. Paper presented at the Ninety-second Annual Convention of the American Psychological Association, Toronto.

11. Staub, *Positive social behavior*, vol. 1.

Idem, *Social behavior and moral conduct*.

12. Buss, A. H. (1971). Aggression pays. In J. L. Singer (Ed.), *The control of aggression and violence*. New York: Academic Press.

13. Bercheid, E., Boye, D., & Walster, E. (1968). Retaliation as a means of restoring equity.

Journal of Personality and Social Psychology, 10, 370–6.

   Walster, E., Walster, G. W., & Berscheid, E. (1978). *Equity: Theory and research.* Boston: Allyn & Bacon.

   Staub, The learning and unlearning of aggression.

14. Festinger, L. (1954). A theory of social comparison processes. *Human Relations, 7*, 117–40.

15. Toch, H. (1969). *Violent men.* Chicago: Aldine.

16. Moore, B. (1978). *Injustice: The social bases of obedience and revolt.* White Plains, N. Y.: M. E. Sharpe.

17. Eron, L. D. (1982). Parent–child interaction, television violence, and aggression of children. *American Psychologist, 37*, 197–211.

   Copeland, A. (1974). Violent black gangs: Psycho- and sociodynamics. *Adolescent Psychiatry, 3*, 340–53.

   Bond, T. (1976). The why of fragging. *American Journal of Psychiatry, 133*, 1328–31.

18. Dodge, K. A., & Frame, C. L. (1982). Social cognitive biases and deficits in aggressive boys. *Child Development, 53*, 620–35.

   Parke, R. D., & Slaby, R. G. (1983). The development of aggression. In P. Mussen (Ed.), *Manual of child psychology*, vol. 4. 4th ed. New York: Wiley.

19. Perry, D. G., & Perry, L. C. (1974). Denial of suffering in the victim as a stimulus to violence in aggressive boys. *Child Development, 45*, 55–62.

20. Des Pres, T. (1976). *The survivor: An anatomy of life in the death camps.* Oxford: Oxford University Press.

21. Gelinas, D. J. (1983). The persisting negative effects of incest. *Psychiatry, 46*, 312–32.

   Denise Gelinas expanded the information provided in her article in the course of our discussion about incestuous fathers in the spring of 1986.

22. Becker, E. (1975). *Escape from evil.* New York: Free Press.

23. Epstein, S. (1973). The self-concept revisited: Or a theory of a theory. *American Psychologist, 28*, 404–16.

   Idem. (1980). The self-concept: A review and the proposal of an integrated theory of personality. In E. Staub (Ed.), *Personality: Basic aspects and current research.* Englewood Cliffs, N. J.: Prentice-Hall.

24. Janoff-Bulman, R. (1985). The aftermath of victimization: Rebuilding shattered assumptions. In C. R. Figley (Ed.), *Trauma and its wake.* New York: Bruner/Mazel.

25. Reykowski, J., & Jarymowitz, M. (1976). Elicitation of the prosocial orientation. Unpublished manuscript, University of Warsaw.

26. Isen, A. M., Horn, N., & Rosenhan, D. L. (1973). Effects of success and failure on children's generosity. *Journal of Personality and Social Psychology, 27*, 239–48.

27. Fromm, E. (1954). *Escape from freedom.* New York: Avon Books.

28. Tajfel, H. (Ed.). (1982). *Social identity and intergroup relations.* Cambridge: Cambridge University Press.

   Tajfel, H., & Turner, J. C. (1979). An integrative theory of intergroup conflict. In W. G. Austin and S. Worchel (Eds.), *The social psychology of intergroup relations.* Monterey, Calif: Brooks-Cole.

29. Milgram, S. (1974). *Obedience to authority: An experimental view.* New York: Harper & Row.

30. Lifton, R. J. (1986). *The Nazi doctors: Medical killing and the psychology of genocide.* New York: Basic Books.

31. De Jonge, A. (1978). *The Weimar chronicle: Prelude to Hitler.* New York: New American Library, p. 12.

32. Hovland, C. I., & Sears, R. R. (1940). Minor studies of aggression: Correlation of lynchings with economic indices. *Journal of Psychology, 9*, 301–10.

33. Hepworth, J. T., & West, S. G. (1988). Lynchings and the economy: A time-series reanalysis of Hovland and Sears (1940). *Journal of Personality and Social Psychology*, *55*, no. 2, 239–47.
34. Landau, S. F. (1982). Trends in violence and aggression: A cross-cultural analysis. Paper presented at the Tenth International Congress of Sociology, Mexico City.
35. Peck, M. S. (1983). *People of the lie: The hope of healing human evil.* New York: Simon & Schuster.
36. Sereny, G. (1974). *Into that darkness: From mercy killing to mass murder.* New York: McGraw-Hill, pp. 212–13.
37. Stern, F. (1987). *Dreams and delusions: The drama of German history.* New York: Knopf.
38. Platt, G. M. (1980). Thoughts on a theory of collective action: Language, affect and ideology in revolution. In M. Albin, R. J. Devlin, & G. Haeger (Eds.), *New directions in psychohistory: The Adelphi papers in honor of Erik H. Erikson.* Lexington, Mass: Lexington Books.
39. Egendorf, A., Kadushin, C., Laufer, R. S., Rothbart G., & Sloan, L. (1981). Summary of findings. *Legacies of Vietnam: Comparative adjustment of Vietnam veterans and their peers*, Vol. 1. Washington D. C.: U. S. Government Printing Office.
     Wilson, P. J. (1980). Conflict, stress and growth: The effects of war on psychosocial development among Vietnam veterans. In C. R. Figley & S. Leventman (Eds.), *Strangers at home: Vietnam veterans since the war.* New York: Praeger Press.
     Fletcher, K. E. (1987). Belief systems, exposure to stress, and posttraumatic stress disorder among Vietnam veterans. Ph.D. diss., University of Massachusetts, Amherst.
40. Fletcher, Belief systems.
41. Card, J. J. (1983). *Lives after Vietnam: The personal impact of military service.* Lexington, Mass.: Lexington Books.
42. Hendin, H., and Haas, A. P. (1984). Combat adaptations of Vietnam Veterans without posttraumatic stress disorders. *American Journal of Psychiatry*, *141*, 956–60.
43. Fletcher, K. E. (1987). Personal communication.
44. Allport, G. (1954). *The nature of prejudice.* Reading, Mass.: Addison-Wesley.
45. Staub, E. (1985). The psychology of perpetrators and bystanders. *Political Psychology*, *6*, 61–86.
46. Sherif, M., Harvey, O. J., White, B. J., Hood, W. K., & Sherif, C. W. (1961). *Intergroup conflict and cooperation: The Robbers' Cave experiment.* Norman, Okla.: University of Oklahoma Book Exchange.
47. Stoessinger, J. G. (1982). *Why nations go to war.* New York: St. Martin's Press.
48. Tajfel, H. (1982). Social psychology of intergroup relations. *Annual Review of Psychology*, *33*, 1–39; quotations, p. 24.
49. Zimbardo, P. G. (1969). The human choice: Individuation, reason, and order versus deindividuation, impulse, and chaos. In D. Levine (Ed.), *Nebraska symposium on motivation.* Lincoln: University of Nebraska Press.
50. Ajzen, I., & Fishbein, M. (1980). *Understanding attitudes and predicting social behavior.* Englewood Cliffs, N. J.: Prentice-Hall.
     Staub, E. (1974). Helping a distressed person: Social, personality and stimulus determinants. In L. Berkowitz (Ed.), *Advances in experimental social psychology*, vol. 7. New York: Academic Press;
     Idem, *Positive social behavior*, vol. 1.
     Erkut, S., Jaquette, D., & Staub, E. (1981). Moral judgment–situation interaction as a basis for predicting social behavior. *Journal of Personality*, *49*, 1–44.
51. See endnote 8.
52. Davitz, J. R. (1952). The effect of previous training on postfrustration behavior. *Journal of Abnormal and Social Psychology*, *47*, 309–15.

53. Sherif, M. (1958). Superordinate goals in the reduction of intergroup conflict. *American Journal of Sociology*, *63*, 349–58.

Sherif et al., *The Robbers' Cave experiment.*

Tajfel, Social psychology of intergroup relations.

Worchel, S. (1979). Cooperation and the reduction of intergroup conflict: Some determining factors. In W. G. Austin & S. Worchel (Eds.), *The social psychology of intergroup relations.* Monterey, Calif.: Brooks-Cole.

See Chapter 18, as well as 16 and 17.

Chapter 4

1. Milgram, S. (1961). Nationality and conformity. *Scientific American*, *205*, 45–51.

Perrin, S., & Spencer, C. (1981). Independence and conformity in the Asch experiments as a reflection of cultural and situational factors. *British Journal of Psychology*, *20*, 205–9.

2. Garbarino, J., & Bronfenbrenner, U. (1976). The socialization of moral judgment and behavior in cross-cultural perspective. In T. Lickona (Ed.), *Moral development and behavior.* New York: Holt.

Bixenstine, V. E., DeCorte, M. S., & Bixenstine, B. A. (1976). Conformity to peer-sponsored misconduct at four grade levels. *Developmental Psychology*, *12*, 226–36,

Staub, E. (1979). *Positive social behavior and morality.* Vol. 2, *Socialization and development.* New York: Academic Press.

3. Maslow, A. (1971). *The farther reaches of human nature.* New York: Viking Press, see Chap. 14 on Synergy in society and in the individual.

4. Whiting, B., & Whiting, J. W. M. (1975). *Children of six cultures.* Cambridge: Harvard University Press.

5. McClelland, D. (1961). *The achieving society.* Princeton: Van Nostrand.

6. Slavson, S. R. (1965). *Reclaiming the delinquent.* New York: Free Press.

Toch, H. (1969). *Violent men.* Chicago: Aldine.

Buss, A. H. (1971). Aggression pays. In J. L. Singer (Ed.), *The control of aggression and violence.* New York: Academic Press.

7. Wilson, E. O. (1978). *On human nature.* New York: Bantam Books.

8. Ibid., p. 116.

9. Lowentin, R. C., Rose, S., & Kamin, L. (1984). *Not in our genes: Biology, ideology and human nature.* New York: Pantheon Books.

10. Rushton, J. P., Fulker, D. W., Neale, M. C., Nias, D. K. B., & Eysenck, H. J. (1986). Altruism and aggression: The heritability of individual differences. *Journal of Personality and Social Psychology*, *50*, 1192–8.

11. Masserman, J. H., Wechkin, S., & Terris, W. (1964). "Altruistic" behavior in rhesus monkeys. *American Journal of Psychiatry*, *121*, 584–5.

Staub, E. (1978). *Positive social behavior and morality.* Vol. 1, *Social and personal influences.* New York: Academic Press, for a general discussion of the effects of experience on animal "altruism."

12. MacDonald, K. (1984). An ethological-social learning theory of the development of altruism: Implications for human sociobiology. *Ethology and Sociobiology*, *5*, 9–109.

13. Dentan, R. K. (1968). *The Semais: A nonviolent people of Malaysia.* New York: Holt, Rinehart & Winston.

14. Ibid.

15. Leggett, G. (1981) *The Cheka.* New York: Oxford University Press, p. 68. Quoted in Peters, E. (1985). *Torture.* New York: Basil Blackwell.

16. Rotter, J. B. (1944). The nature and treatment of stuttering: A clinical approach. *Journal*

of Abnormal and Social Psychology, *39*, 150–73.

17. Copeland, A. (1974). Violent black gangs: psycho- and sociodynamics. *Adolescent Psychology*, *3*, 340–53.

   Gillooly, D., & Bond, T. (1976). Assaults with explosive devices on superiors. *Military Medicine*, *141*, 700–2.

   Newman, D. E. (1974). The personality of violence: Conversations with protagonists. *Mental Health and Society*, *1*, 5–6, 328–44.

   Toch, *Violent men*.

18. Newman, *The personality of violence*.

   Toch, *Violent men*.

19. Allport, G. (1954). *The nature of prejudice*. Reading, Mass.: Addison-Wesley.

20. Jarymowitz, M. (1977). Modification of self-worth and increment of prosocial sensitivity. *Polish Psychological Bulletin*, *8*, 45–53.

   Reese, H. (1961). Relationships between self-acceptance and sociometric choices. *Journal of Abnormal and Social Psychology*, *62*, 472–4.

   Staub, *Positive social behavior*, vol. 2.

   Staub, E. (1986). A conception of the determinants and development of altruism and aggression: Motives, the self, and the environment. In C. Zahn-Waxler, Cummings, E. M., & Iannotti, R. (Eds.), *Altruism and aggression: Social and biological origins*. New York: Cambridge University Press.

21. De Jonge, A. (1978). *The Weimar chronicle: Prelude to Hitler*. New York: New American Library, p. 12.

22. Maslow, *Farther reaches of human nature*.

23. Lewis, M. (1978). *The culture of inequality*. New York: New American Library.

24. Douglas, M., & Wildovsky, A. (1982). *Risk and culture: An essay on the selection of technical and environmental dangers*. Berkeley & Los Angeles: University of California Press.

25. Durkheim, E. (1961). *Moral education*. New York: Free Press.

   Gilligan, C. (1982). *In a different voice: Psychological theory and women's development*. Cambridge: Harvard University Press.

   Idem. (1984). Remapping the moral domain in personality research and assessment. Paper presented at the Ninety-second Annual Convention of the American Psychological Association, Toronto.

   Hoffman, M. L. (1970). Conscience, personality, and socialization technique. *Human Development*, *13*, 90–126.

   Staub, *Positive social behavior*, vol. 2.

   Staub, E. (1980). Social and prosocial behavior: Personal and situational influences and their interaction. In E. Staub (Ed.), *Personality: Basic aspects and current research*. Englewood Cliffs, N. J.: Prentice-Hall.

   Staub, E. (Forthcoming). *Social behavior and moral conduct: A personal goal theory account of altruism and aggression*. Century Series. Englewood Cliffs, N. J.: Prentice-Hall.

26. Baron, R. A. (1977). *Human aggression*. New York: Plenum Press.

27. Staub, E. (1974). Helping a distressed person: Social, personality and stimulus determinants. In L. Berkowitz (Ed.), *Advances in experimental social psychology*, vol. 7. New York: Academic Press.

   Staub, *Positive social behavior*, vol. 1.

   Idem, Social and prosocial behavior.

   Erkut, S., Jaquette, D., & Staub, E. (1981). Moral judgment-situation interaction as a basis for predicting social behavior. *Journal of Personality*, *49*, 1–44.

   Feinberg, J. K. (1978). Anatomy of a helping situation: Some personality and situational determinants of helping in a conflict situation involving another's psychological distress. Ph.D. diss., University of Massachusetts, Amherst.

Grodman, S. M. (1979). The role of personality and situational variables in responding to and helping an individual in psychological distress. Ph.D. diss., University of Massachusetts, Amherst.

28. Kohlberg, L. (1969). Stage and sequence: The congitive-developmental approach to socialization. In D. Goslin (Ed.), *Handbook of socialization theory and research.* Chicago: Rand McNally.

29. Kohlberg, L., & Candee, L. (1984). The relationship of moral judgment to moral action. In J. L. Gewirtz & W. M. Kurtines (Eds.), *Morality, moral behavior, and moral development*, New York: Wiley-Interscience, pp. 52–73.

30. Gilligan, *In a different voice.*

31. Gilligan, Remapping the moral domain.

32. Whitbourne, S. K. (1986). *The me I know: A study of adult identity.* New York: Springer-Verlag.

33. Lerner, M. (1980). *The belief in a just world: A fundametal delusion.* New York: Plenum Press.

34. Tajfel, H., Flamant, C., Billig, M. Y., & Bundy, R. P. (1971). Societal categorization and intergroup behavior. *European Journal of Social Psychology*, *1*, 149–77.

Tajfel, H. (Ed.). (1982). *Social identity and intergroup relations.* Cambridge: Cambridge University Press.

35. Hornstein, H. A. (1984). Out of the wilderness. *Contemporary Psychology*, *29*, 11–12; quotation, 11. (A review of Tajfel, *Social identity and intergroup relations.*)

36. Brewer, M. B. (1978). Ingroup bias in the minimal intergroup situation: A cognitive-motivational analysis. *Psychological Bulletin*, *86*, 307–24.

Tajfel, *Social identity and intergroup relations.*

Hornstein, H. A. (1976). *Cruelty and kindness: A new look at aggression and altruism.* Englewood Cliffs, N. J.: Prentice-Hall.

37. Ainsworth, M. D., Blehar, M. C., Waters, E., & Wall, S. (1978). *Patterns of attachment: A psychological study of strange situations.* Hillsdale, N. J.: Lawrence Erlbaum Associates.

Thompson, W. R., & Grusec, J. (1970). Studies of early experience. In P. H. Mussen (Ed.), *Carmichael's manual of child psychology*, vol. 2. 3d ed. New York: Wiley.

38. Shaffer, D. R. (1979). *Social and personality development.* Monterey, Calif.: Brooks-Cole.

39. Sroufe, L. A. (1979). The coherence of individual development: Early care, attachment, and subsequent developmental issues. *American Psychologist*, *34*, 834–42.

Waters, E., Wippmann, J., & Sroufe, L. A. (1979). Attachment, positive affect, and competence in the peer group: Two studies in contrast validation. *Child Development*, *50*, 821–9.

40. Zajonc, R. B. (1968). Attitudinal effects of more exposure. *Journal of Personality and Social Psychology, Monograph Supplement 1*, *9* (2).

41. Allport, *Nature of predjudice*, p. 28.

42. Piaget, J., & Weil, A. (1951). The development in children of the idea of the homeland and of relations with other countries. *International Social Science Bulletin*, *3*, 570.

43. Russell, C., & Russell, W. M. S. (1968). *Violence, monkeys and man.* London: Macmillan.

44. Becker, E. (1975). *Escape from evil.* New York: Free Press.

Hornstein, *Cruelty and kindness.*

45. Haritos-Fatouros, M. (1979). The official torturer: Learning mechanisms involved in the process. Relevance to democratic and totalitarian regimes today. Unpublished manuscript, University of Thessaloniki, Greece.

Gibson, J. T., & Haritos-Fatouros, M. (1986). The education of a torturer. *Psychology Today*, *20*, 50–58.

46. Brewer, Ingroup bias.
    Tajfel et al., Social categorization.
    Tajfel, *Social identity and intergroup relations*.
47. Bandura, A., Underwood, B., & Fromson, M. E. (1975). Disinhibition of aggression through diffusion of responsibility and dehumanization of victims. *Journal of Research in Personality*, 9, 253–69.
48. Duster, T. (1971). Conditions for guilt-free massacre. In N. Sanford & C. Comstock (Eds.), *Sanctions for evil*. San Francisco: Jossey-Bass, p. 27.
49. Fein, H. (1979). *Accounting for genocide: Victims and survivors of the Holocaust*. New York: Free Press.
50. Cited in Krauthammer, C. (1981). The humanist phantom. *New Republic*, July 25, p.21.
51. Garbarino, L., & Bronfenbrenner, U. (1976). The socialization of moral judgment and behavior in cross-cultural perspective. In Lickona, T. (Ed.), *Moral development and behavior: Theory, research, and social issues*. New York: Holt, Rinehart & Winston, p. 95.
52. Ibid. A limitation of the Garbarino and Bronfenbrenner research was that most of the pluralistic societies were Western democracies and most of the monolithic ones communist countries.
53. Kohlberg, Stage and sequence.
    Kohlberg and Candee, Relationship of moral judgment to moral action.
    Elms, A. C., & Milgram, S. (1966). Personality characteristics associated with obedience and defiance toward authoritative command. *Journal of Experimental Research in Pensonality*, 2, 282–9.
54. Milgram, Nationality and conformity.
    Perrin and Spencer, Independence and conformity.
55. Adorno, T. W., Frenkel-Brunswik, E., Levinson, D. J., & Sanford, R. N. (1950). *The authoritarian personality*. New York: Norton & Co.
    Sanford, N. (1973). Authoritarian personality in contemporary perspective. In J. N. Knutson (Ed.), *Handbook of political psychology*. San Francisco: Jossey-Bass.
    Cherry, F., & Byrne, D. (1977). Authoritarianism. In T. Blass (Ed.), *Personality variables in social behavior*. Hillsdale, N. J.: Lawrence Erlbaum Associates.
56. Holmes, D. S. (1978). Projection as a defense mechanism. *Psychological Bulletin*, 85, 677–88.
    Idem. (1981). Existence of classical projection and the stress-reducing function of attributive projection: A reply to Sherwood. *Psychological Bulletin*, 90, 460–6.
    Sherwood, G. G. (1979). Classical and attributive projection. *Journal of Abnormal Psychology*, 88, 635–40.
    Sherwood, G. G. (1981). Self-serving biases in person perception: A reexamination of projection as a mechanism of defense. *Psychological Bulletin*, 90, 445–59.
57. Schwartz, G. E. (1983). Disregulation theory and disease: Applications to the repression/cerebral disconnection/cardiovascular disorder hypothesis. In J. Matarazzo, N. Miller, & S. Weiss (Eds.), special issue on behavioral medicine of *International Review of Applied Psychology*, 32, 95–118.
58. Davis, P. J., & Schwartz, G. E. (1987). Depression and the inaccessibility of affective memories. *Journal of Personality and Social Psychology*, 52, 155–62.
59. Miller, A. (1983). *For your own good: Hidden cruelty in child-rearing and the roots of violence*. New York: Farrar, Straus, Giroux, pp. 187–8.
60. Lewis, *Culture of inequality*.
61. Heider, F. (1958). *The psychology of interpersonal relations*. New York: Wiley.
    Festinger, L., & Freedman, J. L. (1964). Dissonance reduction and moral values. In P. Worchel & D. Byrne (Eds.), *Personality change*. New York: Wiley.

Rokeach, M. (1973). *The nature of human values*. New York: Macmillan.

Rokeach, M. (1985). Inducing change and stability in belief systems and personality. *Journal of Social Issues, 41*, 153–71.

62. Asch, S. E. (1951). Effects of group pressure upon the modification and distortion of judgments. In H. Guetzkow (Ed.), *Groups, leadership, and men*. Pittsburgh: Carnegie Press.

Milgram, Nationality and conformity.

Perrin and Spencer, Independence and conformity.

63. Bickman, L. (1972). Social influence and diffusion of responsibility in an emergency. *Journal of Experimental Social Psychology, 8*, 438–45.

Staub, Helping a distressed person.

Idem, *Positive social behavior*, vol. 1.

64. Arendt, H. (1963). *Eichmann in Jerusalem: A report on the banality of evil*. New York: Viking Press.

65. Benesh, M., & Weiner, B. (1982). On emotion and motivation: From the notebooks of Fritz Heider. *American Psychologist, 37*, 887–95.

Rotter, J. B. (1954). *Social learning and clinical psychology*. Englewood Cliffs, N. J.: Prentice-Hall.

Staub, *Positive social behavior*, vol. 1.

Idem, *Social and prosocial behavior*.

Idem, *Social behavior and moral conduct*.

66. Hilberg, R. (1961). *The destruction of the European Jews*. Chicago: Quadrangle Books.

67. Titmus, R. *The gift relationship: From human blood to social policy*. New York: Pantheon Books.

Chapter 5

1. Janis, I. (1983). *Victims of groupthink*. Boston: Houghton Mifflin.

2. Borofsky, G. L., & Brand, D. J. Personality organization and psychological functioning of the Nuremberg criminals: The Rorschach data. In J. E. Dimsdale (Ed.), *Survivors, victims and perpetrators: Essays on the Nazi Holocaust*. New York: Hemisphere Publishing Co.

3. Lanzman, C. (1985). *Shoah: An oral history of the Holocaust*. New York: Pantheon Books, p. 106.

4. Zimbardo, P. G., Haney, C., Banks, W. C., & Jaffe, D. (1974). The psychology of imprisonment: Privation, power, and pathology. In Z. Rubin (Ed.), *Doing unto others*. Englewood Cliffs, N. J.: Prentice-Hall.

5. Idid., p. 65.

6. Peck, M. S. (1983). *People of the lie: The hope of healing human evil*. New York: Simon & Schuster, pp. 227–8.

7. Haritos-Fatouros, M. (1979). The official torturer: Learning mechanisms involved in the process. Relevance to democratic and totalitarian regimes today. Unpublished manuscript, University of Thessaloniki, Greece.

Gibson, J. T., & Haritos-Fatouros, M. (1986). The education of a torturer. *Psychology Today, 20*, 50–58.

Haritos-Fatouros, M. (1988). The official torturer: A learning model for obedience to the authority of violence. *Journal of Applied Social Psychology, 18*, 1107–20.

8. Hilberg, R. (1961). *The destruction of the European Jews*. Chicago: Quadrangle Books.

Lifton, R. J. (1986). *The Nazi doctors: Medical killing and the psychology of genocide*. New York: Basic Books.

9. Hilberg, R. *Destruction.*
10. Staub, E. (1978). *Positive social behavior and morality.* Vol. 1, *Social and personal influences.* New York: Academic Press.
11. Oliner, S. B., & Oliner, P. (1988). *The altruistic personality: Rescuers of Jews in Nazi Germany.* New York: Free Press, p. 152.
12. Huesmann, L. R., & Eron, L. D. (1984). Cognitive processes and the persistence of aggressive behavior. *Aggressive behavior, 10,* 243–51.
13. Masters, B. (1986, orig. 1985). *Killing for company: The case of Dennis Nielson.* London: Maddox & Stoughton.
14. Eliasz, H. (1980). The role of empathy, activity, and anxiety on interpersonal aggression. *Polish Psychological Bulletin, 3,* 169–78.
15. Peck, *People of the lie,* p. 76.
16. Ibid., p. 74.
17. Bandura, A., & Walters, R. H. (1959). *Adolescent aggression: A study of the influence of child training practices and family interrelationship.* New York: Ronald Press.

    Eron, L. D. (1982). Parent–child interaction, television violence, and aggression of children. *American Psychologist, 37,* 197–211.

    Parke, R. D., & Slaby, R. G. (1983). The development of aggression. In P. Mussen (Ed.), *Manual of child psychology,* Vol. 4. 4th ed. New York: Wiley.
18. Patterson, G. R. (1982). *Coercive family processes.* Eugene, Ore.: Castilla Press.

    Reid, J. B. (1986). Social-interactional patterns in families of abused and nonabused children. In C. Zahn-Waxler, E. M. Cummings, & R. Iannotti (Eds.). *Altruism and aggression: Social and biological origins.* New York: Cambridge University Press.
19. Hoffman, M. L. (1970). Conscience, personality, and socialization technique. *Human Development, 13,* 90–126.
20. Staub, E. (1979). *Positive social behavior and morality.* Vol. 2, *Socialization and development.* New York: Academic Press.

    Idem. (1981). Promoting positive behavior in schools, in other educational settings, and in the home. In J. P. Rushton & R. M. Sorrentino (Eds.), *Altruism and helping behavior.* Hillsdale, N. J.: Lawrence Erlbaum Associates.

    Idem. (1986). A conception of the determinants and development of altruism and aggression: Motives, the self, and the environment. In Zahn-Waxler et. al., *Atruism and aggression.*

    Idem. (Forthcoming). *Social behavior and moral conduct: A personal goal theory account of altruism and aggression.* Century Series. Englewood Cliffs, N. J.: Prentice-Hall.

    Grusec, J. (1981). Socialization processes and the development of altruism. In Rushton & Sorrentino, *Altruism and helping behavior.*

    Zahn-Waxler et al., *Altruism and aggression.*
21. Staub, E. (1975). To rear a prosocial child: Reasoning, learning by doing, and learning by teaching others. In D. DePalma & J. Folley (Eds.), *Moral development: Current theory and research.* Hillsdale, N. J.: Lawrence Erlbaum Associates.

    Staub, *Positive social behavior,* vol. 2.
22. Adorno, T. W., Frenkel-Brunswik, E., Levinson, D. J., & Sanford, R. N. (1950). *The authoritarian personality.* New York: Norton & Co.

    Cherry, F., & Byrne, D. (1977). Authoritarianism. In T. Blass (Ed.), *Personality variables in social behavior.* Hillsdale, N. J.: Lawrence Erlbaum Associates.

    Sanford, N. (1973). Authoritarian personality in contemporary perspective. In J. N. Knutson (Ed.), *Handbook of political psychology.* San Francisco: Jossey-Bass.

    For a review of measurement problems as well as later research see:

    Cherry and Byrne, Authoritarianism.

For a discussion of issues related to the authoritarian personality, see also:

Samuelson, R. (1986). Authoritarianism from Berlin to Berkeley: On social psychology and history. *Journal of Social Issues, 42,* 191–208:

Ray, J. J. (1988). Why the F scale predicts racism: A critical review. *Political Psychology, 9,* no. 4, 671–80.

Eckhardt, W. (1988). Comment on Ray's "Why the F scale predicts racism: A critical review." *Political Psychology, 9,* no. 4, 681–91.

23. Elms, A. C., & Milgram, S. (1966). Personality characteristics associated with obedience and defiance toward authoritative command. *Journal of Experimental Research in Personality, 2,* 282–9.

24. Miller, A. (1983). *For your own good: Hidden cruelty in child-rearing and the roots of violence.* New York: Farrar, Straus, Giroux, p. 70.

25. DeMause, L. (Ed.). (1974). *History of childhood.* New York: Psychohistory Press.

Stone, L. (1977). *The family, sex and marriage in England, 1500–1800.* New York: Harper & Row.

26. Devereux, E. D. (1972). Authority and moral development among German and American children: A cross-national pilot experiment. *Journal of Comparative Family Studies, 3,* 99–124.

Miller, *For your own good.*

27. Hoffman, Conscience, personality, and socialization.

28. von Maltitz, H. (1973). *The evolution of Hitler's Germany: The ideology, the personality, the moment.* New York: McGraw-Hill.

29. Lewis, B. (1985). The Shiites. *New York Review of Books, 32,* no. 13, pp. 7–10.

30. Sargant, W. (1957). *Battle for the mind: A physiology of conversion and brain-washing.* London: Pan Books.

31. Zimbardo, P. G. (1969). The human choice: Individuation, reason, and order versus deindividuation, impulse, and chaos. In *Nebraska symposium on motivation.* Lincoln: University of Nebraska Press.

32. Kren, G. M., & Rappoport, L. (1980). *The Holocaust and the crisis of human behavior.* New Haven: Yale University Press.

Gibson and Haritos-Fatouros, The education of a torturer.

Dyer, G. (1985). *War.* New York: Crown Publishers.

Chapter 6

1. Lerner, M. J., & Simmons, C. H. (1966). Observer's reaction to the "innocent victim": Compassion or rejection? *Journal of Personality and Social Psychology, 4,* 203–10.

Lerner, M. (1980). *The belief in a just world: A fundamental delusion.* New York: Plenum Press.

Smith, R. E., Keating, J. P., Hester, R. K., & Mitchell, H. E. (1976). Role and justice considerations in the attribution of responsibility to a rape victim. *Journal of Research in Personality, 10,* 346–57.

2. Lerner and Simmons, Observer's reaction.

3. Rubin, Z., & Peplau, L. A. (1973). Belief in a just world and reactions to another's lot: A study of participants in the national draft lottery. *Journal of Social Issues, 29,* 73–93.

Idem. (1975). Who believes in a just world? *Journal of Social Issues, 31,* 65–89.

4. Staub, E. (1978). *Positive social behavior and morality.* Vol. 1, *Social and personal influences.* New York: Academic Press.

5. Ibid.

6. Lerner and Simmons, Observer's reaction.
   Lerner, *Belief in a just world*.
7. Staub, E. (1975). To rear a prosocial child: Reasoning, learning by doing, and learning by teaching others. In D. DePalma & J. Folley (Eds.), *Moral development: Current theory and research*. Hillsdale, N. J.: Lawrence Erlbaum Associates.
   Idem. (1979). *Positive social behavior and morality*. Vol. 2, *Socialization and development*. New York: Academic Press, Chap. 6.
8. Staub, To rear a prosocial child.
   Idem. *Positive social behavior*, vol. 2, Chap. 6.
9. DeJong, W. (1979). An examination of self-perception mediation of the foot-in-the-door effect. *Journal of Personality and Social Psychology, 34*, 578–82.
   Freedman, J. L., & Fraser, S. C. (1966). Compliance without pressure: The foot-in-the-door technique. *Journal of Personality and Social Psychology, 4*, 195–202.
   Harris, M. B. (1972). The effects of performing one altruistic act on the likelihood of performing another. *Journal of Social Psychology, 88*, 65–73.
   Staub, *Positive social behavior*, vol. 2, Chaps. 5 and 6.
10. Bem, D. J. (1972). Self-perception theory. In L. Berkowitz (Ed.), *Advances in experimental social psychology*, vol. 6. New York: Academic Press.
11. Freedman and Fraser, Compliance without pressure.
    DeJong, Examination of self-perception mediation.
12. Keneally, T. (1983). *Schindler's List*. New York: Penguin Books.
13. As an example of this finding see: Buss, A. H. (1966). The effect of harm on subsequent aggression. *Journal of Experimental Research in Personality, 1*, 349–55.
    For a list of relevant references see:
    Goldstein, J. H., Davis, R. W., & Herman, D. (1975). Escalation of aggression: Experimental studies. *Journal of Personality and Social Psychology, 31*, 162–70.
14. Goldstein et al., Escalation.
15. Bem, Self-perception theory.
    Eisenberg, N., & Cialdini, R. B. (1984). The role of consistency pressures in behavior: A developmental perspective. *Academic Psychology Journal, 6*, 115–26.
    Staub, *Positive social behavior*, vol. 2.
16. Arendt, H. (1963). *Eichmann in Jerusalem: A report on the banality of evil*. New York: Viking Press.
17. Bettelheim, B. (1979). Remarks on the psychological appeal of totalitarianism. In *Surviving and other essays*. New York: Vintage Books.
18. Haritos-Fatouros, M. (1979). The official torturer: Learning mechanisms involved in the process. Relevance to democratic and totalitarian regimes today. Unpublished manuscript, University of Thessaloniki, Greece.
    Gibson, J. T., & Haritos-Fatouros, M. (1986). The education of a torturer. *Psychology Today, 20*, 50–58.
19. For a review see:
    Fishbein, M., & Ajzen, I. (1975). *Belief, attitude, intention and behavior*. Reading, Mass.: Addison-Wesley.
20. Orwell, G. (1949). *1984*. New York: Harcourt & Brace, p. 151.
21. Lifton, R. J. (1986). *The Nazi doctors: Medical killing and the psychology of genocide*. New York: Basic Books.
22. Latane, B., & Darley, J. (1970). *The unresponsive bystander: Why doesn't he help?* New York: Appleton-Crofts.
    Staub, *Positive social behavior*, vol. 1.
    Tilker, H. A. (1970). Socially responsive behavior as a function of observer responsibility and victim feedback. *Journal of Personality and Social Psychology, 4*, 95–100.

23. Poliakov, L. (1954). *Harvest of hate: The Nazi program for the destruction of the Jews in Europe.* Syracuse, N. Y.: Syracuse University Press, pp. 12–13.
24. Hilberg, R. (1961). *The destruction of the European Jews.* Chicago: Quadrangle Books.
    Davidowicz, L. S. (1975). *The war against the Jews: 1935–1945.* New York: Holt, Rinehart & Winston.
25. Amnesty International Report. (1980). *Testimony on secret detention camps in Argentina.* London: Amnesty International Publications.
26. Tilker, Socially responsive behavior.
27. Staub, *Positive social behavior,* vol. 1.
    Bickman, L. (1972). Social influence and diffusion of responsibility in an emergency. *Journal of Experimental Social Psychology, 8,* 438–45.
    Staub, E. (1974). Helping a distressed person: Social, personality, and stimulus determinants. In L. Berkowitz (Ed.), *Advances in experimental social psychology,* vol. 7. New York: Academic Press.
28. Wilson, J. P. (1976). Motivation, modeling and altruism: A person × situation analysis. *Journal of Personality and Social Psychology, 34,* 1078–86.
    Schwartz, S. H., & Clausen, G. T. (1970). Responsibility norms and helping in an emergency. *Journal of Personality and Social Psychology, 16,* 299–310.
29. Hilberg, *Destruction.*
30. Peck, M. S. (1982). *People of the lie: The hope of healing human evil.* New York: Simon & Schuster.
31. Lewin, K. (1938). *The conceptual representation and measurement of psychological forces.* Durham, N. C.: Duke University Press.
    Lewin, K. (1948). *Resolving social conflicts.* New York: Harper.
    Hornstein, H. A. (1976). *Cruelty and kindness: A new look at aggression and altruism.* Englewood Cliffs, N. J.: Prentice-Hall.
32. Heider, F. (1958). *The psychology of interpersonal relations.* New York: Wiley.
    Festinger, L. (1957). *A theory of cognitive dissonance.* Evanston, Ill.: Row-Peterson.
33. Becker, E. (1975). *Escape from evil.* New York: Free Press.
34. For example, in Hungary:
    Lacko, M. (1976). *Nyilasok, Nemzetiszocialistak, 1935–1944* (The Arrow Cross, National Socialists). Budapest.
35. Beck, F., & Godin, W. (1951). *Russian purge and the extraction of confession.* New York: Viking Press.
36. Arens, R. (1982). The Ache of Paraguay. In J. N. Porter (Ed.), *Genocide and human rights: A global anthology.* New York: University Press of America.
37. Stoessinger, J. G. (1982). *Why nations go to war.* New York: St. Martin's Press.
38. Staub, *Positive social behavior,* vol. 1.
39. Latane and Darley, *Unresponsive bystander.*
40. Ibid.
41. Asch, S. E. (1951). Effects of group pressure upon the modification and distortion of judgements. In H. Guetzkow (Ed.), *Groups, leadership, and men.* Pittsburgh: Carnegie Press.
42. Staub, Helping a distressed person.
43. Fein, H. (1979). *Accounting for genocide: National responses and Jewish victimization during the Holocaust.* New York: Free Press.
    Davidowicz, *War against the Jews.*
    Lifton, *Nazi doctors.*
44. Fein, *Accounting for genocide.*
45. Wyman, D. S. (1984). *The abandonment of the Jews: America and the Holocaust, 1941–1945.* New York: Pantheon Books.

Chapter 7

1. Girard, P. (1980). Historical foundations of anti-Semitism. In J. Dimsdale (Ed.), *Survivors, victims and perpetrators: Essays on the Nazi Holocaust*. New York: Hemisphere Publishing Co., p. 75.
2. De Jonge, A. (1978). *The Weimar chronicle: Prelude to Hitler*. New York: New American Library, p. 12.
3. Ibid.
4. Abel, T. [1938] (1966). *The Nazi movement: Why Hitler came into power*. Reprint. Englewood Cliffs, N.J.: Prentice-Hall.
    Moore, B. (1978). *Injustice: The social bases of obedience and revolt*. White Plains, N. Y.: M. E. Sharpe.
5. De Jonge, *The Weimar chronicle*, p. 215.
6. Ibid., p. 218.
7. Ibid., p. 232.
8. Mosse, G. L. (Ed.). (1966). *Nazi culture: Intellectual, cultural and social life in the Third Reich*. New York: Schocken Books, p. 6.
9. Hitler, A. (1923). *Mein Kampf*. Translated by Ralph Manheim. Boston: Houghton Mifflin Co., p. 328.
10. Ibid., p. 329.
11. Ibid.
12. Allport, G. (1954). *The nature of prejudice*. Reading, Mass.: Addison-Wesley, p. 40.
13. Ibid.
14. Meinecke, F. (1950). *The German catastrophe: Reflections and recollections*. Boston: Beacon Press.
15. From von Kotze, H., & Krausnick, H. (Eds.). (1966). *Es spricht der Führer* (The führer speaks). Gütersloh: S. Mohn.
    Cited in Davidowicz, L. S. (1975). *The war against the Jews: 1933–1945*. New York: Holt, Rinehart & Winston, p. 93.
16. In the *Volkischer Beobachter*, August 26, 1932, quoted in De Jonge, *Weimar chronicle*, p. 212.
17. von Maltitz, H. (1973). *The evolution of Hitler's Germany: The ideology, the personality, the moment*. New York: McGraw-Hill.
18. Quoted in Feingold, H. L. (1982). *An American Jewish history*. Albany: State University of New York Press, p. 50.
19. Quoted on p. 19 of Waite, R. G. L. (1981). The perpetrator: Hitler and the Holocaust. In M. D. Ryan (Ed.), *Human responses to the Holocaust*. New York: E. Mellen Press.
20. Benesh, M., & Weiner, B. (1982). On emotion and motivation: From the notebooks of Fritz Heider. *American Psychologist*, *37*, 887–95.
21. Meinecke, *German catastrophe*, pp. 73–74.

Chapter 8

1. Davidowicz, L. S. (1975). *The war against the Jews: 1933–1945*. New York: Holt, Rinehart & Winston.
2. Girard, P. (1980). Historical foundations of anti-Semitism. In J. Dimsdale (Ed.), *Survivors, victims, and perpetrators: Essays on the Nazi Holocaust*. New York: Hemisphere Publishing Co.
    Hilberg, R. (1961). *The destruction of the European Jews*, Chicago: Quadrangle Books.

See also Hilberg's revision (1985), 3 vols. New York: Holmes & Meier.

Davidowicz, *War against the Jews.*

3. Girard, Historical foundations of anti-Semitism, pp. 57–8.
4. Brown, R. W. (1965). *Social psychology.* New York: Free Press.
5. Paul, B. B., & Demerast, W. J. (1984). The operation of a death squad in La Jaguna, Guatemala. Paper presented at the meetings of the American Anthropological Association, Denver, November 15–19.

    Amnesty International Report. (1980). *Testimony on secret detention camps in Argentina.* London: Amnesty International Publications.

6. Brewer, M. B., & Kramer, R. M. (1985). The psychology of intergroup attitudes and behavior. *Annual Review of Psychology, 36,* 219–43.
7. Rothbart, M. (1981). Memory processes and social beliefs. In D. L. Hamilton (Ed.), *Cognitive processes in stereotyping and intergroup behavior.* Hillsdale, N. J.: Lawrence Erlbaum Associates.
8. Brewer and Kramer, Psychology of intergroup attitudes.
9. Merton, R. K. (1957). *Social theory and social structure.* Rev. ed. New York: Free Press, p. 428.
10. Luther, M. (1955–75). *Works.* Vol. 47, *On the Jews and their lies.* Muhlenberg Press. Quoted in Hilberg, *Destruction,* rev. ed., vol. 1, pp. 15–16.
11. Girard, Historical foundations of anti-Semitism, p. 71.
12. Abel, T. [1938] (1966). *The Nazi movement: Why Hitler came into power.* Reprint. Englewood Cliffs, N. J.: Prentice-Hall.

    Merkl, P. H. (1975). *Political violence under the swastika.* Princeton: Princeton University Press.

13. Bar-Tal. D. (1986). Group political beliefs. Paper presented at the Annual Meeting of the International Society for Political Psychology, Amsterdam, June.
14. Craig, G. A. (1980). *The Germans.* New York: New American Library, p. 31.
15. Fishman, J. A. (1983). Language and ethnicity in bilingual education. In W. McCready (Ed.), *Culture, ethnicity, and identity.* New York: Academic Press.
16. Craig, *The Germans,* p. 31.
17. Chamberlain, H. S. [1899] (1936). *Die Grundlagen des neunzehnten Jahrhunderts* (The genesis of the nineteenth century). Munich: F. Bruckman.
18. Mayer, M. (1955). *They thought they were free: The Germans 1933–1945.* Chicago: University of Chicago Press.

    Craig, *The Germans.*

19. Craig, *The Germans.*
20. Ibid.
21. Nathan, O., & Norden, H. (Eds.). (1968). *Einstein on peace.* New York: Avenel Books, p. 3.
22. Ibid., pp. 3–4.
23. Nathan and Norden, *Einstein.*
24. Craig, *The Germans,* pp. 323, 332.
25. Hilberg, *Destruction.*

    Davidowicz, *War against the Jews.*

26. Craig, *The Germans,* pp. 22, 23.
27. Ibid., p. 23.
28. Quoted in Steiner, J. M. (1980). The SS yesterday and today: A sociopsychological view. In J. Dimsdale (Ed.), *Survivors, victims and perpetrators: Essays on the Nazi Holocaust.* New York: Hemisphere Publishing Co., p. 413.
29. Kren, G. M., & Rappoport, L. (1980). *The Holocaust and the crisis of human behavior.* New York: Holmes & Meier, p. 23.

30. Kren and Rappoport, *Holocaust*, p. 24.
31. Quoted in Girard, Historical foundations of anti-Semitism, p. 66.
32. Fromm, E. (1965). *Escape from freedom*. New York: Avon Books.
33. Miller, A. (1983). *For your own good: Hidden cruelty in child-rearing and the roots of violence*. New York: Ferrar, Straus, Giroux.

    Dicks, H. V. (1972). *Licensed mass murder*: A sociopsychological study of some SS killers. New York: Basic Books.

    Steiner, The SS yesterday and today.
34. Miller, *For your own good*.
35. Sulzer, J. (1748). Versuch von der Erziehung and Unterweisung der Kinder (An essay on the education and instruction of children). In Miller, *For your own good*, pp. 1–2.
36. Kruger, J. G. (1752). Gedanken von der Erziehung der Kinder (Some thoughts on the education of children). In Miller, *For your own good*, p. 2.
37. Miller, *For your own good*, p. 61.
38. DeMause, L. (Ed.). (1974). *History of childhood*. New York. Psychohistory Press.

    Stone, L. (1977). *The family, sex and marriage in England, 1500–1800*. New York: Harper & Row.
39. Staub, E. (1986). A conception of the determinants and development of altruism and aggression: Motives, the self, and the environment. In C. Zahn-Waxler, E. M. Cummings, & R. Iannotti (Eds.), *Altruism and aggression: Social and biological origins*. New York: Cambridge University Press.

    Idem. (Forthcoming). *Social behavior and moral conduct: A personal goal theory account of altruism and aggression*. Century Series. Englewood Cliffs, N. J.: Prentice-Hall.
40. Dicks, *Licensed mass murder*.
41. Steiner, The SS yesterday and today.
42. Devereux, E. D. (1972). Authority and moral development among German and American children: A cross-national pilot experiment. *Journal of Comparative Family Studies, 3*, 99–124.
43. MacDonald, K. (1984). An ethological-social learning theory of the development of altruism: Implications for human sociobiology. *Ethology and Sociobiology, 5*, 97–109.
44. Wesley, F., & Karr, C. (1968). Vergleich der Ansichten und Erziehung-haltungen deutscher und amerikanischer Mutter. *Psychologische Rundschau, 19*, 35–46.
45. Adelson, J. (1971). The political imagination of the young adolescent. *Daedalus, 100*, 1031–50.
46. Kaufmann, W. (1950). *Nietzsche: Philosopher, psychologist, antichrist*. Princeton: Princeton University Press.
47. Quoted in Russell, B. (1945). *A history of Western philosophy*. New York: Simon & Schuster, p. 763.

    My review is partly based on Russell's review, partly on Kaufmann, *Nietzsche*, and partly on material from the anthology:

    The philosophy of Nietzsche. (1927, 1945). New York: Modern Library.
48. Kren and Rappoport, *Holocaust*.
49. Lowenberg, P. (1971). The psychosocial origins of the Nazi youth cohort. *American Historical Review, 76*, 1457–1502.
50. There is beginning interest in the effects of economic stress and unemployment, one aspect of difficult life conditions, on the family and children. See:

    Elder, G. H., & Caspi, A. (1988). Economic stress in lives: Developmental perspectives. In D. Dooley & R. Catalano (Eds.), Psychological effects of unemployment. *Journal of Social Issues, 44*, no. 4, 25–45.
51. Reich, W. (1970). *The mass psychology of fascism*. New York: Farrar, Strauss, Giroux.

52. Abel, *Nazi movement*.
    Merkl, P. H. (1980). *The making of a stormtrooper*. Princeton: Princeton University Press.
53. Merkl, *Stormtrooper*.
54. Lifton, R. J. (1986). *The Nazi doctors: Medical killing and the psychology of genocide*. New York: Basic Books.

Chapter 9

1. Craig, G. A. (1982). *The Germans*. New York: New American Library, pp. 68–69.
2. Littell, F. H. (1980). Invited lecture at the Jewish Community of Amherst, Amherst, Mass.
3. Dimont, M. I. (1962). *Jews, God and history*. New York: New American Library of World Literature.
    Po-chia Hsia, R. (1988). *The myth of ritual murder: Jews and magic in Reformation Germany*. New Haven: Yale University Press.
4. Axel, L. A. (1979). Christian theology and the murder of the Jews. *Encounter, 40*, no. 2.
    Flannery, E.H. (1965). *The anguish of the Jews: Twenty-three centuries of antisemitism*. New York: Paulist Press.
    A sociological account of the roots and continuity of anti-Semitism is provided by:
    Fein, H. (Ed.). (1987). *The persisting question: Sociological perspectives and social contexts of modern antisemitism*. New York: Walter de Gruyter.
5. Dimont, *Jews, God and history*; Po-chia Hsia, *The myth*.
6. Hilberg, R. 1961. *The destruction of the European Jews*. Chicago: Quadrangle Books.
7. Davidowicz, L. S. (1975). *The war against the Jews: 1933–1945*. New York: Holt, Rinehart & Winston.
    Lifton, R. J. (1986). *The Nazi doctors: Medical killing and the psychology of genocide*. New York: Basic Books.
8. London, P. (1970). The rescuers: Motivational hypotheses about Christians who saved Jews from the Nazis. In J. Macaulay & L. Berkowitz (Eds.), *Altruism and helping behavior*. New York: Academic Press.
9. Oliner, S. P., & Oliner, P. M. (1988). *The altruistic personality: Rescuers of Jews in Nazi Europe*. New York: Free Press.
10. Friedrich, V. (1989). From psychoanalysis to the "great treatment": Psychoanalysts under National Socialism. *Political Psychology 10*, 3–26.
    Staub, E. (1989). The evolution of bystanders, German psychoanalysts and lessons for today. *Political Psychology 10*, 39–52.
11. Lifton, *Nazi doctors*.
12. Stotland, E. (1969). Exploratory studies of empathy. In L. Berkowitz (Ed.), *Advances in experimental social psychology*, vol. 4. New York: Academic Press.
    Regan, D., & Totten, J. (1975). Empathy and attribution: Turning observers into actors. *Journal of Personality and Social Psychology, 32*, 850–6.
13. Hilberg, *Destruction*.
14. Staub, E. (1975). To rear a prosocial child: Reasoning, learning by doing, and learning by teaching others. In D. DePalma & J. Folley (Eds.), *Moral development: Current theory and research*. Hillsdale, N. J.: Lawrence Erlbaum Associates.
    Idem. (1979). *Positive social behavior and morality: Socialization and development*, vol. 2. New York: Academic Press, Chap. 6.
15. Kramer, B. M. (1950). Residential contact as a determinant of attitudes toward Negroes. Ph.D. diss., Harvard University.
    Deutsch, M., & Collins, M. E. (1951). *Interracial housing: A psychological evaluation*

of a social experiment. Minneapolis: University of Minnesota Press.
16. Hilberg, R. (1980). The nature of the process. In J. Dimsdale (Ed.), *Survivors, victims, and perpetrators: Essays on the Nazi Holocaust*. New York: Hemisphere Publishing Co.
   Lifton, *Nazi doctors*.
17. Bloch, S., & Reddaway, P. (1977). *Psychiatric terror: How Soviet psychiatry is used to suppress dissent*. New York: Basic Books.
   Idem. (1985). Psychiatrists and dissenters in the Soviet Union. In E. Stover & E. O. Nightingale (Eds.), *The breaking of bodies and minds*. New York: Freeman.
18. Lifton, *Nazi doctors*.
   Proctor, R. (1988). *Racial hygiene: Medicine under the Nazis*. Cambridge: Harvard University Press.
19. Lifton, *Nazi doctors*, p. 46.
20. Proctor, *Racial hygiene*.
21. Binding, L., & Hoche, A. (1920). *Die Freigabe der Vernichtung lebensunwerten Lebens: Ihr Mass und ihre Form*. Leipzig: F. Meiner.
   quoted in Lifton, *Nazi doctors*, p. 47.
22. Friedrich, From psychoanalysis to the "great treatment."
23. Lorenz, K. (1940). Durch Domestikation verursachte Störungen arteigenen Verhaltens, *Zeitschrift fur angewandte Psychologie und Charakterkunde* (Journal of Applied Psychology and the Science of Character), *59*, 66, 71.
   See also Craig, *The Germans*, for an account of the enthusiastic production of ideas supporting National Socialism by German academics.
24. Sargent, S. (1957). *Battle for the mind: A physiology of conversion and brain washing*. London: Pan Books.
25. Latane, B., & Darley, J. (1970). *The unresponsive bystander: Why doesn't he help?* New York: Appleton-Crofts.
   Piliavin, J. A., Dividio, J. F., Goertner, S. L., & Clark, R. D. (1981). *Emergency intervention*. New York: Academic Press.
   Staub, E. (1974). Helping a distressed person: Social, personality and stimulus determinants. In L. Berkowitz (Ed.), *Advances in experimental social psychology*, vol. 7. New York: Academic Press.
   Staub, E. (1978). *Positive social behavior and morality*. vol. 1, *Social and personal influences*. New York: Academic Press.
26. Staub, Helping a distressed person.
27. Davidowicz, *War against the Jews*.
   Lifton, *Nazi doctors*.
28. Bettelheim, B. (1979). *Surviving and other essays*. New York: Vintage Books, pp. 260, 265.

Chapter 10

1. Kren, G. M., & Rappoport, L. (1980). *The Holocaust and the crisis of human behavior*. New York: Holmes & Meier Publishers, p. 69.
2. Davidowicz, L. S. (1975). *The war against the Jews: 1933–1945*. New York: Holt, Rinehart & Winston.
   Lifton, R. J. (1986). *The Nazi doctors: Medical killing and the psychology of genocide*. New York: Basic Books.
3. Kren and Rappoport, *Holocaust*.
4. Ibid., p. 51.
5. Segev, T. (1977). The commanders of the Nazi concentration camps. Ph.D. diss., Boston University (University Microfilms, Ann Arbor, Mich., 77–21, 618).

6. Kren and Rappoport, *Holocaust*, p. 43.
7. Hilberg, R. (1980). The nature of the process. In J. Dimsdale (Ed.), *Survivors, victims, and perpetrators: Essays on the Nazi Holocaust*. New York: Hemisphere Publishing Co.
8. Merkl, P. H. (1980). *The making of a stormstrooper*. Princeton: Princeton University Press, pp. 218–22.
9. Segev, The commanders.
10. Hoess, R. (1959). *Commandant of Auschwitz*. New York: World.
11. Sereny, G. (1974). *Into the darkness: From mercy killing to mass murder*. New York: McGraw-Hill.
12. Dicks, H. V. (1972). *Licensed mass murder: A sociopsychological study of some SS killers*. New York: Basic Books.
13. Steiner, J. M. (1980). The SS yesterday and today: A sociopathological view. In J. Dimsdale (Ed.), *Survivors, victims, and perpetrators: Essays on the Nazi Holocaust*. New York: Hemisphere Publishing Co.
14. Ibid.
15. Ibid., pp. 431–2.
16. Kren and Rappoport, *Holocaust*, p. 58.
17. Kren and Rappoport, *Holocaust*.
    Davidowicz, *The war against the Jews*.
    Hilberg, R. (1961). *The destruction of the European Jews*. Chicago: Quadrangle Books.
18. Sereny, *Into the darkness*.
19. Kren and Rappoport, *Holocaust*, p. 61.
20. Perry, D. G., & Perry, L. C. (1974). Denial of suffering in the victim as a stimulus to violence in aggressive boys. *Child Development*, *45*, 55–62.
    Staub, E. (Forthcoming). *Social behavior and moral conduct: A personal goal theory account of altruism and aggression*. Century Series. Englewood Cliffs, N. J.: Prentice-Hall.
21. Keneally, T. (1983). *Schindler's list*. New York: Penguin Books.
22. Gelinas, D. J. (1985). Unexpected resources in treating incest families. In M. A. Karpel (Ed.), *Family resources: The hidden partner in family therapy*. New York: Guilford Press.
23. Karski, J. (1944). *Story of a secret state*. Boston: Houghton Mifflin, p. 330.
24. Ibid., pp. 331–2.
25. Keneally, *Schindler's list*, p. 292.
26. Marton, K. (1982). *Wallenberg*. New York: Ballantine Books.
27. Kren and Rappoport, *Holocaust*.
28. Keneally, *Schindler's list*.
29. Lifton, *Nazi doctors*.
30. Ibid.
31. Lifton, R. J. (1986, November). Personal communication.
32. Lifton, *Nazi doctors*, p. 425.
33. Ibid., p. 175, from interview with the SS Doctor B.
34. Ibid., p. 176, from interview with SS Doctor B.
35. Ibid., p. 425.
36. Durkheim, E. (1961). *Moral education*. New York: Free Press.
    Gilligan, C. (1982). *In a different voice: Psychological theory and women's development*. Cambridge: Harvard University Press.
    Staub, E. (1978). *Positive social behavior and morality*. Vol. 1, *Social and personal influences*. New York: Academic Press.
    Idem. (1980). Social and prosocial behavior: Personal and situational influences and their interactions. In E. Staub (Ed.), *Personality: Basic aspects and current research*. Englewood Cliffs, N. J.: Prentice-Hall.

37. Lifton, *Nazi doctors*.
    Hilberg, Nature of the process.
    Steiner, The SS yesterday and today.
38. Eliach, Y. (Ed.). (1982). *Hassidic tales of the Holocaust*. New York: Oxford University Press.
39. Becker, E. (1975). *Escape from evil*. New York: Free Press.
40. Lewin, R. (1938). *The conceptual representation and measurement of psychological forces*. Durham, N. C.: Duke University Press.

Chapter 11

1. Heider, F. (1958). *The psychology of interpersonal relations*. New York: Wiley.
    Festinger, L. A. (1957). *A theory of cognitive dissonance*. Evanston, Ill.: Row-Peterson.
2. Hilberg, R. (1980). The nature of the process. In J. Dimsdale (Ed.), *Survivors, victims, and perpetrators: Essays on the Nazi Holocaust*. New York: Hemisphere Publishing Co.
    Davidowicz, L. S. (1976). *The war against the Jews: 1933–1945*. New York: Holt, Rinehart & Winston.
    Lifton, R. J. (1986). *The Nazi doctors: Medical killing and the psychology of genocide*. New York: Basic Books.
3. Kren, G. M., & Rappoport, L. (1980). *The Holocaust and the crisis of human behavior*. New York: Holmes & Meier.
4. Hilberg, R. (1961). *The destruction of the European Jews*. Chicago: Quadrangle Books.
5. Fein, H. (1979). *Accounting for genocide: National responses and Jewish victimization during the Holocaust*. New York: Free Press.
6. Kren and Rappoport, *Holocaust*.
7. Fein, *Accounting for genocide*.
8. Lukas, R. (1986). *The forgotten Holocaust: The Poles under German occupation, 1939–1944*. Lexington: University Press of Kentucky.
    Gross, J. T. (1979). *Polish society under German occupation: The Generalgouvernment, 1939–1944*. Princeton: Princeton University Press.
9. Fein, *Accounting for genocide*.
10. Hilberg, *Destruction*, pp. 386–7.
11. Fein, *Accounting for genocide*.
12. Arendt, H. (1951). *The origins of totalitarianism*. New York: Harcourt Brace Jovanovich, p. 269.
    See:
    U. S. Government. (1946). *Nazi conspiracy and aggression*. Washington, D. C.: U.S. Government Printing Office, vol. 6, pp. 87ff.
13. Wyman, D. S. (1984). *The abandonment of the Jews: America and the Holocaust, 1941–1945*. New York: Pantheon Books.
14. Hilberg, Nature of the process.
15. Wyman, *Abandonment*.
16. Moscovici, S. (1973). *Social influence and social change*. London: Academic Press.
    Moscovici, S. (1980). Toward a theory of conversion behavior. In L. Berkowitz (Ed.), *Current issues in social psychology*. New York: Academic Press.
17. Wyman, *Abandonment*.
18. A report by D. Yankelovich on polls taken at the time, described in Bernstein, R. (May 22, 1988). U.S. articles on prewar Jews of Germany found wanting, *New York Times*, p. 24.

19. Wyman, D. S. (1968). *Paper walls: America and the refugee crisis, 1938–1941*. Amherst: University of Massachusetts Press.
20. Taylor, F. (Trans. and Ed.). (1983). *Goebbels' diaries, 1933–1941*. New York: G. P. Putnam's Sons.
21. Marcus, M. R. (1987). *The Holocaust in history*. Hanover: University Press of New England & Brandeis University Press.
22. Fein, *Accounting for genocide*.
23. Ibid.
24. Arendt, H. (1963). *Eichmann in Jerusalem: A report on the banality of evil*. New York: Viking Press.
25. Fein, *Accounting for genocide*, p. 126.
26. Ibid.
27. Arendt, *Eichmann in Jerusalem*.
28. Fein, *Accounting for genocide*, p. 131.
29. Bettelheim, B. (1952). *Surviving and other essays*. New York: Vintage Books.
    Davidowicz, *War against the Jews*.
    Hilberg, *Destruction*.
30. Fein, *Accounting for genocide*, p. 204.
31. Fein, H. (March/April 1980). Beyond the heroic ethic. *Culture and Society*, pp. 51–55.
32. Kren and Rappoport, *Holocaust*.
33. Des Pres, T. (1976). *The survivor: An anatomy of life in the death camps*. Oxford: Oxford University Press.
34. Ibid.
    Fein, Beyond the heroic ethic, pp. 51–55.
35. An up-to-date source is:
    Schindler, J., & Freud, A. (1985). *The analysis of defense: The ego and the mechanism of defense revisited*. New York: International Universities Press.
    See also:
    Goleman, D. (1985). *Vital lies, simple truths: The psychology of self deception*. New York: Simon & Schuster.
36. Arendt, *Eichmann in Jerusalem*.
37. Fein, *Accounting for genocide*.
38. Bluhm, H. O. (1948). How did they survive? Mechanisms of defense in Nazi concentration camps. *American Journal of Psychotherapy, 2*, 32.
    Bettelheim, B. (1943). Individual and mass behavior in extreme situations. *Journal of Abnormal and Social Psychology, 38*, 417–52.
39. Seligman, M. (1975). *Helplessness: On depression, development and death*. San Francisco: Freeman Press.
40. Levin, N. (1973). *The Holocaust: The destruction of European Jewry, 1933–1945*. New York: Shocken Books.
41. Warmbrunn, W. (1963). *The Dutch under German occupation, 1940–1945*. Stanford: Stanford University Press.
    See also Arendt, *Eichmann in Jerusalem*.
42. Hallie, P. P. (1979). *Lest innocent blood be shed: The story of the village of Le Chambon and how goodness happened there*. New York: Harper & Row, p. 114.
43. Ibid., p. 245.
44. London, P. (1970). The rescuers: Motivational hypotheses about Christians who saved Jews from the Nazis. In J. Macaulay & L. Berkowitz (Eds.), *Altruism and helping behavior*. New York: Academic Press.
    Fogelman, E., & Weiner, V. L. (1985). The few, the brave, the noble. *Psychology Today, 19*, 60–65.

Tec, N. (1986). *When light pierced the darkness: Christian rescue of Jews in Nazi-occupied Poland*. New York: Oxford University Press.

45. Oliner, S. B., & Oliner, P. (1988). *The altruistic personality: Rescuers of Jews in Nazi Europe*. New York: Free Press.

46. Staub, E. (1978). *Positive social behavior and morality*. Vol. 1, *Social and personal influences*. New York: Academic Press.

    Idem. (1984). Steps toward a comprehensive theory of moral conduct: Goal orientation, social behavior, kindness and cruelty. In J. L. Gewirtz & W. M. Kurtines (Eds.), *Morality, moral behavior, and moral development*. New York: Wiley-Interscience.

47. London, Rescuers.

    Tec, *When light pierced the darkness*.

48. Oliner & Oliner, *Altruistic personality*, p. 210.

49. Tec, *When light pierced the darkness*.

50. Keneally, T. (1983). *Schindler's list*. New York: Penguin Books.

51. Marton, K. (1982). *Wallenberg*. New York: Ballentine Books.

52. Staub, E. (July 1988). The roots of altruism and heroic rescue. *The World and I*, pp. 398–401, 399.

53. Staub, E. (1988). The evolution of caring and nonaggressive persons and societies. In R. V. Wagner, J. deRivera, & M. Watkins (Eds.), Psychology and the promotion of peace. *Journal of Social Issues*, *44*, 81–101.

Chapter 12

1. Issawi, C. (1980). *The economic history of Turkey, 1800–1914*. Chicago: University of Chicago Press.

2. Karpat, K. H. (1985). *The Ottoman population, 1830–1914: Demographic and social characteristics*. Madison: University of Wisconsin Press.

3. Mears, E. G. (1924). *Modern Turkey: A political-economic interpretation*. New York: Macmillan, see especially Chap. 19.

4. Miller, W. (1923). *The Ottoman Empire and its successors 1901–1922*. Cambridge: Cambridge University Press.

    Ahmad, F. (1969). *The Young Turks: The Committee of Union and Progress in Turkish Politics, 1908–1914*. Oxford: Clarendon Press.

5. Issawi, *Economic history*.

6. Mears, *Modern Turkey*.

7. Lewis, R. (1971). *Everyday life in Ottoman Turkey*. New York: G. P. Putnam & Sons.

    Ramsauer, E. E., Jr. (1957) *The Young Turks: Prelude to the revolution of 1908*. New York: Russell & Russell.

8. Issawi, *Economic history*.

9. McCarthy, J. (1983). *Muslims and minorities: The population of Ottoman Anatolia and the end of the empire*. New York: New York University Press.

10. Toynbee, A. J. (1915). *Armenian atrocities: The murder of a nation*. London: Hodder & Stoughton.

    Toynbee, A. J. (Ed.). (1916). *The treatment of the Armenians in the Ottoman Empire, 1915–1916*. London: His Majesty's Stationery Office. (The author of the material compiled by Toynbee was Viscount Bryce.)

11. *Encyclopedia Britannica*. (1922). Vol. 27, p. 458.

12. Greene, F. D. (1895). *The Armenian crisis in Turkey: The massacre of 1894, its antecedents and significance*. New York: G. P. Putnam's Sons.

13. Ibid.

14. Lewis, *Everyday life*.
15. Ramsauer, *Young Turks*, pp. 119–20.
16. Ibid., pp. 42–43.
17. Ibid.
18. Krikorian, M. K. (1977). *Armenians in the service of the Ottoman Empire, 1860–1908*. London: Routledge & Kegan Paul.
19. Ibid.
20. Hartunian, A. (1968). *Neither to laugh nor to weep*. Boston: Beacon Press, pp. 18 & 20.
21. Miller, *Ottoman Empire*, p. 479.
22. Quoted in Boyajian, D. H. (1972). *Armenia: The forgotten genocide*. Westwood: Educational Book Crafters, p. 50.
23. For a discussion of this position and an argument against it see:
    Melson, R. (1986). Provocation or nationalism: A critical inquiry into the Armenian genocide of 1915. In R. G. Hovannisian (Ed.), *The Armenian genocide: A perspective*. New Brunswick, N. J.: Transaction Books.
24. Miller, *Ottoman Empire*, pp. 428–30.
25. Sarkisian, E. K., & Sahakian, R. G. (1965). *Vital issues in modern Armenian history*. West Concord, Mass.: Concord Press.
26. Miller, *Ottoman Empire*.
27. Ramsauer, *Young Turks*, pp. 40–42.
28. Ibid., pp. 64–70.
29. Toynbee, *Treatment of the Armenians*, p. 81.
30. Trumpener, U. (1968). *Germany and the Ottoman Empire, 1914–1918*. Princeton: Princeton University Press.
31. Bedrossyan, M. D. (1983). *The first genocide of the twentieth century: The perpetrators and the victims*. Voskedar Publishing Co.
    Boyajian, *Armenia*.
    Melson, Provocation or nationalism.
32. Missakian, J. (1950). *A searchlight on the Armenian question (1878–1950)*. Boston: Haisenik Publishing Co.
33. Gurun, K. (1985). *The Armenian file: The myth of innocence exposed*. New York: St. Martin's Press.
34. McCarthy, *Muslims and minorities*, pp. 118–19.
    Emin, A. (1930). *Turkey in the World War*. New Haven: Yale University Press.
35. McCarthy, *Muslims and minorities*, p. 119.
    Allen, W. E. D., & Muratoff, P. (1953). *Caucasian battlefields*. Cambridge: Cambridge University Press.
36. Buxton, C. R. (1909). *Turkey in revolution*. New York: Charles Scribner's Sons.
37. Miller, *Ottoman Empire*, p. 476.
38. Ibid., pp. 161–3.
39. Knight, E. F. (1909). *The awakening of Turkey: A history of the Turkish revolution*. Philadelphia: Lippincott, pp. 278–81.
40. Ahmad, *Young Turks*, pp. 162–3.
41. Lepsius, J. (1919). *Deutschland und Armenian*. Potsdam: Tempelverlag.
    Quoted in Boyajian, *Armenia*, pp. 106–7.
42. Gokalp, Z. (1968, first published in Ankara in 1920). *The principles of Turkism*. Leiden: E. J. Brill.
43. Smith. R. W. (1986). Denial and justification of genocide: The Armenian case and its implications. Paper presented at the Annual Meetings of the American Political Science Association, Washington, August 28–31.
44. Sarkisian and Sahakian, *Vital issues*, pp. 35–36.

45. Nazer, J. (1968). *The first genocide of the twentieth century: The Armenian massacre.* New York: T. and T. Publishing Co.

46. Morgenthau, H., Sr. (1918). *Ambassador Morgenthau's story.* New York: Doubleday.

47. Dadrian, V. N. (1986). The Naim-Andonian documents of the World War I destruction of Ottoman Armenians: The anatomy of a genocide. *International Journal of Middle East Studies, 18,* 311–60.

48. A number of sources quote the memoirs, for example:
    Sarkisian and Sahakian, *Vital issues.*
    Bedrossyan, *First genocide.*
    Nazer, *Armenian massacre.*

49. See Sarkisian and Sahakian, *Vital issues.*

50. Dadrian, The Naim-Andonian documents, pp. 340–1.

51. Ibid.

52. Ibid., pp. 71–72.

53. Quoted in Missakian, *A searchlight,* pp. 44–45.

54. Lepsius, J. (Ed.). (1919). *Deutschland und Armenien, 1914–1918.* Potsdom: Der Tempelverlag.
    Quoted in Boyajian, *Armenia.*

55. Gladstone, W. E. (1876). *Bulgarian horrors and the question of the East.* London, J. Murray Press, p. 38.

56. Boyajian, *Armenia.*

57. Quoted in Bedrossyan, *First genocide,* p. 132.

58. Ibid., p. 130.

59. Miller, *Ottoman Empire,* p. 538.

60. Trumpener, *Germany and the Ottoman Empire.*

61. Ibid., p. 214.

62. *New York Herald Tribune,* quoted in Bedrossyan, *First genocide,* p. 131.

63. Ibid., p. 131.

64. According to the Archives of the Nuremberg Proceedings, this statement was made by Hitler at a meeting of SS units at Obersalzberg, on August 22, 1939, instructing them "to kill, without pity, men, women and children" in their march against Poland. See:
    Bedrossyan, *First genocide,* pp. 136 & 459.
    Lochner, L. (1942). *What about the Germans.* New York.

65. Smith, Denial and justification.

Chapter 13

1. Osborne, M. E. (1969). *The French presence in Cochinchina and Cambodia: Rule and response (1859–1905).* Ithaca: Cornell University Press.

2. Etcheson, C. (1984). *The rise and demise of democratic Kampuchea.* Boulder: Westview Press.

3. Kiernan, B., & Boua, C. (Eds.). (1982). *Peasants and politics in Kampuchea, 1942–1981.* New York: M. E. Sharpe, p. 7.

4. Vickery, M. (1984). *Cambodia: 1975–1982.* Boston: South End Press.

5. For tax collecting, see:
   Etcheson, *Rise and demise,* p. 70.
   Ponchaud, F. (1978). *Cambodia: Year Zero.* New York: Holt, Rinehart & Winston.

6. Etcheson, *Rise and demise,* p. 71.

7. Ibid.

8. Vickery, *Cambodia.*

9. For example, by Henry Kissinger, as noted in:
Shawcross, W. (1979). *Sideshow: Kissinger, Nixon, and the destruction of Cambodia.* New York: Simon & Schuster.

10. Becker, E. (1986). *When the war was over: The voices of Cambodia's revolution and its people.* New York: Simon & Schuster.

11. Sihanouk, Prince Norodom (1980). *War and hope: The case for Cambodia.* New York: Pantheon Books.

12. Barron, J., & Paul, A. (1977). *Murder of a gentle land: The untold story of communist genocide in Cambodia.* New York: Readers Digest Press.

13. Ibid., as well as other sources.

14. Becker, *When the war was over.*

15. Etcheson, *Rise and demise.*

16. Vickery, *Cambodia.*, p. 139.

17. Vickery, *Cambodia.*

18. Hildebrand, G., and Porter, G. (1976). *Cambodia: Starvation and revolution.* New York: Monthly Review Press.

19. Vickery, *Cambodia.*

20. Ibid., p. 26.

21. Barron and Paul, *Murder of a gentle land.*

22. Chandler, D. P. (1983). *A history of Cambodia.* Boulder: Westview Press.

23. Osborne, *French presence.*

24. Vickery, *Cambodia*, Chap. 1.

25. Burchett, W. (1981) *The China, Cambodia, Vietnam triangle.* Chicago: Vanguard Books, p. 122.
Quoted in Vickery, *Cambodia*, p. 17.

26. Osborne, *French presence.*

27. Chandler, *A history*, p. 59.

28. Ibid., p. 81.

29. Myrdal, J., & Kessle, G. (1971). *Angkor: An essay on art and imperialism.* London: Chatto & Windus.

30. Osborne, *French presence*, p. 284.

31. Ibid., p. 19.

32. Ibid.
Becker, *When the war was over.*

33. Becker, *When the war was over*, p. 54.

34. Kamm, H. (September 1987). A broken country. *New York Times Magazine*, p. 110.

35. Becker, *When the war was over.*

36. Ibid., p. 84.

37. Bun Chan Mol. (1973). *Charit Khmer.* Phnom Penh.

38. Chandler, D. (1973). Cambodia before the French. Ph. D. diss., University of Michigan.
Vickery, *Cambodia*, p. 7.

39. Cited in Chomsky, N., & Hermann E. S. (1979). *After the cataclysm: Postwar Indochina and the reconstruction of imperial ideology.* Boston: South End Press.

40. Kiernan, B. (1982). The Samlaut rebellion, 1967–68. In Kiernan and Boua, *Peasants and politics*, p. 195.

41. Ibid.

42. Cattell, D. C. (1956). *Communism and the Spanish Civil War.* Berkeley & Los Angeles: University of California Press. p. 2.
Vickery, *Cambodia*, p. 282.

43. Vickery, *Cambodia*, p. 284.

44. Chandler, *A history.*

45. Etcheson, *Rise and demise.*

46. Vickery, *Cambodia.*
47. Ibid. p. 281.
48. Meisner, M. J. *Mao's China: A history of the People's Republic,* pp. 205, 212. Quoted in Vickery, *Cambodia,* p. 273.
49. Burchett, *Triangle,* p. 64.
    Quoted in Vickery, *Cambodia,* pp. 272–3.
50. Hou Youn. (1955). The Cambodian peasants and their prospects for modernization. Part of it reprinted in Kiernan and Boua, *Peasants and politics.*
51. Hou Youn. (1964). Solving rural problems. Described in Etcheson, *Rise and demise,* p. 51.
52. Khieu Samphan's 1959 thesis is described in Hildebrand and Porter, *Cambodia.*
53. Etcheson, *Rise and demise.*
54. Ibid.
55. Ibid., p. 101.
56. In Becker, *When the war was over,* p. 155.
57. Ibid., p. 155.
58. Barron and Paul, *Murder of a gentle land.*
59. Ibid., p. 44.
60. Ibid.
61. Ibid., pp. 46–47.
62. Becker, *When the war was over,* p. 71.
63. Sihanouk, *War and hope.*
64. Becker, *When the war was over,* p. 21.

Chapter 14

1. Inter-American Commission on Human Rights. General Secretariat. (April 11, 1980). *Report on the situation of human rights in Argentina.* Washington, D.C.: Organization of American States, p. 14.
2. Hodges, D. C. (1976). *Argentina, 1943–1976: The national revolution and resistance.* Albuquerque: University of New Mexico Press.
3. Bernard, J. P., et al. (1973). *Guide to the political parties of South America.* Rev. ed. New York: Penguin Books, p. 35.
4. Dworkin, R. (1986). Introduction. In *Nunca Mas: The Report of the Argentine National Commission on the disappeared.* New York: Farrar, Straus, Giroux.
5. San Martin, S. (1983). *El poder militar y la nación* (The military power and the nation). Buenos Aires: Editorial Troquel S. A.
6. Potash, R. A. (1969, 1980). *The army and politics in Argentina.* Vol. 1, 1928–1945; vol. 2, 1945–1962. Stanford, Calif.: Stanford University Press. Potash's two-volume history of the military in Argentina has been highly regarded both by the military rulers of Argentina and by the present civilian government.
7. Ibid., vol. 2.
8. Ibid., vol. 2, p. 298.
9. Caviedes, C. (1984). *The Southern Cone: Realities of the authoritarian state in South America.* Totowa, N. J.: Rowman & Allenheld.
    Commission on Human Rights, *Report on the situation.*
10. Bernard et al., *Guide.*
11. Potash, R. A. (1970). Argentina. In L. N. McAlister et al. (Eds.), *The military in Latin American sociopolitical evolution.* Washington, D. C.: Center for Research in Social Systems.
12. Bernard et al., *Guide,* pp. 103–4, 105.

13. Hodges, *Argentina*, p. 18.
14. Ibid., p. 14.
15. Secretaria de Guerra (Secretary of War). (1966). *Operaciones de Asuntos Civiles (Operation of Civil Affairs)*. RC-19-1 Publico. Instituto geográfico militar. Republic Argentina.
16. Potash, Argentina.
17. Weil, T. E. et al. (1974). *Area handbook for Argentina*. 2d ed. DA pamphlet 550–73. Prepared by Foreign Area Studies of the American University. Washington, D. C.: U.S. Government Printing Office.
18. Potash, Argentina, p. 98.
19. Ibid.
20. San Martin, *El poder militar*.
21. Weil et al., *Area handbook*.
22. Caviedes, *Southern Cone*.
23. Ibid.
      Keegan, J. (1983). *World armies*. 2d ed. London: Macmillan.
24. *Terrorism in Argentina*. (January 7, 1980). República Argentina. Poder ejecutivo nacional.
25. Crawley, E. (1984). *A house divided: Argentina 1880–1980*. New York: St. Martin's Press, p. 423.
26. *Terrorism in Argentina*, p. 398.
27. Crawley, *A house divided*, p. 423.
28. Zalaquett, J. (1985). *New Republic*, issue 3700. Washington, D.C.
29. *Nunca Mas*, p. 363.
30. Cox, R. (December 8, 1983). The second death of Perón. *New York Review of Books*.
31. Caviedes, *Southern Cone*.
32. Ibid.
33. Keegan, *World armies*.
34. Potash, R. A. (1977). The impact of professionalism on the twentieth century Argentine military. Program in Latin American Studies Publication. Occasional Papers no. 3. International Area Studies Programs. University of Massachusetts, Amherst, p. 15.
35. San Martin, *El poder militar*.
36. Caviedes, *Southern Cone*.
37. *Nunca Mas*, pp. 254–63.
38. I refer to decrees 261, 2770, and 2771. One of them appears in *Terrorism in Argentina*. I am grateful to Robert Potash, who showed me copies of the decrees and translated them for me.
39. *Nunca Mas*, pp. 386, 387.
40. Keegan, *World armies*.
41. Weil et al., *Area handbook*, pp. 320–30.
42. *Nunca Mas*.
43. Ibid.
44. Commission on Human Rights, *Report on the situation*, p. 19.
45. Gillespie, R. (1982). *Soldiers of Perón: Argentina's Montoneros*. Oxford: Clarendon Press, p. 250.
46. Sabato, E. (1986). Prologue. In *Nunca Mas*, p. 4.
47. Ibid., p. 3.
48. Commission on Human Rights. *Report on the situation*.
      Nunca Mas.
49. *Nunca Mas*, p. 22.
50. Ibid., p. 38.
51. Ibid., p. 42.

52. Ibid., p. 37.
53. Amnesty International Report. (1980). *Testimony on secret detention camps in Argentina.* London: Amnesty International Publications.
54. Ibid.
55. *Nunca Mas*, p. 72.
56. Ibid.
57. Commission on Human Rights, *Report on the situation*, especially pp. 55–57, 104–16, 199–201.
    Gillespie, *Soldiers of Perón*, pp. 244–50.
    Nunca Mas.
58. *Nunca Mas*, p. 21–22.
59. Ibid., p. 62.
60. Ehlstein, J. (December 1986). Reflections on political torture and murder: Visits with the Mothers of the Plaza del Mayo. Invited lecture, Department of Psychology, University of Massachusetts, Amherst.
61. *Nunca Mas*, p. 340.
62. Dworkin, Introduction to *Nunca Mas*, p. xvii.
    Simpson, J., & Bennett, J. (1985). *The disappeared and the Mothers of the Plaza.* New York: St. Martin's Press.
63. Sartre, J. P. (1958). Preface. In H. Alleg, *The Question*, an account of torture during the French-Algerian war, discussed in:
    Peters, E. (1984). *Torture.* New York: Basil Blackwell.
64. *Nunca Mas*, p. 95.
65. Peters, *Torture.*
    Staub, E. (In press). The psychology of torture and torturers. In P. Suedfeld. (Ed.) *Psychology and Torture.* Washington, D. C.: Hemisphere Publishing Co.
66. Amnesty International Report, *Testimony.*
67. *Nunca Mas*, p. 122.
68. Ibid., see e.g., pp. 122–8.
69. Ibid., p. 60.
70. Dworkin, Introduction, p. xiii.
71. *Nunca Mas*, p. 197.
72. Hopkins, J. W. (Ed.). (1981–82). *Latin American and Caribbean contemporary record.* Vol. 1, *1981–1982.* New York: Holmes & Meier.
73. Ehlstein, Reflections.
74. Ibid.
75. *Nunca Mas*, p. 444.
76. Ibid., p. 426.

Chapter 15

1. *Time* magazine, December 1986, p. 34.
2. Hoffer, E. (1951). *The true believer.* New York: Harper, p. 59.
3. Toch, H. (1965). *The social psychology of social movements.* New York: Bobbs-Merrill.
4. Staub, E. (1987). Commentary. In N. Eisenberg & J. Strayer (Eds.), *Empathy and its development.* New York: Cambridge University Press.
5. Plutchik, R. (1987). Evolutionary bases of empathy. In Eisenberg & Strayer, *Empathy.*
6. Egendorf, A. (1986). *Healing from the war: Trauma and transformation after Vietnam.* Boston: Shambhala.
7. Grover, G. (1961). *Inside the John Birch Society.* Greenwich, Conn.: Fawcett Publica-

tions, p. 143.
8. Staub, E. (1975). To rear a prosocial child: Reasoning, learning by doing and learning by teaching others. In D. DePalma and J. Folley (Eds.), *Moral development: Current theory and research.* Hillsdale, N. J.: Lawrence Erlbaum Associates.
   Idem. (1979). *Positive social behavior and morality.* Vol. 2, *Socialization and development.* New York: Academic Press.
   Idem. (1986). A conception of the determinants and development of altruism and aggression: Motives, the self, the environment. In C. Zahn-Waxler, E. M. Cummings, & R. Iannotti, (Eds.), *Altruism and aggression: Social and biological origins.* New York: Cambridge University Press.
9. Staub, E., & Kellett, D. S. (1972). Increasing pain tolerance by information about aversive stimuli. *Journal of Personality and Social Psychology, 21,* 198–203.
10. Staub, E., & Baer, R. S., Jr. (1974). Stimulus characteristics of a sufferer and difficulty of escape as determinants of helping. *Journal of Personality and Social Psychology, 30,* 279–85.
11. Egendorf, *Healing,* p. 102.
12. Bandura, A. (1973). *Aggression: A social learning analysis.* Englewood Cliffs, N. J.: Prentice-Hall.
13. Bellah, P. N., Madsen, R., Sullivan, W. M., Swindler, A., & Lipton, S. M. (1985). *Habits of the heart: Individualism and commitment in American life.* New York: Harper & Row.
14. Suedfeld, P. (Ed.). (In press). *Psychology and Torture.* Washington D. C.: Hemisphere. Publishing Co.
   Peters, E. (1985). *Torture.* New York: Basil Blackwell.
15. Staub, E. (In press). The psychology of torture and torturers. In Suedfeld, *Psychology and torture.*

Chapter 16

1. White, R. K. (1984). *Fearful warriors: A psychological profile of U.S. – Soviet relations.* New York: Free Press.
2. Deutsch, M. (1983). The prevention of World War III: A psychological perspective. *Political Psychology, 4,* 3–31.
3. Stoessinger, J. G. (1982). *Why nations go to war.* New York: St. Martin's Press.
4. Ibid., pp. 120–1.
5. Ibid.
6. Berlin, I. (1979). Nationalism: Past neglect and present power. *Partisan Review, 45,* 350.
7. Davidson, S. (1985). Group formation and its significance in the Nazi concentration camps. *Israeli Journal of Psychiatry and Related Sciences, 22,* 41–50.
8. Staub, E. (1978). *Positive social behavior and morality.* vol. 1, *Social and personal influences.* New York: Academic Press. Ainsworth, M. D. S. (1979). Infant–mother attachment. *American Psychologist, 34,* 932–69.
9. Mack, J. (1983). Nationalism and the self. *Psychoanalytic Review, 2,* 47–69.
10. Pinderhughes, C. A. (1979). Differential bonding: Toward a psychophysiological theory of stereotyping. *American Journal of Psychiatry, 136,* 33–37.
    Idem. (1981). Paired biological, psychological and social bonding. Paper presented at the 134th Annual Meetings of the American Psychiatric Association, May 9–12.
11. Barnet, R. J. (Winter, 1985). The ideology of the national security state. *Massachusetts Review.*
12. Ibid., p. 490.

13. Mack, Nationalism, p. 57.
14. James, W. [1910] (1970). The moral equivalent of war. In R. A. Wasserstrom (Ed.), *War and morality*. Reprint. Belmont, Calif.: Wadsworth.
15. Dyson, F. (1984). *Weapons and hope*. New York: Colophon Books/Harper & Row, p. 19.
16. Morgenthau, H. J., & Thompson, K. (1984). *Politics among nations: The struggle for power and peace*. New York: Alfred A. Knopf.
17. Walzer, M. (1977). *Just and unjust war: A moral argument with historical illustrations*. New York: Basic Books.
18. Lebow, R. N. (1986). Deterrence reconsidered: The challenge of recent research. In R. K. White (Ed.), *Psychology and the prevention of nuclear war: A book of readings*. New York: New York University Press.
19. Janis, I. (1983). *Victims of groupthink*. Boston: Houghton Mifflin.
20. Morgenthau & Thompson. *Politics among nations*.
21. Hoffman, S. (1985). Realism and its discontents. *New Republic*, November, p. 134.
22. Stover, E., & Nightingale, E. O. (1985). *The breaking of bodies and minds: Torture, psychiatric abuse and the health professions*. New York: W. H. Freeman.
23. Bloch, S., & Reddeway, P. (1984). *Soviet psychiatric abuse: The shadow over world psychiatry*. London: Victor Gollancz.
24. Sorokin, P. A. (1971). The powers of creative, unselfish love. In A. H. Maslow (Ed.). *New knowledge in human values*. Chicago: Henry Regnery Co.
    Staub, *Positive social behavior*, vol. 1.
25. Schopler, J. (1970). An attribution analysis of some determinants of reciprocating a benefit. In J. Macaulay & L. Berkowitz (Eds.), *Altruism and helping behavior*. New York: Academic Press.
    Staub, *Positive social behavior*, vol. 1.
26. Mallick, S. K., & McCandless, B. R. (1966). A study of catharsis of aggression. *Journal of Personality and Social Psychology, 4,* 591–6.
    Pastore, N. (1952). The role of arbitrariness in the frustration-aggression hypothesis. *Journal of Abnormal and Social Psychology, 47,* 728–31.
    Staub, E. (1971). The learning and unlearning of aggression: The role of anxiety, empathy, efficacy and prosocial values. In J. Singer (Ed.), *The control of aggression and violence: Cognitive and physiological factors*. New York: Academic Press.

Chapter 17

1. Tomkins, S. S. (1965). The constructive role of violence and suffering for the individual and for his society. In S. S. Tompkins & C. E. Izard (Eds.), *Affect, cognition, and personality*. New York: Springer.
   Dyson, F. (1984). *Weapons and hope*. New York: Colophon Books/Harper & Row.
2. Moscovici, S. (1973). *Social influence and social change*. London: Academic Press.
   Moscovici, S. (1980). Toward a theory of conversion behavior. In L. Berkowitz (Ed.), *Current issues in social psychology*. New York: Academic Press.
3. Schmookler, A. B. (1984). *The parable of the tribes: The problem of power in social evolution*. Berkeley & Los Angeles: University of California Press, pp. 23, 20. 286.
4. Niebuhr, R. [1932] (1960). *Moral man and immoral society: A study in ethics and politics*. Reprint. New York: Charles Scribner's Sons, p. ix.
5. Ibid., pp. xxii–xxiii.
6. Ibid, pp. 91, 88.
7. Maslow, A. H. (1970). *Motivation and personality*. 2d ed. New York: Harper & Row.

8. Lefcourt, H. M. (1973). The functions of the illusion of control and freedom. *American Psychologist, 28,* 417–26.
9. Bellah, P. N., Madsen, R., Sullivan, W. M., Swindler, A., & Lipton, S. M. (1985). *Habits of the heart: Individualism and commitment in American life.* New York: Harper & Row.
10. Maslow, A. (1962). *Toward a psychology of being.* Princeton: Van Nostrand.
11. Maslow, A. H. (1965). Some basic propositions of a growth and self-actualization psychology. In G. Lindzey & C. S. Hall (Eds.), *Theories of personality: Primary sources and research.* New York: John Wiley & Sons.
12. Harmon, J. D. (Ed.). (1982). *Volunteerism in the eighties.* Washington, D. C.: University Press of America.
13. Packard, V. (1972). *A nation of strangers.* New York: David McKay, pp. 6–7.
14. Etzioni, A. (1983). *An immodest agenda: Rebuilding America before the twenty-first century.* New York: McGraw-Hill.
15. Kinkead, E. (1959). *In every war but one.* New York: Norton, pp. 165, 168.
16. Garbarino, J., & Bronfenbrenner, U. (1976). The socialization of moral judgment and behavior in cross-cultural perspective. In T. Lickona (Ed.), *Moral development and behavior: Theory, research and social issues* New York: Holt, Rinehart & Winston.
17. Janis, I. (1983). *Victims of groupthink.* Boston: Houghton Mifflin.
18. Lear, N. (1985). Goldwater is true protector of our rights. *San Diego Tribune,* October 29.
19. Gans, H. (1980). *Deciding what's news.* New York: Vintage, p. 194.
20. Aronson, J. (1970). *The press and the cold war.* Boston: Beacon, p. 201.
21. Ellul, J. (1973). *Propaganda: The formation of men's attitudes.* New York: Vintage.
22. Rosten, L. (1937). *The Washington correspondents.* New York: Harcourt & Brace.
23. Mackenzie, A. (1981). Sabotaging the dissident press. *Columbia Journalism Review,* March/April, pp. 57–63.

Chapter 18

1. Deutsch, M. (1973). *The resolution of conflict: Constructive and destructive processes.* New Haven: Yale University Press.
2. Sherif, M., Harvey, D. J., White, B. J., Hood, W. K., & Sherif, C. W. (1961). *Intergroup conflict and cooperation: The Robbers' Cave experiment.* Norman: University of Oklahoma Books Exchange.
    Sherif, M. (1958). Superordinate goals in the reduction of intergroup conflict. *American Journal of Sociology, 63,* 349–58.
3. Worchel, S. (1979). Cooperation and the reduction of intergroup conflict: Some determining factors. In W. G. Austin & S. Worchel (Eds.), *The social psychology of intergroup relations.* Monterey, Calif.: Brooks-Cole.
4. Stroebe, W., Lenkert, A., and Jonas, K. Familiarity may breed contempt: The impact of student exchange on national stereotypes and attitudes. In W. Stroebe, A. W. Kruglanski, D. Bar-Tal, & M. Hewstone (1988). *The social psychology of intergroup conflict: Theory, research, and applications.* New York: Springer-Verlag.
5. Cook S. W. (1970). Motives in conceptual analysis of attitude-related behavior. In W. J. Arnold and D. Levine (Eds.), *Nebraska symposium on motivation.* Lincoln: University of Nebraska Press.
6. Ben-Ari, R., & Amir, Y. (1988). Intergroup contact, cultural information and change in ethnic attitudes. In Stroebe et al., *Social psychology of intergroup conflict.*
7. Crosby, T. L. (1986). *The impact of civilian evacuation in the Second World War.* London: Croom Helm.

8. Boyer, E. (1983). *High school: A report on secondary education in America*. New York: Harper & Row, p. 213.

9. Harmon, J. D. (Ed.). (1982). *Volunteerism in the eighties*. Washington, D.C.: University Press of America.

10. Titmus, R. (1971). *The gift relationship: From human blood to social policy*. New York: Pantheon Books.

11. Heber, R. F., & Heber, M. E. (1957). The effect of group failure and success on social status. *Journal of Educational Psychology, 48*, 129–34.
    Staub, E. (1979). *Positive social behavior and morality*. Vol. 2, *Socialization and development*. New York: Academic Press.

12. Gross, A. E., Wallston, B. S., & Piliavin, I. M. (1980). The help recipient's perspective. In D. H. Smith & J. Macauley (Eds.), *Participation in social and political activities*. San Francisco: Jossey-Bass.

13. Moynihan, D. P. (1986). *Family and nation*. New York: Harcourt Brace Jovanovich.

14. Bronfenbrenner, U. (1960). The mirror image in Soviet–American relations: A social psychologist's report. *Journal of Social Issues, 16*, 45–56.

15. For a review of research and for a theory of the origins of caring and of prosocial orientation, see:
    Staub, *Positive social behavior and morality*, vol. 2.
    Idem. (1981). Promoting positive behavior in schools, in other educational settings, and in the home. In J. P. Rushton, & R. M. Sorrentino (Eds.), *Altruism and helping behavior*. Hillsdale, N. J.: Lawrence Erlbaum Associates.
    Idem. (1986). A conception of the determinants and development of altruism and aggression: Motives, the self, the environment. In C. Zahn-Waxler, E. M. Cummings, & R. Iannotti (Eds.), *Altruism and aggression: Social and biological origins*. New York: Cambridge University Press.
    Staub, E. (Forthcoming). *Social behavior and moral conduct: A personal goal theory account of altruism and aggression*. Century Series. Englewood Cliffs, N. J.: Prentice-Hall.
    Grusec, J. (1981). Socialization processes and the development of altruism. In J. P. Rushton & R. M. Sorrentino (Eds.), *Altruism and helping behavior*. Hillsdale, N. J.: Lawrence Erlbaum Associates.
    Radke-Yarrow, M. R., Zahn-Waxler, C., & Chapman, M. (1983). Children's prosocial dispositions and behavior. In P. H. Mussen (Ed.), *Carmichael's manual of child psychology*, vol. 4. 4th ed. New York: Wiley.
    Zahn-Waxler et al., *Altruism and aggression*.
    Eisenberg, N. (1986). *Altruistic emotion, cognition and behavior*. Hillsdale, N. J.: Lawrence Erlbaum Associates.
    Hoffman, M. L. (1976). Empathy, role-taking, guilt, and development of altruistic motives. In T. Lickona (Ed.), *Moral development and behavior: Theory, research and social issues*. New York: Holt, Rinehart & Winston.

16. Staub, *Positive social behavior*, vol 2.
    Staub, A conception.

17. Straus, M. A., Gelles, R. J., & Steinmetz, S. K. (1980). *Behind closed doors: Violence in the American family*. New York: Anchor Books.

18. Meyerholt, M. K., & White, B. L. (1986). Making the grade as parents. *Psychology Today, 20*, 38–45.

19. Hertz-Lazarowitz, R., & Sharan, S. (1984). Enhancing prosocial behavior through cooperative learning in the classroom. In E. Staub, D. Bar-Tal, J. Karylowski, & J. Reykowski (Eds.), *Development and maintenance of prosocial behavior*. New York: Plenum.
    Johnson, D. W., Maruyama, G., Johnson, R., Nelson, D., & Skon, L. (1981). The effects of cooperative, competitive, and individualistic goal structures in achievement: A meta analysis. *Psychological Bulletin, 89*, 47–62.

Sharan, S., Hare, P., Webb, C., & Hertz-Lazarowitz, R. (Eds.). (1980). *Cooperation in education*. Provo: Brigham Young University Press.
20. Staub, A conception.
    Idem. *Social behavior and moral conduct.*
21. Alpokrinsky, A. (1986). Paper presented at the conference on the "Social causes and effects of the nuclear arms race," Budapest, June.

Index